James P. Clark
2529 Foraker DR.
Anchorage AK.
99503

The Saudi Arabian Economy

Ramon Knauerhase

The Saudi Arabian Economy

PRAEGER SPECIAL STUDIES IN INTERNATIONAL ECONOMICS AND DEVELOPMENT

Praeger Publishers New York Washington London

Library of Congress Cataloging in Publication Data

Knauerhase, Ramon.
The Saudi Arabian economy.

(Praeger special studies in international economics and development)
Bibliography: p.
Includes index.
1. Saudi Arabia—Economic conditions. I. Title.
HC497.A6K57 330.9'53'805 75-8407
ISBN 0-275-0900-0

PRAEGER PUBLISHERS
111 Fourth Avenue, New York, N.Y. 10003, U.S.A.

Published in the United States of America in 1975
by Praeger Publishers, Inc.

Printed in the United States of America

For Keith and Todd
. . . who liked to go "shoufing"

PREFACE

"What's Past Is Prologue."

This study has been undertaken for five reasons: first, to present in an orderly manner the development of the Saudi Arabian economy over the past two and a half decades; second, with a basis of fact to show the real progress that has been made in the Kingdom's economic development; third, by discussing the various economic, cultural, and political constraints, to place the Kingdom's economic advancement in its proper perspective; fourth, through analysis of the economic aspects of Saudi Arabia's oil policy to expose the historical roots and the timing of recent OPEC actions; fifth, to make the general statistical data issued by the Saudi government more accessible through the inclusion of extensive tables on all types of economic problem. Finally, it is hoped that the information and analysis presented in this study will lead to a better understanding of Saudi Arabia and reduce the amount of misinformation about the Kingdom.

To achieve the first objective Parts II and III of this book deal with all aspects of the Saudi Arabian economy. Part II covers the private sector and Part III the public sector. A detailed analysis of the major components of each sector shows the manner in which the economy has grown.

The second objective is achieved by a comparative analysis of the various sectors. In each case the course of interrelated events is traced to the present. Thus, the information given explains the measurable past achievements and how they are related to current conditions.

A discussion of the Kingdom's economic development is incomplete without a firm knowledge of the constraints retarding the development process. To accomplish the third objective, therefore, Part I presents a brief history of Saudi Arabia as well as a discussion of the major cultural aspects that exert an influence on the development process. The information contained in Chapters 2 and 3 has been integrated into the subsequent economic analysis. Thus, the conclusions reached in this study reflect the economic as well as cultural, historical, and political factors that shaped the course of economic development in the past and shape it in the present.

To understand the timing of Saudi Arabia's role in the current international energy crises one must be familiar with the adversary relationship between the government and Aramco as it developed since 1933 and the economic problems facing the Kingdom during the second half of the 1950s and following the War of 1967. At least since 1950 the most important issue between the government and the company has been the division of profits. From 1950 to 1960, hard-bargaining sessions between the two antagonists led to an increasing share of the profits from oil exploitation.

In 1956/57 the country experienced a foreign-exchange crisis endangering the nation's stability and survival. Owing to a decline of oil revenues because of excess supplies in the world markets without a corresponding cut in expenditures on imports, the value of the Saudi Riyal fell on the international money markets. To meet the increasing financial difficulties two steps were taken. First, the government formulated and implemented an austerity program to eliminate the deficit in the state budget and to pay off the rising national debt. Second, to assure success to the stabilization effort without major declines in national well-being, Saudi Arabia became a leader in the drive to increase the share of oil profits flowing to the oil-producing nations. To gain more leverage vis-a-vis the companies, the oil-producing states united in the Organization of Petroleum Exporting Countries (OPEC). Saudi Arabia became a moving force within this organization.

From the formation of OPEC to the Arab-Israeli War of 1967 the oil-producing countries negotiated within the framework of OPEC a number of important agreement changes. In each case the share of oil revenues due the host countries rose as a result of the negotiations.

The War of 1967 created a number of problems for Saudi Arabia, and within 18 months the country faced increasing economic difficulties. The subsidy payments to Egypt and Jordan quickly depleted the reserves, and in the budget year 1969/70 the state budget ran a deficit of S.R. 70 million. The support payments to Egypt and Jordan came in addition to the expenditures for economic development, and in 1968 and 1969 the balance of payments was in deficit on current account. At about the same time a decision was made to formulate a five-year plan to accelerate economic development. It soon became apparent that, given the country's external obligations, current revenues would at best finance the implementation of a very modest plan. Faced with these difficulties, the government reacted as it had in the late 1950s. Operating within the framework of OPEC, the government forced an increase in the tax-reference prices and weakened the oil companies' control over the prices. In quick succession control over posted prices was wrested from the oil companies, and the oil cartel began raising the price of petroleum. Concurrently with that action, the Saudi government advanced its claim for participation in the ownership of Aramco, and it appears at this writing (January 1975) that Saudi Arabia will take over complete ownership of the oil industry located in the country. Thus, the events of the past three years are the culmination of an effort that began in 1950. The timing in each case was triggered by economic difficulties facing the nation.

In some respects this study is a beginning in the analysis of Saudi Arabia's economic development. It is a base on which other studies can rely in investigations concerned with Saudi Arabia. It brings together numerous statistics and exposes their strength and weaknesses. In some cases the official data are completely reorganized to make more effective analytical tools. Furthermore, as redesigned these statistical series can be used by any interested individual, because the reorganization in each case brings the statistics more into line with generally accepted methods of data presentation.

Unfortunately, however, the dearth of important statistical series and the time lags before the data become available forced the curtailment of the investigation of a number of important and interesting aspects of Saudi Arabia's economy. But, again, this study meets an important need: the analysis contained in it offers a firm base for additional investigations as the base of required data is enlarged.

The study reaches the fifth objective because all economic problems and issues have been treated in great detail. Discussions of the Saudi Arabian economy are often influenced by the fact that the available information is either misleading, incomplete, or distorted by all manner of prejudgments. The analysis in this book has been presented with as little bias as possible. Therefore, it can be trusted as a source of information by anyone interested in the economy of Saudi Arabia. It can also be used as a check on many of the overblown claims and statements made by individuals or published in various sources of information. (An example is the recent statement by a high Saudi Arabian government official published in the New York Times [January 5, 1975] that expenditures on the coming development plan may rise to $70 billion. Anyone who has taken the most superficial look into the facts presented in this book would realize that this statement is a bit of hyperbole. The absorptive capacity of the economy is simply not high enough to make such expenditures feasible.)

Throughout this book only the official statistics have been used. This means that in most cases the analysis begins in the late 1950s. Information given by D. Van der Menlen, Lipskey et al., or in the extensive publications of H. St.-John Philby are by and large impressionistic and of doubtful reliability. The data published by the Saudi Arabian government, on the other hand, are in most cases consistent and are prepared by qualified statisticians. Thus, to avoid possible errors and conflicts, nonofficial statistics have been ignored.

It is necessary to make brief reference to the differences in the Islamic and Gregorian calendars. With very few exceptions all dates have been given in Gregorian terms. Very often this practice leads to an overlap of a given Islamic year with two Gregorian ones. For example, the Hijra year 1380 covers seven months of 1960 A.D. and five months of 1961 A.D. Thus, the year 1380 A.H. is given in this book as 1960/61 A.D. The reader is urged to consult Appendix A for a complete explanation of the problems and a statement on the method followed by the author in translating Hijra years into Gregorian years.

Finally, it must be mentioned that to simplify the spelling of Arabic place names and words no attention was paid to diacritical marks. The spelling of Arabic words approximates as much as possible the most common non-Arab usage.

I would like to thank several persons whose assistance and advice has made my task easier and improved the content of this study. Much of the understanding of Saudi society and economic issues is due to Mohammad el-Bassam with whom I worked for two years during my stay in Saudi Arabia. Phillip E. Taylor and Gerald Sazama read various chapters of this study. Their critique and advice added significantly to the undertaking. Thanks are also owing to Sheila Carney, who typed many of the first drafts, and to Jean Hankins, who typed the final draft.

Of course, none of the persons mentioned is responsible for the final product. I alone am responsible for the content and any errors that may be contained in this book.

CONTENTS

LIST OF TABLES

Table Page

LIST OF MAPS AND FIGURE

LIST OF ABBREVIATIONS

A.H.	Anno Hijri
AOC	Arabian Oil Company (Japan)
API	American Petroleum Institute
Aramco	Arabian American Oil Company
Auxirap	Societe Auxiliaire de la Regie Autonome des Petroles
Bbl.	Barrel (= 42 U.S. gallons)
BPD	Barrels per day
Casoc	California Arabian Standard Oil Company
CDS	Central Department of Statistics
c.i.f.	Cost, insurance, and freight
CPO	Central Planning Organization
FAO	Food and Agricultural Organization, United Nations
GDP	Gross domestic product
GNP	Gross national product
Ha	Hectare (= 2.5 acres)
IBRD	International Bank for Reconstruction and Development
IPA	Institute of Public Administration
Km.	Kilometer (= 1,000 meters; 0.621 miles)
Kwh.	Kilowatt hours
LPG	Liquified petroleum gas
MEES	Middle East Economic Survey
OPEC	Organization of Petroleum Exporting Countries
Rls.	Riyals
Safco	Saudi Arabian Fertilizers Company
SAMA	Saudi Arabian Monetary Agency; Central Bank
Socal	Standard Oil of California
S.R.	Saudi riyal
Tapline	Trans Arabian Pipe Line
UAR	United Arab Republic

GLOSSARY

Al-Hasa	The eastern region of Saudi Arabia bordering on the Arabian (Persian) Gulf. Most of the country's oil fields are located in this region.
API gravity	A numerical scale developed by the American Petroleum Institute (API) for stating the weight or density of liquid petroleum.
Crude Oil	Oil as pumped out of the ground. Saudi Arabian oil is divided into three types, by API gravity range: Arabian Light, 34.0° to 34.9°; Arabian Medium, 31.0° to 31.9°; Arabian Heavy, 27.0° to 27.9°.
Dhahana	A narrow band of sand mountains from Rub al-Khali to the Great Nafud.
Dunum	Measure of surface used in agriculture, equal to 1,000 square meters. One hectare equals ten dunums.
Fatwa	Legal decision of the ulema.
Flaring	The burning of natural gas.
Haditha	Oral tradition that can be traced to a companion of the Prophet or to the Prophet Mohammed.
Hadj	Pilgrimage to Mecca.
Hejaz	The western region of Saudi Arabia along the Red Sea coast. It extends roughly from the Jordanian border south about 100 miles past Jedda.
Hijra	The flight of the Prophet Mohammed from Mecca to Medina, 622 A.D. It is the first year of the Moslem calendar.
Ijma	Consensus of the community.
Ikhwan	The brethren. Bedouin who were settled by Abd al-Aziz in agricultural villages. They were to cultivate the soil and study and practice their faith. They became known for their overzealous, uncompromising belief in Islam.
Immam	Religious leader.
Jihad	Holy War.
Malik	King.

Mushaa	Land jointly owned by an extended family.
Mutawwa	Unitarian missionaries. Today, in Saudi Arabia, the term is applied to the enforcers of public morality; i.e., officials who enforce the observance of prayer.
Nejd	The central part of Saudi Arabia. It is bounded in the north by the Nafud desert, in the west by the coastal mountain ranges, in the south by the Rub al-Khali, and in the east by the Dhana.
Neutral Zone	There are two neutral zones, one between Kuwait and Saudi Arabia, and the other between Iraq and Saudi Arabia. They were created to resolve complex border problems. Within the zones the two neighbors share 50-50 rights in the resources.
Posted prices	Tax-reference prices that form the base upon which the oil companies' income-tax liability is calculated.
Quaseem	The area around the cities of Onaiza and Buraida.
Qujas	Analogy
Ramadan	The ninth month of the Hijra year. It is the month of fasting from sunrise to sunset.
Rub al-Khali	The Empty Quarter, the southern desert of the Arabian Peninsula: Largely sandy, it contains numerous sand mountains, many of which rise 1,000 feet or more.
Sabka	Salt flats.
Sadakut	Voluntary alms.
Shammal	Sandstorm.
Sharia	Religious Law, upon which the Saudi Arabian legal system is based.
Sub-Khah	Salt marshes.
Sunna	Practice of the Prophet and his companions.
Suq	Central marketplace.
Ulema	The religious establishment.
Wadi	A dry river bed.

Wahhabi	The followers of Shaikh Muhammad ibn Abd al-Wahhab. They are unitarian in outlook and advocate a return to the strict interpretation of the Koran and the simple ways of the Prophet.
Waqf	The endowment of a piece of land to a religious or charitable institution.
Zakat	Obligatory alms.

PART I

SAUDI ARABIA: ITS LAND, SOCIETY, AND HISTORY

CHAPTER

1

GEOGRAPHY, RESOURCES, CLIMATE, AND POPULATION

INTERNATIONAL BOUNDARIES

Saudi Arabia covers most of the Arabian Peninsula, which is located in Southwestern Asia. It is bounded on the north by Jordan, Iraq, and Kuwait; on the east by the Arabian Gulf, Qatar, the Trucial States, Muscat and Oman, Southern Yemen, and Yemen; and on the west by the Red Sea and the Gulf of Aquaba (see Map 1). The western coast along the Red Sea and the Gulf of Aquaba is 1,100 miles long, and the northern boundary, which extends from the head of the Gulf of Aquaba to Ras Mishab on the Arabian Sea near the Neutral Zone with Kuwait, is 850 miles long. The eastern boundary extends for about 300 miles along the Arabian Gulf, from Ras Mishab to Qatar, and the southern boundary extends for 800 miles, from the Arabian Gulf to Maydi on the Red Sea. Estimates of the area enclosed by these boundaries vary because of several disputed border lines. The official estimate is 865,000 square miles.[1]

The determination of boundaries between Saudi Arabia and its neighbors has been complicated. Prior to the establishment of the Kingdom national boundaries meant very little. The various tribes knew the location of their home territory but paid very little attention to nontribal national borders. Disputes over boundaries were a frequent cause of warfare between tribes. Thus, after the national boundaries had been drawn it took some time before the tribes honored the imaginary lines across the deserts as limits to their wanderings. In two areas the inability to reach agreement on the precise location of the international borders led to the establishment of Neutral Zones. One zone is between the Kingdom and Iraq, and the other is with Kuwait. In the zones neighbors share all rights and resources equally.

MAP 1

Major Cities in the Kingdom of Saudi Arabia

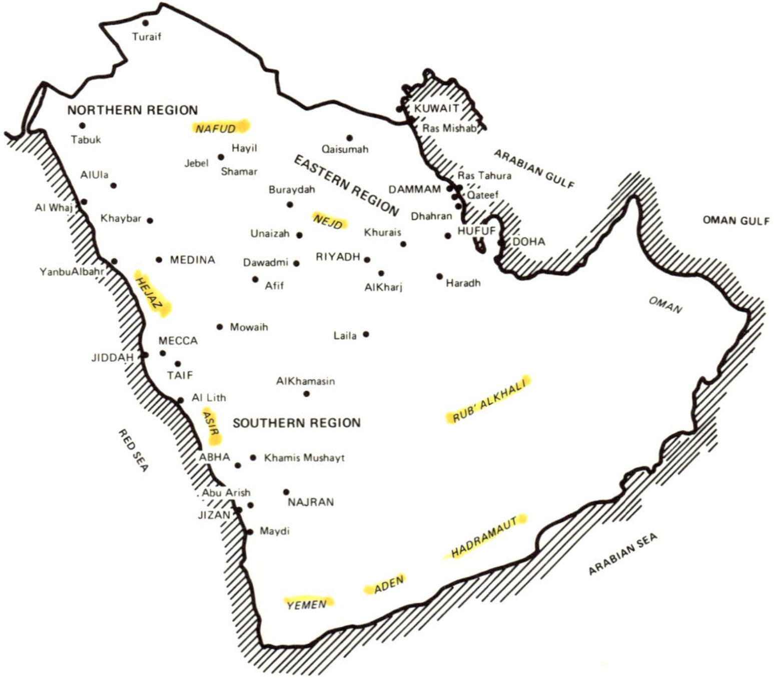

Source: CDS, Annual Report, vol. 9 (1393 A.H.), p. 260.

GEOLOGICAL FORMATION

The Arabian Peninsula is mostly desert. Along the west coast a narrow, fertile plain of varying width extends from the border with Yemen to the Gulf of Aquaba. From the Yemen border to Jizan it is about 40 miles wide; it narrows to about 30 miles from Jizan to Al-Lith and further narrows to 10 miles near Al Whaj, at which width it remains to the Gulf of Aquaba (see Map 2).

East of the plains and parallel to the coast runs a mountain range whose western side rises almost vertically out of the coastal plain. This mountain chain is broken by a number of great valleys (wadis) that are a reminder of the time—about 15,000 years ago—when the climate of the Arabian Peninsula was less hot, and rain was more plentiful than today. The mountains' abrupt rise explains the relative fertility of the coastal plain. Over the millennia the annual rainfall has washed silt from the mountains, fertilizing the plains. In the Asir the highest mountains rise about 9,000 feet; west of Mecca they decline to 8,000 feet, and from Medina north to the frontier they average about 3,000 feet.

To the east of the Hejazi mountain range stretches the Nejd Plateau with an average elevation between 4,000 and 6,000 feet. The height of this plateau falls from its western borders to the Arabian Sea. Its cross section can best be illustrated by the height above sea level of a number of major cities. Jedda, located at the Red Sea, is about 36 feet above sea level. Taif, the summer capital, about 100 miles east of Jedda, is located 4,500 feet above sea level. From this point eastward the height of the plateau declines to 1,950 feet at Riyadh (about 950 miles east of Raif) and 72 feet at Dhahran. The Nejd extends from the Rub al-Khali (the Empty Quarter) in the South to the Jordanian and Iraqui borders. It contains a number of mountain ranges running from the southwest to the northwest.

The Dhahana is a narrow band of sand mountains of varying width extending from the Rub al-Khali northwest to the Great Nafud. It is also called the river of sand, because the traveler going from the west to the east, or in the opposite direction, suddenly comes upon these large sand mountains, and it appears as he travels onward that the road forms a bridge upon which he crosses a river. Just as the mountains of the west mark one border of the Nejd, so does the Dhahana in the east. A number of large salt marshes called sub-khah are scattered throughout the Nejd. East of the Dhahana the elevation falls quickly to sea level; this is the area in which most of the country's oil reserves are located.

The Rub al-Khali is the most forbidding desert in the world. It consists of sand mountains, many of which reach over 1,000 feet in height. Although Arabian American Oil Company (Aramco) explora-

MAP 2

The Geography of the Arabian Peninsula

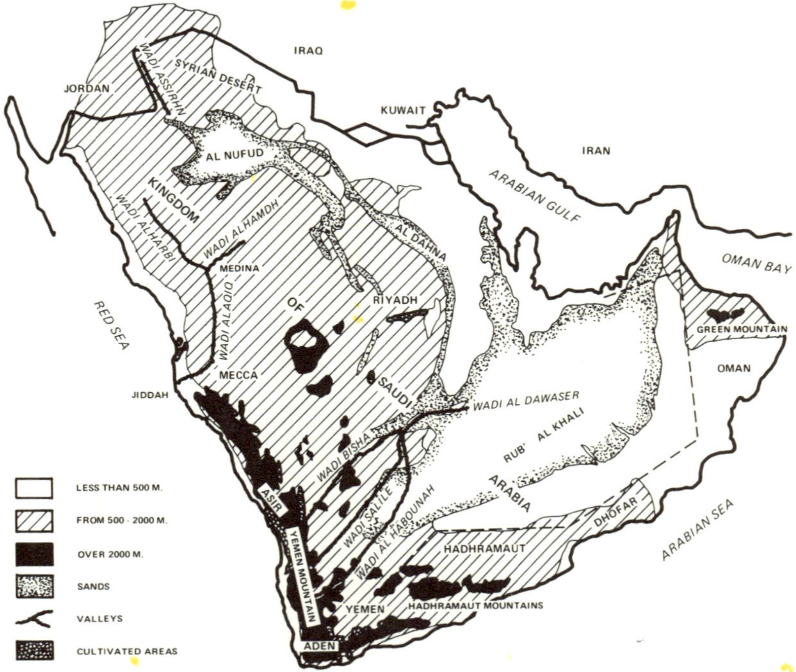

Source: CDS, Statistical Yearbook, vol. 6 (1390 A.H.), p. 13.

tion teams have been searching for oil in the southeastern part of the desert, by far the largest part is still terra incognita and has never been explored. The Great Nafud is a barren, stony desert in the north. It blooms during the rainy season and provides animal pasturage for a short period of time; for the rest of the year it remains dry, hot, and barren.

WATER RESOURCES

Water is by far the most precious resource in the Kingdom. Without its presence the desert is a harsh, desolate place, but where it is found in adequate amounts and in the right quality the desert blooms, and agriculture and animal husbandry are possible. Water is the main constraint on the nation's development. When Aramco, drilling for oil near Riyadh several years ago, found not oil but several huge aquifers of fossil water, the discovery was greeted with the same satisfaction that would greet the discovery of a major oil field.

The water resources depend on the geological composition of the area.[2] In some areas—for example, Buraidah and Qateef—abundant sources of water exist, but improperly drilled wells have led to leaching and improper runoff, reducing the potential usefulness of the land. In other areas the amount of water is large, but its quality is poor. Usable water resources are divided into four classes: confined aquifers, free-flowing aquifers, springs, and valleys (wadis). Confined aquifers store water under pressure; when a bore hole strikes the water, it will rise freely in the bore hole, depending on the pressure in the aquifer. Their depth varies between 250 and 8,000 feet. Free-flowing aquifers contain water without pressure; pumping is required to bring the water to the surface. Their depth rarely exceeds 150 feet. Sources of water flowing above ground in channels but originating below ground are called springs. Certain parts of the Kingdom are rich in springs; the majority are located in the Eastern Province, especially in the area of Al-Hasa where at least 160 springs provide plenty of water. The flow rate of springs varies from a few gallons to 27,000 gallons per minute. Wadis are water courses that fill up with runoff during the rainy season. The water subsides very quickly because there is no vegetation along the wadis that can absorb it and hold it back. In some areas dams have been built to catch the runoff for use in agricultural irrigation and for drinking water. The most important wadis are Wadi Assirhn, along the frontier with Jordan; Wadi Alharbi; Wadi Alhamdh; Wadi Alaqiq; and Wadi Fatima, in the Hejaz. In the southern region Wadis Bisha, Salile, Al Dawasar, and Al Habounah are of major importance (see Map 2).

OIL RESOURCES

The search for oil is a game of blindman's bluff with a few geological clues available that reduce the search to certain areas of the world. Oil is found in the world's sedimentary basins, the location of ancient seas that covered certain regions of the globe millions of years ago. Today these basins are covered by hundreds of feet of soil and rock, and oil pools are located by examination of the microfossils contained in various geological strata, the evaluation of geological structures, and drilling. Saudi Arabia covers part of the world's largest oil reserves, bounded on the north by the Taurus Mountains, by the mountains of Lebanon and Syria and the central highlands of Saudi Arabia on the west, and on the east by the mountains of Iran, Muscat, and Oman. With the exception of two fields, the country's producing fields are located in the Paleozoic stratum east of Riyadh. There is some evidence that oil may also be present under the Red Sea off the western coast of Saudi Arabia, but at this time of writing (October 1974) oil has not been found in commercial quantities.

The quality of crude oil is partially measured by its degree of API gravity and the amount of sulfur and wax it contains. API gravity is a measure of the density of crude oil as established by the American Petroleum Institute and must not be confused with specific gravity. Crude oil lifted in Saudi Arabia is divided into three density classes: Arabian Heavy (27.0° to 27.9° API gravity), Arabian Medium (31.0° to 31.9°), and Arabian Light crude oil (34.0° to 34.9°). The lighter the crude oil (that is, the higher the API gravity), the more desirable it is, because a larger quantity of the higher-valued light products can be refined from it. The degree of gravity of a given crude can be used as a rough measure of the yield of various refined products and is thus an indicator of the relative value of various crudes lifted. Table 1.1 lists Aramco producing fields by API gravity in 1973. Of the 12 fields on stream, seven produce Arabian Light, four produce Arabian Medium, and one produces Arabian Heavy. In addition to the fields located in Saudi Arabia proper, the government has claim to one-half of the undivided share of the oil lifted in the Neutral Zone between the Kingdom and Kuwait. The oil lifted from this area is classified as Arabian Heavy.

Two of the fields listed in Table 1.1 warrant special attention. The Safania field, discovered in May 1951, is the largest known offshore field in the world, and the Ghawar field, first tapped in 1948, is the largest onshore field in the world. The latter stretches 150 miles, from Haradh to Ain Dar, and is up to 22 miles wide.

Sulfur is an undesirable contaminant of crude oil, and its presence lowers the quality of the various products distilled. It is

MAP 3

The Oil Fields of Eastern Saudi Arabia

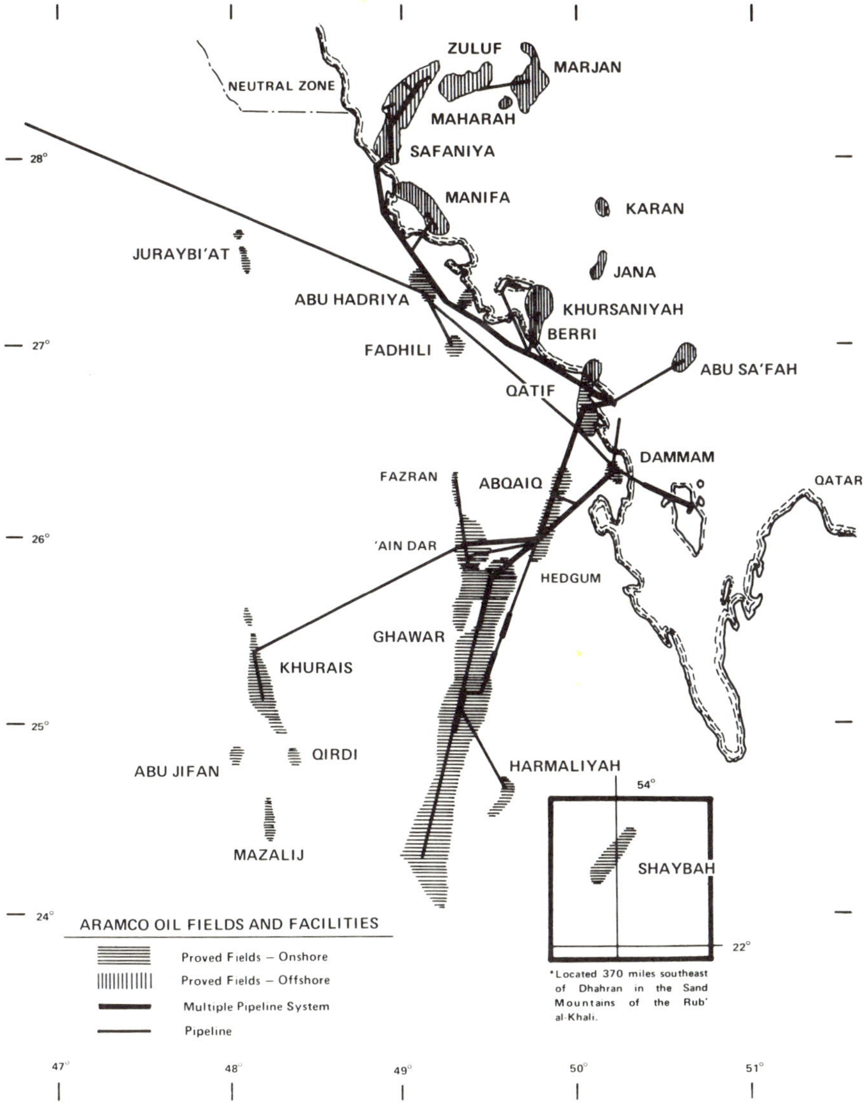

<u>Source</u>: Aramco, <u>Annual Report for 1973</u> (1973), p. 9.

TABLE 1.1

Classification of Aramco Producing Fields, by API Gravity

Arabian Light	Arabian Medium	Arabian Heavy
Berri (1968)	Abu Safah (1966)	Safaniyah (1957)
Fadhili (1963)	Manifa (1966)[b]	
Abu Hadriyah (1962)	Khursaniyah (1960)	
Ghawar (1948)[a]	Khurais (1963)[c]	
Quateef (1938)		
Dammam (1938)		
Abqaiq (1945)		

[a]The extent of this field was not established until 1952. The year 1948 was the year in which a well sunk at Ain Dar first tapped the wealth of the Ghawar field.

[b]A small amount of crude was lifted in 1964.

[c]Small amounts of crude were lifted in 1959 and 1960.

Note: Except in the cases of Abqaiq and Qateef, which were discovered during World War II and began production with completion of the Ras Tanura loading facility at the end of the war, the years in which a field produced a significant amount of crude for sale is given in parentheses.

Source: Ministry of Petroleum and Mineral Resources, Petroleum Statistical Bulletin, 1974 (Dammam: Al-Mutawa Press Co., n.d.), p. 8.

contained in crude either in gaseous form as hydrogen sulfide or as chemical compounds that remain in solution in the crude. Sulfur in crude oil corrodes refinery equipment and produces noxious fumes. Thus, the lower the sulfur content, the more desirable the crude. Saudi Arabian crude oil contains a relatively high amount of sulfur, averaging about 1.77 percent.

There is some controversy regarding the Kingdom's known oil reserves, and various sources publish slightly different figures. In any case, Saudi Arabia has the largest known and proven oil reserves in the world. Proven reserves are defined as those pools of crude known and recoverable with current technology and available equipment in place. In 1973 proved reserves amounted to 97 billion barrels, or more than 50 percent of known world reserves (see Table 1.2). Probable reserves (including proved reserves) amounted to 164.5 billion barrels. Since 1957 proved reserves have risen about 700 percent, from 12 to 97 billion barrels.

In addition to crude oil, Saudi Arabia owns huge amounts of natural gas in association with the oil in the ground. In the past this gas was flared (burned), except for relatively small amounts, which were sold in the local markets as liquified petroleum gas (LPG) for industrial and home use. In recent years natural gas has been collected and used for the manufacture of fertilizer.

MINERAL RESOURCES

In addition to the crude oil resources minerals have been located in commercial quantities. The government is currently undertaking extensive geological exploration to determine the nature of the known deposits and search for additional mineral deposits. The search has been successful: Copper, gold, silver, iron, sulfur,

TABLE 1.2

Proved Oil Reserves at Year's End, 1951-73

Year	Million Barrels	Year	Million Barrels
1951	12,000	1963	61,000
1952	16,000	1964	62,000
1953	28,000	1965	67,000
1954	36,000	1966	78,000
1955	37,000	1967	80,000
1956	40,000	1968	88,000
1957	45,000	1969	89,000
1958	47,000	1970	88,000
1959	50,000	1971	90,000
1960	46,000	1972	93,000
1961	50,000	1973	97,000
1962	60,000	1974	n.a.

Sources: 1951-59: Kamal S. Sayegh, Oil and Arab Regional Development (New York: Praeger, 1968), p. 297; 1960-69: CDS, Statistical Yearbook, 1390 A.H., vol. 8 (Riyadh), p. 230; 1970-73: 1970-73: Aramco, Aramco 1973, annual report, p. 8.

phosphates, and rare earths have been found in commercial quantities. A major iron deposit estimated to contain 1.5 billion tons of low-grade (30 to 40 percent) iron ore has been discovered west of Jedda. Additional iron deposits have been found in Wadi Fatima and Jebel Idsas. The geological surveys currently under way have discovered geological formations that indicate that more minerals are to be found, especially in the western part of the nation.

CLIMATE

Saudi Arabia's climate is controlled by the subtropical high-pressure system. In the interior sections summer is hot and dry, and winter is relatively cool. Despite the Kingdom's geographical location, variations between summer and winter temperatures are significant.

In the Nejd, the Quaseem, and other interior sections summer temperatures average about 100° F, but daily temperature variations are quite large. In the Riyadh area temperatures over 130° F are quite common during July and August; in the winter temperatures rarely fall below 32° F, but wind and low humidity often combine to produce bone-chilling weather conditions during January and February; spring and fall are very pleasant, with daily highs in the 80s and 90s and very low humidity.

In the eastern and western coastal regions temperature differences are modified by the presence of the seas. Humidity is high and temperatures go rarely above 100° F. Nevertheless, the author recalls one day in July 1970 when the temperature in Jedda reached 128° F, and the humidity stood at 98 percent.

Except for the southwestern coastal region, rainfall is scarce. The number of rainy days varies considerably and has no significant pattern. For example, in 1972 the capital city Riyadh had a total of 36 rainy days, of which 11 occurred in April and seven each in January and March. There was no rain from June through October, and the total rainfall amounted to 0.91 inches for the year.

In the eastern province sandstorms (shammals) occur frequently during late spring and early summer, reaching their peak in June, when it is not uncommon to have 23 out of 30 days with blowing dust and strong northwesterly winds.

POPULATION

No figure has been agreed upon for the population size. Estimates vary between 3 and 15 million. The government has used population estimates ranging from 6 to 12 million. In all probability any figure over 6 million is incorrect, and outside sources such as the International Bank for Reconstruction and Development (IBRD) place the figure between 5 and 5.5 million.[3] Even that estimate appears too high in our opinion. Based on conversations with various officials, our estimate is 3.75 to 4 million, with an absolute upper limit of 4.5 million persons in 1974.

Ethnically, the population is relatively homogeneous. Non-Saudi Arabs are concentrated in the major cities, among them Palestinian refugees and Yemeni laborers. The number of non-Arab residents has increased owing to the increasing demand for skilled technicians. Most non-Arabs are located in the major east- and west-coast cities and in Riyadh. The proportion of non-Saudis in the population has been estimated to be between 15 and 20 percent in Mecca, Medina, and Taif, and 23 percent and 35 percent in Riyadh and Jedda, respectively.[4]

More than 45 percent of the population is under 15 years of age. The birthrate is about 2.75 percent, and the deathrate is about 20 per 1,000 per annum.[5]

Because most of the country consists of wasteland, the settled population is concentrated in a few major cities and in three belts running southeast to northwest. In the west the population is concentrated on the coastal plain from north of Medina to about Taif, with a small band in the Asir running south to the Yemeni border. The second concentration is located in the Nejd; it begins north of Burayda and stretches south along the Tuwaig escarpment past Al-Kharj. The third area is located along the Arabian Gulf coast from Ras Tanura south and west to the Haradh agricultural settlement. Even within those belts the population is concentrated in the areas where water is available. In addition to the three population belts, small areas of permanent settlement are scattered throughout the country.

In recent years the rural-urban shift has accelerated the growth of the major cities. Originally, all towns had the same characteristics. They were walled and strongly fortified. The marketplace (suq) was located in the center of town, and dwellings were clustered around it, separated by small alleys. In the suq small shops opened onto covered lanes and alleys with various specialties clustered together. All carpet sellers, jewelers, cloth merchants, and so on, carry out their activities in a specific area of the market. The population size of the 12 major cities is unknown, but it is reasonable to assume that the three largest cities, Riyadh, Mecca, and Jedda, each have populations of more than 200,000. It has been estimated that Riyadh has grown twelvefold in the last 40 years.[6] The move to the cities has led to the abandonment of whole villages. During a trip from Medina to Jedda the author saw the remains of at least three completely deserted, rapidly deteriorating villages whose inhabitants had moved into the cities.

Western observers frequently label as slums the mudbrick dwellings and narrow streets and alleys of the older sectors of towns and villages, but such labeling is often incorrect. No doubt, slums exist, as anyone with a normal amount of perception can see, but mudbrick buildings and narrow streets and alleys are not necessarily evidence of slums. On the average, mudbrick buildings are cooler inside than similar buildings constructed of concrete blocks, and narrow streets offer protection from heat and dust storms. Because of the lack of a cloud cover, nights in the desert are often rather cool. This coolness is trapped in the narrow streets and released slowly during the day, providing some protection from the heat of the day. Furthermore, the crooked, narrow streets of the old sector provide excellent protection from wind and dust. Clearly, the old quarters are an example of town building designed to modify the environment, rather than evidence of slums.

The Bedouin population has been estimated to be between 200,000 and 300,000. However, observers who have had contact with the various tribes believe that this estimate is too low. The Bedouin wander with their herds of camels and goats from the northern fringes of the Rub al-Khali to the Jordanian border and from the Hejazi mountains east to the coastal areas along the Arabian Gulf. Attempts have been made to settle the nomads. There are now semipermanent settlements clustered along the Trans Arabian Pipeline (Tapline) in the east. The completion of the road links west from the Onaiza-Buraida area to Mecca has attracted some nomads. The author traveled this route before and after completion of the road. During the first trip he met almost no one along the road and saw only a few villages. About 14 months later he found that numerous tent-villages had sprung up along the highway, and in two or three locations mudbrick houses had been built. Another area of Bedouin concentration is east of Riyadh in the Khurais oil field where the availability of water has attracted the nomads from the surrounding desert.

NOTES

1. CDS, Statistical Yearbook, 1390 A.H., vol. 6 (Riyadh), p. 8.
2. For additional detail, see ibid., pp. 9-10.
3. Norman C. Walpole et al., Area Handbook for Saudi Arabia (Washington, D.C.: Government Printing Office, 1971), p. 18.
4. Ibid., p. 19.
5. CPO, Development Plan, 1390 A.H. (Riyadh, n.d.), p. 65.
6. Ibid.

CHAPTER

2

SAUDI ARABIAN SOCIETY

To appreciate the course of Saudi history, the direction of the nation's economic development, and the problems facing the Kingdom today, it is necessary to gain some understanding of Saudi society. In developing countries social and economic factors combine to place severe constraints on economic progress. Among the economic constraints, one stands out above all: the lack of capital. However, in Saudi Arabia capital has been available in adequate amounts at least since 1960 to support brisk economic activity and a high growth rate. Social and cultural factors, however, have been a major constraint on economic development.

ISLAM

Saudi Arabia is by far the most conservative of the Arab states. Two mutually reinforcing factors account for this conservatism. First, Arabia is the birthplace and cradle of Islam and the site of the two Holy Cities, Mecca and Medina. Second, it is also the place of origin of a reform movement known as Wahhabism in the Western world. Together, those factors have given the Saudis a sense of uniqueness in the Moslem world: They are the stewards of Moslem heritage and, therefore, have an obligation to reform Islam.

The Origin of Islam

Islam rose in the western part of Arabia, the Hejaz. Before the time of the Prophet Mohammed, the Arabian Peninsula was populated by nomads who followed the rains across the desert with their flocks of goats and camels, eking out a meager subsistence standard of living. There were a few fortified towns and villages whose walls protected the sedentary population against incursions from roving bands of Bedouin. Life in the desert was short and harsh, and the threat of starvation was ever present. In time some of the towns grew and became centers of trade. Among these towns, Mecca and Medina were the most important. In addition to its commercial importance, Mecca was also the focal point of Arab polytheism. In Mecca pilgrims came to worship at the Kaaba, a small temple built of stones.

Mohammed was born in Mecca in April, 571 A.D. His youth and early manhood were spent in and around Mecca, first as a shepherd and later as a merchant. He traveled widely in connection with his business activities and was known as an honest and fair man. By the time Mohammed turned 40 his lifestyle had changed. Now and again he withdrew from society for quiet and undisturbed meditation in the desert surrounding the city. It was during one of these periods of meditation, in 610 A.D., that he underwent a religious experience that led him to preach against the prevailing immorality and paganism. He offended the local power structure, which plotted to assassinate him, and he was forced to flee to Medina in 622 A.D. The first year of the Moslem calendar dates from this event. Mohammed stayed in Medina and continued to preach his doctrine. Slowly, he attracted followers to his cause, and at the time of his death in the eleven Hijra year (633 A.D.) he had unified most of the Bedouin tribes and inspired them with fervent zeal to spread his teachings.

The Koran

The central core of Mohammedanism is laid down in the Koran.[1] It records "those formal utterances and discourses which Mohammed and his followers accept as directly inspired. Muslim orthodoxy, therefore, regards them as the literal Word of God mediated through the angel Gabriel."[2] The Koran outlined the basis for a new religion that is neither Christian nor Jewish but is influenced to some extent by both faiths.

The Koran lays down a way of life to which the believer must adhere if he is to enter into paradise. The system, as presented in the Koran:

> . . . is rigid, positive, and emphatic. The rigidity, the special emphasis upon the compulsory performance of legal and religious duties, the demand for unquestioning obedience, can be explained as a reaction

> against the social and spiritual anarchy of Arabia.
>
> There is a reality in the suggestion that the ceremonial bowings and prostrations in unison of the daily powers were a means of physical as well as spiritual discipline.[3]

The belief that the Koran is the literal Word of God has raised many problems. For example, the Koran prohibits the taking of interest. In Saudi Arabia this injunction is honored in the basic rules governing the Saudi Arabian Monetary Agency (SAMA, the central bank). It is possible to enforce the Koranic injunction against interest taking at least with respect to non-Moslems whenever a governmental organization is involved. (The agency does collect interest on funds invested in the international money market.) Considerable pressure from the religious establishment exists to extend the ban to private banking institutions. One solution proposed has been to establish banks on the principle of "Free Partnership" and "Limited Partnership" as determined by the Koran.[4] Briefly, the organization would be as follows. Suppliers of capital will contribute funds on the basis of "Free Partnership," which is defined as "A form of company organization in which two or more persons own implements or animals for the purpose of using them for profit and every one of the partners receives a share in the profits."[5] The bank will use these funds for investment purposes according to the principle of Limited—or silent—Partnership. That is, the bank enters into a partnership with the borrower and provides the required loan. The bank may or may not participate in the operation. Its share of the profits is fixed by contract. By sharing in the borrower's profit, the bank does not collect interest and the earnings from the partnership are divided among the bank's shareholders as determined in its charter.

Another example of the constraining influence of the Koran is the treatment of the Nabatean cliff tombs near the village of Madain Salih, in the northern part of the Hejaz. According to the Koran, the area around the village was once the territory of the pagan Thamud who "carve houses out of [rocky] mountains with great skill." Displeased with their licentious way of life, God sent the prophet Saleh among them to lead them back to a righteous way of life. They refused to heed the prophet's warning, and God punished them: "The (mighty) Blast overtook the wrong doers, and they lay prostrate in their homes before morning."

It has been known for some time that the "rooms" hewn into the cliffs around Madain Salih are Nabatean tombs similar to those found in Petra.[6] Yet in the government-authored pamphlet Saudi Arabia: Land of Achievement this is the description of the tombs that is given: "Famous for its magnificent beauty is the ancient city of Madain Salih, where the people carved their homes from solid rock and chiseled decorations into the exteriors."[7]

The Teaching of Islam

The center of Islamic teaching is the belief in the absolute oneness of God. He has certain attributes that are not separate from Him but are an integral part of God, and to recognize these virtues as separable from God is to associate other gods with Him, which is to deny the oneness of God and is thus blasphemy. God is eternal; everything and everyone depends on Him, and He causes things in accordance with His will. The prophets were messengers of God sent among men to teach them how to lead a righteous life and to warn them away from sin.

All prophets preached approximately the same doctrine. Adam was the first and Mohammed the last of the prophets. Five prophets—Muhammed, Noah, Abraham, Moses, and Jesus—stand out among them and are held in special honor. The Prophet's teachings were delivered orally by him but written down at a later date. The best known of the Holy Books are the Old and New Testaments, the Psalms, and the Koran. The Koran is the transcript of a tablet in heaven. The prophets received their messages from angels who enforce God's decrees. Death is the end of life, but there will come a Day of Resurrection when all men will be judged. Those who pass will go to heaven and those who are found wanting will go to hell. Anyone who dies in the Cause of Allah will go directly to heaven. God's deeds are all parts of His plan. Thus, Moslems must carry out their daily obligations faithfully: "If they attain their aims they should be thankful to God. If they fail, they should not despair and resent their fate."[8]

Mohammed's teachings found expression in the Five Pillars of Islam to which all Moslems must adhere and whose dictates they must follow. The first obligation is the utterance of the Creed: "There is but one God, Mohammed is the Apostle of God." It is the declaration of faith and occurs in the obligatory prayers, the call to prayer, and other rituals. Second, a believer must say his prayers five times daily: at dawn, at midday, in the afternoon, at sunset, and about two hours after sunset. When praying, the person must face in the direction of Mecca and perform certain prescribed motions. Third, the giving of alms is an important act. The Koran distinguishes between zakat (obligatory alms) and sadakut (voluntary alms). Zakat is not a tax that can be used by the state to meet its own needs. It is a form of income distribution and is to be spent on the poor, the needy, slaves, prisoners, and others. Alms must be given in accordance with certain rates laid down by law. The fourth obligation is fasting. Ramadan, the ninth month of the Hijra year, is the month of obligatory fasting. During the month all Moslems must abstain from food, drink, and sexual intercourse from sunrise to sunset. Exceptions to the abstinence from food and drink are made for the ill, travelers, pregnant women, and others in special circumstances who must make up the missed fast days during the period before the next Ramadan. The final obligation is the hadj (pilgrimage). Every Moslem who has the means to make the journey to Mecca must do so at least once in his lifetime. He must be in Mecca during Dhul Hijra, the twelfth month of the Hijra year, where he must perform specified rituals on certain days of this month.

In addition to the duties imposed on Moslems by the five pillars of the faith, there is the obligation for the struggle for the propagation of the faith. The Jihad (Holy War) has been called the sixth pillar of the faith. Mohammed challenged the Bedouin of Arabia to compose their differences and proceed with the Jihad to bring God's word to the rest of the world, and it is the duty of every believer to continue this effort.

The Traditions

The Koran lays down strict rules governing the behavior of men that were first received by the Arab communities in Mecca and Medina through the Prophet. Mohammed lived among the communities, and by following his example there were few problems of interpretation of the Koranic injunctions. Questions regarding the new faith could always be submitted to the Prophet himself, and he would interpret the law.

A believing Moslem tries to model his life as much as possible after that of the Prophet. But times and communities have changed, and new problems or old problems in new surroundings confront the believer. How is he to react to these when the Koran often offers only vague or contradictory advice or no advice at all? He must turn to the facts known about the Moslem community at the time of the Prophet. Thus, there developed soon after the Prophet's death the practice of referring to those who knew the Prophet directly and asking them for guidance whenever a problem of Koranic interpretation arose. The companions of the Prophet would search their memory and recount a similar event in which Mohammed participated and was known to have explained the Law, or they would repeat a comment on a subject from the Prophet himself. These hadith ("oral tradition which can be traced back to a Companion or to the prophet Mohammed"[9]) are considered the final authority on any subject. The hadith, therefore, can be considered a supplement to the Koran designed to assist the Moslem in his attempt to model his life after that of the Prophet.

The traditions contain the practice of the Prophet and his companions (the sunna). Scholars of Islam have produced prodigious amounts of material dealing with haditha and sunna, and the most important fact for a student of Saudi Arabia to remember is that appeals by the ulema (men learned in religious matters) or the King for a return to the sunna is in effect an attempt to return to the basic content of Mohammedanism as the Prophet lived it.

Early in its history Islam split into two sects: the Shiites and the Sunnites. The schism originated in a political dispute as to whether the legitimate ruler of the Moslem community would come from the descendents of Ali, the Prophet's son-in-law, or from the Ummayyads, who denied the election principle as a legitimate means to the succession, claiming the right to rule the Moslem community because they had been the hereditary rulers of the people before the rise of Islam. As time progressed the Shiites disputed not only politically but also doctrinally with Moslem orthodoxy. Except for a small minority in the Eastern Province, the Kingdom's population belongs to the Sunnite sect.

The Sharia

The Shiites and the Sunnites each developed their own legal systems. The sharia (religious Law) is the law upon which the Saudi Arabian legal system is based. Four schools of legal thought developed within Sunnite thought, each named after its originator: the Hanafite School, the Malikite School, the Shafiite School, and the Hanbalite School. Today, the Hanafi school rules in western Asia (except in Arabia), lower Egypt, and Pakistan; the Shafii rules in Indonesia, and the Maliki in north and west Africa and upper Egypt. The Hanbali school was the last to be developed; it was also "responsible for the most intolerant and fanatical view of a Muslim's duties and responsibilities."[10] It declined in importance during Ottoman rule but has experienced a revival in Saudi Arabia, where it is the predominant school of legal thought today.

WAHHABISM

Following the death of the fourth Caliph, Ali, the Prophet's son-in-law, Arab influence on Islam declined. The spiritual capital remained in Arabia, but the temporal seat of Islam was moved to Damascus and finally to Constantinople. In the course of time Moslem society deteriorated and lost the asceticism that characterized its early years:

> From the simple, rigid, and austere monotheism preached by Mohammed to a small Arab community it had broadened into an intricate complex of legal schools and theological sects, superimposed on a medley of congregations with their own rituals and an extraordinary diversity of religious ideas and practices.[11]

Arabia had become a backwater, and religious practices had turned away from proper Mohammedan beliefs. Islam was ripe for reform and one of the earliest reforms begain the Nejd under the leadership of Muhammad Ibn Abd al-Wahhab.

Muhammad Ibn Abd al-Wahhab was born in 1703 in the Nejdi town Uyainah, near Riyadh. He was the son and grandson of Hanbali judges. Instructed by his father he had memorized the Koran before he was 10 years old. He traveled extensively and made the pilgrimage to Mecca. He visited Medina, as well as Persia and Iraq. He studied Sufism and at one time even taught its message. Everywhere he went he found that the people had turned away from the original content of the Prophet's teaching. Syntheism prevailed, and there were saint worship and other diversions from original Islam. At about the age of 40 he returned home, and following his father's death he began to teach his reformist fundamentalist message. To dramatize his teachings he cut down sacred trees, destroyed the tomb of a locally revered hero, and stoned a woman who had confessed to adultery. Slowly, he gathered converts to his doctrine, and his teachings spread throughout the central Nejd. When it became apparent that the opposition planned to assassinate him, he moved to the neighboring town of Diriyah and gained the protection and support of the leader of the town's ruling family, Muhammed ibn Saud, who publicly accepted his teachings. Inspired by Abd al-Wahhab's cause, the Nejdis set out upon a Jihad designed to reform Islam and force the believers to live in accordance with the Law.

Abd al-Wahhab's message was "puritanical, vigorous and simple": He advocated the return to classical Law "and that in its straightest, most rigid Hanbali version, stripped of all innovation developed through the intervening centuries. Obey the pristine Law, fully, strictly, singly; and establish a society where that Law obtains. This [he] preached is Islam. All else is superfluous and wrong."[12] He rejected "worship of saints and at saint's tombs, reliance upon the intercessions of the Prophet and the saints; indeed, the whole gamut of popular religion."[13] He advocated a return to the message of the Koran and the Prophet's sunna, and demanded that the community live in accordance with these precepts.

Owing to the Wahhabis' fanaticism in implementing their fundamentalist views, they soon offended the orthodox segment of Islam, and following a series of initial military triumphs they were defeated by the troops of the Sublime Porte, and their major stronghold Diriyah was razed to the ground. Despite this setback, Wahhabi doctrine survived: "[I]n its ideal aspect, in the challenge which it flung out to the contamination of pure Islamic monotheism by the infiltration of animistic practices and pantheistic nations, Wahhabism had a salutory and revitalizing effect, which spread little by little over the whole Muslim world."[14]

Throughout the nineteenth century Wahhabism was concentrated in the Nejd. It spread to the rest of Arabia with the conquests of Abd al-Aziz during the first quarter of the twentieth century, but its impact on the lifestyle of the population was uneven. Today, the most fanatical adherents to Wahhabism are located in the Quasim around the town of Buraida. In the rest of the nation the most extreme manifestations of Wahhabism are slowly weakening. For example, at one time the obligation of prayer was rigidly enforced throughout the Kingdom: All activities stopped; stores and shops had to close; workers in industry and other activities had to lay down their tools; traffic came to a virtual standstill. Mutawwa (Unitarian missionaries; religious police) went about to enforce adherence to the custom. In recent years observation of prayer has loosened. While the religious police still try to enforce obedience, an increasing portion of the population does not follow the law. Instead of closing his shop or store to go to the nearest mosque for prayer, the proprietor will reduce the lights, close the door and stay in his shop to carry out any business he may get. Fewer people stop on the road to perform their prayer; rather, they continue on their way until they return home, where they may or may not meet their prayer obligation. Another example illustrating the increasing liberalization of life as well as the differential impact of Wahhabism in the Kingdom is the ban on smoking. Until the early 1960s smokers caught in the streets of Riyadh could be turned over by the mutawwa to the local committee on morality for appropriate action. While the no-smoking ban was rigidly enforced in Riyadh, it was not enforced in Mecca, where anyone could smoke in the street, even in the vicinity of the Holy Mosque. Today, the ban on smoking is also no longer enforced in Riyadh.

The increasing liberalization of life has not proceeded without opposition. The King speaks out upon occasion if a particular trend has gone too far. One such trend was the matter of dress of the young Saudis. A statement issued by the King on proper dress codes is an example of the rear-guard action fought by the traditionalist forces. In his statement King Faisal said:

> We have observed of late that our country has been infiltrated by alien customs which have no relationship whatsoever to our religion and traditions such as clothes put on by women when they go to the marketplace which clothes are repulsive to decorum, inconsistent with Islamic ethics and are designed to reveal feminine charms.
>
> Likewise I have come to understand that some of our young boys have started adopting customs and fashions which, to say the least, are symptoms of moral degeneration and are incompatible with manliness and good conducts.[15]

The King urged all Saudis and foreigners "to observe the regulations of the country and its traditions with respect to their conduct and the way they get dressed." "To enforce decorum the King empowered police and the Mutawin (religious police) to take all measures necessary to eliminate these outrageous manifestations." While this pronouncement did not stop the spread of Western dress, it did slow it down and relegated the wearing of such apparel to the privacy of the home.

Wahhabi influence still controls the entertainment available in the Kingdom. Over strong opposition television stations have now been built in all major population centers. Programing is limited to educational material and some American or European productions. The first moon landing was televised over all stations (in order to reconcile the fact of a moon landing with the Koran, a special series of lectures by religious leaders was screened throughout the Kingdom). Cinemas and dancing are prohibited, but it is possible to rent feature-length films for viewing in the privacy of one's own home. An intensive program of sports is supported by the government. Soccer is a favorite sport among Saudi men and draws thousands of spectators to even the least important intracity games.

The Wahhabi influence has retarded the development of the fine arts. Except for the Holy Mosques in Mecca and Medina, most mosques are extremely plain. In the countryside they are built of unpainted mudbrick without any decoration. The only art form that has developed is the decoration of trucks: Doors, hoods, and bodies of all sizes of trucks are covered with paintings of trees, beaches, and ponds; truck gates and bodies are often decorated with welded metal constructions, sometimes painted in red or white. These decorations are a true folk art. In 1970 the first exhibition of oil and watercolor paintings was held in Riyadh's major hotel. Although most of the artists represented came from Arab countries other than Saudi Arabia, a number of paintings were exhibited by native Saudi artists. As would be expected the subject matter of the Saudi artists avoided paintings of humans and animals. Most of the artists concentrated on calligraphy. The paintings of the Saudi artists were crude and primitive, but they showed the possible beginning of a unique Saudi Arabian school of painting.

Except for non-Saudis, women do not play any public role. They are segregated, and when they appear in public they must cover themselves completely; their dress includes a veil to hide the face. Despite their inferior status, Saudi women are making advances. Some have gone abroad for study; others are being educated in the public girls' schools. Polygamy is on the decline among the younger generation. Maintaining several wives in accordance with the Law has become expensive, and because the men want to consume the modern, imported goods they settle for one wife and spend their increasing discretionary income on goods and services. Furthermore, many educated Saudis do not wish to subject their children to the stresses of growing up in a home with several mothers. There is constant conflict between the siblings and their mothers in such homes. Often, the natural mother will give preference to her own children over those of the other wives. Having been in this predicament, many men have decided that one wife is sufficient. Finally, there appears to be a move toward smaller families among the better-educated Saudis.

Foreigners, primarily Westerners, are by and large welcome, but they are still greeted with suspicion and occasionally may find themselves abused by the mutawwa. People may not approve of foreign customs, but they are willing to accept foreigners as neighbors in their midst. When the author and his family moved into their home in Riyadh, the neighbors gave the customary feast. To assure our comfort and enjoyment one of them went to the market and bought chairs and eating utensils, neither of which are used in a traditional Saudi Arab home.

Adherence to the Hanbali school of legal interpretation with its absolute prohibition of innovation has reduced the liberalizing influence of the ijma (consensus of the community). The Koran and sunna are often contradictory on a particular point. Furthermore, there are many occasions in modern life when a search of the Koran and hadith on a given problem by different individuals leads to differing interpretations and conclusions. To resolve these problems an individual can consult the religious authorities. If upon consultation among the teachers an ijma is achieved, the believer may apply the ruling in his life without fear of violating the spirit of Islam. An ijma arrived at by the members of the community is infallible, because "the people will never agree on an error." The importance of this device to a Moslem community rests on the fact that when the community reaches a consensus and it is in contradiction with the haditha, the existing sunna is abrogated, and the new consensus will be accepted as law.[16] Unfortunately, the Wahhabi tradition restricts the ijma to the consensus reached during the first three centuries of Islam and rejects all subsequent agreements. Thus, the Wahhabis are forced to find solutions to twentieth-century problems in seventh-, eighth-, or ninth-century tradition.

Two examples will suffice to illustrate the difficulties. The Koran prohibits interest, but a modern economy cannot function without a money market governed bythe interest-rate mechanism. Under the prevailing Wahhabi doctrine a formal solution to this predicament has not been found. As was mentioned before, the charter of the SAMA expressly prohibits the taking of interest. In commercial bank legislation the question of interest rates has been ignored. To get around the Koranic injunction, rather than collect interest on loans commercial banks collect service charges--which, of course, is just another name for interest. Another problem is the lack of a body of commercial law. The sharia contains various legal provisions dealing with commerce, but there are many aspects of modern economic activity that are not covered by sharia Law. An attempt to formulate a commercial code failed a number of years ago, owing to strong opposition by the religious establishment. Currently, a second attempt is being undertaken to provide the country with a commercial code based on sharia and drawing on English and Roman law.

Concern with the reconciliation of sharia law with the demands of the modern, secular state is not limited to the ulema. Many Saudi leaders are concerned with the problem, among them Ahmed Zaki Yamani, the Minister of Petroleum and Mineral Resources. In a lecture delivered at the American University in Beirut in February 1967 he took issue with "[t]he statement that it is too late for Sharia to face contemporary issues."[17] He blames this attitude, which predominates among Western observers, on the fact that "centuries before any contact with the West, a reactionary movement took place, and the elaborate dynamic intellectual stream came to an abrupt standstill after closing the doors of the Ijtihad (free investigation). The Shaira became static and confined to the voluminous traditions of the four schools of thoughts (Hanafi, Shafie, Maliki, and Hanbali)."[18] Yamani maintains that this closing off of dynamic intellectual exploration is not inherent in Moslem thought, and he points to the possibilities inherent in the principle of ijma and argument by qiyas (analogy) as a means to make sharia Law relevant to the solution of modern problems. He proposes that to implement sharia Law fully the state should

> select principles from the various juristic schools with no exceptions, the criterion being what is more

> appropriate to the needs of that particular country. Such countries could legislate new solutions for novel problems, deriving such solutions from the general principles of the Sharia and considerations of public interest and communal welfare.[19]

This is clearly a major break with Wahhabi fundamentalism, and when it is remembered that this proposal comes from one of the nation's most powerful ministers, there can be no doubt that Saudi Arabia will find a solution to the vexing problems involved in an integration of Islam with modern problems.

SOCIAL ORGANIZATION

The family is the center of the social structure, and loyalty to the family overshadows all other obligations. Individual members participate in major family decisions, but the final determination of a question lies in the hands of the father or the head of a family. Women are rarely if ever consulted in the decision-making process.

The basic family is the extended family with descent traced through the paternal line. An individual's well-being is the responsibility of the whole family, and the family's well-being is the individual's primary concern. If the head of a household dies, his family is absorbed into the larger family group. The deceased's older children usually join the household of the paternal grandfather or that of the oldest surviving brother. The widow may stay in the husband's family or she may return to her own family, in which case she takes the younger children with her. Although the mother's family has the responsibility for the upbringing of the widow's youngest children, the children return to the father's family between the ages of six and ten. Final responsibility for the individual members of the family does not rest necessarily with the patriarch. It is not unusual for a more distant relative to take in members of a family. A bachelor or a man with a small family may take on the responsibility for needy family members, such as a cousin and his (or her) children.

Women are assigned inferior status in the society. They lead extremely private lives, subject entirely to the will of the men in the family. When a woman appears in public she must wear a long black cloak covering her from head to toe and hide her face behind a veil. The inferior public status of women is underscored by the custom that if two men in company with their wives meet one another in public, they will engage in conversation without the slightest reference to the women. The women will stand some distance away, waiting for the men to finish their discussion. It is considered extremely bad form to inquire about anyone's wife. At best one asks, "How is the family?" and avoids all reference to the wife. Marriages are arranged by the family. When a man is ready to marry, he makes his intention known to his family, and the father or any other close male relative will then inquire among the fathers of eligible daughters. Once a bride has been chosen the future husband may send a relative to see the bride and tell him what impression the prospective bride has made upon the intermediary. Bride and groom ordinarily meet each other for the first time on the wedding day during the marriage ceremony. This custom is slowly changing.

Although in most cases the marriage is still arranged, among the more liberal upper classes the prospective husband may have a chance to meet his bride before the marriage. The automobile has further weakened the strict enforcement of traditional marriage customs. Today, it is even possible for a young man to "date" his prospective wife before the betrothal. The suitor will come calling with his car. Dressed in the appropriate fashion, the future bride will sit in the back seat. The couple will then go for a drive about town, conversing with each other. This practice is not very common, but as long as the suitor does not stop and she does not remove her veil during the ride, their parents will not object.

By and large a man's social standing is determined by his family and the tribe or region from which he originates. There is a small upper class in the nation whose status is determined by the family. The highest social standing is accorded to the members of the royal family and its branches. To this group can be added a small number of the Al-Shaikh family, the descendants of Abd al-Wahhab, and a small number of wealthy merchants who have achieved the lifestyle of the upper class. The lower class consists of Bedouin and herdsmen and semiskilled and unskilled workers employed in the government and private sectors. With the exception of a few merchant families in the major Red Sea and Arabian Gulf port towns, the rise of the middle class has been a recent development.

A middle class is slowly emerging; its growth has been closely associated with the nation's transformation from a traditional economy based on herding to a modern economy based on the exploitation of oil and the expanding role of the government.[20] The new economy requires skilled managers, engineers, and technicians. But until 1950 the Kingdom's educational system was only concerned with the classic Arab education--that is, the study of Arabic, the Koran and the hadith and Arab history. It did not provide an extensive modern education in mathematics, science, engineering, and management. Thus, many young men went abroad for advanced training in these fields. Upon their return they found immediate employment in private industry and government. The middle-class status that they acquired rests almost entirely on the acquisition of an advanced, secular education. Family ties--tribal affiliations--enter into determining anyone's status, but for the vast majority it is a modern education that enables the individual to gain entry into the new middle class.

The importance of tribal and regional origins, in addition to a secular education, can be clearly seen in the way a newly appointed higher-level government official will staff his office. As soon as possible he will choose individuals from his own tribe or area and will place them into jobs held by persons from other tribes or regions. If the new supervisor comes from the Nejd around Buraida, he will seek qualified individuals from that area to replace those from, say, the Asir and Jedda. Sometimes he will even lower standards to attract kindred individuals. The importance of a modern, secular education is found in the increasing retirement of senior government officials with a traditional education, who achieved their positions through experience. Passed over for promotion in favor of younger, better-educated individuals, they become resentful. When they realize that friends and fellow students of their childhood, with advanced education received abroad, have been promoted into far more responsible positions, they give up and retire. This pattern in job competition may well contribute to increasing efficiency in government operations. In nearly every government office or department there exists a small but significant number of higher-ranking civil servants who have outlived their usefulness. Many of these men still have ten or more years of service ahead, and there is no way to eliminate them. They are a dead weight on the more active, aggressive members of the organization, and their contribution to the functions of the office is the negative one of increasing obstructionism.

The growing middle class is stratified into an upper and lower division. The upper stratum consists largely of engineers, accountants, physicians, college teachers, higher-level government officials, and some businessmen. The lower stratum consists of skilled blue-collar workers, primarily schoolteachers and lower-grade government clerks.

The prestige attached to a job is very important in the choice of occupation. A man will accept considerably lower wages for a given job if he considers it socially more prestigious. For example, graduates of the Riyadh Vocational Training Center are given a set of tools required in their trade upon completion of training. It is not unusual for a man to sell these tools and use the proceeds as a down payment for a taxi. Although he could probably earn more as a plumber or other artisan, he prefers driving a taxi for prestige reasons. Because of this, many foreigners, Palestinians, Yemeni, and others hold down well-paying jobs, while there may be some disguised unemployment among Saudis.

THE POLITICAL SYSTEM

Constitutional Framework

The Kingdom of Saudi Arabia is a Moslem state governed by an absolute monarch. Currently the reigning monarch is Faisal ibn-Abdul Aziz al-Saud, the second son of the Kingdom's founder, Abd al-Aziz ar-Rahman al-Faisal al-Saud. He is the third King of Saudi Arabia from the House of Saud.

The nation does not have a constitution as such. The basic constitutional structure rests on four documents: the Constitution of Hejaz (1926); the Decree of January 29, 1927, uniting Hejaz and Nejd and constituting the Hejaz a Kingdom; the Decree of September 18, 1932, announcing the establishment of the Kingdom of Saudi Arabia; and Decree 38, Regulations of the Council of Ministers, May 11, 1958.[21] There is some disagreement among the sources concerning the applicability of the 1926 Constitution of the Hejaz as part of the basic constitutional framework; those who feel that it does not apply omit the Constitution of the Hejaz and instead include the Decree of December 29, 1931, establishing the Council of Ministers.[22]

Since the source of the sovereign power is not mentioned in any of the documents, it must be assumed to rest on the right of conquest. During the early years of his reign Abd al-Aziz defeated the opposition in a series of battles, eliminated the old rulers, and often sent his own men, either loyal retainers or members of his family, to administrate the area in his stead. Thus, he sent Abd Allah ibn Jiluwi to Al Hasa as his governor, and following the conquest of the Hejaz, he appointed his second son, Prince Faisal, as Viceroy of the Hejaz.

The Saud family comes from the sedentary population of the towns. They are connected to the tribes, but their status and power grew almost entirely out of the barrel of a gun or as immams (religious leaders) of Wahhabism, rather than that of sheikh.

The need for a written constitution has been recognized for some time. On November 6, 1962, Crown Prince Faisal issued a ten-point program in which he outlined the tasks ahead of his government. Point 1 deals with the creation of a constitution:

> His Majesty's Government believes that the time has now come for the promulgation of a Basic Law for the Government of the country, drawn from the Koran and the Tradition of His Prophet and the acts of the Orthodox Caliphs, that will set forth explicitly the fundamental principles of government and the relationship between the governor and the governed, or-

> ganize the various powers of the State, and the relationship among these powers, and provide for the basic rights of the citizen, including the right to freely express his opinion within the limits of Islamic belief and public policy.[23]

While many other points contained in the program have been implemented, the "Basic Law" has not yet been issued. In the absence of a written constitutional document the Koran and the haditha are the basic elements of Saudi Arabi's political system. It may well be that the Basic Law has not yet been issued because of the difficulty associated with the reconciliation of the precepts of the Koran and the haditha with the demands of a modern, written constitution. Meanwhile, the Koran and the sunna are the civil and criminal law, and all important decisions are based on them.

The System of Government

The King and the Council of Ministers are the executive and legislative branches of the nation. In addition there exists a judicial branch that is associated with the religious authorities.

The King

All executive powers rest ultimately with the King who unites three leadership roles in his person: Sheikh of Sheikhs and Immam are the traditional roles of an Arab leader; to these was added the role of Malik (King) when Abd al-Aziz turned his conquests into the Kingdom of Saudi Arabia.[24] "[He] is responsible for protecting the institutions of Islam and the Islamic community, for defening the state and for furthering the interests of the nation."[25] As Sheikh of Sheikhs the King establishes his right to rule over the Bedouins. He provides leadership and holds this office as long as he maintains the sheikhly virtues of courage, leadership, and generosity. If he fails and his leadership goes wrong, he can be removed. As Immam the King possesses both secular and religious attributes. It is his duty to administer the state within the dictates of sharia, but he is also obliged "to spread the dominion of the true interpretation of the true faith."[26] In his role of Malik, the Monarch is commander-in-chief of the armed forces and the chief of state. All foreign ambassadors are accredited to him, and he appoints the nation's ambassadors to various governments. As King he is less dependent on tribal relationship, and it is his duty to assure the survival of the secular state.

Although the kingship rests currently with the family of Abd al-Aziz, succession is not based on primogeniture. During his reign the ruling monarch chooses his own successor, who must be approved by the ulema and the Saud family. Thus, Abd al-Aziz chose his eldest son to succeed him. Upon Saud's investiture, he in turn chose Faisal, the second-eldest surviving son, and designated him Crown Prince. The choicc of Saud and that of Faisal were not based on law or custom, rather they were Abd al-Aziz' command, which determined the succession upon his death. The ruling family's legitimacy rests as much on the fact that Mohammed ibn Saud, the first member of the House of Saud to be chosen immam by Abd al-Wahhab, swore an oath promising to defend and spread the true interpretation of Islam and that each successor has sworn the same oath, as it does on the conquests of Abd al-Aziz.

The Council of Ministers

During the early years Abd al-Aziz ruled in the traditional Arab fashion. So long as his domains were limited to the Nejd and Al-Hasa and the economy was based on the nomads, there was no need to establish a government with formal ministries. He appointed governors and other officials in certain areas whose main function it was to take care of the area's day-to-day affairs. He concerned himself personally with the most petty as well as the most pressing problems of his realm, content to consult a small number of trusted advisers. The patriarchal ways of the Arabs sufficed to administer the territories. With the conquest of the Hejaz it was no longer possible to rule in this manner. Furthermore, there existed in the Hejaz a formal structure of government, which he retained, modified, and placed into the hands of his second son, Faisal.

The Council of Ministers was formed late in 1953 by order of Abd al-Aziz. Its functions were redefined by Decree 38, issued May 11, 1958. The Counci is composed of a president and vice-president, ministers in charge of various ministries, ministers without portfolio, and royal councilors. Its functions are as follows:

> [It will] lay down the policy of the state with respect to internal and foreign affairs, finance, the economy, education, defense and all public affairs and shall oversee the execution thereof. It possesses regulatory authority, executive authority, and administrative authority. It is the final authority for financial affairs and for all matters connected with the various Ministries of the State and other Government departments, and shall decide what measures should

> be taken in these matters. Treaties and international agreements shall not be considered effective until approved by the Council. The decisions of the Council of Ministers are final except for those which require the issuing of a Royal Decree or Order in accordance with the Provisions of these Regulations.[27]

Thus, controls over economic and social policies rest with the King and the Council of Ministers. The order pays particular attention to the regulation of financial affairs.

<u>The Religious Establishment</u>

The religious establishment has three distinct levels: the imam, the ulema, and the mutawwa. This division is characteristic of traditional Moslem society, and as a matter of fact the Saud family provided the first imam appointed by Abd al-Wahab, which kept alive its claim to the rule of the Nejd after the Wahhabi's defeat by the Egyptian forces of the Ottoman Empire.

The ulema is the connecting link between the imam and the people, and it is their obligation to guard the purity of the faith and to enforce the observation of the Law. In some ways it parallels the state's political organization. Its influence is not as apparent as that of a member of the Council of Ministers, but it is nevertheless an important factor in the decision-making process. Thus, the ulema was able to limit the imposition of an income tax to foreigners with the argument that income taxes are an un-Islamic tax and that the state should rely on zakat from Saudi citizens. Decisions of the ulema are announced in a fatwa (legal decisions). During the political crisis of the early 1960s that led to the deposition of King Saud, the ulema were consulted and Crown Prince Faisal did not occupy the throne until the ulema issued a fatwa, signed by 12 of the nation's most distinguished religious leaders, sanctioning the deposition as a legitimate solution to a crisis threatening the existence of the Moslem nation. In recent years the power of the ulema has declined, probably because the sharia Law is unsuitable as a base for decision-making in a modern state.

The mutawwa are the teachers of religious practice, and they are the enforcers of the imam in religious and secular matters. Today, they are held somewhat in contempt by an ever-increasing portion of the population, because of their attempts to enforce rigid adherence to religious practice.

Regional Government

There are five major geographical divisions in the Kingdom: the Eastern Province (including Al-Hasa), Nejd, al-Hijaz, Asir, and Northern Frontier Province. Prior to 1963 there was only a tenuous relationship between the central government and the provinces. The boundarics of the various regions were poorly drawn and they were administered by amirs who were directly responsible to the King. In some cases these regions were ruled by someone appointed by the King with little if any reference to the central government. An example of this is the administration of the Eastern Province by members of the ibn Juluwi family. Following the reform of October 1963, the central government gained more control over the regions: "[T]he 'governor' of the province is no longer the King's personal representative, and is no longer called the 'amir' of the province. He has become an administration officer reporting to the Minister of Interior who is a member of the Council of Ministers, so that the governor of the province now represents the Government."[28] As the system of regional, district, and local government grew it developed an intricate system of overlapping relationships tied firmly to the Ministry of Interior's central operations--although in some respects the local governments operate with virtual autonomy.

The governor is nominated by the Minister of Interior and upon acceptance of the nomination by the Council of Ministers is appointed by Royal Decree. The governor administers the province in accordance with the overall national policy. Among his duties are the preservation of law and order and the execution of sharia court decisions. In cooperation with other ministries he is responsible for improving health standards and medical services, irrigation, communications, labor, trade, education, and other matters.

The governor of a province shares his power with the provincial council, whose duties "cover everything of interest to the local population."[29] They supervise and implement anti-illiteracy programs, set up vocational training centers and model farms, and hold local industrial and agricultural fairs. Furthermore, they are empowered "to furnish financial, technical and administrative assistance to social and charitable organizations and to co-operative societies."[30]

The Judiciary and the Law

As has been stated, the basic law of the country is sharia Law as interpreted within the Hanbali code. While this Law provides the basis for the solution of many disputes, it does not cover all activities in a modern state. To circumvent this problem a second type of law, Decree Law, has been developed. It consists of legal provisions enacted by Royal Decree, such as the traffic code or the industrial-accident law. The two types of law are not integrated and are administered separately. For issues covered by sharia Law there is a well-developed system of courts in which justice is pronounced by the religious authorities. Decree Law is administered by the local amir.

Punishment of offenders is prescribed by sharia Law and is carried out in accordance with its provisions. Thievery is punished by jail for the first two offenses, but for a third offense the offender's right hand is cut off. Adultery is still punished by the stoning to death of both culprits. Premeditated murder carries the death sentence, and this is usually executed. Accidental death is usually punished by a fine. Although fines have been increasingly levied for murder or accidental death, some families still insist on private retribution--that is, the family chooses the means and carries out the execution. Minor violations of the law, such as avoidance of prayer, drunkenness, and others are punished by flogging. All sentences are carried out in public, usually on Friday following the prayer service in the mosque.

NOTES

1. The quotations from the Koran have been taken from the Abdullah Yusuf Ali translation (Beirut: Dar Al Arabia, 1968).

2. H. A. R. Gibb, Mohammedanism, 2d ed. (New York: Oxford University Press, 1962), p. 35.

3. Ibid., p. 48.

4. A. Rahman, "Outlines of an Islamic Bank," The Journal of Moslem World League 1, no. 9 (1974): 43-48.

5. CDS, Statistical Yearbook, 1388 A.H., vol. 4 (Riyadh), p. 175.

6. For a detailed description of Madain Salih see Charles M. Doughty, Travels in Arabia Deserta, vol. 1 (London: Cape, 1964), Ch. 4 and the Appendix to Chs. 4, 5, and 6.

7. Kingdom of Saudi Arabia, Ministry of Information, Saudi Arabia: Land of Achievement (n.d.), p. 11.

8. M. A. Rauf, A Brief History of Islam (Kuala Lumpur: Oxford University Press, 1964), p. 9.

9. Alfred Guilliaume, The Traditions of Islam, Khayat's Oriental Reprint, no. 13 (Beirut: Khayats, 1966), p. 10.

10. Alfred Guilliaume, Islam (Baltimore: Penguin Books, 1956), p. 102.

11. Gibb, Mohammedanism, p. 164.

12. Wilfred C. Smith, Islam in Modern History (Princeton, N.J.: Princeton University Press, 1957), p. 42.

13. Fazlur Rahman, Islam (New York: Holt, Rinehart and Winston, 1966), p. 197.

14. H. A. R. Gibb, Modern Trends in Islam (Chicago: University of Chicago Press, 1947), pp. 26-27.

15. Statement of King Faisal, Replica, October 10, 1967, p. 1.

16. Guilliaume, Traditions, pp. 74-75.

17. Ahmed Zaki Yamani, Islamic Law and Contemporary Issues (Jedda: The Saudi Publishing House, 1968), p. 14.

18. Ibid., p. 4.

19. Ibid., p. 7.

20. For an excellent discussion of the new middle class, see William Rugh, "Emergence of a New Middle Class in Saudi Arabia," Middle East Journal 27, no. 1 (1973): 7-20.

21. Secretariat of the Asian-African Legal Consultation Committee, Constitutions of Asian Countries (Bombay: Tripathi Private, 1968), p. 1034.

22. Amos J. Peaslee, Constitutions of Nations, vol. 2, "Asia, Australia and Oceania," 3d ed., rev. (1965), p. 1089.

23. Reprinted in Gerald DeGaury, Faisal, King of Saudi Arabia (London: Barker, 1966), pp. 147-51.

24. For a detailed discussion see George A. Lipsky et al., Saudi Arabia (New Haven, Conn.: HRAF Press, 1959), pp. 106-12.

25. Norman C. Walpole et al., Area Handbook for Saudi Arabia, rev. ed. (Washington, D.C.: The American University, 1971), p. 133. This volume is distributed by the U.S. Government Printing Office.

26. Lipsky et al., Saudi Arabia, p. 110.

27. Peaslee, op. cit., p. 1097.

28. Ahmed Assah, Miracle of the Desert Kingdom (London: Johnson, 1969), p. 128.

29. Ibid., pp. 129-30.

30. Ibid., p. 130.

CHAPTER

3

A BRIEF HISTORY OF SAUDI ARABIA

Recorded Western history began in the Middle East. Long before the Greek city states were established there existed in the Fertile Crescent of the Middle East societies whose economic development had progressed to a level in which small economic surpluses were produced, over and above the population's immediate needs. These surpluses supported a group of individuals whose contribution to society consisted of products of the intellect rather than those of the land. The alphabet was invented; legal systems were developed; the state became strong enough to support and protect long-distance trade. As markets became larger, external economies of scales produced accelerating economic development.

Take a map of Eurasia including northern Africa. Prepare a series of overlays showing the expansion of the various empires that flourished in the area between Lybia and India. Beginning with the Old Babylonian Empire, about 1700 B.C., we can trace the expanding influence of these societies. The Old Babylonian Empire covered the area between the Tigris and Euphrates rivers and some territory on the eastern and western banks of these rivers. Within 250 years the Hittites and Kassites had conquered the Old Babylonian Empire, and by the seventh century B.C. the Assyrian Empire held sway from Lybia to the Indus River. Now shift your focus from the Middle East to Europe about 450 A.D. The Western and Eastern Roman Empires have extended their influence into Europe. In North Africa and the Middle East they control a small strip along the African coast of the Mediterranean Sea, Egypt, Palestine, and Syria.

During this nearly 2,000-year period of history the people of the Arabian Peninsula remained isolated.* In fact, it is the arid deserts of Arabia that give the Fertile Crescent its shape. This isolation ended around the middle of the seventh century. Inspired by their new, militant faith, the tribes of Arabia united and established an empire that at its apogee extended from the Pyrenees in the west to the Indus River in the east. By the beginning of the second millennium control over the Moslem Empire had passed from Mecca and Medina to Baghdad and subsequently into the hands of the Ottoman sultans. Save for the Hejaz around Mecca and Medina, which continued to be the religious focus of Islam, the rest of Arabia lost its importance.

It is important to understand the significance that the Arabs of the Arabian desert attach to the 200-year period of the Arab Empire. The Islamic faith does not distinguish between secular and religious matters; even those individuals who do not have a formal education learn about past glories through informal study of the Koran. The Arabs of the Arabian Peninsula are proud of the civilizing influence exerted by the contributions of their ancestors in law, science, mathematics, literature, and philosophy, and many of the modern descendants of the first four caliphs believe that they can recapture some of this lost glory. They are aware that this cannot be done by reestablishment of the Arab Empire, but they are convinced that they can affect political events and contribute to the reform of Islam: "The internal history of Arabia since the 18th century can best be understood in terms of the efforts of this community [Wahhabi] to spread its doctrine. Modern Saudi Arabia is the political expression of this continuing effort."[1]

The Saudis' firm belief in their mission is reflected in the preamble of the ten-point program for the betterment of the country issued by Crown Prince Faisal in his capacity as Prime Minister on November 6, 1962. After a brief reference to past achievements the proclamation states:

> His Majesty's Government will redouble its efforts in developing and consolidating the structure of this youthful state, and in leading its citizens to the place they deserve as a nation which, from the dawn of Arab history, was the centre of true Arabism and the origin of spreading of the eternal Islamic civilization.[2]

---

*The following narration can be visualized with the help of a series of maps published in Aramco, Aramco Handbook, rev. ed. (Dhahran, 1968), pp. 12-13, 35, and 47.

THE RISE OF THE HOUSE OF IBN SAUD, 1744-45 to 1818

The history of Saudi Arabia can be divided into four time periods: from about 1745 to 1818, from 1819 to 1902, from 1903 to 1953, and from 1953 to the present. The first period began when Mohammad ibn Saud, the Amir of the central Nejdi town of Diriyah, offered protection to the religious reformer Mohammad Abd al-Wahab and accepted his religious reforms. In an effort to spread the Unitarian doctrines of Abd al-Wahab the ruler of Diriyah subdued the Arabian tribes. At its height, about 1810, "the doctrines of Wahhabism held sway in some form or the other from the gates of Damascus and Baghdad to Yemen and the Hadramout and from the Persian Gulf to the Red Sea."[3] In 1801 the Wahhabis captured Karbala, the Holy City of the Shiites, killing many inhabitants and destroying the domes erected over many tombs, and in 1806 Wahabi forces seized Mecca and Medina and evicted the Ottoman Turks and their representatives.

The destruction of Karbala and the occupation of Mecca and Medina goaded the Ottoman forces into action. Sultan Mahmud II ordered Muhammad Ali, his Egyptian viceroy, to recapture the Holy Cities and to break the Wahhabis' power. After a seven-year campaign directed by Mohammed Ali's son, Ibrahim Pasha, the Egyptian army drove the Wahhabi zealots out of Mecca and Medina. They seized and destroyed the Saudi capital, Diriyah, capturing Abd Allah ibn Saud, the fourth ruler of the Saudi line after Mohammad ibn Saud.

THE STRUGGLE FOR SUPREMACY IN THE NEJD, 1819-1902

The second period of Saudi Arabia's history begins with the capture and execution of Abd Allah ibn Saud and ends with the exile of the House of Saud to Kuwait and the coastal towns along the Arabian Gulf. Following the destruction of Diriyah, the Egyptians maintained themselves in the Nejd on and off for 20 brutal years. The long struggle for freedom from Egyptian rule began in 1823 when Turki ibn Abd Allah ibn Muhammad ibn Saud attempted to capture Riyadh. He failed in his first attempt but succeeded the following year and liberated the central part of the Nejd from its Egyptian conquerors. To avoid the cost and effort required for the rebuilding of Diriyah Turki established himself in Riyadh, making it the new capital of the House of Saud.

Following the assassination of Turki on May 19, 1834, the new imam, Faisal ibn Turik, lost control of the central and eastern parts of Arabia to the Egyptian forces of Mohammad Ali. Faisal reestablished himself in 1845 and maintained the Saudi family's authority over the various factions of the Wahhabi state until his death in 1865. From Faisal's death to the turn of the century the nation's history is a confused and confusing story of various factions fighting each other for control. In 1891 the Saudi family again lost control over the Wahhabi state, because fraternal quarrels between Faisal ibn Turki's sons had weakened the family's power. The quarrel had resolved itself eventually in favor of Saud ibn Faisal, who died in 1875 without having united the various factions contending for authority over the state.

While the Saudis quarreled among themselves the House of the Rashid's had consolidated its hold over the north-central part of the Nejd, centering on the town of Hail.

The feuding did not end with Saud's death. Faisal's fourth son, Abd al-Rahman, who was in Riyadh at the time of his father's death, claimed power for himself. His action was disputed by Abd Allah with the support of his brother Mohammad, Faisal's third son, as well as Saud's sons, who also claimed the right to rule. The three brothers, Abd Allah, Muhammad, and Abd al-Rahman, patched up their disagreements and forced their nephews out of Riyadh. An uneasy peace settled over the area and Abd Allah ibn Faisal was installed as imam for the third time. In 1884 the Imam Faisal attempted to curtail the rising Rashidi power. He was defeated in the battle of Hamadah, and soon thereafter Muhammad ibn Rashid established himself as ruler of the central Nejd, exiling Abd Allah to Hail, the Rashidi capital.

Following Abd Allah's death Abd al-Rahman challenged the Rashidi overlords. He lost and was forced to flee to Kuwait. The House of Saud was completely defeated and it seemed that they had been permanently eliminated as a participant in the struggle for control of the Nejd. Rashidi control of the Nejd lasted only a decade, however, before it was again challenged by the Saud family.

THE REIGN OF ABD AL-AZIZ, 1902-53

In 1901 Abd al-Aziz ibn Abd ar-Rahman Al Faisal Al Saud set out from Kuwait, where the Saud family had been granted asylum, to regain his patrimony. He captured Riyadh on January 1, 1902, and inaugurated the third phase of Saudi Arabia's history.

Following a number of months spent in Eastern Arabia, Abd al-Aziz set out for Riyadh. He had hoped to attract additional support for his venture among the tribes along the fringes of the Rub al-Khali and the Haradh area. When it became apparent that this support would not be offered, Abd al-Aziz decided to move to Riyadh with about 60 men but without any particular plan of action once he reached the city.

Approaching from the east he left one-third of his force with the camels about ten kilometers from the city. At the outskirts of Riyadh he left all but six of the remaining men and sneaked into the city with these six under cover of darkness. Once in the city they intended to enter the Rashidi governor's house and seize him. Unfortunately, it was the governor's custom to spend the night in the fortress, called al-Masmak, across the street from his residence. Abd al-Aziz and his six companions entered the governor's home and found only his wife and servants. Abd al-Aziz decided to wait and attack the governor in the morning. He sent for the 30 men he had left at the outskirts of the town and the group spent the remainder of the night in the governor's residence.

The following morning, as governor Ajlan left the fort to return to his residence, Abd al-Aziz and his men attacked. Surprised, the governor's guard attempted to return to the fortress. The assailants managed to prevent that, and Ajlan and his men were forced to fight in the street. Abd al-Aziz faced the governor, who attacked him with his sword. Abd al-Aziz fired his gun, wounding the governor. To prevent Ajlan from reaching safety Abd al-Aziz grabbed his legs and held onto them while the governor's men tried to drag their commander into the fortress. They failed. Instead, some of the attackers managed to enter the fort through a small portcullis. They threw the doors wide open and the remainder of Abd al-Aziz' force entered. Outnumbered two-to-one, they fought a brief skirmish, killing about half of the defenders. With the capture of al-Masmak the city fell to Abd al-Aziz, who proclaimed himself the new ruler. The townspeople accepted his claim, happy to be free of the harsh Rashidi control.

During the struggle for the fort, Abd al-Aziz' cousin ibn-Jiluwi distinguished himself. He threw his spear at Ajlan and missed, killing him later during the attack. The head of ibn Jiluwi's spear is still embedded in the door of the fort. Anyone who visits the fort today need only point to the relic and mention Abd al-Aziz' name, and the old men who stand by the gate will nod and speak the dead King's name proudly, offering the visitor a look inside the fort, which is off-limits to strangers. The younger generation's response to Abd al-Aziz' exploit is decidedly different from the older's. If they admit knowing the stories at all, they depreciate them with a wave of the hand, saying, "That is all old." As far as the fort itself is concerned, they would like to tear it down. It is located in a side street off the main downtown shopping area and is in the wayof progress.

The difference in attitude regarding al-Masmak is illustrative of the change in attitude that has taken place among the younger generation. As far as they are concerned, al-Masmak and the memories it recalls are all part of the primitive past. The sooner forgotten, the better they would like it, because it is a reminder to them of the primitive conditions that existed and still exist in the country. One gets the feeling that they are somewhat ashamed of the past, feeling that it is part of a tradition that is unsuitable for the reputation of a modern nation.

The capture of Riyadh did not assure Abd al-Aziz his patrimony. The Najd was still in ibn Rahid's hands. To recapture it he had to gain the support of the Bedouin tribes of the Southern Najd. Having nothing to offer in material inducements, he attracted them by his personal reputation as a warrior and the implied booty that success in battle promised. His strongest asset was "his own conviction that God was on his side, and that the Moslem world still needed to be purified by Wahhabism. . . . [I]bn Saud drew men to follow him in battle by his faith, and infected them with fervent intolerant zeal."[4]

Ibn Rashid, Abd al-Aziz' opponent, was a talented commander well-versed in desert warfare. His mistake was that he underestimated his young adversary's ability and daring. Between 1902 and 1906 they engaged in a number of battles that ended inconclusively, like most desert battles. Nevertheless, Abd al-Aziz was able to exploit the population's resentment of the harsh Rashidi rule and extended his control throughout the Saud family's original domain.

The strongest challenge to Abd al-Aziz' plans came in mid-1904 when ibn Rashid negotiated an alliance with the Turks. Seeing a chance to reestablish their dominance over Arabia, the Sultan sent eight battalions of troops in support of ibn Rashid. For the first time Abd al-Aziz was faced with a modern armed force equipped with artillery. On June 15, 1904, the two armies met in a day-long battle. Abd al-Aziz' warriors managed to rout the opposing Bedouin forces but could not defeat the Turks.

Abd al-Aziz could not defeat the Turks, but he had only to wait for the summer's heat to accomplish the task for him. The Turkish troops suffered horribly under the heat, which often climbs above 130° F. Unprepared for survival in the desert, many of the soldiers died, and when the Saudi army faced them again, the desert warriors managed to breach the Turkish ranks. Unable to use their cannons, the Turks broke and ran. Abd al-Aziz' forces carried the day. Yet this victory was not conclusive, because the House of Rashid still threatened his control over the Najd. The final contest between them came in April 1906, when the Saudi forces surprised Rashid's army during a raid 20 miles north of Buraida. In a short, bloody skirmish the enemy was defeated, and their leader was killed. Abd al-Aziz had reestablished his power over the family's domain.

Abd al-Aziz' greatest problem during this period was to gain and hold the loyalties of the various tribes in the central Najd. The Bedouin have fickle loyalties. Their first loyalty is to the tribe, and their leader's actions are geared to promote the tribe's well-being.

They think nothing of changing from one side to the other in a contest when they perceive themselves to be on the losing side. At that time, often boredom with the matters at hand would make them leave their allies to return home. They liked action and enjoyed nothing more than a successful raid on an enemy's encampment that gained them the chance for loot. It was one of Abd al-Aziz greatest achievements that he united all factions in support of his cause and that he managed to keep their loyalty after the fighting had stopped and the Kingdom of Saudi Arabia had been established.

The defeat and death of ibn Rashid did not end Abd al-Aziz problems. Between 1906 and 1912 numerous tribal quarrels and other challenges kept him in the field. In the north the House of Rashid still controlled the country. In the east, in al-Hasa, the Turks had maintained themsleves, and in the Hejaz the Turks had installed Hussain ibn Ali, whose presence kept the Saudi prince's ambitions in check. In the south his cousins, the Araif, were unwilling to accept his rule and fomented upheaval. Slowly, however, Abd al-Aziz gained the upper hand. In April 1913 he captured Hofuf and thus eliminated Turkish influence in the al-Hasa region.

Abd al-Aziz succeeded in uniting the various tribal groups by settling the Bedouin on the land in the ikhwan (brethren) settlements: "Some authorities see these settlements as the greatest of his achievements; for the battles and diplomatic intrigues were mainly the means of building a kingdom; the settlements were a means of giving it permanence. The first stage had often been achieved in Arabian history, but the second never."[5] In the ikhwan settlements tribal loyalties were supplemented by a broader loyalty, that of loyalty to Islam. In addition to settlement on the land and the pursuit of agricultural activities, the ikhwan were to study the Koran under the guidance of mutawwa sent to them by the ulema. After initial difficulties were overcome the ikhwan settlements succeeded. With ten years more than 200 settlements had been established whose men owed allegiance only to God and their king: "[T]he settlements gave the ulema new fields for the harshest extremes of their Wahhabi faith, and gave ibn Saud, in the end, a military strength which no other ruler in Arabia could resist, except those who had British support."[6] Furthermore, it created a new segment of the society who had given up the ways of the desert, and it was this group of people upon whom a stable society could be built.

After the conquest of al-Hasa, Abd al-Aziz negotiated a settlement with the Turks. While conceding him the eastern region, the Turks concluded an agreement with Saud ibn Rashid, the new head of the House of Rashid in Hail, offering to supply rifles to the Rashids for a renewed attack on the Najd. To counter the Turkish initiative Abd al-Aziz entered into negotiations with the British that culminated in the Anglo-Saudi treaty of 1915.

Arabia did not play an important role in the events of World War I. To weaken the Turks the British induced Abd al-Aziz to attack the Rashids. In January 1915 the Saudi and Rashidi forces met in a fierce battle at Jirab in the Quasim area, during which the British representative to Abd al-Aziz was killed. Both sides claimed victory, but as usual in desert warfare the battle settled nothing. The House of Saud was still threatened by the Rashids. A second attack on Hail, launched in 1918, also failed.

While the British dealt with Abd al-Aziz in inner Arabia, they also entered into negotiations with the Grand Sharif of Mecca and ruler of the Hejaz, Husain ibn Ali, a member of the Hashimite family. Husain, who had been born in Mecca but spent nearly all his life at the Sultan's court, was appointed Sharif of Mecca by the Turks in an attempt to consolidate Ottoman rule in the Hejaz. The British saw a chance to weaken the Turkish enemy further by inducing Husain to secede from the Ottoman Empire. In July 1916 Husain proclaimed his independence from Constantinople, claiming the title of King of the Arabs. The British, however, recognized him only as King of Hejaz.

At the end of World War I the British faced a choice between their two Arabian allies as the object of support. They opted for support of Hussain in the belief that his better-trained and -equipped army was superior to Abd al-Aziz' warrior force. Encouraged by this support, Hussain launched an attack in May 1919 on the oasis of al-Khurma on the western fringes of Abd al-Aziz' domain. The invading force was met by Saudi ikhwan warriors of the al-Khurma area. The ikhwan struck in the middle of the night, killing almost all of the invading force. It has been estimated that only about 100 of the 4,000-man force escaped the massacre. By the time Abd al-Aziz arrived at the scene the way to Mecca and the Hejaz lay open before him; however, he did not grasp the opportunity. Instead, he turned to the conquest of his northern enemy, the Rashids, and in 1921 conquered Jabal Shammar and its capital, Hail, ending the Rashidi threat.

With the northern frontier secured the limits of the Saudi state between Iraq and Kuwait required definition. The problem was settled late in 1922 by the creation of two Neutral Zones, one between Saudi territory and Iraq and the other between Saudi territory and Kuwait.

After the delineation of the borders with Iraq and Kuwait on the one side and Abd-al-Aziz' territory on the other side there remained only one unsettled problem: the Hejaz. The ikhwan tried to persuade Abd al-Aziz to annex the Holy Cities, Mecca and Medina, and to purge them of the many unholy practices condoned by Hussain. Abd al-Aziz held his troops in check, but when Hussain declared himself caliph, following the abolition of the caliphate by the Turkish Republic, the Saudis decided to act. The mountain city of Taif was captured in September 1924, and Mecca fell in October of that same year. As soon as the ikhwan had established themselves in the Holy City they proceeded to demolish decorative domes over graves and other signs of deviation from fundamental Koranic guidelines.

The port city of Jidda was besieged. The Saudis did not attempt to attack the city, being content with an occasional artillery bombardment. In keeping with ancient practice, Abd al-Aziz lifted the siege for the duration of the Pilgrimage season. In December 1925, Medina surrendered with the stipulation that the dreaded ikhwan would not enter the city. Two weeks later Jidda fell and Hussain's eldest son, Ali, who had succeeded his father, left for Iraq. Saudi sovereignty had been established from al-Hasa in the east to the Hejaz in the west and from the rub-al Khali in the south to the Nafud in the north.

Following his victory in the Hejaz, Abd al-Aziz set up a system of control over the Bedouin. His approach was direct and simple. In cases of lawlessness the chief of each tribe was responsible for the punishment of the malefactors. If the chief failed to punish the offenders, the chief of the neighboring tribe was responsible for taking action; if that failed, Abd al-Aziz was ready to move in with his army. This system of law enforcement was effective, and for the first time in the history of the Arabian Peninsula intertribal warfare and general lawlessness were controlled. Peace had finally come to Arabia.

Throughout the period under discussion Abd al-Aziz was in constant financial difficulties. There were times when his treasury consisted of the silver coins he carried in his saddle bags. With the capture of the Hejaz some financial relief occurred, because taxation of the pilgrims yielded additional revenues. Nevertheless, when Major Frank Holmes* approached him regarding a license for oil exploration, Abd al-Aziz granted him the exploration rights for an area of more than 30,000 square miles in al-Hasa. The search for oil was unsuccessful, but it was only a matter of time until oil would be found in the desert.

After his victory over the Rashidi, Abd al-Aziz was proclaimed Sultan of the Najd and its Dependencies. On January 8, 1926, the citizens of Mecca swore allegiance to him and proclaimed him King of the Hejaz. About a year later the people of the Najd, unwilling to have their ruler carry an inferior title to that of the Hejaz, proclaimed him King of the Najd, and Abd al-Aziz became King of Hejaz and Najd and its Dependencies. In 1927 Great Britain recognized Abd al-Aziz' domain as an independent, sovereign state, and on September 22, 1932, the country was renamed the Kingdom of Saudi Arabia.

---

*See Chapter 7, p. 151.

In naming his realm Saudi Arabia Abd al-Aziz created considerable resentment among the people beyond the original Saudi patrimony. Tribal and regional loyalties are still too strong to have the ruling family's name constantly before people, a reminder of their own lost causes. It may be a minor irritant, but it is one factor keeping regional and tribal differences alive.

Before Abd al-Aziz could consolidate his success and forge the diverse regions and tribes into a coherent nation state he had to solve one final problem: what to do about the ikhwan. The ikhwan had been the mainstay of his army. Inspired by their religious fanaticism, they had fought in the name of God and Abd al-Aziz. Spurred on by their sectarian zeal, they had contributed greatly to his victories. However, their narrow-minded dedication to Wahhabism led to bloody excesses. Believing that their opponents had deviated from the path of the correct faith and that non-Wahhabi Moslems were in the same class as the unbelievers, they murdered and plundered ruthlessly whenever they conquered the opposition. The massacre of more than 300 inhabitants after the victory of Taif is only one example of ikhwan ruthlessness.

Following his victories in the Hejaz Abd al-Aziz no longer needed their services and sent them back to their tribes. Unfortunately, however, he had created an organism beyond his control. When the ikhwan returned home they found life dull. Agricultural activities, which had never appealed to them, could not absorb their energy. The knowledge of the existence of numerous Moslem communities not yet cleansed by submission to the Wahhabi discipline continued to stimulate their spirit. Frustrated in their religious zeal and bored by their humdrum existence as farmers, they disobeyed Abd al-Aziz and raided across the border into Iraq and Kuwait. But they changed the nature of desert raiding. Instead of raiding a community and driving off their herds of camels and goats, leaving the population unharmed, they entered into Iraq killing all men and boys, driving off the herds and leaving the women and children helpless in the desert.

The Iraqi and Kuwait governments protested to Abd al-Aziz in vain: He would not--or could not--restrain his erstwhile supporters. Forced to act, the invaded nations organized a defense. On the Iraqi side John Glubb, later known as Glubb Pasha, organized a defense based on the use of aircraft and truck-mounted cannons. Slowly, the defenders gained the upper hand and the raiding tribes of ikwan turned from raids across the borders to raids of neighboring tribes within the Kingdom. This was a mistake. Now Abd al-Aziz had reasons to oppose them. He left the Hejaz and moved his army into the Eastern Province. On March 29, 1929, the two armies met in the Battle of Sibilla. It was the last act of warfare carried out in the traditional, time-honored desert fashion. The rebels lost. Although some of the rebellious ikhwan held out for another 12 months, Abd al-Aziz had led his last charge. From now on he turned to the establishment of an administrative system for the nation he had created.

No sooner had the ikhwan problem been settled in 1930 than another problem arose: The King had run out of cash. Since the conquest of the Hejaz his main source of income had been from the pilgrims. Although it was inadequate, given the nation's needs, it did provide temporary relief from his money worries. But the pilgrimage depends on the prosperity of the Moslem world. When the Great Depression of the early 1930s spread from Europe and the United States, it reduced the number of pilgrims, and Abd al-Aziz faced a crisis.

The King cared little about fiscal matters and delegated them to his treasurer, al-Sulaiman. The fiscal system was based on the assumption that the national revenues were the King's private income and only after his and his family's needs had been met was the remainder allocated for general administrative purposes. Of course this is not a way to run the government of a nation extending across more than 1 million square miles. By 1931 not only could the Kingdom not repay its foreign debt, but, what is much more important, the minor civil servants were not paid. As their pay fell more and more into arrears they returned to their old habits of swindling King and public alike. This was regrettable, because it was a fall from the high moral standard that Wahhabism was trying to maintain. It created a tradition of corruption and fiscal irresponsibility that even today is one of the features of government in Saudi Arabia.

The Pilgrimage of 1931 drove home the fact that the Hadj is an unreliable source of revenue. Abd al-Aziz finally had to face the unpleasant task of dealing with his fiscal crisis, and the idea of attracting oil prospectors was revived. According to H. S. St.-J. B. Philby, an Englishman who had converted to the Moslem faith and had attached himself to the King as a sometime adviser, the events leading to the decision to look for oil concessionaires began as follows:

> One day I was in the royal car with him, on one of his afternoon excursions, when he let himself go on the subject of his country's prospects. If the pilgrimage was to fail like this in the coming years, the country would be faced by ruin, for it had no other assets of any value. I tried to rally him: "Really," I said, "there is no ground for despair, provided you are prepared to help yourself, instead of waiting for God to save you. For verily God doth not change the state of a people unless they change

> their state themselves'" (this was a favorite Quranic quotation of his). "You are like a man sleeping over a buried treasure and complaining of poverty, while unwilling to do anything about it." "What do you mean?" he asked sharply. "I mean," I replied, "that your country is full of buried riches--oil and gold for instance--which you cannot exploit yourselves and won't allow anyone else to exploit for you." "I tell you, Philby," he answered rather wearily, "that if anyone would offer me a million pounds now he would be welcome to all the concessions he wants in my country." "They are worth a great deal more than that," I said, "and if you really mean what you have just said, I know a man who can help you."[7]

The conversation led to a meeting in May 1931 between the King and Charles Crane, an American with deep interest in Arabia, who in turn made K. S. Twitchell, one of his engineers, available to the government. Following some maneuvering among the international oil companies the Original Concession Agreement between the Saudi Arabian government and Standard Oil of California was signed in May 1933. As far as Abd al-Aziz was concerned, the importance of this agreement rested in the fact that his immediate financial difficulties were reduced, and there was always the hope of large future revenue from oil production, God willing.

While the American geologists and engineers searched for oil, Saudi society continued in its old ways. It has been said that the King never really understood the significance of the foreigners' activities. After a short period of interest he pushed the oil problem out of his mind, and he and the court returned to the routine of picnics and hunting, which he liked most.

In March 1938 test drillings in the Dhamam area of al-Hasa confirmed the presence of oil in commercial quantities. A year later the first oil shipment left Ras Tanura. It appeared that the King's financial problems had been solved, but four months later World War II broke out, and progress in the oil fields came almost to a complete halt.

By 1940 oil operations had stopped, and the number of persons arriving for the Hadj had fallen to a mere trickle. The winter of 1939-40 was a very dry season, and agriculture and animal husbandry suffered severely. Saudi Arabia faced bankruptcy, and the King turned to the British and the oil company for aid. Despite their own desperate needs during the early war years, the British managed to supply Saudi Arabia with some food and cash loans. The country needed more funds, and Abd al-Aziz turned to the oil company with a request for $30 million spread over a five-year period. Unable and unwilling to meet these demands, the parent companies persuaded the U.S. government to include Saudi Arabia in the Lend-Lease Program. After two years of negotiation President Roosevelt ordered the extension of Lend-Lease aid to the Kingdom.

During the war Saudi Arabia stayed neutral, but the King's sympathies were on the Allied side. World War II marks an important turning point in Saudi Arabia's history. Before the war the King's efforts were concentrated on the nation's internal problems and the Kingdom's participation in world affairs was practically nonexistent. After the end of the war Saudi Arabia's voice began to be heard in Middle Eastern and Islamic affairs.

On November 13, 1953, Abd al-Aziz died. He was succeeded on the throne by his eldest son, Saud ibn Abd al-Aziz al Saud, and Faisal ibn Abd al-Aziz, his second son, was named Crown Prince. Although Abd al-Aziz is not widely known in the Western World, he was one of the most important rulers of the Middle East. He unified the Arabian tribes and stopped their intertribal warfare. He created the Saudi state that was a necessary step in the economic development of the Arabian Peninsula. Abd al-Aziz has often been maligned by Western writers as a barbarian, spendthrift ruler of a third-rate nation; he was the last of the medieval rulers, possessed great personal courage, and knew how to deal with the Bedouin. He was honest and straightforward. Judged by the standards of early twentieth-century Arabian society, he was an outstanding individual. His failure to use the immense riches that the exploitation of oil eventually made available to him resulted from the fact that the Bedouin society was not prepared to deal with the new wealth. Socially and economically, Saudi Arabia was not prepared to absorb hundreds of millions of riyals efficiently.

THE KINGDOM SINCE 1953

The history of the country since Abd al-Aziz' death is characterized by several trends. On the international level there is the struggle with Egypt, the Palestinian question, the settlement of a number of border disputes, and the drive to become the leader of the Moslem world. To this must be added Saudi Arabia's leading role in the formation of the Organization of Petroleum Exporting Countries (OPEC). Domestically, the main concern was the establishment of a coherent economic policy designed to stimulate economic development and the continued integration of the various factions among the population.

The reign of Saud lasted 11 years, affording the transition from the Bedouin society to a settled, modern nation. Saud was unprepared to rule the country, however. In 1958 Crown Prince Faisal was appointed Prime Minister, and the government of the nation became his responsibility. On November 5, 1964, Saud was forced to abdicate, and Faisal Ibn Abdul-Aziz Abdul-Rahman Al Faisal was invested as King and Imam of Saudi Arabia.

Contrary to experience in other Arab states, the change of rulers in Saudi Arabia proceeded in an orderly and peaceful fashion. Faisal's appointment as Prime Minister was forced upon Saud by the family in consultation with the ulema. The original plan had been to depose Saud and place Faisal on the throne. Faisal refused the offer of investiture, and accepted the appointment as Prime Minister instead. Although he was well-known in the Hejaz, he was less well-known in the eastern part of the nation. To overcome this handicap it was suggested that he make a series of radio and television addresses. He carried this suggestion several steps further by giving a series of speeches in various parts of the country. This was a novel approach and gained him recognition and support among the populace.

Faisal was a strong and able administrator. Within a few days of his appointment as Prime Minister he issued a communique in which he offered to participate in an effort to settle a number of outstanding issues involving relations with other Arab countries. This effort met with failure. The new Prime Minister was more successful, however, in his attempts to reform the monetary system.

Saudi Arabia's policy with respect to the Palestinian question has not changed since Abd al-Aziz' days. The old King had argued that Palestine was an Arab area and that the Israelis had no right to the land. He felt that the European Jews who had suffered so horribly from Nazi extermination policies should return to their country of origin, because the Allied victory had removed the Nazi threat to their existence. From Abd al-Aziz' point of view this was reasonable, because he believed that the Jewish question was a European problem and that the sins of the Europeans should not be expiated at the expense of the Arabs.

There is considerable doubt that this position will change. King Faisal viewed the Israelis as intruders, and he felt that the time had come to force the major oil-using nations to force Israel into compliance. He did not feel that a settlement would require the elimination of the state of Israel, but it does require that Israel withdraw from all occupied territories. There are at least two reasons behind this policy. First, King Faisal was a devout Moslem, and he was fully committed to Israeli evacuation of East Jerusalem, Islam's third most holy city. He had stated repeatedly that he wanted to pray in the mosque of the Dom of the Rock, and he would hardly do so as long as the city was in Israeli hands. Second, the "Arab Cause"--that is, the Arabs' fight against Israel and other forces threatening Arab culture--is immensely popular among the younger Saudis. To guarantee the survival of a conservative monarchy among the Left-leaning Arab states King Faisal had to prove that he was willing to be in the forefront of the struggle with Israel. Only if he convinced his Leftist critics of his sincerity in his commitment, would he have the opportunity to further the ideal of Pan-Islamism, the creation of a united Islam that cuts across national concern.

Saudi Arabia has been an active participant in the Arab-Israeli conflict. The Kingdom's major contribution has been in the form of cash subsidies to Egypt, Jordan, and certain Palestinian groups. At the Khartoum Summit meeting, Saudi Arabia pledged S.R. 630 million ($140 million) as its contribution to the Arab cause. This generous promise, which the government kept despite continued frictions between the United Arab Republic (UAR) and the Kingdom, contributed to the Saudi fiscal crisis of 1969/70.

Saudi Arabia is the most conservative force in the Middle East. Until 1956 there was no friction between Egypt and Saudi Arabia. Following the overthrow of King Farouk in 1952, relations between the countries continued amicably. In 1956 Nasser nationalized all foreign property in Egypt, including that held by Saudi citizens, and realtions became strained. When Nasser announced his doctrine of Arab socialism following his failure to gain support from the United States and the World Bank for the Aswan high dam project, he turned to the Soviet Union for aid. The Soviets saw a chance to gain a foothold in the Middle East and offered to support the project. Secure in this support, Nasser accused the United States and the other NATO countries of imperialistic behavior. Soon he broadened his attacks to include all Third World countries supporting the Western imperialist. Egypt began a propaganda war against Saudi Arabia, Jordan, and Syria.

The relationship between Saudi Arabia and Egypt reached its low point in the fall of 1962 with Nasser's military intervention in the Yemen. Nasser saw an opportunity to gain the oil riches of Arabia through the back door. Until January 1963 the conflict between the two rival factions was stalemated. Nasser's propaganda attacked Faisal again and again, trying to drive a wedge between the Royal Family and the younger, foreign-educated air force and army officers, as well as foreign educated government employees. Faisal broke off relations with the UAR. By the end of December the Egyptian air force attacked a number of Saudi border towns, and in response to this attack Faisal ordered a general mobilization. A few days later he issued his conditions for ending the war: withdrawal of all foreign armed forces from Yemeni soil, ending all foreign interference in internal Yemen affairs, and allowing the Yemeni to chhose their own government. The war in Yemen continued until the summer of 1965, when the number of Egyptian troops rose to about 60,000 men. Despite this formidable armed force, Egypt could not defeat the resisting loyalist forces commanded by the Imam, Muhammad al Badr. A final offensive of the summer of 1964 failed, and Faisal and Nasser met in Jedda from August 22-24, 1965, to work out a solution to the Yemeni impasse. Following the end of the Jedda Conference, the two sides issued a memorandum laying down the basic conditions for a solution. Unfortunately, a conference in Harad, Saudi Arabia, of all interested Yemeni parties, with Saudi Arabia and Egypt in attendance, failed to reach a complete agreement. It did, however, achieve a ceasefire among the contending Yemeni factions.

Neither Saudi Arabia nor Egypt gained an absolute success in the conflict. President Nasser failed in his attempt to subvert the King's conservative government and to tap the country's vast resources for Egypt's development. Despite Saudi Arabia's failure to dislodge the Egyptian army from its southern border, the war had a salutary effect on the Kingdom. Faisal's firm leadership in the dispute gained him greater recognition within the Kingdom and was one of the factors contributing to his investiture as King and Imam. Although the danger of open warfare between the two Arab countries had been averted, the relationship between them remained strained.

Another important aspect of recent Saudi Arabian history was the eastern-boundary dispute. In 1949 Saudi Arabia advanced a territorial claim, with roots in the nineteenth century, to the major part of Abu Dhabi. There were several reasons for Saudi Arabi's claims in the Buraimi Oasis: First, it was assumed that there exist large oil deposits in the area; second, the Saudi Arabian government was opposed to the presence of British troops in the Trucial States and wished to dislodge their presence; third, there was a faction of the ruling Saudi elite that wanted to pick up where Abd al-Aziz had stopped and desired to extend the Kingdom's rule throughout the Arabian Peininsula.

Many parties were involved in the dispute, and it must be viewed as an Arabian Gulf problem rather than as a local problem involving only Saudi Arabia and Abu Dhabi. The Iraqi government laid claim to Kuwait as part of that country's historical domain. The Shah of Iran advanced claims to certain islands in the gulf, including Bahrain. In addition to the local participants, the United States, Britain, and Egypt also involved themselves in the dispute. During the early 1960s the contending factions each laid down "unalterable" demands for which there appeared no amicable resolution. All these disputed claims and counterclaims were settled between 1964 and 1974. Saudi Arabia recognized Abu Dhabi as an independent state, renounced its claims on the Buraini Oasis, and agreed to a formal boundary between the two areas. Bahrain has become an independent state, and Iran has relinquished its claims on the island. Thus, it appears that at the moment at least peace and harmony will prevail among the Arabian Gulf countries.

On November 6, 1962, Crown Prince Faisal issued a ten-point program outlining his proposed social and economic reforms.[8] Point 1 called for the "promulgation of a Basic Law for the Government of the country, drawn from the Koran and the Tradition of the Prophet and the acts of the Orthodox Caliphs, that will set forth explicitly the fundamental principles of government and the relationship between the governor and the governed, organize the various powers of the State, and the relationship among these powers, and provide for the basic rights of the citizen, including the right to freely express his opinion within the limits of Islamic belief and public policy." Point 2 promises to draw up "legislation that will regulate the system of local government in the various provinces of the Kingdom." Point 3 announced the creation of a Supreme Judicial Council and of a Ministry of Justice, and Point 4 the establishment of "a Judicial Council consisting of twenty members chosen from among the outstanding jurists and ulema to look into the matters referred to it by the State and to consider all the questions and requests for advice directed to it by individual Moslems."

Point 4 is very important. As has been shown, the Koran and the traditions are fixed and cannot be changed. Therefore, they are somewhat limited in their applicability to many modern problems. The new Council was to be a mechanism by which the legal problems of a modern society can be reconciled with the immutable rules laid down by God and His Prophet. The discussion of "important matters of State" in the Council "to arrive at solutions from Sharia and in keeping with the interests of Moslems" opens the way to derive solutions by consensus.

Because the government is aware of its obligation "to spread the call of Islam," Point 5 called for the adoption of "all means necessary for the performance of this noble task." To improve the religious climate within the Kingdom Point 6 announced the resolve "to reform the Committees for Public Morality in accordance with the Sharia and Islam's lofty goals, for which they were originally created, and in such a way as to extirpate to the greatest extent evil motives from the hearts of the people." Point 7 was a promise to improve the lot of the average Saudi citizen by the implementing of various social legislation. Point 8 recognizes the need for intensification and coordination of the economic development effort. To achieve this end "a large number of important regulations will be issued gradually whereby the State will, before long, have a complete body of laws that will make for progress and greater activity and attract capital." Point 9 lists the priority items of the development plan. Among the projects to be undertaken were the creation of a road system; improvement of the water supply, including the construction of dams; and the encouragement of heavy and light industry. Furthermore, the memorandum called for the creation of an agricultural and an industrial bank. Finally, the establishment of the Economic Development Fund was announced. Point 10 ordered the abolition of slavery and the manumission of all slaves.

Since the announcement of this program, nearly 12 years have passed, and many of the promises have been fulfilled. How successful the King had been in realizing his promises, especially the economic promises, is the subject of this book.

King Faisal's efforts in the Islamic cause were based on the assumption that Arabs and Moslems have common problems calling for a common solution. Some of these problems are the Palestinian question, Moslem Kashmir's annexation by India and the denial of self-determination of the Moslem population, and the condition of Moslems in the Soviet Union and the PRC. Because political, social, and religious concerns are all inextricably intertwined in Islam, to solve some of the above problems is to advance the cause of Islam, and that is a sacred burden imposed on all Moslems.

Despite King Faisal's denials that he did not wish to create an aggressive political power bloc to advance the interest of the Moslem countries, the idea of an Islamic call to solidarity will lead to such a development. Although the various Moslem countries have diverse social and political structures, their adherence to Islam gives them a common bond, and in a world where the success or failure of policies is determined by the size of the state or the support of one of the superpowers, a united Moslem bloc could gain satisfaction of its demands for a change, and the "oil weapon" is the sword. The recent use of the oil boycott is a case in point. There can be no doubt that the oil boycott caused a shift in U.S. support of Israel.

The King has been active in his efforts to advance the Islamic cause. He has traveled widely in the Moslem world and his diplomacy has produced some solidarity among the Moslem States. A beginning has been made, and that is a most crucial step.

NOTES

1. George A. Lipsky et al., Saudi Arabia (New Haven, Conn.: HRAF Press, 1959), p. 43.

2. Reprinted in Gerald DeGaury, Faisal, King of Saudi Arabia (London: Barker, 1966), p. 147

3. R. Bayly Winder, Saudi Arabia in the Nineteenth Century (New York: St. Martin's Press, 1965), p. 6.

4. David Horwarth, The Desert King (London: Collins, 1964), p. 32.

5. Ibid., p. 69.

6. Ibid., p. 71.

7. H. S. St.-J. B. Philby, Arabian Days (London: Hale, 1948), pp. 290-91.

8. See DeGaury, Faisal, pp. 147-51.

PART II

THE ECONOMY: THE PRIVATE SECTOR

CHAPTER

4

THE ECONOMY: AN OVERVIEW

In 1940 the wheel was not in general use in most areas of the nation. Saudi Arabia had a pastoral economy based on the raising of goats, sheep, and camels. The majority of the urban population lived in small villages built of mudbrick and earned a living from subsistence agriculture. The nomads drove their herds of animals across the desert in search of forage, carrying their meager belongings on camel back from grazing area to grazing area. If one of the animals became ill, that was Allah's will; it was cut out of the herd and quarantined to prevent the spread of disease among the healthy stock. If the animal died, that, too, was Allah's will. If it recovered, Allah be praised, and it was returned to the herd. There was no industry in the towns, and trade was the most important activity. In the cities of the Hejaz, in Mecca, Medina, and Jedda, the Pilgrimage was by far the most important source of income. For about four months of the year a large number of persons was engaged in supplying various services to the pilgrims, and during the rest of the year trade offered some opportunities for additional employment.

Today, Saudi Arabia is one of the fastest-growing nations in the world, and it has become a world power through its petroleum policy. In the larger towns light industries have been established. In Jedda a small steel mill has been erected, and in Dammam a large fertilizer plant has begun production. Nearly all major cities have been connected by a system of well-constructed, paved roads, as well as by airline service. The nation's airline is equipped with the latest passenger jets, many of which are piloted by Saudi nationals.

This chapter presents a discussion of the progress of the nation's economic development. In addition to the analysis of the structure of the economy by industry groups and major economic sector based on the available gross domestic statistics, the chapter presents

TABLE 4.1

GDP by Industrial Origin, 1962/63 to 1972/73
(S.R. million)

Industry Group	1962/63	1963/64	1964/65	1965/66
Industries and Other Producers, Except for Producers of Government Services				
Agriculture, forestry, fishing	866.2	908.8	874.4	839.4
Mining, quarrying				
Petroleum, natural gas	4,049.2	4,068.8	4,508.8	5,441.5
Other	15.5	18.4	25.1	31.7
Manufacturing				
Petroleum refining	528.6	586.4	658.3	698.2
Other	157.0	172.9	191.3	212.4
Electricity, gas, water	100.9	112.8	128.2	150.3
Construction	310.8	368.3	501.7	633.4
Wholesale and retail trade, restaurants, hotels	516.0	599.7	718.0	823.2
Transport, storage, communication	537.3	636.6	739.4	855.5
Finance, insurance, real estate, business services[c]				
Ownership of dwellings	382.0	405.9	430.0	462.0
Other	n.a.	n.a.	n.a.	n.a.
Community, social and personal service[d]	212.7	222.1	246.2	284.8
Less imputed bank service charge	n.a.	n.a.	n.a.	n.a.
Nongovernment production	7,676.2	8,100.7	8,591.4	10,432.4
Producers of Government Services				
Public administration and defense	659.7	771.7	853.3	900.2
Other services[e]	226.0	285.5	323.7	374.7
Government production	885.7	1,057.2	1,177.0	1,274.9
Total public and private output[f]	8,561.9	9,157.9	9,768.4	11,707.3
Import duties	n.a.	n.a.	n.a.	n.a.
GDP[g]	8,603.7	9,205.2	10,257.5	11,775.6

[a]Overlap with old series.

[b]Preliminary estimate.

[c]For 1962/63 to 1966/67 this item is recorded differently. To make it compatible with the new series only the Ownership of Dwellings component was included here. The remaining items that appear to belong here under the new classification have been omitted.

[d]These figures have been deduced on the assumption that private services in education and health services listed in the old series can be combined to yield an approximation of the new group, Community, Social, and Personal Service. For the private components of the old series see CDS, Gross Domestic Product, pp. 32, 33.

1966/67 Old Series	1966/67 New[a] Series	1967/68	1968/69	1969/70	1970/71	1971/72	1972/73[b]
862.4	846.3	881.0	957.4	984.1	1,015.5	1,058.7	1,138.7
6,052.2	6,130.7	6,892.8	7,269.8	8,106.3	12,581.3	16,931.5	26,980.9
35.4	36.4	43.5	48.9	46.7	50.3	58.7	70.8
736.2	759.8	901.6	984.7	1,240.9	1,474.2	1,441.6	1,926.3
237.0	308.9	344.1	385.3	431.2	483.6	543.0	617.1
166.9	198.7	219.6	247.2	273.1	297.9	302.2	319.1
707.1	727.4	869.1	977.4	933.9	1,007.0	1,173.8	1,415.1
876.3	721.8	806.5	937.8	1,007.5	1,067.5	1,177.0	1,317.8
976.4	937.9	1,009.7	1,173.2	1,242.5	1,479.3	1,567.4	1,667.6
494.0	494.0	545.0	601.0	661.0	727.0	800.0	896.0
n.a.	266.7	314.7	334.9	354.9	376.6	411.4	450.3
310.8	171.0	191.4	214.7	238.3	265.4	297.1	333.9
n.a.	-34.5	-39.1	-43.2	-46.0	-49.6	-50.0	-52.0
11,454.7	11,565.1	12,979.9	14,089.1	15,474.2	20,776.0	25,712.4	37,081.6
1,079.5	752.2	801.0	891.5	942.1	992.7	1,076.4	1,362.6
462.5	613.8	648.3	723.7	736.3	812.4	1,068.5	1,228.3
1,542.0	1,366.0	1,449.3	1,615.2	1,678.4	1,805.1	2,144.9	2,590.9
12,996.7	12,931.1	14,429.2	15,704.3	17,152.6	22,581.1	27,857.3	39,672.5
n.a.	211.4	227.4	271.0	246.0	340.1	400.0	315.0
13,078.6	13,142.5	14,656.6	15,975.3	17,398.6	22,921.2	28,257.3	39,987.5

[e]For 1962/63 to 1966/67 old series it has been assumed that the items called Total Government Education and total contribution of Government Health Services approximate the new category. Other services are listed under producers of Government Service in the new series.

[f]In using the above estimating procedure the total of private and public contributions to GDP are slightly overestimated.

[g]GDP as published in the old series. The discrepancy between this line and the line marked Total (Public and Private) results from an upward bias in the estimates used to make the old and new series as compatible as possible.

Sources: 1962/63 to 1966/67: CDS, Gross Domestic Product of Saudi Arabia, 1382/83 through 1388/89 A.H. (Riyadh, September 1970), p. 2; 1966/67 to 1972/73: SAMA, Annual Report, 1392/93 A.H. (Jedda, 1974), pp. 112-13.

TABLE 4.2

Percent Relatives of the Change in GDP by Industrial Origin, 1962/63 to 1972/73
(1962/63 = 100)

Industry Group	1962/63	1963/64	1964/65	1965/66	1966/67 Old Series	1966/67 New[a] Series
Industries and Other Producers, Except for Producers of Government Services						
Agriculture, forestry, fishing	100.0	104.9	100.9	96.9	99.6	97.7
Mining, quarrying						
Petroleum, natural gas	100.0	100.5	111.4	134.4	149.5	151.4
Other	100.0	118.7	161.9	204.5	228.4	234.8
Manufacturing						
Petroleum refining	100.0	110.9	124.5	132.1	139.3	143.7
Other	100.0	110.1	121.8	135.3	151.0	196.8
Electricity, gas, water	100.0	111.8	127.1	149.0	165.4	196.9
Construction	100.0	118.5	161.4	203.8	227.5	234.0
Wholesale and retail trade, restaurants, hotels	100.0	116.2	139.1	159.5	169.8	139.9
Transport, storage, communication	100.0	118.5	137.6	159.2	181.7	174.6
Finance, insurance, real estate, business services[c]						
Ownership of dwellings	100.0	106.3	112.6	120.9	129.3	129.3
Other	n.a.	n.a.	n.a.	n.a.	n.a.	n.a.
Community, social, and personal service[d]	100.0	104.4	115.7	133.9	146.1	80.4
Less imputed bank service charge	—	—	—	—	—	—
Producers of Government Service						
Public administration and defense	100.0	117.0	129.3	134.5	163.6	114.0
Other services[e]	100.0	126.3	143.2	165.8	204.6	271.6
GDP	100.0	107.0	119.2	136.9	152.0	152.8

	1967/68	1968/69	1969/70	1970/71	1971/72	1972/73[b]
Industries and Other Producers, Except for Producers of Government Services						
Agriculture, forestry, fishing	101.7	110.5	113.6	117.2	122.2	131.5
Mining, quarrying						
Petroleum, natural gas	170.2	179.5	200.2	310.7	418.1	666.3
Other	280.6	315.5	301.3	324.5	378.7	456.8
Manufacturing						
Petroleum refining	170.7	186.3	234.8	278.9	272.7	364.4
Other	219.2	245.4	274.6	308.0	345.9	393.1
Electricity, gas, water	217.6	245.0	270.7	295.2	299.5	316.3
Construction	279.6	314.5	300.5	324.0	377.7	455.3
Wholesale and retail trade, restaurants, hotels	156.3	181.7	195.3	206.9	228.1	255.4
Transport, storage, communication	187.9	218.4	231.2	275.3	291.7	310.4
Finance, insurance, real estate, business services[c]						
Ownership of dwellings	142.7	157.3	173.0	190.3	209.4	234.6
Other	n.a.	n.a.	n.a.	n.a.	n.a.	n.a.
Community, social, and personal service[d]	90.0	100.9	112.0	124.8	139.7	157.0
Less imputed bank service charge	—	—	—	—	—	—
Producers of Government Service						
Public administration and defense	121.4	135.1	142.8	150.5	163.2	206.5
Other services[e]	286.9	320.2	325.8	359.5	472.8	543.5
GDP	170.4	185.7	202.2	266.4	328.4	467.8

[a]Overlap with old series.

[b]Preliminary estimate.

[c]For 1962/63 to 1966/67 this item is recorded differently. To make it compatible with the new series only the Ownership of Dwellings component was included here. The remaining items that appear to belong here under the new classification have been omitted.

[d]These figures have been deduced on the assumption that private services in education and health services listed in the old series can be combined to yield an approximation of the new group, Community, Social, and Personal Service. For the private components of the old series see CDS, Gross Domestic Product, pp. 32, 33.

[e]For 1962/63 to 1966/67 old series it has been assumed that the items called Total Government Education and total contribution of Government Health Services approximate the new category. Other services are listed under producers of Government Service in the new series.

Sources: 1962/63 to 1966/67: CDS, Gross Domestic Product of Saudi Arabia, 1382/83 Through 1388/89 A.H. (Riyadh, September 1970), p. 2; 1966/67 to 1972/73: SAMA, Annual Report, 1392/93 A.H. (Jedda, 1974), pp. 112-13.

TABLE 4.3

Percent Distribution of Industry Groups in GDP, 1962/63 to 1972/73

Industry Group	1962/63	1963/64	1964/65	1965/66	1966/67[a] Old Series	1966/67[a] New Series
Industries and Other Producers, Except for Producers of Government Services						
Agriculture, forestry, fishing	10.1	9.9	8.5	7.1	6.6	6.4
Mining, quarrying						
Petroleum, natural gas	47.1	44.2	44.0	46.2	46.3	46.6
Other	0.2	0.2	0.2	0.3	0.3	0.3
Manufacturing						
Petroleum refining	6.1	6.4	6.4	5.9	5.6	5.8
Other	1.8	1.9	1.9	1.8	1.8	2.4
Electricity, gas, water	1.2	1.2	1.2	1.3	1.3	1.5
Construction	3.6	4.0	4.9	5.4	5.4	5.5
Wholesale and retail trade, restaurants, hotels	6.0	6.5	7.0	7.0	6.7	5.5
Transport, storage, communication	6.2	6.9	7.2	7.3	7.5	7.1
Finance, insurance, real estate, business services[c]						
Ownership of dwellings	4.4	4.4	4.2	3.9	3.8	3.8
Other	—	—	—	—	—	2.0
Community, social, and personal service[d]	2.5	2.4	2.4	2.4	2.4	1.3
Less imputed bank service charge	—	—	—	—	—	—
Producers of Government Service						
Public administration and defense	7.7	8.4	8.3	7.6	8.3	5.7
Other services[e]	2.6	3.1	3.2	3.2	3.5	4.7
Import duties	—	—	—	—	—	1.6
GDP	f	—	—	—	—	100.0

	1967/68	1968/69	1969/70	1970/71	1971/72	1972/73[b]
Industries and Other Producers, Except for Producers of Government Services						
Agriculture, forestry, fishing	6.0	6.0	5.7	4.4	3.7	2.8

Mining, quarrying						
Petroleum, natural gas	47.0	45.5	46.6	54.9	59.9	67.5
Other	0.3	0.3	0.3	0.2	0.2	0.2
Manufacturing						
Petroleum refining	6.2	6.2	7.1	6.4	5.1	4.8
Other	2.3	2.4	2.5	2.1	1.9	1.5
Electricity, gas, water	1.5	1.5	1.6	1.3	1.1	0.8
Construction	5.9	6.1	5.4	4.4	4.2	3.5
Wholesale and retail trade, restaurants, hotels	5.5	5.9	5.8	4.7	4.2	3.3
Transport, storage, communication	6.9	7.3	7.1	6.5	5.5	4.2
Finance, insurance, real estate, business services[c]						
Ownership of dwellings	3.7	3.8	3.8	3.2	2.8	2.2
Other	2.1	2.1	2.0	1.6	1.5	1.1
Community, social, and personal service[d]	1.3	1.3	1.4	1.2	1.1	0.8
Less imputed bank service charge	—	—	—	—	—	—
Producers of Government Service						
Public administration and defense	5.5	5.6	5.4	4.3	3.8	3.4
Other services[e]	4.4	4.5	4.2	3.5	3.8	3.1
Import duties	1.6	1.7	1.4	1.5	1.4	0.8
GDP	100.0	100.0	100.0	100.0	100.0	100.0

[a]Overlap with old series.

[b]Preliminary estimate.

[c]For 1962/63 to 1966/67 this item is recorded differently. To make it compatible with the new series only the Ownership of Dwellings component was included here. The remaining items that appear to belong here under the new classification have been omitted.

[d]These figures have been deduced on the assumption that private services in education and health services listed in the old series can be combined to yield an approximation of the new group, Community, Social, and Personal Service. For the private components of the old series see CDS, Gross Domestic Product, pp. 32, 33.

[e]For 1962/63 to 1966/67 old series it has been assumed that the items called Total Government Education and total contribution of Government Health Services approximate the new category. Other services are listed under producers of Government Service in the new series.

[f]For 1962/63 to 1966/67 the old series has been used. The percentages will not add to 100 percent because of adjustment errors. Beginning with the new series, the omission of the imputed bank service charge will overstate the total by less than ± 0.03 percentage points.

Sources: 1962/63 to 1966/67: CDS, Gross Domestic Product of Saudi Arabia, 1382/83 Through 1388/89 A.H. (Riyadh, September 1970), p. 2; 1966/67 to 1972/73: SAMA, Annual Report, 1392/93 A.H. (Jedda, 1974), pp. 112-13.

an estimate of physical capital formation and a discussion of the general standard of living.

Before we begin the discussion, it is necessary to comment briefly on the statistical sources. By far the most detailed presentation of GDP figures is contained in CDS, The Gross Domestic Product of Saudi Arabia, 1382/83 to 1388/89 A.H. published in September 1970. This series was kept up to date until 1974, when a revised series was published in the SAMA's Annual Report of 1392/93 A.H.[1] Unfortunately, the central bank did not publish an explanation of the changes in assumptions and method underlying the new data, nor did it publish any detailed figures for the various components of GDP. Finally, the new data only go back to 1966/67, while the old statistics begin in 1962/63. Comparison between the old and new series shows that, in addition to a change in the content of the various classifications, the figures for the new GDP series are only about 1 percent higher for the years 1966/67 to 1969/70 than those in the older series, while for 1970/71 they were about 8 percent higher. To facilitate the discussion of GDP by industrial origin the two series have been spliced in 1966/67, and the various subclassifications for the years prior to '966/67 have been adjusted whenever possible to conform with the new series, while the analysis of GDP by sectors, as well as the detailed analysis of various subclassifications, has been based on the older statistical series.

GDP BY INDUSTRY CLASSIFICATION

Today, Saudi Arabia's major product is oil. But oil is a wasting asset, and assuming that no additional major oil fields are discovered and that oil exploitation continues at present rates, the country's oil resources will be exhausted around the turn of the century. Thus, the aim of economic policy must be to diversify the economy to free the nation from its dependence on oil.

The beginning of Saudi Arabia's effort to industrialize dates from about 1962, the year of Faisal's elevation to the throne. What has been the growth rate of the economy? These questions are easily stated but, unfortunately, the answers are not always readily available.

GDP BY INDUSTRIAL ORIGIN

Tables 4.1 to 4.3 present GDP by industrial origin in current prices for 1962/63 to 1972/73. These data offer a means to examine changes in the industrial structure prior to the beginning of the first development plan in the budget year 1970/71. In this chapter we will concentrate our attention on the pre-plan years. In Chapter 15 a comprehensive review of the plan, as well as of the success or failure of the planning mechanism, will be presented. Although the fiscal year 1970/71 is the beginning of the first operational five-year plan, it is included in the pre-plan period, because numerous difficulties delayed total implementation of the plan until 1971/72.

GDP has risen steadily since 1962/63 (see Table 4.2). From that date to 1972/73 it rose S.R. 31.4 billion, or 365 percent, at an average annual rate of change of 16.6 percent. The figures given in Table 4.1 are recorded in current riyals, reflecting the underlying real growth as well as changes in relative prices. Unfortunately, the real GDP statistics on the new basis are only available since 1966/67 so that a comparison over the whole period since 1962/63 is impossible. Real GDP rose more than 100 percent from 1966/67 to 1972/73, at an annual rate of 12.9 percent. Most of this growth occurred since 1970/71. From 1966/67 to 1969/70 real DGP rose 28.3 percent, at an annual rate of 8.6 percent. Since 1970/71 it rose 40.4 percent, for an annual rate of growth of 18.6 percent. Considering the many economic and social obstacles in the way of development, this growth rate is truly phenomenal.

The agriculture, forestry, and fishing classification contains five product groups: field crops and fodder, vegetables, fruits, livestock (including fish), and firewood. In 1967/68, the benchmark year for value added in the old series, 37 percent of total value came from field crops and fodder, 30 percent from livestock raising (primarily goats, camels, and chickens, and some fishing), and 18.9

TABLE 4.4

Estimated Value Added in Agriculture, 1967/68, by Major Group

Product Group	S.R. Million	Percent
Field crops, fodder	332.1	37.0
Vegetables	72.3	8.1
Fruits	169.3	18.9
Livestock, including fish	270.3	30.2
Firewood	51.5	5.7
Total	895.7	100.0

Source: CDS, Gross Domestic Product of Saudi Arabia, 1382/83 Through 1388/89 A.H. (Riyadh: September 1970), p. 9.

percent from fruit production (mainly dates, 8.1 percent from vegetable culture, and the remaining 5.7 percent from firewood production (see Table 4.4).

Agricultural progress reflects the tremendous difficulties associated with the development of an agricultural base in a desert region. Total value added by agriculture rose from S.R. 866.2 million in 1962/63 to S.R. 1,138.7 million in 1972/73, an increase of 31.5 percent, the lowest total increment of all 11 industry groups. Progress was not smooth in the agricultural sector. It rose to S.R. 908.8 in 1963/64, declined during the next two years, rose again in 1966/67, and surpassed the level of the beginning of the period in 1968/69. Since that year value added by agriculture to GDP has risen in each year. In terms of relative shares of all industry groups in GDP, agriculture fell from 10.1 percent at the beginning of the period to 2.8 percent in 1972/73. The average rate of growth in agricultural value added was about 3 percent.

The agricultural sector is the least efficient sector of the economy despite the large sums the government has allocated for improvements in that industry. It would probably be better to give up attempts to improve cereal growing in the Kingdom and concentrate on fruit and vegetable production, because in the past the average world price for wheat was considerably lower than that in Saudi Arabia. The main reason for support of agricultural activity appears to be the attempt to settle the nomad population, but that reason is dubious, because there is some evidence that the nomads can adapt easily to city life. Unfortunately, socially acceptable employment opportunities are insufficient in the cities. Therefore, until employment opportunities in the cities are enhanced the government will have to continue its support of agriculture to avoid unemployment.

The mining and quarrying industrial group is divided into two parts: crude oil and natural gas production and other mining activities. Value added to GDP rose by 550 percent from 1962/63 to 1972/73 in petroleum and natural gas production and more than 300 percent in the other mining category. The average growth rate of petroleum and natural gas production was almost 21 percent, and that of the nonpetroleum component 16.4 percent. As would be expected, the three-year period since 1970/71 accounted for most of the increase in the petroleum sector, but it is interesting that from 1962/63 to 1969/70 petroleum exploitation grew only 10.4 percent per annum, while the nonpetroleum grew at 17.1 percent per year. Despite the fact that the nonpetroleum component began at a lower base, the higher growth rate indicates that attempts at diversification within this component had been implemented.

The petroleum sector has always been the most important part of the Kingdom's economy. It is interesting, however, that the relative share of the oil sector actually declined between 1962/63 and 1969/70. In the beginning of the period crude oil extraction accounted for 47.1 percent of value added. It fell to a low of 44 percent and surpassed its earlier high in 1970/71. By 1972/73 value added by crude oil and natural gas extraction constituted 67.5 percent, and there is every indication that this share will continue to rise in the future.

Nonoil mining and quarrying is by far the least important industry group, contributing annually about 0.2 percent to total value added.

The manufacturing industry group is divided into two subsections: petroleum refining and other manufacturing. Within the Kingdom itself refining takes place at Ras Tanura (Aramco) and, since the end of fiscal year 1968/69, at Jedda (Petromin). A third refinery at Riyadh was expected to be on stream by the end of 1974. In addition, one-half of the output produced from the operation of refineries in Mina Saud (Getty) and Khafji (Arabian Oil Company [Japan]) in the Kuwaiti Neutral Zone must be added to GDP.

Value added by petroleum refining rose from S.R. 528.6 million in 1962/63 to S.R. 1,926.3 million in 1972/73, a total increase of 264 percent, at an annual average growth rate of 13.8 percent. The industry's relative share in GDP rose slightly from 1962/63 to 1964/65, declined to 5.6 percent in 1966/67, rose to a high of 7.1 percent in 1969/70, and declined to 4.8 percent in 1972/73. Value added by petroleum refining is a function of refinery capacity. With the completion of the expansion of the Jedda refinery and the Riyadh refinery value added by this industry group will increase both absolutely and relatively.

Other manufacturing increased by almost 300 percent during the period under discussion. Its relative importance in terms of value added rose from 1.8 percent of GDP in 1962/63 to 2.5 percent in 1969/70 and declined to 1.5 percent in 1972/73.

Total value added by construction rose 355 percent, from S.R. 310.8 million in 1962/63 to S.R. 1,415.1 million in 1972/73. It increased from year to year without significant slowdowns in the rate of growth at an average annual rate of 16.4 percent. In 1962/63 construction ranked seventh in relative contribution to GDP with 3.6 percent in value added. By 1968/69 construction contributed 6.1 percent to GDP, and by 1972/73 its contribution had fallen to 3.5 percent, ranking fourth behind transport, storage, and communications.

The construction component consists of seven subsegments. Table 4.5 presents the contributions to value added to GDP of each of these segments for the years 1962/63 to 1968/69. In 1962/63 residential construction stood in first place, with 32.9 percent of value added, followed by government (including Petromin), with 31.2 percent. In third place stood oil companies' construction (excluding Petromin), with 23.7 percent, and in fourth place was maintenance

TABLE 4.5

Estimated Contribution to GDP (Old Series) of Construction by Subclasses, 1962/63 to 1968/69
(S.R. million)

	1962/63	1963/64	1964/65	1965/66	1966/67	1967/68	1968/69	Percent Change, 1962/63 to 1968/69
Oil companies, excluding Petromin	73.8	77.3	119.5	152.4	130.7	121.5	121.6	64.8
Other manufacturing; trade services (private sector)	11.8	13.4	15.2	17.4	19.8	22.8	26.2	122.0
Electric power industry	2.5	3.8	9.2	15.5	17.5	14.9	15.1	504.0
Farms	4.2	4.4	4.2	4.7	5.4	5.8	6.1	45.2
Residential construction	102.3	116.2	131.3	155.4	181.2	206.7	232.2	127.0
Government, including Petromin	97.0	113.0	200.7	265.0	327.7	397.2	403.0	314.5
Maintenance (private sector)	19.1	20.2	21.5	23.1	24.7	27.2	30.0	57.1
Total	310.8	368.3	501.7	633.4	707.1	796.1	834.2	168.4

Source: CDS, Gross Domestic Product of Saudi Arabia, 1382/83 Through 1388/89 A.H. (Riyadh, September 1970), p. 19.

of private sector dwellings. Except for the switch of residential and government construction projects the structure of construction activity remained about the same in 1968/69: government construction projects accounted for nearly 0.5 percent of value added; residential construction, in second place, contributed 27.8 percent, and oil company construction 14.6 percent. The remainder had become almost insignificant.

The continued predominance of government construction underscores the relative failure to raise the level of participation of private persons in the development process. Four reasons account for this failure. First, the number of actual and potential entrepreneurs is small, and those who participate in business activities concentrate by and large in trade and residential-housing construction. Second, it is considerably easier to identify construction projects that tend to be considered the government's obligation. Hospitals, schools, and roads are easier to conceive and execute than manufacturing projects. Given the thin markets for most private-consumption goods and the lack of trained personnel, it is understandable that private enterprises are reluctant to invest large amounts of funds in risky projects. Third, government construction projects tend to be large undertakings. It takes only one port expansion project, the building of a refinery, or any number of military projects to raise the government's contribution to value added in construction well above that of the private sector. Finally, the housing shortage, caused by the rising expectations of the growing middle class, makes investment in the construction and sale or rental a relatively riskless endeavor, thus drawing activity away from other parts of the construction sector.

The contribution of the small sector of electricity, gas, and water rose from S.R. 100.9 million in 1962/63 to S.R. 319.1 million in 1972/73, an increase of 216 percent. In relative contribution to value added this segment fluctuated between 0.8 and 1.6 percent throughout the period. It is interesting that this sector's share rose from 1.2 percent in 1962/63 to 1.6 percent in 1969/70—a clear indication that the government was trying to provide enough power, gas, and water to meet the needs of the expanding economy. The decline in 1972/73 resulted from the tremendous increases in the oil exploitation and manufacturing sectors that overshadowed the absolute growth of S.R. 46 million.

Table 4.6 presents a breakdown of the electricity, gas, water, and sanitary services component. By far the largest portion of value added by this category was water and sanitary services. It rose 98.3 percent, from S.R. 59.6 million in 1962/63 to 118.2 million in 1968/69, and accounted for 59.1 percent of the total at the beginning of this seven-year period and 60.4 percent at the end. There can be little doubt that the bulk of the value added came from the water com-

TABLE 4.6

Contribution of Gas, Water, and Sanitary Services to GDP, 1962/63 to 1968/69 (S.R. million)

Year	Electricity	Gas	Water and Sanitary Services	Total
1968/69	72.4	5.0	118.2	195.6
1967/68	66.9	4.0	110.4	181.3
1966/67	61.4	3.1	102.4	166.9
1965/66	53.2	2.3	94.8	150.3
1964/65	47.9	1.9	78.4	128.2
1963/64	43.1	1.6	68.1	112.8
1962/63	40.1	1.2	59.6	100.9

Source: CDS, The Gross Domestic Product of Saudi Arabia, 1382/83 Through 1388/89 A.H. (Riyadh: September 1970), p. 23.

ponent, because observation has shown that the sanitary facilities in towns and villages are still in a very rudimentary state.

The transportation, storage, and communication sector's contribution to GDP rose 350 percent, at an annual rate of 12 percent, from S.R. 537.3 million in 1962/63 to S.R. 1,667.6 million in 1972/73. Except for the year 1966/67, this component rose in each year throughout the period. The decline in 1966/67 was probably a result of the switch from the old to the new GDP series. The relative share of transportation, storage, and communications in GDP rose steadily from 6.2 percent in 1962/63 to 1968/69 and declined to 4.2 percent in 1972/73.

By far the largest percentage of value added in this group came from the mechanized road transport and the airline, railway, and storage components (see Table 4.7). The overwhelming importance of road transportation, which rose 150 percent, from S.R. 379 million to S.R. 947.9 million, reflects the country's inhospitable terrain. Only cars, trucks, and aircraft are efficient means of transportation in the Kingdom's deserts. In 1962/63 the contribution of mechanized road transport within the sector amounted to 70.5 percent,

TABLE 4.7

Contribution of Transportation, Storage, and Communications to GDP, 1962/63 to 1968/69
(S.R. million)

Year	Tapline	Mechanized Road Transport	Post, Telephone, Telegraph	Airline, Railway, and Other	Total
1968/69	45.0	947.9	47.8	131.4	1,172.1
1967/68	48.3	836.8	50.7	124.3	1,060.1
1966/67	54.9	761.3	48.6	111.6	976.4
1965/66	44.7	659.4	52.5	98.9	855.5
1964/65	40.9	566.6	45.7	86.2	739.4
1963/64	42.1	470.3	47.5	76.7	636.6
1962/63	50.2	379.0	39.9	68.2	537.3

Source: CDS, Gross Domestic Product of Saudi Arabia, 1382/83 Through 1388/89 A.H. (Riyadh: September 1970), p. 24.

followed by airline, railway and storage* (12.7 percent), tapline (9.3 percent) and post, telephone, and telegraph (7.4 percent). In 1968/69 mechanized road transport and airline, railway, and storage still stood in first and second place respectively, but road transport had risen to 80.9 percent, and airline, railway, and storage had fallen to 11.2 percent of the four subdivisions in this sector, while post, telephone, and telegraph and tapline had declined to 4.1 and 3.8 percent, respectively.

The value of goods entering wholesale and retail trade is the sum of four separate subgroups: locally manufactured agricultural products, petroleum products, local manufactures (except for oil refining), and imports (see Table 4.8). Total wholesale and retail contributions to value added rose 155.4 percent, from S.R. 516 mil-

*The other component in the transportation, storage, and communications sector contains--in addition to storage contributions to GDP by the activities in the minor ports--lighterage and coastal shipping.

lion in 1962/63 to S.R. 1,317.8 million in 1972/73, at an average annual growth rate of 11.5 percent. The value added for wholesale and retail trade was calculated on the basis of the estimated value of goods entering the economy through trade. Both in 1962/63 and in 1968/69 imports accounted for the largest percentage by far, about 66 percent, of the value of goods entering trade. In 1962/63 local manufactures accounted for 17 percent and local agricultural products for 13.6 percent, while in 1968/69 locally produced agricultural products stood in second place, with 15.4 percent, and local manufactures had slipped to third place with 14.2 percent.

The finance, insurance, real estate, and business services group has undergone considerable content change during the reorganization of the GDP statistics. In the old series this subgroup consisted of three components: banks, real estate offices, and insurance. In the new statistics ownership of dwellings has been added to this classification, and together with a group called "other" it forms the only two subdivisions of this sector of GDP. The precise meaning of the content of this sector is further obscured by the lack of figures for the period 1962/63 to 1966/67 for the other subdivision.

Imputed value added by ownership of dwellings rose 135 percent from 1962/63 to 1972/73, from S.R. 382 million to S.R. 896 million. In relative terms value added through ownership of dwellings accounted for 4.4 percent at the beginning of the period and 2.2 percent at the

TABLE 4.8

Estimated Value of Goods Entering Trade Through Wholesale and Retail Trade, 1962/63 to 1968/69
(S.R. million)

Year	Local Agricultural Products	Petroleum Products	Local Manufactures (except for oil refining)	Imports	Total
1968/69	564.9	161.9	521.3	2,425.4	3,673.5
1967/68	471.7	150.5	463.1	2,016.8	3,102.1
1966/67	415.5	121.0	413.0	1,788.2	2,737.7
1965/66	362.7	100.9	370.2	1,726.6	2,560.4
1964/65	312.2	83.2	333.3	1,500.3	2,228.9
1963/64	270.2	72.5	301.3	1,220.2	1,864.2
1962/63	218.6	63.1	273.6	1,049.5	1,604.8

Source: CDS, Gross Domestic Product of Saudi Arabia, 1382/83 Through 1388/89 A.H. (Riyadh, September 1970), p. 27.

end. Statistics on finance, insurance, real estate, and business services are only available since 1966/67. From that date to 1972/73 this subdivision rose nearly 70 percent, from S.R. 266.7 million to S.R. 450.3 million, and its relative share fell from 2 to 1.1 percent.

Fortunately, there is some detail in the old GDP series on the contribution of banking, real estate offices, insurance, and other financial institutions available for the mid-1960s (see Table 4.9). The most significant fact is the 134.6 percent increase in value added registered by the banking component. Despite its large income from oil exploitation, Saudi Arabia must still be classified as a developing nation. The increase in banking value added clearly shows that the development of the banking system is in step with the country's overall economic development effort.

TABLE 4.9

Contribution of Banking, Insurance, and Real Estate to GDP, 1962/63 to 1968/69
(S.R. million)

Year	Banks	Real Estate Establishments	Banks and Other Financial Institutions	Total
1968/69	86.1	8.0	8.6	102.7
1967/68	78.0	7.3	7.8	93.0
1966/67	68.6	6.4	6.9	81.9
1965/66	57.5	5.0	5.8	68.3
1964/65	50.6	3.4	5.1	59.1
1963/64	41.9	2.2	4.2	48.2
1962/63	36.7	1.4	3.7	41.8

Source: CDS, Gross Domestic Product of Saudi Arabia, 1382/83 Through 1388/89 A.H. (Riyadh, September 1970), p. 28.

The community, social, and personal services classification is an entirely new item published only in the new GDP series, which divides the service sector between private and governmental activities beginning in 1966/67. It was possible, however, to splice the old and new series to arrive at the figures given in Table 4.1. The value added to GDP by private service activities rose 57 percent, from S.R. 212.7 million in 1962/63 to S.R. 333.9 million in 1972/73, at an average annual rate of 4.6 percent. During the same time period its relative share in GDP fell steadily from 2.5 to 0.8 percent.

At first glance the relative unimportance of the public sector is surprising. However, further examination of the figures given in Table 4.1 reveals that the low contribution by the public administration and defense sector resulted from the switch to the new statistics. From 1962/63 to 1972/73 contributions by this sector more than doubled, rising from S.R. 659.7 million to S.R. 1,362.6 million, while its relative importance fell from 7.7 percent to 3.4 percent over the period. The average growth rate was about 7.9 percent.

NET FACTOR PAYMENTS ABROAD

Net factor payments abroad* are income payments to foreigners (individuals, companies, and governments) accruing to them from ownership of productive resources in Saudi Arabia, or the provision of services to producers in Saudi Arabia, less payments to the Saudi government or Saudi individuals arising from ownership of productive resources outside the Kingdom. Unfortunately, the revised GDP series does not give net factor payments abroad, so we must turn to the old series, which covers the period 1962/63 to 1968/69 (see Table 4.10).

Net factor payments abroad rose from S.R. 2,119 million, or 24.6 percent of GDP, in 1962/63 to S.R. 6,988.5 million, or 26.7 percent of GDP in 1972/72, a total increase of 228.9 percent. When viewed from the Saudi Arabian government's point of view, the percentage of GDP going abroad supplies an additional reason for the rapid takeover of the oil companies. To a Saudi these figures meant but one thing: The payment of one-quarter of GDP for the use of foreign capital is too much! And from that conviction rose a strong demand for total takeover of the oil companies by the government. It might be argued that there is no basis for the feeling that an "excess" amount of GDP is lost abroad so long as it is not accurately known how much foreign capital has been invested. But to the dedicated nationalist this argument is irrelevant; he sees but one fact: the portion of GDP going to foreigners could be used domestically. That is all he needs to know to demand the transfer of ownership from foreigners to Saudi nationals.

---

*Net factor payments abroad are given in Gregorian years to take advantage of the detail published in addition to the figures that form part of the budget-year GDP figures.

TABLE 4.10

Net Factor Income Payments Abroad, 1962/69
(S.R. million)*

	1962	1963	1964	1965	1966	1967	1968	1969
Factor income payments								
Oil companies (other than Aramco) disbursed or retained abroad	5.9	24.3	29.7	24.8	37.4	36.0	37.4	n.a.
Investment income payments (including Aramco)	1,845.0	2,056.5	1,732.5	1,984.5	2,727.0	2,709.0	3,141.0	n.a.
Other services	175.5	182.3	216.0	459.0	481.5	513.0	506.3	n.a.
Total payments	2,026.4	2,263.1	1,978.2	2,469.3	3,245.9	3,258.0	3,684.7	3,934.8*
Factor income receipts								
Foreign investments of SAMA (estimated)	—	—	22.5	45.0	90.0	157.5	225.0	n.a.
Private Saudi investments abroad (estimated)	11.3	22.5	22.5	45.0	45.0	67.5	67.5	n.a.
Total estimated receipts	11.3	22.5	45.0	90.0	135.0	225.0	292.5	270.0*
Net factor income payments abroad	2,015.1	2,240.6	1,933.2	2,378.3	3,110.9	3,033.0	3,392.2	3,669.3*

*Preliminary figure.

Note: Figures have been recalculated from U.S. dollar figures at the rate of S.R. 4.50 per dollar.

Source: CDS, Gross Domestic Product of Saudi Arabia 1382/83 Through 1388/89 A.H. (Riyadh, September 1970), p. 37.

By far the largest portion of the factor income payments left the country as investment income payments to the owners of the foreign oil companies. These payments rose 70.2 percent, from S.R. 1,845 million in 1962 (91 percent of total payments) to S.R. 3,141 million (85.2 percent) in 1968.

SUMMARY AND CONCLUSIONS

GDP rose from S.R. 8.6 billion in 1962/63 to S.R. 21.3 billion in 1972/73, an increase of 147.6 percent in value added (new series). Subtracting net factor payments abroad, GNP rose from S.R. 6.5 billion to S.R. 19.2 billion in 1971/72, an increase of almost 200 percent (old series).

Throughout the period under discussion there was little change in the nation's industrial structure. Oil exploitation dominated the economy. With two exceptions, agriculture and private services, the various industry groups registered increases in value added of well over 100 percent.

Ranking of all industry groups by percent of contributions to GDP indicates some change in the structure of industry between 1962/63 and 1972/73 (see Table 4.11). At the beginning of the period crude oil and natural gas production stood in first place, with 47.1 percent of total value added. In second place stood agriculture (10.1 percent), followed by public administration and defense (7.7 percent), transport, storage, and communications (6.2 percent), and petroleum refining (6.1 percent). Wholesale and retail trade, food services, and hotels stood in sixth place (6 percent), ownership of dwellings (4.2 percent), construction (3.6 percent), other government services (2.6 percent), community, social, and personal services (2.5 percent), other manufacturing (1.8 percent), electricity, gas, and water stood in twelfth place, and other mining and quarrying in thirteenth.

In 1972/73 the ranking had changed somewhat. Agriculture had fallen to eighth place, and petroleum refining had risen to second place. Transport, storage, and communications had moved into third from fourth place, public administration had fallen from third to fifth place. Wholesale and retail trade, food services, and hotels had remained in sixth place, followed by other government services in seventh place, ownership of dwellings in ninth place, and other manufacturing in tenth place. Other finance, insurance, real estate, and business source occupied eleventh place and community, social, and personal service and electricity, gas, and water were tied for twelfth place. Other mining and quarrying had remained in thirteenth place.

The above statistics do not suggest a major trend. Oil and oil-related industries still stood in first place. The rise in transport

TABLE 4.11

Ranking of Industry Groups, Including and Excluding the Oil Industry, 1962/63 and 1972/73

	Including Oil				Excluding Oil			
	1962/63		1972/73		1962/63		1972/73	
Industry Group	Rank	Percent*	Rank	Percent*	Rank	Percent*	Rank	Percent*
Agriculture, forestry, fishing	2	10.1	8	2.8	1	21.5	6	10.2
Mining, quarrying								
Petroleum, natural gas	1	47.1	1	67.5	Omitted		Omitted	
Other	13	0.2	13	0.2	11	0.4	12	0.6
Manufacturing								
Petroleum refining	5	6.0	2	4.8	Omitted		Omitted	
Other	12	1.8	10	1.5	9	3.9	8	5.5
Electricity, gas, water	12	1.2	12	0.8	10	2.5	11	2.9
Construction	8	3.6	4	3.5	6	7.7	2	12.7
Wholesale and retail trade, restaurants, hotels	6	6.0	6	3.3	4	12.8	4	11.8
Transport, storage, communication	4	6.2	3	4.2	3	13.3	1	15.0
Finance, insurance, real estate, business services								
Ownership of dwellings	7	4.2	9	2.2	5	9.5	7	8.0
Other	n.a.	n.a.	11	1.1	n.a.	n.a.	9	4.0
Community, social, and personal service	10	2.5	12	0.8	8	5.3	10	3.0
Public administration and defense	3	7.7	5	3.4	2	16.4	3	12.2
Other government service	9	2.6	7	3.1	7	5.6	5	11.0

*Detail does not add to 100 percent because of omission of import duties and imputed bank service charge.

Sources: 1962/63 to 1966/67: CDS, Gross Domestic Product of Saudi Arabia, 1382/83 Through 1388/89 A.H. (Riyadh, September 1970), p. 2; 1966/67 to 1972/73: SAMA, Annual Report, 1392/93 A.H. (Jedda, 1974), pp. 112-13.

from fourth to third place and the rise of construction from eighth to fourth place indicates generally quickening economic activity. Particularly disappointing is the fact that nonoil manufacturing is still in last place, suggesting that attempts to reduce the predominance of the leading sector have not yet reached a significant stage.

It can be argued that the presence of the oil industry obscures a structural analysis, because it distorts changes by its overwhelming size. Therefore, this industry should be treated as an enclave and excluded from structural analysis, because it is under foreign control and its development has been determined by exogenous factors. This has never been a convincing argument, however, and recent changes in the oil industry have made it even less important. Regardless of who owns and operates the Kingdom's oil industry (excluding control over posted prices) its growth is determined by international factors, because the domestic market is not large enough to affect the oil industry. Nevertheless, a ranking of industry groups excluding oil and oil-related industries is helpful. It shows that transportation and construction have moved into first and second place among nonoil industry groups, that public administration and defense has declined somewhat in importance, and that the importance of wholesale and retail trade, restaurants, and hotels has remained the same. It is interesting that other manufacturing has risen in importance, suggesting that our evaluation including the oil industry obscured the changes taking place in the private, nonoil industrial sector. Government contributions to GDP show that the attempts to reduce the government's participation in the nation's economic life have been ineffective. Overall, however, it must again be concluded that there is no strong, discernible trend showing diversification of the economy and less reliance on oil.

THE ECONOMIC SECTORS

Table 4.12 presents contributions to GDP by major economic sectors: public sector; private sector, oil; and private sector, nonoil. Because this classification is unavailable in the new GDP series, the old series must be used in the following analysis.

On the average the private oil sector contributed about 54 percent, the private nonoil sector 30 percent, and the public sector 15 percent of value added for the period 1962/63 to 1968/69. There was a slight shift in the relative shares of the three sectors away from the private and to the public sector. The public sector grew fastest during the period under discussion: It rose at an average annual rate of 13 percent, from S.R. 1.2 billion in 1962/63 to S.R. 2.5 billion in 1968/69, an overall increase of about 110 percent. During the same time the private nonoil sector grew 81.3 percent, and the private oil sector 78.7 percent.

Some changes in the relative shares within the major economic sectors have occurred. In 1962/63 public administration and defense accounted for more than half of the contribution within the public sector, and in 1968/69 this contribution had fallen to 48.5 percent. Despite the absolute increase of S.R. 535.4 million during this seven-year period, its relative share fell, clearly indicating that the government had been giving more emphasis to nonpublic administration and defense in its domestic policy. During the same period the relative contribution to public-sector value added nearly doubled, from 8.3 percent to 16.4 percent, and education rose slightly from 14.7 to 16.5 percent. The largest decline within the government's contribution to GDP occurred in the transport, storage, and communications group, which fell from 9.2 to 7.3 percent. The remaining groups maintained essentially the same relative position within the public sector.

Very little needs to be said about the private oil sector. Crude petroleum, natural gas extraction, and petroleum refining accounted for well over 95 percent of total value added within this sector. The remaining activities, construction, services, and so on, reflect the petroleum industry's contribution to GDP in the course of its own activities.

In the private nonoil sector agriculture made the largest contribution in 1962/63 (32.5 percent). By 1968/69, it had fallen to second place, with 20.1 percent, and the wholesale and retail trade component stood in first place, up from 17.8 percent in 1962/63. There are several reasons for the premier position of wholesale and retail trade within the private, nonoil sector. First, among the settled population trade has been the main activity for as long as one cares to remember. Thus, when the increasing oil income quickened the tempo of economic activity it was fairly easy to draw additional entrepreneurs into this industry group. Second, as personal income grew, the people demanded consumer goods produced outside Saudi Arabia, offering existing traders an opportunity to expand and drawing new private capital into the sector. Thus, tradition and the nature of demand combined to stimulate wholesale and retail trade.

Next in importance within the nonoil sector stands the transport, storage, and communications group. It rose from 14.2 percent in 1962/63 to 19.6 percent in 1968/69. The expansion of this group reflects the increasing economic activity in the Kingdom. Without transport, storage, and communications services, economic growth would be retarded, and it may well be that the growth of trade has stimulated the growth of this component.

The remaining industry groups did not change significantly.

TABLE 4.12

Contributions to GDP by Economic Sectors, 1962/63 to 1968/69
(S.R. million)

Economic Sector and Industry Group	1962/63	1963/64	1964/65	1965/66	1966/67	1967/68	1968/69
Public Sector							
Petroleum refining	—	—	—	—	—	—	18.9
Construction	97.0	133.0	200.7	265.0	327.7	397.2	403.0
Electricity, gas, water, sanitary services	49.6	56.2	63.9	76.4	82.5	88.9	95.1
Transport, storage, communications	108.1	124.2	131.9	151.4	160.2	175.0	179.2
Public administration and defense	659.7	771.7	853.3	900.2	1,079.5	1,096.3	1,195.1
Services							
Education	172.1	219.6	248.7	290.4	361.7	393.4	405.7
Medical and health	53.9	65.9	75.0	84.3	100.8	100.5	104.1
Other	32.3	29.7	38.1	47.8	53.6	55.9	60.6
Total government	1,172.7	1,400.3	1,611.6	1,815.5	2,166.0	2,307.2	2,461.7
Private Sector, Oil							
Crude oil, natural gas	4,049.2	4,068.8	4,508.8	5,441.5	6,052.2	6,772.9	7,360.6
Petroleum refining	528.6	586.4	658.3	698.2	736.2	870.6	948.2
Construction	73.8	77.3	119.5	152.4	130.7	121.5	121.6
Transport, storage, communications	50.2	42.1	40.9	44.7	54.9	48.3	45.0
Wholesale and retail trade	40.4	52.3	55.8	37.5	26.4	13.2	4.0
Services							
Medical and health	7.2	6.6	5.3	5.1	4.3	4.1	4.2
Other services	12.9	11.6	12.0	21.7	20.6	40.5	27.0
Total private sector, oil	4,762.5	4,845.1	5,400.6	6,401.1	7,025.3	7,871.1	8,510.6

Private Sector, Nonoil							
Agriculture, forestry, fishing	866.2	908.8	874.4	839.4	862.4	895.7	974.4
Other mining and quarrying	15.5	18.4	25.1	31.7	35.4	39.8	41.7
Other manufacturing	157.0	172.9	191.3	212.4	237.0	265.6	299.0
Construction	140.0	158.0	181.5	216.0	248.7	277.4	309.6
Electricity, gas, water, sanitary services	51.3	56.6	64.3	73.9	84.4	92.4	100.5
Transport, storage, communications	379.0	470.3	566.6	659.4	761.3	836.8	947.9
Wholesale and retail trade	475.6	547.4	662.2	785.7	849.9	975.7	1,171.9
Banking, insurance, real estate	41.8	48.2	59.1	68.3	81.9	93.0	102.7
Ownership of dwellings	382.0	405.0	430.0	462.0	494.0	545.0	601.0
Services							
Education	8.6	11.0	12.5	14.5	18.1	19.7	20.3
Medical and health	16.5	20.2	23.0	25.9	30.9	30.8	31.9
Other	135.0	143.0	155.3	169.8	183.3	207.9	237.0
Total private sector, nonoil	2,668.5	2,959.8	3,245.3	3,559.0	3,887.3	4,279.8	4,837.9
Total GDP	8,603.7	9,205.2	10,257.5	11,775.6	13,078.6	14,458.1	15,810.2
Economic Sectors as Percent of GDP							
Public sector	13.6	15.2	15.7	15.4	16.6	16.0	15.6
Private sector, oil	55.4	52.6	52.7	54.4	53.7	54.4	53.8
Private sector, nonoil	31.0	32.2	41.6	30.2	29.7	29.6	30.6
Total GDP	100.0	100.0	100.0	100.0	100.0	100.0	100.0

Source: CDS, Gross Domestic Product of Saudi Arabia, 1382/83 Through 1388/89 A.H. (Riyadh, September 1970), pp. 5-6.

TABLE 4.13

The Growth of Real GDP by Industry Group, 1966/67 to 1972/73
(S.R. million 1969/70)

Industry Group	Real GDP 1966/67	Real GDP 1972/73
Industries and Other Producers, Except for Producers of Government Services		
Agriculture, forestry, fishing	884.6	1,088.7
Mining, quarrying		
Crude oil, natural gas	6,177.0	16,707.1
Other	39.7	61.4
Manufacturing		
Petroleum refining	780.4	1,389.0
Other	308.9	610.3
Electricity, gas, water	198.0	381.0
Construction	846.8	1,185.2
Wholesale and retail trade, restaurants, hotels	755.0	1,264.6
Transport, storage, communication	918.9	1,631.6
Finance, insurance, real estate, business services		
Ownership of dwellings	520.5	773.6
Other	289.1	396.5
Community, social, and personal service	180.2	291.9
Less imputed bank service charge	-38.5	-45.0
Nongovernment production	11,860.6	25,735.8
Producers of Government Services		
All government services	1,475.3	1,980.4
Total public and private output	13,335.9	27,716.3
Import duties	228.3	240.8
GDP	13,564.2	27,957.1

		Average Annual Growth Rate	Percent Relative Shares of Industry			
			Including Oil Sector		Excluding Oil Sector	
1966/67	1972/73		1966/67	1972/73	1966/67	1972/73
100.0	123.1	3.1	6.5	3.9	13.3	10.9
100.0	270.5	18.1	45.5	59.8	Omitted	
100.0	154.7	8.3	0.3	0.2	0.6	0.6
100.0	178.0	10.1	5.8	5.0	Omitted	
100.0	197.6	12.0	2.3	2.2	4.6	6.1
100.0	192.4	11.5	1.5	1.2	3.0	3.8
100.0	140.0	5.8	6.2	4.2	12.7	11.9
100.0	167.5	9.0	5.6	4.5	11.4	12.7
100.0	177.6	10.0	6.8	5.8	13.8	16.4
100.0	148.6	6.7	3.8	2.8	7.8	7.7
100.0	137.1	5.4	2.1	1.4	4.4	4.0
100.0	162.0	8.4	1.3	1.0	2.7	2.9
—	—	—	—	—	—	—
100.0	217.0	13.8	87.4	92.1	74.2	77.1
100.0	134.2	5.0	10.9	7.1	22.3	20.0
100.0	207.8	13.0	98.3	99.1	96.5	97.1
100.0	105.5	0.9	1.7	0.9	3.5	2.4
100.0	206.1	12.9	100.0	100.0	100.0	100.0

Source: Appendix Table C.1.

THE REAL GROWTH OF THE PRODUCTIVE SECTORS

The Kingdom's economy has grown rapidly since 1966/67. GDP in real terms grew at an average annual rate of 12.9 percent, from S.R. 13.5 billion to S.R. 28 billion in 1972/73. Considering the relative backwardness of the nation's economic institutions and the economy's low absorptive capacity, this rate of growth represents a remarkable achievement rivaled only by the growth rates of Japan and West Germany during the 1960s.

By far the smallest growth rate was experienced by agriculture, with an average annual rate of 3.1 percent. The fastest growing industry group was crude oil and natural gas exploitation, with 18.1 percent per annum, followed by other manufacturing, electricity, gas, and water, 11.5 percent; petroleum refining, transport, storage, and communications, 10 percent, and wholesale and retail trade, restaurants, and hotels, with 9.0 percent. The remaining industry groups ranked as follows: community, social, and personal services, 8.4 percent; other mining and quarrying 8.3 percent; ownership of dwellings 6.7 percent; construction, 5.8 percent; other finance, insurance, and real estate, 5.4 percent, and all government services, 5 percent.

The pattern of growth, as reflected by real growth rates, has been satisfactory (see Table 4.13). Except for the growth of the agricultural sector, the annual growth has been well balanced. Excluding the oil sector, the high growth rates achieved by transport, storage, and communications, electricity, gas, and water, and other infrastructure sectors is important, because it guarantees that future development efforts will probably not be constrained by low absorptive capacity owing to slow growth of the infrastructure.

In terms of relative shares the petroleum sector increased its contribution from 51.3 percent in 1966/67 to 64.8 percent in 1972/73. Agriculture's share fell from 6.5 to 3.9 percent, and government services fell from 10.9 to 7.1 percent during the period under discussion. Despite the 12-percent growth rate of nonoil manufacturing, during the seven-year period under discussion its relative share of GDP declined slightly as a percent of all industry groups and rose from 4.6 to 6.1 percent when measured in terms of the nonoil components of GDP. In view of the need to diversify to reduce the dependence on oil, this small change in the relative share on the nonoil manufacturing group is disappointing and underscores the need for a planned effort to raise nonoil manufacturing. The relative share of transport, storage, and communication rose from 13.8 percent in 1966/67 to 16.4 percent in 1972/73, indicating the relatively rapid growth of the physical infrastructure. The remaining industry groups held their relative position without significant changes. Thus, it can be concluded that omission of oil-related activities in GDP does not show a significantly different alignment of relative shares of industry group.

There was no significant change in real terms in the relationship between the public and private sectors either including or excluding oil companies.

CAPITAL FORMATION

Official estimates of capital formation are not available. Table 4.14 is an attempt to use some of the existing data to construct a time series of capital formation. The estimates are based on three assumptions (see Appendix C). First, it is assumed that the construction component of GDP (old series) accurately reflects additions to the capital stock by the building industry. Second, it is assumed that almost all machinery and other capital goods are imported from abroad. Third, it is assumed that the values for capital goods other than building are understated by omission of in-country costs, such as transportation, installation, and so on. Given these assumptions, it is possible to use certain published index number series of foreign trade and extrapolate capital formation. It is impossible to evaluate the reliability of the resulting data, and they should be used very carefully. Nevertheless, they can be used to gain some tentative insight into the process of capital formation.

Total real capital rose from S.R. 933.5 million in 1963/64 to S.R. 2,481.4 million in 1970/71, a total increase of 165.8 percent at an average annual rate of 15 percent. The relative shares of these two types of capital changed dramatically during that period. In 1963/64 construction accounted for 45.9 percent of capital formation, and imported capital goods for 54.1 percent. From 1963/64 to 1966/67 the two types of capital drifted toward a 50-50 division, with construction rising and imported goods as a percent of total capital formation falling. From 1967/68 to the end of the period capital goods imported increased its share, from 55.1 percent to 70.7 percent of total capital formation. The large shift away from construction to imported capital goods may have resulted from the addition to production of the Abu Safah and Manifa fields in 1966 and the Berri field in 1968. In addition to an increase in the demand for capital goods associated with oil exploitation, the building of the steel mill and desalinization plants in Jedda and the fertilizer plant near Dammam and other capital projects throughout the country raised the value of machinery imports since 1967/68.

Comparison of GNP and capital formation clearly shows that Saudi Arabia has crossed the threshold of capital formation, from be-

TABLE 4.14

Estimated Total Capital Formation in Constant Prices, 1963/64 to 1971/72
(S.R. million 1966/67)

Year	Construction	Imported Capital Goods	Total
1963/64	428.8	504.7	933.5
1964/65	555.2	654.9	1,210.1
1965/66	666.3	769.7	1,436.0
1966/67	707.1	778.3	1,485.4
1967/68	756.7	927.8	1,684.5
1968/69	756.8	1,228.0	1,984.8
1969/70	722.3	1,467.5*	2,189.8
1970/71	727.7	1,753.7*	2,481.4
Average percent change	8.9	19.5	15.0

*Projection based on average annual growth of 19.5 percent.

Source: See Appendix C.

low 10 percent of national income to over 10 percent. Capital formation as a percent of GNP rose from 12.4 percent in 1963/64 to 17.7 percent in 1970/71. During the same timespan GNP rose 87.3 percent and capital formation 165.8 percent.

THE STANDARD OF LIVING

Data on family incomes and expenditures for the Kingdom as a whole are not available. The only systematic study of consumption patterns available is that made by the late Thomas W. Shea.[2] It is limited because Shea concentrated his investigation on Saudi Arab employees of Aramco living in the Eastern Province near company installations. By far the majority of Aramco's Saudi employees are skilled workers whose income is greater than that of the average worker, both because of their skills and because Aramco salaries tend to be higher for any given type of job than the salaries for the same skills paid outside the company. Nevertheless, Shea states that "so long as comparisons are made only in terms of broad expenditure categories, the Aramco data may be regarded as broadly representative of Saudi Arab urban workers as a whole."[3] Shea's findings will be briefly summarized.

Household Size

Because the extended family is the basic unit of social organization, households contain a large number of individuals. Between 1962 and 1968 the number of family members rose from 7.7 to 8.7 members per household. The number of working adults remained the same (1.2 per household), while the number of dependent adults declined slightly. The expansion in the number of members per family resulted entirely from a large increase in the number of children under 18 years of age, which rose about 31 percent, from 4.2 per family in 1962 to 5.5 per family in 1968. During the same period the model size of Armaco employees' families rose from 7 and 8 to 8 and

TABLE 4.15

Estimated Capital Formation as a Percent of GNP, 1963/64 to 1970/71 (S.R. million 1966/67)

Year	GNP (1)	Capital Formation (2)	(2) as Percent of (1)
1963/64	7,504.1	933.5	12.4
1964/65	8,383.6	1,210.1	14.4
1965/66	9,109.7	1,436.0	15.8
1966/67	10,117.6	1,485.4	14.7
1967/68	11,000.0	1,684.5	15.3
1968/69	11,751.8	1,984.8	16.9
1969/70	12,775.2	2,189.8	17.1
1970/71	14,052.1	2,481.4	17.1
Percent change	87.3	165.8	--

Sources: GNP 1963/64 to 1968/69: CDS, Gross Domestic Product of Saudi Arabia, 1382/83 Through 1388/89 A.H. (Riyadh, September 1970), p. 39; 1969/70 to 1970/71: SAMA, Annual Report 1390/91, A.H. (Jedda, 1972), p. 105; capital formation: Table 4.14.

9. The number of households with two or more wives stayed about the same--10 percent in both survey years.

Home Ownership

In 1962, 85.3 percent of all employees owned a house, and in 1968 this percentage had risen to 86.8 percent. This relatively small increment was achieved despite a 10 percent decline in the number of employees. Employees living in rented houses declined from 11.5 percent in 1962 to 8.2 percent in 1968, while the proportion renting part of a house rose from 0.8 percent to 4.2 percent.

In 1962, 70.8 percent of the employees lived in stone or cement block houses, and in 1968, 84.3 percent. The high proportion of cement block or stone houses is an important indicator of the standard of living, because nearly all of these houses are equipped with tiled floors, electricity, indoor plumbing, and cooking ranges. The number of houses with electricity and running water more than doubled, from 36 percent in 1962 to 81.2 percent in 1968, an average annual rate of growth of 10.6 percent. Houses equipped with running water and no electricity fell from 47.4 percent in 1962 to 16.6 percent in 1968, and houses with neither electricity nor running water declined to 1.8 percent from 15.8 percent. In view of the many projects undertaken by the government to provide the urban population with electricity, sewers, and running water, it is reasonable to assume that all urban households have electricity and running water, the latter being supplied either by municipal line or gravity-fed storage tanks supplied with water by truck.

Earnings and Expenditures

Although the earnings of Aramco employees are not comparable with those of noncompany workers in the rest of the country, the comparison of gross earnings and expenditure reveals an interesting fact (shown in Table 4.16): On the average the savings rate is much higher than in most developing countries. Expenditures as a percent of earnings varied considerably among the eight job classifications, from 70 percent for job-grade 28 to 96.3 percent for job-grade 27. More interesting, however, is the fact that on the average for all grades expenditures as a percent of earnings amounted to only 83.8 percent. This statistic supports the opinion of many Saudi economists who claim that the savings rate in the Kingdom may exceed 20 percent.

Table 4.17 presents average expenditures by major categories. Overall, expenditures rose 47.1 percent from 1962 to 1968. By far the largest increase, 116.1 percent, occurred in the furniture and durables group. This increase reflects to some extent the increasing

TABLE 4.16

Average Gross Earnings and Expenditures of Aramco Employees, by Job Grade, 1962 and 1968
(Saudi riyals per year)

Job Grade	Average Gross Earnings*	Expen-ditures*	Earnings Less Ex-penditures	Expenditures as Percent of Earnings
23	8,699.7	8,158.8	541.0	93.8
24	10,311.7	7,991.8	2,319.9	77.5
25	12,167.6	11,292.7	874.9	92.8
26	14,299.6	12,232.6	2,067.0	85.5
27	17,272.5	16,631.7	641.0	96.3
28	20,565.4	14,404.6	6,160.8	70.0
29	24,430.4	19,217.4	5,212.9	78.7
30	26,402.2	22,425.3	3,976.9	85.4
All grades	16,768.7	14,044.4	2,724.3	83.8

*Converted from U.K. pounds at the rate of 10.8 riyals per pound.

Source: Thomas W. Shea, "Measuring the Changing Family Consumption Patterns of Aramco's Saudi Arab Employees, 1962 and 1968," in The Arabian Peninsula, Derek Hopwood, ed. (Totowa, N.J.: Rowman and Littlefield, 1972), p. 250.

Westernization of the population. Traditionally, Arabs live on their carpets; that is, the Arab household does not use chairs, tables, or other furniture. In recent years, however, more and more households have purchased all types of furnishings. The relatively large increase, 88.2 percent, of household expenditures resulted from the rising cost of operating a household associated with the general availability of electricity and running water. Despite the large overall increase in total average expenditures, the distribution of the various expenditure items has changed very little between 1962 and 1968.

Wholesale Prices

A reliable consumer price index does not exist. There is, however, a wholesale price index for the years 1963/64 (1962/63 = 100)

TABLE 4.17

Aramco Employees' Average Expenditures, by Major Category, 1962 and 1968

Item	1962 Riyals*	1962 Percent of Total	1968 Riyals*	1968 Percent of Total	Percent Change 1962-68
Housing	1,410.5	16.5	2,104.9	16.7	49.2
Food	4,399.9	51.4	6,208.9	49.4	41.1
Clothing	729.0	8.5	1,067.0	8.5	46.4
Household expenses	490.3	5.7	922.3	7.3	88.2
Furniture and durables	609.1	7.1	1,315.4	10.5	116.1
Transportation	316.4	3.7	278.6	2.2	-11.7
Miscellaneous	599.4	7.0	682.6	5.4	14.0
Total	8,554.7	100.0	12,579.7	100.0	47.1

*Converted from U.K. pounds at the rate of 10.8 riyals per pound.

Source: Thomas W. Shea, "Measuring the Changing Family Consumption Patterns of Aramco's Saudi Arab Employees, 1962 and 1968," in The Arabian Peninsula, Derek Hopwood, ed. (Totowa, N.J.: Rowman and Littlefield, 1972), p. 251.

that gives some insight into price movements.[4] The general wholesale price index rose 17.1 percent between 1962/63 and 1971/72, at an annual rate of 1.8 percent.

Among the six subgroups contained in the wholesale price index construction materials rose 26.5 percent, followed by food wholesale prices (24.6 percent). The increase--26.5 percent--between 1962/63 and 1971/72 of the wholesale price index for construction materials is considerably lower than that for the period 1962/63 to 1969/70, during which the index registered a 36.4 percent increase. Textiles and miscellaneous classes each rose slightly over 4 percent, and fuels declined nearly 13 percent during the period under discussion.

According to SAMA, inflationary pressures from abroad as well as those generated internally have led to a considerable increase in the cost of living. To alleviate the effect of rising prices on the population the government reduced or eliminated many tariffs, increased salaries and pensions of government employees, as well as social-relief payments, and imported large quantities of basic commodities to raise supply and thus reduce pressure on prices and reintroduced subsidies on flour, rice, and sugar.

Summary

Despite the sketchiness of the available statistics, it can be shown that the quality of life of the urban population has increased in recent years. Based on a survey of Aramco employees, it has been shown that better housing and higher salaries, combined with the removal or reduction of tariffs and subsidies of major food items, have contributed to an increase in living standards. In addition to these items, better medical care, the building of municipal water- and electrical-generating systems and other improvements of the physical and social infrastructures have maintained or contributed to increases of the quality of life.

NOTES

1. SAMA, Annual Report, 1392/93 A.H. (Jedda, 1974), pp. 114-15.
2. Thomas W. Shea, "Measuring the Changing Family Consumption Patterns of Aramco's Saudi Arab Employees, 1962 and 1968," in The Arabian Peninsula, Derek Hopwood, ed. (Totowa, N.J.: Rowman and Littlefield, 1972), pp. 231-54.
3. Ibid., p. 232.
4. SAMA, Annual Report, 1392/93 A.H., p. 109.

CHAPTER

5

THE PHYSICAL INFRASTRUCTURE

The creation of a physical infrastructure is one of the major goals--if not the major one--of the early phases of economic development. Without adequate public utility services, transportation, and communications systems, economic development is severely constrained, and even the most ambitious and concentrated and best financed effort to create a modern, industrialized economy is doomed to failure. Although information on the major sectors of Saudi Arabia's physical infrastructure is scarce and of uneven quality, an attempt will be made in the following pages to present a discussion of the Kingdom's infrastructure.

ELECTRIC POWER

As of 1973 (1393 A.H.) eight electric companies served the larger urban areas, and seven smaller companies served some of the nation's smaller towns.[1] The industry is rather inefficient. Unofficial estimates of "plant factors" and "load factors" indicate that the Saudi Arabian electric utilities operate at efficiency levels considerably below those achieved by other developing countries.* The service is spotty and plagued by power failures, voltage fluctuations, and

---

*"Plant factor" is the amount of electricity produced during a given period and the amount that could have been produced, if the generating equipment had been operating at full capacity. "Load factor" is the electricity produced in a given period and the amount that could have been produced with the equipment working at peak demand levels.

inability to provide repair services. In some towns the service, voltage, and frequency differs from area to area, preventing standardization of equipment used by consumers.

Most of the electric companies are privately owned. The rate structure is poorly designed, resulting in uneconomic demands on the available capacity. An important problem is the poor collection procedure. For some companies uncollected bills amount to as much as 50 percent or more of total revenue. To eliminate these problems the government established a Department of Electricity Services on May 1972, whose main function is to design a rational rate structure, to write uniform regulations, to introduce standardized accounting procedures, and to examine license applications. To assist the department in this task and to establish a training program for Saudi engineers, the Ministry of Commerce and Industry entered into a contract with a foreign consulting firm.

Table 5.1 presents the generating capacity, number of users, and power generated from 1966/67 to 1972. Total capacity and power generated rose 162.1 and 165.9 percent, respectively, at an average annual growth rate of 17.4 and 18 percent. The close agreement between total capacity and power generated indicates that operating efficiency did not improve and stayed at about the same level as the industry expanded. During the same period the number of users rose from 134,324 to 247,746, or 84.4 percent, at an average annual growth rate of 10.7 percent.

Consumption of electric power by major types of users is one way to measure the progress of industrialization. Although, unfortunately, the statistics cover only seven years, they allow some tentative conclusions regarding the progress of economic development in the Kingdom (see Table 5.2). Household consumption of electricity rose 180.9 percent, from 272 million kilowatt hours (kwh) to 764 million kwh, at an annual average rate of 18.8 percent, during the period April 21, 1966, to January 5, 1973. This growth is quite satisfactory, indicating that in terms of benefits to the general population the economic development effort has improved the quality of life. Industrial consumption of electrical energy showed little progress in the growth of the industrial sector. In fact, the growth of industrial energy consumption suggests that there was virtually no growth in this sector from 1966/67 to 1970. Industrial consumption of electricity rose only 0.2 percent during this period. It declined 29.6 percent between 1967 and 1969, rose to 37.2 million kwh in 1969, and declined to 34.2 million kwh in 1970. Industrial consumption of electrical energy has grown rapidly since 1970, increasing 55.6 percent, from 34.2 million kwh to 53.3 million kwh. There is no readily available explanation of this erratic behavior; the author can only suggest that many industrial users generate their own energy. In view of the con-

TABLE 5.1

Electric Generating Capacity, Number of Users, and Power Generated, 1966/67 to 1972

Year	Total Capacity at Year End (thousand kwh)	Number of Users	Power Generated (thousand kwh)
1966/67	130.0	134,324	376,792
1967/68	150.1	150,599	430,168
1968/69	188.2	167,521	528,446
1969/70[a]	239.8	200,838	653,379
1970	251.0	215,471	724,325
1971	275.7	232,884	802,131
1972	340.6	247,746	999,819
1973	—	—	1,186,200[b]
Percent change	162.0	84.4	165.4
Annual rate of growth	17.4	10.7	17.9

[a]From 1389 A.H. on the figures include seven smaller electric companies.

[b]The figure on power generated for 1973 is probably understated by about S.R. 15 million, because SAMA does not include the smaller cities.

Note: For the second and third columns the corresponding Gregorian dates are April 21, 1966 to January 5, 1973, and for the fourth column, April 21, 1966 to December 25, 1973.

Sources: 1386-90 A.H.: CDS, Statistical Yearbook, 1391 A.H., vol. 7 (Riyadh, 1971), pp. 237, 240, and 1390 A.H., vol. 6 (1970), p. 251; 1392/93, power generated: SAMA, Annual Report, 1392/93 A.H. (Jedda, 1973), p. 110.

stant voltage fluctuations and interruptions in service, it may be more efficient for these users to supply their own energy needs. As far as the increase since 1970 is concerned, it was the completion of several large industrial ventures (such as the desalinization of sea water in Jedda and the Saudi Arabian Fertilizer Company in Dammam) that increased demand considerably. Industrial use of electricity shows that the smaller cities and towns have made little progress in industrialization. In 1971 and 1972 industrial users in the smaller cities consumed less than 0.1 percent of the energy sold.

TRANSPORTATION AND COMMUNICATIONS

It is tempting to observe that a solution to the communications problem was the single most important task confronting the country at the beginning of the 1960s. This is, however, only the case so long as one looks at this sector in isolation. The Saudi economy was so far behind in its development in 1960 that an examination of any sector identifies several candidates for the title of "most important bottleneck." Nevertheless, it is correct to consider the creation of a well-functioning system of communications as the prime problem

TABLE 5.2

Electric Energy Sold, by Type of User, 1966/67 to 1972
(thousand kwh)

Year	Household Consumption	Industrial Consumption	Total
1966/67	271,969	34,152	306,121
1967/68	322,916	27,613	350,529
1968/69	399,642	24,036	423,678
1969/70*	492,390	37,234	529,624
1970	548,928	34,237	583,165
1971	629,996	36,287	666,283
1972	764,046	53,276	817,322
Percent change	180.9	56.0	167.0
Annual rate of growth	18.8	7.9	17.8

*From 1389 on, the figures include seven smaller electric companies.

Note: The period covered is from April 21, 1966 to January 5, 1973.

Source: CDS, Statistical Yearbook, 1390 A.H., vol. 6 (Riyadh, 1970), p. 251; 1391 A.H., vol. 7 (Riyadh, 1971), pp. 237, 240; 1392 A.H., vol. 8, pp. 235, 238; 1393 A.H., vol. 9 (Riyadh, 1973), pp. 251, 254.

area, because of the many economic, social, and political externalities resulting from a well-developed, integrated system of communications and transport.

Total budget appropriations for transport and communications rose at an annual rate of 21.2 percent, from S.R. 209.9 million in 1960/61 to S.R. 2,113 million in 1972/73 (Appendix Table C.5). Except for the budget years 1965/66, 1967/68, 1969/70, and 1970/71, the total amounts allocated for transport and communications rose from year to year throughout the period, and the declines in the four years mentioned above were so small as to be negligible.

There has been considerable variation in allocations for this sector with respect to total budget appropriations (see Table 5.3). Transportation and communications appropriations as a percent of the total budget fluctuated between 11.8 percent in 1960/61 and 23 percent in 1964/65. Appropriations for this sector reached the second-highest level, 21.7 percent, in 1968/69 and declined until 1970/71, rose in the following year, and declined in 1972/73. The variability of the figures results from the nature of this sector. With the exception of postal activities, investment in transportation and communications takes place in large amounts, and thus in any one given year the initiation of a major project will raise the share of this sector considerably, and as it nears completion, its share will decline.

Post, Telephone, and Telegraph

Unfortunately, the postal system and the telecommunications system were operated by the same government agency until 1971/72 when the postal service was turned into the Directorate General of Posts within the Ministry of the Interior. As a result, the available data on these two different activities have not been broken down by category. Overall appropriations for post and telecommunications rose on the average 18.6 percent, from S.R. 42.6 million in 1960/61 to S.R. 329.2 million in 1972/73. Within the category transport and communications, post and telecommunications fluctuated between 20.3 percent of total appropriations in 1960/61 and 8.3 percent in 1967/68. An estimate, based on the percent distribution of estimated revenues derived from this classification, suggests that about 85 percent of the appropriations between 1969/70 to 1970/71 were allocated to the telecommunications systems, and for the period 1966/67 to 1968/69 about 77 percent were used to improve the telecommunications system.

The first step in the establishment of a modern telecommunications system was taken in 1956 when the country's major cities were linked by a wireless radio system using teleprinters. This system was expanded during the next five years by the addition of more domes-

TABLE 5.3

Percent Distribution of Transport and Communications Budget Appropriations

Budget Year	Ministry of Communications	Post, Telephone, and Telegraph	Railways	Roads, Bridges, and Ports	Civil Aviation, Saudi Airlines, and Meteorological Department	As Percent of Total Appropriations
1960/61	5.9	20.3	16.1	31.3	26.3	11.8
1961/62	0.9	13.0	12.3	29.8	44.0	16.6
1962/63	0.9	14.5	9.9	40.2	34.6	14.6
1963/64	1.0	18.9	8.8	35.9	35.4	15.4
1964/65	0.7	17.1	5.3	51.8	25.0	23.0
1965/66	0.3	11.9	4.8	53.9	29.1	16.8
1966/67	0.2	8.7	5.4	52.3	33.3	18.0
1967/68	0.2	8.3	3.9	52.4	35.2	18.3
1968/69	0.2	12.1	3.2	54.0	30.5	21.7
1969/70	0.2	14.3	3.7	48.5	33.2	18.6
1970/71	0.2	13.7	3.9	47.2	34.9	16.2
1971/72	0.1	19.1	2.1	55.1	23.6	18.5
1972/73	0.1	15.6	2.6	50.7	30.9	16.0

Source: Appendix Table C.5.

tic and international circuits. The first automatic telephone system went into operation in Jedda, and by 1971 ten major urban areas had been supplied with modern automatic telephone systems. During the budget year 1970/71, 32,000 additional lines were installed, bringing the total number of lines to 76,600.[2] It has already become apparent that this system is too small, and further expansion of the network has begun. In Riyadh an additional 17,000 lines should have been completed during 1973/74. All told, an additional 80,400 lines are projected for the ten major cities. Furthermore, automatic telephone service will be introduced in 13 minor cities, with a total of 17,700 lines.[3]

The quality of telecommunications, especially telephone service, is poor. A lack of trained personnel results in delays and interrupted messages. This lack of trained persons has been responsible for slow installation and repair of equipment, as well as slowness of billing.

The postal service is probably the most inefficient government department in the Kingdom. During the period 1955/56 to 1972 the total number of pieces of mail handled by the system rose from 6.5 million to 92.4 million.[4] The main cause of the poor service is the gross inefficiency of management, followed closely by lack of trained manpower. The difficulty of the training of manpower is compounded by the fact that mail handlers must be taught to read the Roman alphabet to handle mail from the non-Arab world. The result of these shortcomings has been delay, confusion, and numerous pieces of lost mail.

Roads and Vehicles

In addition to the economic benefits to be derived from a first-class road system, political benefits have resulted from the Kingdom's system. As has been pointed out, the only unifying force in modern times among the various regions of the Arabian desert has been allegiance to the Royal Family. The people of the Arabian Peninsula have much in common, but distance between the various population centers and the great difficulty in crossing the inhospitable desert terrain reinforces the tendency toward separatism. The construction of a good road system has reduced this trend. Distances that took several days of arduous travel to traverse can now be comfortably crossed by air-conditioned car in several hours. The basic trunk roads must still be completed in several regions, but where they have been completed, feeder roads have been added, and communications within population concentrations have risen sharply.

At the beginning of the 1950s the Kingdom had 45 kilometers (km) of asphalted roads; by 1960/61 the amount had grown to 1,708 km.[5]

TABLE 5.4

Main Roads and Agricultural Roads Constructed,
1961/62 to 1972
(kilometers)

Year	Main Roads	Agricultural Roads
1961/62	3,245	—
1962/63	3,420	—
1963/64	3,600	—
1964/65	3,715	1,500
1965/66	4,744	1,700
1966/67	5,700	1,950
1967/68	6,813	1,992
1968/69	7,654	2,786
1969/70	8,021	3,739
1970/71	8,323	4,000
1971/72	8,614	4,601
1972	10,007	n.a.

Sources: 1962/63: CDS, Statistical Yearbook, 1391 A.H., vol. 7 (Riyadh, 1971), p. 251; 1962/63 to 1971/72: Ibid., 1393 A.H., vol. 9 (Riyadh, 1973), p. 265; main roads, 1972: SAMA, Annual Report, 1392/93 A.H. (Jedda, 1973), p. 48.

Table 5.4 tells the story of the rapid growth of the road system since that year. The length of asphalted main roads increased threefold, from 3,245 km in 1961/62 to 10,007 km in 1972, and the length of nonasphalted secondary roads grew from 1,500 km in 1964/65 to 4,601 km in 1971/72. Except for the links from Buraydah to Hail, from Riyadh to Najran and Khamis Mushait in the south, and the connection from Jedda south along the Red Sea to Najran, the main trunk roads connecting the main population centers have been completed (see Map 4). Appendix Table C.6 gives a summary of the road-building program from December 1964 to August 1972.

The quality of design and construction of these roads has been rather uneven. Poor construction methods during the early years of the building program, as well as nonenforcement of load limits, forced the redesign and reconstruction of the road from Medina to Khaybar, from Khurays to the east, as well as smaller stretches elsewhere. Roads built since 1967 have been of first quality, partic-

MAP 4

Kingdom of Saudi Arabia Road Map

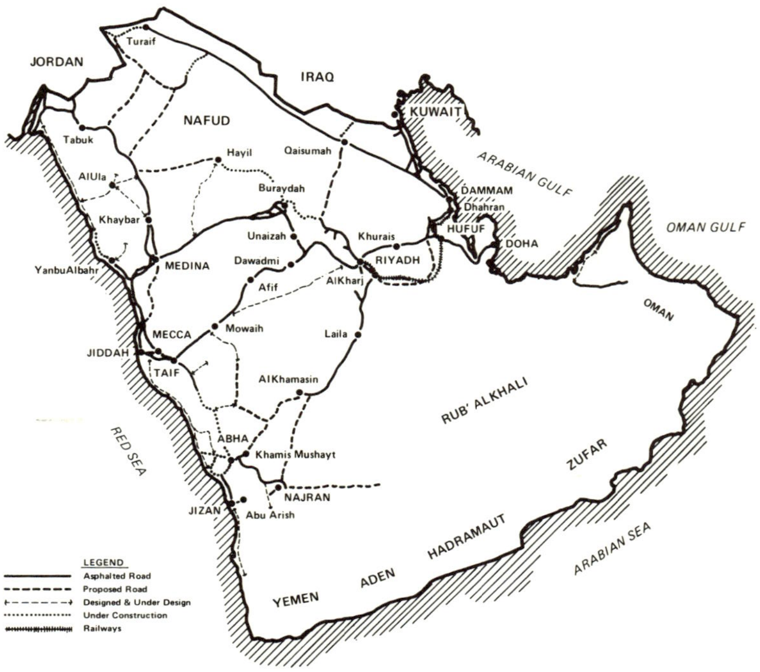

Source: SAMA, Annual Report 1392-93 A.H., p. 49.

ularly the 541-km stretch from Buraydah in the central Najd to Medina.

Because of the nature of the terrain and the long distances between major population centers, motor vehicles and airplanes are the only efficient means of transportation. This is reflected in the rapid growth of all types of vehicle registrations (see Table 5.5).* The total number of registered vehicles rose at an annual rate of 15.4 percent, from 44,766 at the end of 1960/61 to 248,737 at the end of 1972. The total number of passenger cars rose nearly fourfold at an annual rate of 16.2 percent, from 23,560 at the end of 1960/61 to 142,123 at the end of 1972. In 1960/61, 38.2 percent of these vehicles were used as taxis, and 26.4 percent served the same purpose in 1972. The number of buses rose about 300 percent, from 2,125 at the end of 1960/61 to 8,585 at the end of 1972. The number of trucks, fire engines, and other transport vehicles rose more than fourfold, from 19,081 to 98,029, during the same period.

The statistics on motor-vehicle registrations clearly reveal the structure of the nation's transportation system. With the exception of those that pass along the railroad connection between Dammam and Riyadh, nearly all goods move by truck. There is no public mass transport system between or within the cities. People move either by private motor vehicle or by taxi. Even intercity transportation consists largely of privately operated taxi service and some privately operated minibuses. Most of the buses are engaged in the transportation of pilgrims from Jedda to Mecca, Arafat, and Medina during the Hadj, and the remainder are school buses. The decline of the percentage of taxis in passenger-car registration is a clear indication of the increasing well-being of the people.

Railroads

Two railroads have been built in the Kingdom, one in the western region, connecting Medina with Aman in Jordan, and another from Dammam to Riyadh. The Aman-Medina line has not been in operation since World War I. Over the years proposals have been made to revive this railroad and re-establish the link with Jordan. For various reasons, among them the fact that the gauges in the two countries are different, these proposals have never moved beyond the talking stage. The second railway, from Dammam to Riyadh, was built for the government by Aramco. It was inaugurated in 1951

*Given the known inefficiency of the various municipal traffic departments handling motor vehicle registrations, these statistics are considered estimates of actual registrations.

TABLE 5.5

Estimated Number of Motor Vehicles Registered, by Type, 1960/61 to 1972

Year	Private Passenger Cars	Taxis	Transport Vehicles (e.g., trucks)	Buses	Total
1960/61	14,561	8,999	19,081	2,125	44,766
1961/62	17,701	10,119	19,496	2,519	49,835
1962/63	19,940	12,199	24,738	3,023	59,900
1963/64	26,642	14,105	30,282	3,648	74,677
1964/65	32,765	16,161	35,878	4,070	88,874
1965/66	40,137	18,698	42,013	4,803	105,651
1966/67	49,168	21,634	49,197	5,666	125,665
1967/68	55,888	23,708	52,709	5,981	138,286
1968/69	65,447	27,049	56,762	6,288	155,546
1969/70	75,183	30,363	62,626	6,697	174,869
1970/71	83,992	32,984	73,980	7,213	198,169
1971/72	92,834	35,205	81,693	7,671	217,403
1972	104,652	37,471	98,029	8,585	248,737

Note: Year-end figures are by Hijra year, beginning 1380 A.H. The years 1385 and 1386 have been estimated by application of the average (geometric) growth of the period 1380-84. The Hijra year 1380 ended May 16, 1961 A.D. and the year 1390 ended January 1, 1971 A.D.

Sources: 1960/61 to 1966/67: CDS, Statistical Yearbook, 1387 A.H., vol. 3 (Riyadh, 1967), p. 188; 1967/68 to 1969/70: Ibid., 1391 A.H., vol. 7 (Riyadh, 1971), p. 258; 1970/71 to 1972: Ibid., 1393 A.H., vol. 9 (Riyadh, 1973), p. 271.

and run by Aramco during the early years. Later it was taken over by the government and became a government corporation in 1966.

The road passes through Dhahran, Abqaiq, Hofuf, Ain-Haradh, and Al-Kharj and ends in Riyadh, for a total length of 565 km. In addition, there are a number of subsidiary lines that probably add about 100 km to the length. The railroad is closely associated with Dammam port, where it is a primary means of moving freight from the pier to various inland storage and distribution centers.

Precise data on the rolling stock are not available. It appears, however, that the amounts have not changed significantly during the last decade. The only major exception is in the number of flat cars, which rose from 259 in 1965/66 to 452 in 1970.*

Table 5.6 tells the story of the decline of the Saudi railroad. It illustrates the fate of prestige projects undertaken by the government of a developing country, intended as a status symbol. The decline of freight and passenger service was not due to poor management; rather, it was a direct consequence of the completion of the road system. As soon as the roads connecting the major eastern population centers were completed, the railroad began to lose its customers. Freight revenue fell 73 percent, from a high of S.R. 21.7 million in 1958/59 to a low of S.R. 5.8 million in 1967/68, and ton km declined 84 percent. The amount of freight carried actually rose from 614,000 tons in 1957/58 to 1,063,000 tons in 1972. This 73-percent increase reflects the incresing importance of the port of Dammam, from which the railroad carried freight to the nearby cities as well as to staging terminals from which the goods are carried inland by truck.

Passenger traffic also suffered from the completion of the Dammam Riyadh road network. The number of passengers carried fell from 113,000 in 1957/58 to 27,000 in 1961/62. It recovered in the following years, and in 1972 more than 130,000 persons were carried by the railroad. A better indication of the rising importance of passenger traffic is the number of passenger-kilometers, because it reflects the distances passengers are carried as well as their number. Passenger-kilometers fell 77 percent between 1957/58 and 1961/62. It recovered in the following years, reached a high of 59.7 million in 1968/69, and stood at 48.3 million in 1970.

The railroad has not produced a profit. Operating costs exceed operating revenues by a substantial margin, and the government has been forced to cover the losses. Unofficial data suggest that the subsidy paid to the railroad amounted to S.R. 9 or S.R. 10 million during the budget years 1966/67 and 1967/68.

Air Transportation

The long distances between population centers and the inhospitable terrain have been important factors in the growth of air transportation. In February 1968 there were three international and 19 domes-

---

*The Statistical Yearbook does not give the date as 1965/66. However, because the number was published in the 1385 A.H. volume, it is assumed that it applies to that year.

TABLE 5.6

Freight and Passenger Services Supplied by the Railroad, 1957/58 to 1972

	Freight			Passengers		
Year	Revenue from Freight (S.R. thousand)	Ton Kilometers (million)	Tons Carried (thousand)	Revenue from Passengers (S.R. thousand)	Passenger Kilometers (million)	Passengers Carried (thousand)
1957/58	19,436	211.3	614	2,572	42.8	113
1958/59	21,711	233.0	691	2,665	42.6	110
1959/60	19,887	202.1	678	2,699	44.1	98
1960/61	19,844	237.5	721	1,486	25.6	58
1961/62	13,303	171.6	671	364	9.8	27
1962/63	9,826	115.0	650	512	16.4	40
1963/64	7,158	77.0	633	874	24.0	63
1964/65	7,273	64.4	845	902	27.5	75
1965/66	8,463	55.8	850	1,049	31.9	89
1966/67	7,612	52.1	809	1,104	33.9	96
1967/68	5,776	34.3	672	1,229	37.4	97
1968/69	9,071	45.7	862	1,475	59.7	116
1969/70	8,656	45.0	941	1,537	43.0	115
1970	6,240	34.0	733	1,413	38.8	117
1971	7,589	39.0	949	1,493	41.8	114
1972	11,355	68.4	1,063	1,742	48.3	133

Note: The Hijra year 1377 covered the period July 28, 1957, to June 18, 1958, and the Hijra year 1392 the period February 16, 1972, to January 5, 1973.

Sources: 1957/58 to 1960/61: CDS, Statistical Yearbook, 1385 A.H., vol. 1 (Riyadh, 1965), p. 125; 1961/62 to 1970: Ibid., 1391 A.H., vol. 7 (Riyadh, 1971), p. 267; 1971 to 1972: Ibid., 1393 A.H., vol. 9 Riyadh, 1973), p. 282.

tic airports in operation.[6] Nine of these ariports had either asphalt or concrete runways, and seven of the nine had lighting systems for night operations. The three international airports, Jedda, Riyadh, and Dhahran, can accommodate any type of airplane, including the "jumbo jets." The remaining airports had dirt landing strips and no lighting facilities. The operation of several of these airports is not justified on economic grounds alone: In 1970 five airports generated fewer than 1,000 passengers; in such instances current social and political as well as anticipated needs associated with the development program determine the continued operation.

The increasing importance of air transportation is reflected in the movement of cargo and mail through Dhahran International Airport. Between 1964 and 1972 the total volume of domestic and foreign mail loaded and unloaded rose on the average 4.9 percent, from 146.4 to 212.5 tons. During the same period the total volume of domestic and foreign cargo loaded and unloaded rose from 1,800 tons to 8,100 tons, a 350-percent increase, at an average annual growth rate of 21 percent.[7] Changes in the volume of passenger traffic are more difficult to evaluate, because the available statistics cover only the three-year period 1968-70. It appears, however, that passenger traffic declined at Dhahran International Airport, with the non-Saudi carriers losing passengers and Saudi Airlines gaining passengers.

General air transportation was inaugurated by the Saudi Arabian Airline with DC-3-type planes in the late 1940s. Originally, the airline was attached to the Ministry of Defense, but it was separated from the ministry, and in 1963 it was turned into a semiautonomous government corporation. In 1954 the airline's fleet of aircraft consisted of four Bristols, seven DC-3s, three DC-4s, and ten Convairs. By 1972 the fleet consisted of 24 planes, of which five were DC-3s, six Convairs, five Boeing 737s, two Boeing 707s, two Boeing 720s, two Champions, and two Apaches. Of the 158 pilots flying this fleet, 104 were Saudi nationals.

As measured in seat-kilometers, Saudi Airlines has grown on the average about 15 percent over the 17-year period 1954-70. Table 5.7 gives a more detailed overview of the airline's activities since 1966. Capacity-ton-kilometers rose from 76.1 million in 1966 to 205.8 millionin 1972, while the weight-load factor—a performance measure that includes cargo, mail, and passengers carried—amounted to 45 and 42 percent in 1966 and 1972, respectively. During the same period capacity-seat-kilometers rose from 605.4 million to 1,691.2 million, and the passenger-load factor fell from 51 percent to 46 percent. The decline in the passenger-load factor reflects a change in policy. In the past the airline increased capacity in response to increases in demand. In recent years, however, it has been adding capacity to its fleet in anticipation of demand.

TABLE 5.7

Passenger-Seat-Kilometers and Cargo-Ton-Kilometers on Saudi Aircraft, 1966-70

Year	Ton-Kilometers			Seat-Kilometers		
	Revenue-Ton-Kilometers	Capacity-Ton-Kilometers	Weight Load Factor	Revenue-Seat-Kilometers	Capacity-Seat-Kilometers	Passenger-Load Factor
1966	34,543	76,114	45	308,752	605,395	51
1967	40,135	128,124	35	339,965	752,880	48
1968	58,004	146,258	40	543,149	1,221,388	44
1969	55,903	140,683	40	529,365	1,176,048	45
1970	64,886	159,844	41	566,995	1,314,935	43
1971	74,359	161,791	46	623,191*	1,332,989*	46*
1972	86,038	205,800	42	777,390	1,691,234	46

*Excludes pilgrims.

Note: Revenue-ton-kilometers, capacity-ton-kilometers, revenue-seat-kilometers, and capacity-seat-kilometers are in thousands; weight-load factor and passenger-load factor are in percentages.

Source: CDS, Statistical Yearbook, 1393 A.H., vol. 9 (Riyadh, 1973), p. 296.

The airline probably operates at a loss. Statistics on costs of operation and revenues are not available, but it is known that it is a relatively high-cost operation. Currently, the maintenance and many of the flight operations are carried out under contract by Trans World Airlines. Because of the small number of qualified Saudi personnel, the majority of technical positions are staffed by expatriates requiring higher compensations than Saudi technicians would demand. Higher personnel costs and the known high cost of operating the smaller DC-3s and Convairs suggest that revenues do not cover costs. The difference is made up by government subsidies.

Seaports

Except for the relatively small air-freight shipments, most general cargo entering or leaving the Kingdom goes through three major ports: Jedda and Yenbo on the Red Sea coast and Dammam on the Arabian Gulf coast. In addition, there is the Aramco oil terminal at Ras Tanura.

Jedda is the oldest and most important general cargo port of the Kingdom. For hundreds of years it has been the major port of entry for pilgrims, as well as the focal point of the Red Sea trade and some of the internal trade. The amount of goods unloaded rose about 125 percent, from 454,800 tons in 1960/61 to 1,021,500 tons in 1972, an annual rate of growth of 6 percent (Table 5.8). In March 1967 a major expansion program of the Jedda port facilities was begun, raising the number of piers to ten of more than 1,000 meters, six transit sheds with 33,120 square meters, and 10,000 square meters of additional covered warehousing facilities. As a result of this expansion the annual capacity for dry-cargo handling will rise from about 600,000 tons to 1.8 million tons. The success of the expansion program is underlined by the fact that Red Sea Lines Conference of shippers removed the freight surcharge that had been placed on goods destined to Jedda, because of the constant delays experienced in the unloading of goods in the port. The expansion was officially completed in January 1973.

To relieve the demands on the facilities of Jedda the port of Yenbo has been expanded considerably. Cargo unloaded rose at an annual rate of nearly 24 percent, from 17,400 tons in 1960/61 to 211,000 tons in 1972. To divert traffic from Jedda to Yenbo, which is 360 km north of Jedda, certain duties and charges levied on cement imports were canceled if the cargo was off-loaded in Yenbo. These exemptions were extended for an additional year beginning in June 1972. A reception hall for pilgrims, customs sheds, and an electric power station are currently under construction.

TABLE 5.8

Goods Unloaded to Major Ports, 1960/61 to 1972
(tons)

Year	Jedda	Dammam	Yenbo
1960/61	454,772	399,878	17,375
1961/62	518,221	369,333	29,423
1962/63	624,220	343,485	38,141
1963/64	653,600	361,124	33,561
1964/65	766,572	477,464	n.a.
1965/66	937,583	758,117	62,026
1966/67	1,029,322	732,583	151,891
1967/68	800,161	482,899	192,479
1968/69	752,406	681,719	412,522
1969/70	783,742	803,711	381,349
1970	920,895	657,656	207,461
1971	998,486	876,545	356,988
1972	1,021,527	987,016	211,048

Note: The Hijra year 1380 covers the period from June 25, 1960 to May 16, 1961, and the year 1392 the year 1972 A.D.

Sources: 1960/61 to 1965/66: CDS, Statistical Yearbook, 1387 A.H., vol. 3 (Riyadh, 1967), pp. 192-95; 1966/67 to 1972: Ibid., 1393 A.H., vol. 9 (Riyadh, 1973), pp. 278-80.

Dammam is the second largest port in the Kingdom. It is the port of entry for all goods imported for the oil industry and general cargo destined for the eastern and central regions. Although Dammam is located only 467 km from Riyadh, as opposed to 1,061 km from Jedda, considerable amounts of cargo destined for the capital have been shipped via Jedda. This abnormal situation developed because the port duties imposed by the government favored Jedda.

Cargo unloaded in Dammam rose from 399,900 tons in 1960/61 to 987,000 tons in 1972, an increase of 147 percent. To alleviate the crowded crowded conditions in Dammam port a major expansion program has been initiated. A sea wall and a pier equipped to handle fertilizer shipments by the Saudi Arabian Fertilizer Company have been completed, and additional piers, transit sheds, and customs facilities are under construction. Upon completion of this work the port will have an annual cargo capacity of 1.8 million tons.

THE URBAN INFRASTRUCTURE

Very little is known about the urban infrastructure. As in most developing countries, municipal services are inadequate. However, these conditions are slowly changing, owing to intensive efforts to build public water systems and to improve traffic control and sanitation.

The efforts to provide adequate water supplies in the cities has been successful. Forty-three water projects have been completed. In most of the major cities and towns modern water projects have been under construction for a number of years and are nearing completion. In addition to shallow and deep wells, three water-desalination plants are in operation; a fourth one was expected to be completed by the end of 1973, and a fifth plant is under construction.

Most of the larger cities are divided into two sections. The older parts consist of one- or two-story mud buildings with very narrow streets and alleys, many of which are not passable for modern vehicles. In the modern sections most houses are constructed of concrete blocks strengthened by steel reinforcement bars. Nearly every major town contains several shanty towns occupied primarily by expatriate Yemen laborers and some newly arrived Bedouin.

The road networks in most cities are inadequate. In the older quarters many roads are so small that trucks and often even automobiles cannot be used. In the newer sections broad streets and avenues exist but quite often are not properly placed with respect to traffic needs. Traffic jams are endemic, caused in part by the lack of proper signs and lights and in part by the almost complete disregard of traffic rules by the driving public.

Despite the many inconveniences associated with city life, the number of inhabitants of the major cities continues to grow. Because of the prevailing building technology, most of this growth takes place horizontally rather than vertically. Because of the continuous influx of relatively young job seekers from the rural areas, the average age of the urban population is rather low. It has been estimated that more than 50 percent of Riyadh's population is below 20 years of age.

NOTES

1. This account is based on the statistics published in CDS, Statistical Yearbook 1393 A.H., vol. 9 (Riyadh, 1973), pp. 251, 254.
2. SAMA, Annual Report, 1391/92 A.H. (Jedda, 1973), p. 43.
3. SAMA, Annual Report, 1392/93 A.H. (Jedda, 1974), p. 50.
4. CDS, Statistical Yearbook, 1393 A.H., pp. 298, 300.
5. CDS, Statistical Yearbook, 1388 A.H., vol. 4 (Riyadh, 1968), p. 268.

6. CDS, Statistical Yearbook, 1388 A.H., p. 277.
7. Ibid., 1391 A.H., vol. 7 (Riyadh, 1971), p. 275.

CHAPTER

6

AGRICULTURE, INDUSTRY, COMMERCE, AND INTERNATIONAL TRADE

Saudi Arabia is a one-crop economy: It exports oil and imports nearly all its needs from abroad. Oil dominates everything. In the budget year 1971/72 it accounted for 64 percent of GDP and for more than 90 percent of government revenues and foreign-exchange earnings. But, as has been mentioned, oil is a wasting asset: It does not replace itself. Thus, the country must use its currently ample oil revenues to develop and diversify its economy in anticipation of the day when the oil stops. In this chapter the nonoil sector of the economy will be discussed. It will be shown how far agriculture, industry, and commerce have developed. Although the nation is still entirely dependent on oil, a beginning has been made in the nonoil sectors, and the foundation for rapid advances has been laid. The chapter will close with an analysis of foreign trade.

AGRICULTURE

Scattered throughout the Kingdom are a number of areas in which agricultural production is possible (see Map 5). Except for the Asir, an area stretching southward along the Red Sea coast from below Taif to the Jizan-Zaharan region, agriculture is based on irrigation; in the Asir rainfall is sufficient to permit crop and livestock production without irrigation. There is ample evidence that agriculture has been a part of economic activity in the Arabian Peninsula for hundreds of years. Aerial surveys have revealed the outline of fields and gardens abandoned long ago in the Hejaz, Nejd, Hasa, and Asir. In the vicinity of Taif and Khaibar remains of dams and irrigation ditches have been discovered, testifying to the existence of agricultural activities in times past.

MAP 5

Main Agricultural Areas

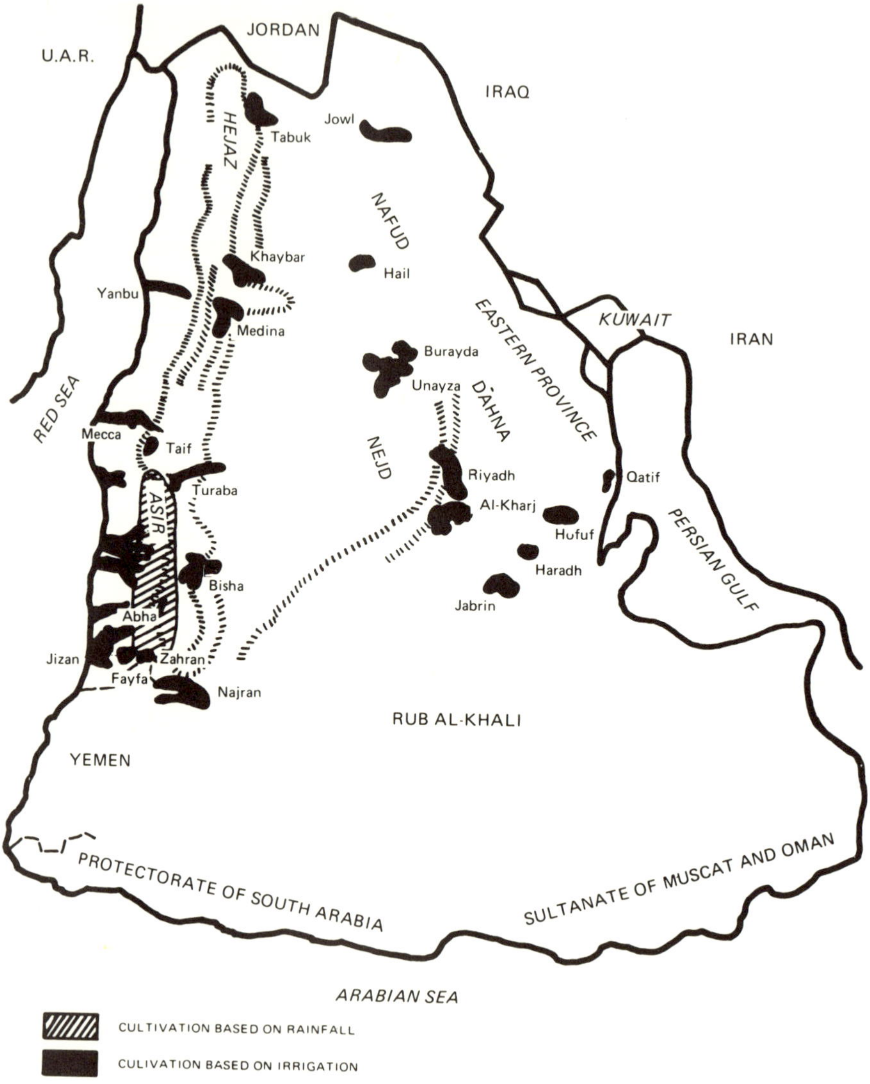

Source: Norman C. Walpole et al., Area Handbook for Saudi Arabia (Washington, D.C.: U.S. Government Printing Office, 1971), p. 216.

Although oil is the basis of Saudi Arabia's current wealth, agriculture plays a dominant role in the life of the majority of her citizens. There are currently 3,084 agricultural villages in the Kingdom, with a total number of holdings amounting to 4.5 million dunums.* of these holdings, 1.6 million dunums, or 34.7 percent, are under cultivation.[1] It has been estimated that in 1969/70 about 65 percent of the total population lived in rural areas and that 46 percent of the total labor force was engaged in agriculture, including crop cultivation and livestock production, fishing, and forestry.[2] Employment in agriculture has been declining slowly in recent years as the economic development of the country has created new demands for nonagricultural goods, which can only be satisfied by factory production.

Reliable, up-to-date agricultural statistics are not available. By far the most important sources of information are a series of surveys carried out by CDS during the early 1960s, a study by A. Y. Asfour, published in 1965, and the information gathered in 1969/70 for the GNP statistics. These statistics are used in the analysis as published in the Statistical Yearbooks. Because the surveys were carried out over a period of several years, they are not strictly comparable. No attempt has been made to reconcile and explain small discrepancies for the same statistic between different time series, because the basic survey data are not available to the author.

Land Use

Despite the arid climate, there are some areas where weather conditions and water supply are such that it is possible to raise two or more crops annually. It has been estimated that multiple cropping has raised the average number of crops to 1.08 per annum.[3]

Table 6.1 gives the land-use pattern in agricultural production by major crops. During the survey period (November 1960 to October 1964) 17.4 percent or 302,100 dunums of the area under cultivation were planted in vegetables, 59.5 percent in field crops, and 23.1 percent in perennial crops, such as fruit trees, coffee, henna,** and clover. By far the largest part of the area under vegetable cultivation was planted in watermelon, followed by squash, pumpkins, tomatoes, onions, and melon. Of the approximately 300,000 dunums

---

*Dunum is a measure of area equal to 1,000 square meters. Ten dunums equal one hectare or 2.471 acres.

**Henna is the Egyptian privet. The shoots and leaves of this plant are used to manufacture a dye that is used as a cosmetic on various parts of the body, such as the hands and the beard.

TABLE 6.1

Land Use by Major Type of Crop, Early 1960s

	Vegetables (dunums)	Annual Field Crops		Perennial Crops	
		Dunums	Percent	Dunums	Percent
Summer	—	182,974	17.8	—	—
Winter	—	846,768	82.2	—	—
Total	302,179	1,029,742	100.0	—	—
Henna and coffee	—	—	—	541	0.1
Clover	—	—	—	207,833	51.9
Palm and fruit trees	—	—	—	191,862	47.9
Total	—	—	—	400,236	100.0
Major uses as percent of total area	17.4	59.5		23.1	

Source: CDS, Statistical Yearbook, 1386 A.H., vol. 2 (Riyadh, 1966), p. 122.

under vegetable cultivation 235,300 dunums or 76.3 percent were planted in the central and Quaseem regions. Next in importance was the area around Jedda and Mecca, followed by Medina. This is to be expected, because these regions have the nation's largest population density, and the road system is excellent, thus encouraging truck farming.[4]

Among the summer crops millet, sorghum, rice, and corn are the most important products, and of the winter crops wheat and barley account for nearly all production. In terms of area under field-crop cultivation the Central Region accounted for 329,200 dunums or 32 percent of the total, followed by the Southern Region, with 261,300 dunums (25.4 percent), the Quaseem, with 186,300 dunums (18.1 percent), and the Taif Region, with 154,900 dunums (15.1 percent).[5]

Palm trees predominate among the permanent crops, with about 8 million trees. By far the majority of palms are of the fruit-bearing variety, and of these trees nearly one-half are found in the eastern region. In addition to palm trees there are grapevines, plum, apple, figs, and several other fruit-bearing varieties under cultivation.

Animal Husbandry

Statistics on livestock are even scarcer than those for grain, vegetables, and trees. Table 6.2 gives the result of the census of livestock carried out as part of the agricultural surveys. Unfortunately, the numbers exclude the animal holdings of the nomadic population and were collected for one point in time. The omission of the nomads' holdings is a serious defect. It has been estimated that the actual sheep population is about four to five times higher than that shown in Table 6.2. The same is true for the number of camels. Production statistics on wool, meat, milk, and eggs are not known. However, it is not unreasonable to assume that 70 percent of the population's meat consumption is met by Saudi-raised sheep, goats, and chickens. In recent years egg production has been growing. Eggs are in plentiful supply, and fresh eggs are available at low prices in all major cities. In the eastern region egg production has increased so much that a thriving export business to Baharain and the Trucial coast areas has been established. As far as sheep, goats, and camels are concerned, their number probably decreased during the early 1960s because of lack of rain. Recently, however, rainfall has increased again, and it is safe to assume that the decline has been reversed.

TABLE 6.2

Livestock and Poultry in Saudi Arabia

Poultry	Number	Livestock	Number
Turkeys	3,764	Goats	294,098
Rabbits	41,146	Sheep	535,164
Pigeons	45,100	Donkeys	52,358
Ducks	3,664	Horses	780
Geese	672	Camels	50,030
Chickens	398,564	Cows	102,952

Source: CDS, Statistical Yearbook, 1386 A.H., vol. 2 (Riyadh, 1966), p. 134.

Water Resources

There are no free flowing, permanent rivers in Saudi Arabia. The nation's water supply depends on rainfall and ground water. Distribution of water varies widely. Except for the western and central regions, ground water resources are sufficient enough to encourage further agricultural development.

Irrigation is primarily carried out by flooding. Distribution technology is simple, consisting for the most part of small earth and sod dams that are opened or closed to regulate water diversion from the main irrigation ditches. Lack of understanding of water requirements and poor water management have led to considerable waste of water. In the Khybar region, for example, large areas of land have been taken out of production because poor water management raised the saline content of the soil, leading to the formation of salt flats (sabkha). Of the total irrigated area 16.6 percent is irrigated by rainfall, 2.5 percent by springs, and 80.9 percent by wells (see Table 6.3). Nearly 1.2 million dunums of land are irrigated by wells, of which 60,088 were artesian wells and 811,734 were ordinary shallow dug wells. Of the shallow dug wells 20.3 percent were used without engines, and 79.7 percent operated with engines.

To increase agricultural output and to control the flash-floods that occur in the desert the government decided to build dams in a number of wadis. Based on a UN Food and Agricultural Organization (FAO) survey, it was decided to build nine dams. In 1971 the first of these projects, the Wadi Jizan project, was finished. The dam is located west of the city of Jizan at an elevation of 450 feet above sea level. It is 1,036 feet across from bank to bank, 131 feet wide at the base, and rises about 100 feet from the base. The dam created a manmade lake containing about 19 billion gallons of water. When released through the two spillways the water will irrigate more than 3,000 acres of land. Eight additional dams are under construction or in the planning stages. Seven of the dams will be used to recharge wells and one is for flood control.[6]

Agricultural Machinery

Agricultural technology used in farm operations varies widely. Use of modern technology is more intense in the vicinity of large urban areas, because the equipment dealers are located there. This is probably more important than the presence of dealerships, because repair and maintenance services are more easily available in these areas.

The technology in use reflects the need for water. By far the largest number of machines in use—21,251—are irrigation machines

TABLE 6.3

Irrigated Land, by Water Source and by Agricultural Region

				Land Irrigated by Wells					
				Area Irrigated (dunums)				Number of Wells	
					Ordinary				
Region	Total Irrigated Area (dunums)	Rainfall Area (dunums)	Area Irrigated by Springs (dunums)	Total	Without Engines	With Engines	Arte-sian	Ordi-nary	Arte-sian
Northern	104,682	16,883	4,031	83,768	26,214	55,129	2,425	7,385	46
Eastern	n.a.	n.a.	n.a.	n.a.	n.a.	n.a.	n.a.	n.a.	n.a.
Medina	44,819	4,381	12,621	27,817	3,343	22,994	1,480	3,021	33
Jedda-Mecca	35,112	24,929	5,893	4,290	736	3,491	63	353	3
Taif	172,167	106,584	322	65,261	36,231	27,273	1,757	7,544	85
Quaseem	319,635	2,174	7,870	309,591	n.a.	n.a.	n.a.	n.a.	3,958
Central	515,128	11,140	5,098	498,890	9,376	435,151	54,363	6,787	522
Southern	268,711	75,768	1,147	191,796	88,881	102,915	—	17,684	—
All regions	1,460,254	241,859	36,982	1,181,413	164,781	646,953	60,088	43,732	4,647

Source: CDS, Statistical Yearbook, 1386 A.H., vol. 2 (Riyadh, 1966), p. 131.

(see Table 6.4). Cultivation before planting is increasingly more often done by machine, but mostof the crop land is still prepared by hand. In those areas where mechanization is spreading, government-owned and privately owned machinery is used. The importance of machinery in the land-preparation phase is underscored by the fact that plowing tractors and plows constitute 22.1 percent of the number of agricultural machines owned by the Ministry of Agriculture, as opposed to 1.1 percent for drillers and threshers.[7] The follow-up cultivation, such as planting, weed control, and harvesting, is done almost completely by manual operations.

Table 6.4 offers an insight into the distribution of irrigation machinery and tractors throughout the country at the time of the agricultural census. There were 48,343 wells in use, of which 44 percent (21,251) were equipped with irrigation machinery. The distribution of irrigation machinery among the regions varied considerably. In the southern region 24.7 percent of the wells were equipped with irrigation machinery, and in the central region 89.5 percent were provided with this equipment. The small proportion of irrigation machinery in the southern region is not surprising, because this is the country's only region where rainfall is adequate for agricultural pursuits.

The agricultural census revealed only 277 tractors in use during the survey period, giving 5,638 dunums of cultivated land per tractor and 254 holdings per tractor. The largest number of tractors—68 and 119—were found in the Quaseem and central regions. This greater use of machinery is probably due to the greater incidence of commercial farming and the employment of agricultural workers on the farms. In recent years the number of tractors has increased considerably. In 1964/65 and 1965/66, 377 and 1,071 tractors, respectively, were imported. If all these tractors were for agricultural use, the number of dunums per tractor declines to 88 and the number of holdings to 41. The increase in mechanization may have led to an increase in agricultural productivity. However, in the absence of corroborating statistics this conclusion cannot be made automatically. The level of education among farmers is very low, and until the training of farmers is improved it is most likely that increasing mechanization will have little effect on output.

Land Tenure and Farm Size

Any Saudi citizen may own, buy, and sell land, subject only to a few government regulations and the restrictions of sharia Law. Primogeniture is not part of sharia Law. Upon the death of a landowner his land is divided among all heirs; sons receive an equal num-

TABLE 6.4

Agricultural Machinery in Use in Saudi Arabia

Region	Wells	Irrigation Machines	Wells with Machines (percent)	Cultivated Area (dunums)	Number of Holdings*	Tractors	Cultivated Dunums per Tractor	Holdings per Tractor
Northern	7,431	2,187	29.4	104,682	8,624	28	3,739	308
Eastern	n.a.	n.a.	n.a.	101,593	9,098	n.a.	n.a.	n.a.
Medina	3,054	1,695	55.5	44,819	7,036	18	2,490	391
Jedda-Mecca	356	200	56.2	35,112	1,501	14	2,508	107
Taif	7,629	2,484	32.6	172,167	9,076	13	13,244	698
Quaseem	4,916	3,794	77.2	319,635	4,950	68	4,701	73
Central	7,309	6,540	89.5	515,128	8,020	119	4,329	67
Southern	17,648	4,351	24.7	268,711	22,047	17	15,807	1,297
Total	48,343	21,251	44.0	1,561,847	70,352	277	5,638	254

*The term is used as defined by FAO in the 1960 World Agricultural Census: "A holding . . . is all land which is used wholly or partly for agricultural production and is operated by one person (the holder) alone or with the assistance of others, without regard to title, size or location. Livestock kept for agricultural purposes without agricultural land is to be considered as constituting a holding. . . . The holding as defined is an operational agricultural holding." FAO, Report on the 1960 World Census of Agriculture, vol. 5 (Rome, 1971), p. 13.

Sources: Wells: Table 6.3; agricultural machinery: CDS, Statistical Yearbook, 1386 A.H., vol. 2 (Riyadh, 1966), p. 129; cultivated areas: Ibid., p. 119; number of holdings: Ibid., p. 121.

ber of shares, and daughters receive half shares. Because this type of inheritance law leads to extreme fragmentation of holdings, most land is held in forms of ownership that avoid distribution of land among the heirs—for example, land may be jointly owned by an extended family (mushaa land). Cultivation rights to various sections of the land may be rotated among family members; however, cultivation is more often entrusted to a son or other individuals, and the harvest is divided each year in accordance with the inheritance laws. This has reduced the size of the individual shares in the harvest from generation to generation.

The most interesting and unique type of landholding is the waqf. A waqf is the endowment of a piece of land to a religious or charitable institution. Once a piece of property has been declared a waqf, ownership is inalienable. Eventually, all rights to this land fall to the institution to which the land is deeded, but during his lifetime the founder of the waqf has the right to say to whom the usufruct of the land is to fall.

Between 80 and 90 percent of the land is pasture land. Traditionally, pasture lands were jointly owned by the various tribes. In the past disputes over the right to the pasture land was one of the main sources of friction among the tribes. In 1925 King Abd al-Aziz abolished the tribal rights to pasture land. The various tribes continue to graze their herds, but the government has the final word in the disposition of the range land. The government owns all subsoil rights and it has the right to move the tribes from this land in order to exploit subsurface minerals or oil.

There is considerable regional variability in the average area per holding. The average size of the total area per holding is 64 dunums, while the average area under cultivation per holding is only 22.2 dunums (see Table 6.5). It is estimated that an area of 10 dunums is sufficient in most regions to sustain an average family. In at least three regions the average area of cultivated holdings approaches that figure, and in only one region, Medina, does it fall below the minimum. Taken as a whole, it is clear that agriculture in the Kingdom is carried out on small farms, at or slightly above subsistence size. This observation is further substantiated by the distribution of holdings by size groups. Out of 70,352 holdings (excluding livestock holdings), 33,242, or 47.3 percent, are between 0 and 5 dunums, and 13,661, or 19.4 percent, are between 5 and 10 dunums in size.[8] The average size of holdings is "distorted" by the presence of two regions, Quaseem and central, with average holdings considerably in excess of the other six regions. The difference is explained by the fact that more capital equipment is in use in these regions than anywhere else (see Table 6.4), as well as the use of more hired hands than in the other regions.

TABLE 6.5

Size and Tenure of Agricultural Holdings in the Mid-1960s
(area in dunums)

Region	Area of Holdings		Number of	Area per Holding		Percent of
	Total	Cultivated	Holdings*	Total	Cultivated	Area Rented
Northern	326,507	104,682	8,624	37.9	12.1	0.1
Eastern	126,136	101,593	9,098	13.9	11.2	18.6
Medina	111,987	44,819	7,036	15.9	6.4	5.0
Jedda-Mecca	39,786	35,112	1,501	26.5	23.4	9.9
Taif	187,875	172,167	9,076	20.7	19.0	2.8
Quaseem	2,695,748	319,635	4,950	544.6	64.6	9.3
Central	680,274	515,128	8,020	84.8	64.2	16.4
Southern	336,213	268,711	22,047	15.2	12.2	2.2
Total	4,504,526	1,561,847	70,352	64.0	22.2	9.0

*Excludes livestock holdings.

Source: CDS, Statistical Yearbook, 1386 A.H., vol. 2 (Riyadh, 1966), pp. 119, 120.

Agriculture in Saudi Arabia is carried out almost completely by the owner; only 9 percent of agricultural area is rented. This is a notable difference from the rest of the developing world where the majority of peasants eke out their living on rented land. In recent years the government has distributed fallow land to farmers. By 1972, 5,610 persons located in different regions of the country had received a total of 342,385 dunums.[9]

Cost of Production and Returns

Although there are no comparative statistics on production costs and income from agriculture, the agricultural census yielded a cost breakdown and income figures for four types of crop in several regions (see Table 6.6). Tomatoes and watermelons showed the highest profit per dunum cultivated. Of the two field crops, clover earned a profit in all four regions for which data are available, and wheat produced a loss in three of the four regions. The largest profit differential between field crops and fruit and vegetables is also shown by the average gross return per hectare of the four major crop groups, as follows:[10]

	Gross Return per ha.
Field crops*	S.R. 1,547
Other field crops (including alfalfa)	806
Vegetables	5,073
Dates	4,162
Fruits	7,187

There is evidence that a shift from field crops to vegetable and fruit cultivation has taken place.[11] There were two reasons for this shift. The first was the observed difference in profits per dunum of cultivated land. Even in the absence of time series for production of various crops, it is certain that this profit differential will lead to a change in cropping patterns as long as the farmer tries to maximize his return on land. The second factor favoring vegetables and fruit production is the 16.7-percent import subsidy on the c.i.f. price paid since 1359 A.H. (1959/60). The subsidy was granted to about 20 food products, including 12 cereals, 5 oil products, dairy products, sugar, and live animals for food. It was instituted to compensate

*Wheat, barley, rice, sorghum, millet, alfalfa.

TABLE 6.6

Expenditure and Income per Dunum from Cultivation of Various Crops, 1960-63
(Saudi riyals)

Crop and Region	Total Cost	Total Income	Profit (+) or Loss (-)
Tomatoes			
Taif Region	955	1,350	+395
Central Region	826	1,125	+299
Watermelon			
Central Region	653	938	+285
Quaseem Region	709	975	+266
Jedda Region	634	975	+341
Northern Region	541	900	+359
Wheat			
Central Region	235	240	+ 5
Quaseem Region	144	104	- 40
Taif Region	159	140	- 19
Northern Region	161	133	- 28
Clover			
Central Region	930	1,200	+270
Quaseem Region	646	813	+167
Medina Region	503	800	+297
Northern Region	498	729	+231

Source: CDS, Statistical Yearbook, 1386 A.H., vol. 2 (Riyadh, 1966), 11. 135-38.

grain importers for potential losses associated with the devaluation of the Saudi riyal, from S.R. 3.75 to S.R. 4.50 per U.S. dollar. In April 1966 the subsidy was removed from all items except for wheat, rice, and meat "in order to encourage local production of foodstuffs. Available evidence indicates that this reduction in subsidies has provided some price incentive to local agriculture, and agricultural output has been gradually increasing."[12] In September 1968 the subsidy on the remaining items was reduced to 12.5 percent for wheat and rice and to 7.5 percent for meat. Further reductions took place in September 1969, and in September 1970 the last vestiges were eliminated. According to SAMA, the elimination of the subsidies had led to the desired increase in domestic agricultural production.

To facilitate the adoption of modern agricultural practices subsidies on domestic production were reintroduced for rice, flour, and sugar. This program was adopted in place of a tariff increase to avoid the inflationary pressures that would result from higher tariffs. In addition to crop subsidies, the government instituted a 50-percent subsidy on fertilizer imports and raised subsidies paid to individual farmers purchasing agricultural machinery, from 25 percent to 45 percent, and that paid to cooperatives was raised 50 percent. Additional subsidies will be paid to wheat and rice producers, in addition to a 50 percent payment of cost for livestock feed.

The cost breakdown of the four types of crop reveals an interesting puzzle. The highest cost element in the cultivation of watermelon, tomatoes, and clover was rent. In the Taif area land rent accounted for 47.1 percent of the cost of tomato production, and in the Central region it was 40 percent. In watermelon-production land rent amounted to between 66.1 and 45.9 percent in the four regions surveyed. Except for the Medina region, where land rent amounted to about 24 percent of production costs, the other regions show similar proportions of rent paid to total costs.

In view of the low percentage of agricultural land rented for production, as shown earlier in the chapter, this observation throws considerable doubt on the tenure statistics. However, the observation may not be an important contradiction of these statistics. Vegetables and fruits are highly perishable commodities, and given the very inadequate transportation facilities at the time of the surveys, it is reasonable to assume that most of these crops were grown close to the major population centers. Observation has shown that around the population centers land is often owned by individuals whose main occupation is not in agriculture. If they rent out their holdings, competition for the available land in the vicinity of population centers could have resulted in the rather high land-rent component of costs.

Special Agricultural Projects

It is the government's aim to make the nation as self-sufficient in agricultural products as the inhospitable climate will allow. To accomplish this goal a number of agricultural projects have been implemented. Two projects deserve to be singled out: the al-Kharj project in the Nejd and the King Faisal Settlement Scheme at Haradh in the Eastern Province. The al-Kharj project was begun in an attempt to provide Riyadh, located about 90 km. north of Al-Kharj, with a supply of fruits and vegetables. In 1942 a U.S. agricultural mission surveyed the area for water resources and an irrigation system.[13] Following the mission's return to Washington, the U.S.

Department of Agriculture sent a number of experts to supervise and manage the project. After the completion of the irrigation and drainage system under the supervision of these advisers the government asked Aramco to assume management of the project. In July 1955 the company relinquished control, and since then it has been managed by Saudi agriculturalists. Today, the farm produces eggs, chickens, and other poultry. A small dairy farm produces pasteurized milk, butter, and some beef for the Riyadh market.

An important aspect of social change is the settlement of the Bedouin population. The first attempt was made by King Abd al-Aziz with the Ikhwan settlement in the second and third decade of the twentieth century. Since that time many Bedouin have settled in and around various cities, and others have curtailed their wanderings considerably. An example of the latter type of settlement is the Bedouin population along the Tapline. Here the company has drilled a number of wells, and the availability of water has induced many nomads to restrict their movement to the vicinity of these wells.

The King Faisal Model Settlement Project was designed to speed up Bedouin settlement in the Eastern Province. It was completed about the end of 1970. Fifty deep wells were sunk. Fields have been laid out, and a complete irrigation and drainage system was built, bringing 4,000 ha. of land under cultivation. The project includes a training center and an experimental farm, cultural centers, and housing for 1,000 Bedouin families.

Another settlement project is the homestead development program carried out in the northern sector. There, Bedouin were offered land for settlement. Several hundred families took advantage of the offer and settled on those lands. Unfortunately, the project had only limited success. The homesteads were scattered, making it difficult to develop an effective infrastructure of agricultural extension and education programs. Wells were drilled and pumping equipment installed, but the lack of trained maintenance and repair technicians led to equipment failure that could not be repaired immediately, creating severe problems for the novice farmers and discouraging extensive resettlement.

During the budget year 1970/71 the Ministry of Agriculture began a program to replace the old, low-yield types of wheat used by the nation's farmers with the high-yielding Mexipack strain. The experimental phase of this program began in 1965/66 in collaboration with FAO and the Ford Foundation on a few selected farms in various agricultural regions. In 1972/73 the program covered 2,000 dunums of land on which the average yield rose from 1.5 tons to four tons per hectare. It is anticipated that eventually 55 percent of the land under wheat cultivation will be sown with the new strain. To insure success the Ministry of Agriculture has launched a number of training programs designed to teach the farmers the new methods of cultivation required to make the new wheat a commercial success.

The Agricultural Development Bank

To facilitate the development of agriculture the government established the Agricultural Development Bank, which began operating in 1964/65 with a nominal capital of S.R. 30 million and a paid-in capital of S.R. 10 million. By 1969/70 the bank's capital stood at S.R. 53 million, and in 1972/73 the bank maintained eight branches and 37 rural offices.

Article 2 of Royal Decree 58 provides that:

> The bank give loans and the necessary facilities needed for the growth and encouragement of agriculture, including:
> 1. Farming, growing, storing and marketing of products, poultry, domestic animals, fishes and forest products.
> 2. Land reclamation.
> 3. Necessary facilities for securing water needed for above purpose.

The bank is authorized to make short-, medium-, and long-term loans, depending on the purpose for which the loan is to be used. In the case of loans for land reclamation, loans of up to 25 years may be made, provided that the bank makes a thorough feasibility study of the project.

Since its inception in 1964/65 the bank has made about 30,000 loans, totaling well over S.R. 110 million (see Table 6.7). The number of annual loans grew by more than 600 percent, from 625 in 1964/65 to 4,477 in 1972/73, and the total annual value of loans extended rose nearly fivefold, from S.R. 4.4 million to S.R. 19.6 million. The small increase in the value of loans from 1969/70 to 1970/71 has been attributed to the lack of rain in the Jizan and other areas.[14]

The average size of loans fell from S.R. 7,000 in the first year of operations to S.R. 4,400 in 1972/73. It can be expected that the size of the average loan will increase in the future, because the board of directors recently raised the limit on medium-term loans from S.R. 12,000 to S.R. 20,000. Furthermore, the rural offices were allowed to make short-term loans of up to S.R. 2,000 per borrower without consultation with the main office.

The proportion of short-term to medium-term loans has changed. During the first two years of operations the value of short-term loans

TABLE 6.7

Lending Activities of the Agricultural Bank

Year	Number of Loans	Value (S.R. thousand)				
		Total	Average	Short-term (0 to 2 years)	Medium-term (2 to 5 years)	Long-term (over 5 years)
1964/65	625	4,390	7.0	131	4,259	—
1965/66	1,922	9,927	5.2	295	9,632	—
1966/67	3,149	13,292	4.2	1,082	12,100	110
1967/68	3,732	12,000	3.2	1,542	10,458	—
1968/69	3,667	13,863	3.8	1,675	12,188	—
1969/70	4,356	16,134	3.7	3,007	13,127	—
1970/71	4,381	16,627	4.0	2,575	14,052	—
1971/72	3,865	16,558	4.3	2,266	14,292	—
1972/73	4,477	19,593	4.4	2,916	16,677	—

Source: SAMA, Annual Report, 1392/93 A.H. (Jedda, 1974), p. 85.

accounted for only 3 percent of the value of all loans made. In 1966/67 it amounted to 8.1 percent, reached a high of 18.6 percent in 1969/70, declined to 13.7 percent in 1971/72, and rose to about 15 percent in 1972/73. This increase in the proportion of short-term to medium-term loans resulted from two factors: First, a policy change raised the maximum amount of a loan a branch manager was permitted to grant from S.R. 1,500 to S.R. 6,000, and, second, the bank was permitted to make short-term loans in cash as well as in kind.

Repayment of loans due has been very high. According to SAMA, 96.5 percent of the amount due on outstanding loans was collected at the end of 1972/73.

The bank has contributed substantially to capital formation in the agricultural sector (see Table 6.8). Unfortunately, much of the bank's loan portfolio is concealed in the other loans classification, which rose from 2.2 percent in 1964/65 to 21.4 percent in 1972/73, but it is safe to assume that a major portion of this category represents cash loans. As would be expected, loans associated with irrigation dominate the loan portfolio. In 1964/65 loans for irrigation purposes accounted for 82.4 percent of all loans. This proportion fell during the period under study, and in 1972/73 it amounted to 42 percent. During the same period livestock loans rose from 0.8 percent to 9.5 percent of the total value of loans. This increase in the share of all loans reflects the farmers' attempt to increase the size of herds following the drought of the early 1960s.

The Ministry of Agriculture and Water

Because the Ministry of Agriculture and Water plays an important role in the development of the agricultural sector, a brief outline of its functions and activities is indicated. The ministry is headed by the Minister of Agriculture assisted by two deputy ministers, one for agriculture and the other for water. The Deputy Minister for Agricultural Affairs supervises four major departments: the Department for Public Land Management; the Agricultural Training Department, which provides in-service training for ministry employees; the Research and Development Department; and the Agricultural Extension and Services Department. The Deputy Minister for Water Affairs also has four departments under his control: the Water Resources Development Department; the Water Services Department, which operates and maintains water supply and distribution systems; the Water Conservation Department; and the Projects Department.

The ministry is in charge of a number of projects designed to improve the efficiency of the agricultural sector. Among them are the reorganization of the water and drainage system of the al-Hasa oasis in the eastern region, the construction of dams and irrigation systems in the Wadi Jaizan, and Abha in the southern region, the building of a drainage system at Quatif to reclaim saline land, sand stabilization, and area studies in various regions to assess future development possibilities.

INDUSTRY AND COMMERCE

As was shown in Chapter 4, nonoil industry and commerce play a relatively small role in the Kingdom's economic structure. In terms of GDP nonpetroleum manufacturing has hovered around 2 percent since the early 1960s, and mining and quarrying around 0.3 percent. Electricity, gas, and water contributed about 1 percent; finance, insurance, real estate, and business services (except ownership of dwellings) contributed 1.5 percent; community, social, and personal services contributed a declining share, from 2.5 percent in 1962/63 to less than 1 percent in 1972/73. Construction rose to a high of 6.1 but declined to 3.5 percent in 1972/73, and even wholesale and retail trade, restaurants, and hotels declined during the period. Clearly, the growth of the nonoil industrial and commercial sectors has been slow and the economy has remained a one-crop operation: oil dominates everything.

Information regarding commerce and industry can be found in the Census of Establishments of 1967/68 and the one of 1971.* Unfortunately, comparisons of the statistics published in those censuses are somewhat limited, because the 1971 census included 37 more cities than the earlier one. Nevertheless, the information contained in the censuses will be used, because they offer an opportunity to see what changes have taken place in the business sector. Despite the difference in the number of cities included in the two censuses, they can be used in a comparative analysis: A comparison of the number of establishments and workers enumerated in 1971 on the basis of the number of cities included in the 1967/68 census with all cities in the 1971 census leads to the conclusion that the additional towns in the 1971 census do not significantly affect the totals for that year

---

*According to the Statistical Yearbook, 1388 A.H., vol. 4 (p. 173): "an establishment [is] defined as a unit organized for a specific activity at a location. Agricultural holders other than poultry farms [are] excluded [as well as] all vendors, hawkers, pavement sellers and taxi drivers, etc."—those without a fixed place of business.

TABLE 6.8

Loans Granted by the Agricultural Bank According to Purpose, 1964/65 to 1971/72

Purpose	1964/65		1965/66		1966/67		1967/68	
	Value	Percent	Value	Percent	Value	Percent	Value	Percent
Engines	1,755.5	38.7	4,758.2	47.9	5,449.1	41.0	5,140.9	42.8
Pumps	1,659.4	36.5	2,855.8	28.8	2,360.7	17.8	1,805.4	15.0
Drilling, deepening, casing of wells	325.9	7.2	752.6	7.6	1,400.7	10.5	1,141.8	9.5
Construction	62.7	1.4	166.9	1.7	422.1	3.2	475.0	4.0
Fertilizer, seed, and shrubs	219.8	4.8	295.3	3.0	414.3	3.1	389.4	3.3
Livestock	36.0	0.8	170.4	1.7	486.9	3.7	522.3	4.3
Poultry	22.0	0.5	12.6	0.1	98.0	0.7	116.1	1.0
Fodder	102.4	2.3	111.1	1.1	524.6	4.0	320.1	2.7
Plowing	88.3	1.9	133.7	1.3	405.2	3.1	246.8	2.0
Installation and carriage	135.8	3.0	174.6	1.8	231.9	1.7	366.7	3.1
Fuel	33.9	0.7	35.1	0.4	152.0	1.1	249.6	2.1
Other	99.4	2.2	461.1	4.6	1,346.9	10.1	1,225.7	10.2
Total	4,541.1	100.0	9,927.4	100.0	13,292.4	100.0	11,999.8	100.0

	1968/69		1969/70		1970/71		1971/72		1972/73	
	Value	Per-cent	Value	Per-cent	Value	Per-cent	Value	Per-cent	Value	Per-cent
Engines	4,521.9	32.6	4,587.8	28.4	3,962.8	23.8	3,653.0	22.1	4,048.1	20.7
Pumps	2,024.8	14.6	1,998.9	12.4	2,103.8	12.7	1,766.0	10.7	2,367.6	12.1
Drilling, deepening, casing wells	1,114.4	8.1	1,309.4	8.1	1.714.2	10.3	1,811.6	10.9	1,816.1	9.2
Construction	645.9	4.7	628.0	3.9	501.9	3.0	534.2	3.2	613.6	3.1
Fertilizer, seed, and shrubs	668.4	4.8	780.2	4.8	899.0	5.4	913.9	5.5	1,172.7	6.0
Livestock	1,632.9	11.7	1,706.0	10.6	1,944.7	11.7	1,570.4	9.5	1,853.9	9.5
Poultry	98.6	0.7	56.0	0.3	74.8	0.5	507.1	3.1	133.0	0.7
Fodder	516.8	3.7	373.8	2.3	889.2	5.3	812.2	4.9	758.2	3.9
Plowing	700.2	5.1	1,234.9	7.7	926.0	4.6	401.7	2.4	362.5	1.8
Installation and carriage	330.7	2.4	545.0	3.4	269.7	1.6	1,312.1	7.9	1,973.8	10.1
Fuel	171.7	1.3	189.0	1.2	270.2	1.6	270.5	1.6	301.7	1.5
Other	1,437.2	10.3	2,725.0	16.9	3,071.3	18.5	3,005.4	18.2	4,192.3	21.4
Total	13,863.5	100.0	16,134.0	100.0	16,627.6	100.0	16,558.1	100.0	19,593.5	100.0

Sources: 1964/65 to 1967/68: SAMA, Annual Report, 1389/90 A.H. (Jedda, 1971), p. 82; 1968/69 to 1971/72: Ibid., 1391/92 A.H. (Jedda, 1973), p. 80; 1972/73: Ibid., 1392/93 A.H. (Jedda, 1974), p. 86.

TABLE 6.9

Growth in the Number of Establishments and Workers in Major Cities, 1967/68 and 1971

Geographical Region	Number of Workers		Number of Establishments	
	1967/68	1971	1967/68	1971
Central	24,741	33,767	10,023	14,039
Western	51,409	63,995	21,856	26,173
Eastern	19,035	25,326	7,198	8,870
Northern	3,015	7,084	2,173	2,840
Southern	3,369	4,691	1,536	2,704
Total based on number of cities in 1967/68 survey	101,569	135,260	42,886	54,626
Total based on number of cities in 1971 survey	101,569	146,710	42,886	60,929

Source: CDS, Statistical Yearbook, 1392 A.H., vol. 8 (Riyadh, 1972), pp. 371-72.

(see Table 6.9). Taking the number of workers and firms in the 1971 census, we find that the number of workers in those cities listed in the 1967/68 census was 135,260, while the total number of employed workers in all towns listed in the 1971 census amounted to 146,710. Thus, the inclusion of more towns in the 1971 census added only 11,450 workers to the census results in terms of the 1967/68 survey. This amounts to 7.8 percent of the total number of workers enumerated in the 1971 census. The same analysis carried out for the number of establishments shows that the additional towns in the 1971 census raised the number of establishments by 6,303, or slightly more than 10 percent. Given that the additional towns accounted for such small proportions, the conclusions reached by a comparison of the data in the two censuses should be valid.

Table 6.10 gives the distribution of establishments by region and economic activity for the years 1967/68 and 1971. Business activity is concentrated primarily in the central, western, and eastern regions. In 1967/68 these three regions accounted for 90 percent of the total number of business firms, with 23 percent of the establishments located in the central region, 50 percent in the western, and 17 percent in the eastern region. By 1971 the distribution had changed slightly. The proportion of establishments in the three regions fell to 87.4 percent, with 16.9 and 43.6 percent in the eastern and western regions, respectively, and 26.9 percent in the central region.

By far the largest number of establishments is located in the western region. This should not come as a surprise. The western region has been an important focus of economic activity in the Arabian Peninsula for the last thousand years and has managed to hold onto that premier position in the Kingdom. In 1967/68 about 62 percent of all establishments were found in the commerce classification. This category includes all wholesale and retail activities. Within that group more than 50 percent of the establishments were in the food, beverage, and other consumption-goods retail trade, followed by retail trade in textiles, clothing, and home furnishings (17.2 percent). Comparable figures for 1971 are not available, but it is likely that these percentages have not changed significantly.

The inclusion of additional towns in the survey reduced the average number of establishments in each of the five regions. This suggests that the additional towns included in the second survey were smaller than those included in the survey of 1967/68. This assumption is strengthened by the fact that the towns included in both surveys accounted for 86 percent of the establishments in central region, 98 percent of those in the western region, 86 percent of those in the eastern region, 87 percent of those in the northern region, and 64 percent of those in the southern region.

By far the largest increase in the number of establishments occurred in the southern region. In addition to the fact that the survey of 1971 contained nine more towns than that of 1967/68, the increase probably reflects an attempt by the government to tie this region closer to the central government. It is here that the border disputes with the People's Republic of the Yemen have taken place, and the large increase in business establishments must in part, at least, be associated with the military build-up in the region. The next largest increase in the number of establishments took place in the central region. This increase was associated with the expansion of the capital city, Riyadh, and the build-up of the area around the towns of Unaizah and Buraida.

Of the various economic activities the largest increase in the number of establishments occurred in the transportation and storage classification. Within this class the western region registered the sharpest rise. The increase in the number of establishments in this group resulted from the expansion of the road network. The western region is the most densely populated, and the 130 percent rise in establishments engaged in transportation and storage reflects that fact.

TABLE 6.10

Distribution of Business Establishments, by Region and Economic Activity, 1967/68 and 1971

	Southern Region		Northern Region		Eastern Region	
	1967/68	1971	1967/68	1971	1967/68	1971
Agriculture, forestry, fishing	2	7	2	3	11	19
Mining, quarrying	1	2	1	—	1	5
Manufacturing	412	758	415	465	1,587	1,819
Electricity, gas, water	4	23	6	8	17	29
Construction	6	6	5	12	69	151
Commerce	1,426	3,088	1,577	2,339	4,598	6,660
Transport, storage	4	11	5	7	36	92
Financial institutions, insurance, real estate	28	20	18	16	78	162
Services	252	497	143	426	1,020	1,395
Communications	—	n.a.	—	n.a.	1	n.a.
Activities not adequately described	—	n.a.	1	n.a.	2	n.a.
Total	2,135	4,412	2,173	3,276	7,431	10,332
Number of cities surveyed	4	13	5	9	7	14

	Western Region		Central Region		Total	
	1967/68	1971	1967/68	1971	1967/68	1971
Agriculture, forestry, fishing	15	41	6	15	36	85
Mining, quarrying	5	7	2	1	10	15
Manufacturing	4,691	4,272	2,068	2,324	9,173	9,638
Electricity, gas, water	16	26	35	36	82	122
Construction	172	252	157	275	416	696
Commerce	12,945	17,610	6,331	10,923	26,877	40,620
Transport, storage	92	211	4	60	141	381
Financial institutions, insurance, real estate	216	433	239	473	519	1,104
Services	3,670	3,802	1,159	2,328	6,264	8,448
Communications	3	n.a.	21	n.a.	25	n.a.
Activities not adequately described	8	n.a.	2	n.a.	13	n.a.
Total	21,853	26,654	10,024	16,435	43,616	61,109
Number of cities surveyed	5	9	3	16	24	61

Sources: 1967/68: CDS, Statistical Yearbook, 1388 A.H., vol. 4 (Riyadh, 1968), p. 181; 1971: Ibid., 1388 A.H., vol. 8 (Riyadh, 1972), p. 374.

It is interesting that the number of establishments in banking, insurance, and real estate rose by more than 100 percent between 1967/68 and 1971. In the central, western, and eastern regions this activitiy rose about 100 percent, while it declined slightly in the southern and northern areas. This change indicates that the financial infrastructure is growing to meet the increasing demands for this service as economic development progresses. It is also an indication that the population is accepting the banking system and that the "cash-and-carry" sector of the economy is shrinking. Finally, to the extent that this increase reflects increases in the number of real estate offices, it shows the rising standard of prosperity that has provided many a Saudi an opportunity to purchase his own villa.

On the average the size of the establishments as measured by the number of employees is small (see Table 6.11). In 1967/68 business establishments averaged 2.3 employees, including paid and unpaid workers: 1.42 paid employees and 0.91 unpaid employees.[15] In 1971 the averages were about the same. As far as the geographical distribution of establishments is concerned there was no major difference in size distribution. In the central, western, and eastern regions for more than half of all business establishments fell into the group employing one worker. The number of establishments in the two-to-four-employee category was 28 percent in 1967/68 and 30 percent in 1971 for all regions. In the central, western, and eastern regions the distribution in 1967/68 and 1971 was approximately that of all regions. In the southern region the percentage of establishments with two to four workers remained about the same (23 percent), and in the northern region the proportion rose from 16 percent in 1967/68 to 23 percent in 1971.

The small size of the business establishments is a result of the "suq mentality" and the limited size of the markets and their fragmentation. For centuries economic activity has taken place in the suq, where each merchant specialized in the sale of one or two commodities, maintaining a small stall under the owner's supervision, with all his wares displayed to the potential customers. The inventory was small and the tempo of trade was slow, so that one person could handle all business activities easily without help, and if any assistance was needed the merchant would employ close relatives, often as unpaid family help. This observation is supported by the fact that in 1967/68 more than 92 percent of all establishments were registered as individually owned.[16]

The distribution of the business establishments by economic activity and employment size again shows the slow development of the business sector (see Table 6.12). Of the 9,174 enterprises enumerated in the manufacturing classification of the 1967/68 census of establishments, 8,163 (89 percent) employed four or fewer workers.

TABLE 6.11

Distribution of Establishments, by Employment Size and Region, 1967/68 and 1971

Number of Employees	Central Region		Western Region		Eastern Region		Northern Region		Southern Region		All Regions	
	1967/68	1971	1967/68	1971	1967/68	1971	1967/68	1971	1967/68	1971	1967/68	1971
1	6,555	10,664	13,948	15,924	4,735	6,865	1,764	2,458	1,623	3,250	28,935	39,161
2 to 4	2,836	4,796	6,717	9,145	1,937	2,831	363	742	501	1,041	12,303	18,555
5 to 9	435	688	824	1,082	278	376	29	54	56	105	1,627	2,305
10 to 19	109	175	201	263	90	134	5	12	2	13	409	597
20 to 49	55	74	103	156	56	77	9	4	1	1	217	312
50 and more	33	48	61	84	33	49	—	6	3	2	130	179
All groups	10,023	16,435	21,856	26,654	7,433	10,332	2,173	3,276	2,136	4,412	43,621	61,109
Number of cities in survey	4	13	5	9	7	14	5	9	3	16	24	61

Sources: 1967/68: CDS, Statistical Yearbook, 1389 A.H., vol. 5 (Riyadh, 1969), p. 201; 1971: Ibid., 1389 A.H., vol. 8 (Riyadh, 1972), p. 373.

TABLE 6.12

Distribution of Business Establishments, by Economic Activity and Employment Size, 1967/68 and 1971

	1		2 to 4		5 to 9		10 to 19	
	1967/68	1971	1967/68	1971	1967/68	1971	1967/68	1971
Agriculture, forestry, fishing	9	32	18	42	4	8	4	1
Mining, quarrying	3	—	—	—	—	5	1	1
Manufacturing	4,394	4,251	3,769	4,308	729	746	169	194
Electricity, gas, water	22	38	29	30	14	19	3	16
Construction	191	321	106	212	31	51	27	40
Commerce	20,838	29,612	5,509	9,833	351	925	95	103
Transport, storage	40	135	71	138	23	43	15	35
Banks, insurance, real estate	267	503	239	408	33	89	15	44
Services	3,066	4,267	2,654	3,584	413	419	71	113
Communications	—	—	—	—	1	—	—	—
Activities not adequately described	13	—	6	—	—	—	1	—
Total	28,843	39,161	12,401	18,555	1,599	2,305	401	597

	20 to 49		50 to 99		100 and Over		Unspecified		Total	
	1967/68	1971	1967/68	1971	1967/68	1971	1967/68	1971	1967/68	1971
Agriculture, forestry, fishing	1	1	—	1	—	—	1	—	34*	85
Mining, quarrying	1	2	—	3	3	2	—	—	8	15
Manufacturing	79	105	12	16	17	18	5	—	9,174	9,638
Electricity, gas, water	3	8	4	2	7	9	—	—	82	122
Construction	22	29	10	13	24	30	5	—	416	696
Commerce	41	66	15	23	10	8	11	—	26,870	40,620
Transport, storage	4	17	3	5	4	8	1	—	161	381
Banks, insurance, real estate	25	42	4	12	3	6	—	—	586	1,104
Services	33	42	8	16	9	7	—	—	6,254	8,448
Communications	2	—	—	—	—	—	—	—	3	—
Activities not adequately described	3	—	—	—	—	—	2	—	25	—
Total	214	312	56	91	77	88	25	—	43,616	61,109

*The source gives the total as 37 establishments. Therefore, the total figure for row and column do not match.

Sources: 1967/68: CDS, Statistical Yearbook, 1388 A.H., vol. 4 (Riyadh, 1968), pp. 190-91; 1971: Ibid., 1391 A.H., vol. 7 (Riyadh, 1971).

In the commerce category 98.1 percent and in the service group 91.5 percent of the firms fell into the one-to-four-worker group. In the 1971 censuses the corresponding figures were 88, 97.1, and 92.9 percent for manufacturing, commerce, and services, respectively.

The censuses of establishments do not show the important gains made in recent years in the creation of a modern business sector because the statistics are dominated by the traditional sector. Statistics reflect the business sector, whose small shops and enterprises make up the largest portion of the survey statistics. There is, however, some information available on the development of the business sector in recent years that indicates the pace of modernization of this sector: the firms licensed under the Foreign Capital Investment Law and the protection and encouragement of National Industries Ordinance. Licenses issued under those two acts tend to be for modern, up-to-date types of businesses necessary to advance the nation's economic development.

Table 6.13 shows that in the modern, industrial sector considerable progress has been made on the road to development since the promulgation of the Protection and Encouragement of National Industries Ordinance in May 1962. By the end of 1971, 188 firms had been licensed to engage in business under the ordinance. They represent a diverse group ranging from food and beverage manufacture to construction and transportation equipment. Their size varies from 64 workers per establishment in food and beverages manufacture to seven per establishment in the machinery, appliances, and maintenance groups. The average number of workers per establishment was 29. The relatively large size of the firms established under the ordinance is also mirrored in the capital of the firms registered. The average capital per firm was S.R. 1.1 million, with the largest amount of capital invested in the construction and building group, followed by food and beverages and by leather, rubber, plastic, and chemical products. In terms of capital per establishment, construction and building stood in first place with S.R. 2.1 million, followed by food and beverages and by textile and wearing apparel with S.R. 1.6 million apiece. The smallest amount of capital per establishment, about S.R. 100,000, was invested in the machinery, appliances, and maintenance classification.

By the end of 1971, 66 industrial establishments had been set up under the Foreign Capital Investment Law. Although the number of employees in establishments licensed under this law is not available, it is certain that these firms employ larger numbers of workers per establishment than those enumerated in the Census of Establishments. At the end of 1971 S.R. 103.4 million, averaging S.R. 1.6 million per firm, had been invested in those 66 firms.[17]

TABLE 6.13

Operating Industrial Establishments Licensed Under the Protection and Encouragement of National Industries Ordinance, End of 1971
(capital in S.R. thousand)

Economic Activity	Number of Establishments	Total Capital	Capital per Establishment	Employment	Number of Workers per Establishment
Food, beverages	29	45,722	1,577	1,841	64
Textiles, wearing apparel	6	9,365	1,561	329	55
Furniture, fixtures (wood, metal)	29	6,678	230	514	18
Paper products, printing	26	10,905	419	420	16
Leather, rubber, plastic, chemical products	13	18,784	1,445	416	32
Construction, building materials	50	103,611	2,072	1,408	28
Metals, metal products	16	5,108	319	329	21
Machinery, appliances, maintenance	6	695	116	44	7
Transport equipment, supplies, repairs	4	684	171	40	10
Others	9	1,426	158	101	11
Total	188	202,978	1,080	5,442	29

Source: SAMA, Annual Report, 1391/92 A.H. (Jedda, 1973), p. 61.

In 1970 the Industrial Studies and Development Center carried out a survey of establishments with ten or more workers (see Table 6.14). The results offer an overview of the size, geographical distribution, and capital structure of the larger establishments. By far the largest proportion of establishments employing ten or more workers was concentrated on the west coast (50 percent), followed by the central and the eastern regions (29 and 19 percent, respectively). In terms of capital invested, the Eastern Province accounted for 58 percent of the paid-up capital and for nearly 70 percent of total capital. Compared to the Western and Central provinces the enterprises in the Eastern Province are more capital intensive, employing only 34 percent of the workers. The greater labor intensity of the economic activities located in the Western Province can be explained in part at least by the proximity of the Holy Cities to Jedda. Jedda is the point of entry and departure for most of the hadjis making the annual pilgrimage. To accommodate the hundreds of thousands of visitors requires a large service industry whose peak period of output is concentrated in the 60 days before and after the month of Dhul-Hijjah (the twelfth month of the Moslem year).

On the whole it appears that Saudi industry suffers from capacity underutilization. It has been estimated that the 271 plants surveyed operated at only about 64 percent of capacity.[18] The cause of this condition is not entirely known, but it has been suggested that "shortages of skilled manpower or raw materials, the small size of the product market, and intense competition from imports" are the main factors.[19]

There is some information available on the output of a small number of selected industries.[20] Cement production rose nearly 300 percent, from 30,300 tons in 1957/58 to 911,100 tons in 1972. Owing to this sharp increase in cement production, imports were reduced from 92 percent of consumption in 1958/59 to 44 percent in 1971. Other industries also registered important gains in production: Gypsum production rose 29 percent from 1966/67 to 1972; iron-bar production rose 114.9 percent, from 4,700 tons in 1968/69 to 10,100 tons in 1972; fertilizer output rose from 20,000 tons to 75,200 tons during the period 1970-72. The rises in iron-bar and fertilizer production are particularly significant, because they show that two of Petromin's largest nonoil investments have been successfully completed.

The above discussion of the private business sector has shown that despite the overwhelming influence of the traditional sector with its small, one-man establishments engaged in trade and related fields, there has developed a modern business sector in which future expansion will occur.

TABLE 6.14

Regional Distribution and Capital Structure of Selected Industries, 1970
(capital in S.R. thousand)

Region	Ten or More Workers		Paid-up Capital		Total Employed Capital*		Employment	
	Number	Percent	Amount	Percent	Amount	Percent	Number	Percent
Central Province	85	29	96,843	13	106,464	7	2,574	20
Western Province	149	50	221,560	29	353,783	24	5,666	45
Eastern Province	55	19	443,290	58	1,010,255	69	4,304	34
Other areas	5	2	87	—	90	—	61	1
Total	294	100	761,780	100	1,470,592	100	12,605	100

*Includes paid-up capital reserves accumulated through retained earnings plus borrowing and trade liability.

Source: SAMA, Annual Report, 1391/92 A.H. (Jedda, 1973), p. 60.

On November 30, 1962, the government established the General Petroleum and Mineral Organization (Petromin), because "[t]he Ministry of Petroleum and Mineral Resources could not, because of its governmental capacity, function as a business organization and participate in joint ventures involving foreign investment."[21] The organization was established to meet the country's need in five areas:

1. Implementing and administering public petroleum and mineral projects,
2. Importing (directly or through agents) all needed minerals,
3. Preparing needed studies dealing with mineral resources and planning and implementing various operations associated with oil exploration, exploitation, distribution, and marketing,
4. Undertaking, in cooperation with private domestic and foreign companies, the advancement of the activities not undertaken by the Ministry of Petroleum and Mineral Resources that are required to accelerate the growth of the oil and minerals sector,
5. Establishing inside and outside the Kingdom "companies with the purpose of engaging in all phases of the industry of petroleum and minerals and their derivatives and by-products including trade transactions, transportation, sales distribution and marketing."[22]

The establishment of Petromin represents a major break with past practice. The contracts with Aramco and Arabian Oil Company (Japan) (AOC) were concluded between a private company and the government creating certain legal problems (see Chapter 7). The creation of Petromin interposed an agent for the government, thus eliminating the legal questions arising out of a direct, contractual relationship between the government and a private company. The rules governing Petromin's activities are general enough to allow the company "to hold interest or participate, in any manner whatsoever, in companies or organizations which are engaged in activities similar to its own or which may assist it in the attainment of its objectives, whether in the Kingdom or abroad."[23]

Since its inception Petromin has been active in many sectors of the economy. In addition to its activities in the oil sector, the organization has operated in a number of industries (for its oil sector operations see Chapter 9). To exploit the abundant amounts of natural gas found in the oil field, much of which is flared, Petromin established the Saudi Arabian Fertilizers Company (Safco). Construction of the plant began in 1967 and experimental production began in 1970 with an output of 20,000 tons of urea. By 1972 output had reached over 75,000 tons of urea, and in 1973 output almost doubled to 150,000 tons, of which 112,000 tons were exported.

The Jedda steel-rolling mill began production toward the end of 1967. Designed to produce 45,000 tons of steel products per annum with three shifts of workers, the mill has made rather slow progress toward capacity operation. In 1970 the plant produced 8,500 tons of iron bars, 9,841 in 1971, and 13,00 tons in 1973. It is estimated that output will reach the 15,000-ton mark in 1974. Currently, Petromin is planning a second steel mill in al-Jubail on the Arabian Gulf.

In June 1971 the Petromin Sulphuric Acid Plant began operations with a design capacity of 50 tons per day, producing 3,000 tons of sulfuric acid by the end of 1971 and 5,700 tons in 1972.

INTERNATIONAL TRADE

Balance of Payments

Table 6.15 gives the balance of payments from 1963 to 1973. In 1963 total receipts on current account amounted to S.R. 5.2 billion and total payments to S.R. 4.5 billion, generating a surplus of S.R. 738 million. In 1973 total receipts were S.R. 35.9 billion and total payments S.R. 25.9 billion, resulting in a surplus of S.R. 10 billion. Except for the two-year period 1968-69 Saudi Arabia had a surplus on current account.

The changes in the current account of the balance of payments must be divided into two time periods: 1963-69, when the oil companies controlled all aspects of the exploitation and sale of petroleum, and since 1970, when, following the Teheran Conference, the oil-producing states wrested control of the industry from the companies. From 1963 to 1967 total receipts on current account grew about 9.7 percent per year, and total payments about 14 percent. The deficit of S.R. 549 million in 1968 and S.R. 535 million in 1969 resulted from a number of events, the most important of which was the Arab-Israeli conflict of 1967. From 1967 to 1969 total receipts on current account rose 17.4 percent and total payments 31.4 percent. The sharp increase in total payments resulted from a 38-percent rise in the value of imports and a 19.9-percent rise in investment-income payments. The addition in the value of imports was the consequence of an increase in the absorptive capacity associated with the development effort, which led to a sharp augmentation of the demand for all types of goods.* In addition, the closing of the Suez Canal led to in-

*The Index of Quantum of Imports rose about 60 percent, from 147.6 in 1967/68 to 235.8 in 1969/70 (1963/64 = 100).

TABLE 6.15

Balance of Payments Estimates of Saudi Arabia, 1963-73
(S.R. million)

	1963	1964	1965	1966	1967	1968	1969	1970	1971	1972	1973
Current Account											
Receipts											
Exports, f.o.b.[a]	4,761	4,675	5,373	6,930	7,038	8,028	8,303	9,810	16,294	21,795	33,409
Oil royalties other than Aramco	162	189	203	202	225	248	243	297	333	420	448
Pilgrimage	180	239	256	266	284	324	423	459	485	653	909
Miscellaneous	95	126	198	234	333	360	315	405	478	655	1,123
Total receipts	5,198	5,229	6,030	7,632	7,880	8,960	9,248	10,971	17,610	23,523	35,889
Payments											
Imports, c.i.f.	1,440	1,773	2,259	2,830	2,912	3,838	4,018	4,010	4,226	5,769	7,359[b]
Nonmonetary gold	50	54	63	72	67	50	58	81	42	40	50
Investment income payments	2,056	1,733	1,985	2,727	2,709	3,118	3,245	4,018	6,446	8,496	12,350
Government expenditures abroad[c]	243	315	342	365	621	1,215	1,251	1,206	1,232	1,240	2,986
Travel and personal transportation	176	198	243	302	374	428	468	554	649	793	1,050
Tapline expenditures abroad	117	99	99	99	103	108	104	72	212	195	180
Other services	378	436	598	643	689	752	675	747	798	1,138	1,932
Total payments	4,460	4,608	5,589	7,038	7,475	9,509	9,819	10,688	13,605	17,671	25,907

Current account surplus or deficit	+ 738	+ 639	+ 441	+ 594	+ 405	- 549	- 535	+ 283	+4,005	+5,852	+9,982
Capital and Financing Account											
Direct investment liability[d]	- 50	- 63	- 243	- 342	- 167	- 81	- 22	- 14	- 490	-1,487	- 220[e]
Other foreign capital[f]	- 544	+ 117	- 104	+ 230	- 157	- 428	- 45	- 446	+ 762	+1,050	+3,978
Gold, foreign exchange holdings and investments of SAMA[g]	+1,066	+ 401	+ 630	+ 508	+ 293	- 306	- 572	+ 392	+3,573[h]	+5,480	+6,044
Commercial banks net foreign position[g]	+ 149	+ 27	- 121	- 68	+ 220	- 54	+ 45	+ 104	+ 103	+ 741	+ 125
Errors and omissions	+ 117	+ 157	+ 279	+ 266	+ 216	+ 320	+ 59	+ 247	+ 57	+ 68	+ 55

[a]Realized prices.
[b]Provisional.
[c]Including the aid to other Arab countries.
[d](-) = increase; (+) = decrease.
[e]Valuation at parity rate prior to third week of December 1971.
[f](-) = inflow; (+) = outflow.
[g](-) = decrease; (+) = increase.
[h]Net of compensation paid to Aramco for 25 percent in its oil production facilities.

Source: SAMA, Annual Report, 1392/93 A.H. (Jedda, 1974), pp. 100-01.

creases in freight charges. By far the most important rise in payments on current account, however, was the rise in government expenditures abroad. It rose by more than 100 percent, from S.R. 621 million in 1967 to S.R. 1,251 million in 1969, primarily because of the subsidies paid to Egypt and Jordan following the War of 1967.*

The deficits of 1968 and 1969 are important, because they strengthened the government's contention that under the prevailing arrangements between the government and the oil companies the income from oil exploitation was insufficient to meet all demands made on the government. Both guns and butter could not be had unless the government's influence in the oil industry supplanted that of the oil companies. It is certain that the deficits in the balance of payments together with the deficit in the budget were important factors in the timing of the takeover of the price-setting mechanism, beginning with the Teheran Conference. Furthermore, by 1970 the country had enough adequately trained Saudi citizens to reduce the reliance on foreign experts in the day-to-day operation of the industry.

The generally favorable balance-of-payments position since 1963 has been reflected in the gold and foreign-exchange holdings of SAMA. In 1963 gold, foreign-exchange holdings, and investments abroad rose S.R. 1.1 billion. It reached a low point in 1969, when SAMA's holdings declined S.R. 572 million, and reached a high in 1973 with a positive balance of S.R. 6 billion.

The Composition of Imports

The value of total imports into Saudi Arabia between 1958/59 and 1972 rose nearly threefold, from S.R. 965 million to S.R. 4.7 billion, at an average annual growth rate of 15.5 percent. Except for 1967/68, imports rose in every year. The slight decline in 1967/68 was the consequence of the restructuring of the Kingdom's international transportation pattern, owing to the War of 1967. During the 12-year period under discussion the value of imported foodstuffs rose from S.R. 317 million to S.R. 1.2 billion, at an average annual rate of growth of 13.2 percent. This substantial increase reflects the increasing prosperity of the population, which has led to a switch from the traditional diet of rice, lamb, and goat to a more varied diet including beef, canned fruits and vegetables, ice cream, and so on. The slight decline in the value of food imports from 1968/69 to 1969/70 was associated with the slowdown in the frantic

---

*The Arab subsidies amounted to S.R. 157.5 million in 1967, S.R. 630 million in 1968, and S.R. 661.5 million since 1968.

pace of development caused by cutbacks in government spending necessitated by the Arab subsidy program (see Table 6.16).

The rapid pace of the development effort during the 1960s is shown by the imports of building materials and machinery. The value of imports of building material rose 439 percent, at an annual rate of 16.3 percent, from 1958/59 to 1972. The effect of the building of cement factories and the steel-rolling mill in Jedda is clearly reflected in the relatively small increase in the value of cement and iron bars and sheets imported. While the value of imports of wood and timber rose more than 340 percent, from S.R. 17 million to S.R. 75 million, cement imports rose only slightly more than 50 percent during the period 1958/59 to 1972, and if we take the period 1968/69 to 1972, there was a decrease in the value of cement imports. The value of iron bars and sheets imported rose more than sevenfold from 1958/59 to 1972, but it rose only 22 percent from 1970 to 1972, reflecting the completion of the Jedda steel mill. The value of machinery and electrical- and transport-equipment imports rose more than 5.5 times from 1958/59 to 1972. Within this group the value of transportation equipment imports rose nearly 700 percent, machinery 1,650 percent, and agricultural machinery more than 1,000 percent.

As far as the distribution of imports by major classes is concerned, there was very little change. In 1958/59 food, textiles, and clothing accounted for 43.8 percent of the value of imports; building materials, 9.2 percent; machinery, etc., 26.5 percent; chemical products (including toiletries), 5.9 percent; and miscellaneous commodities, 14.5 percent. By 1965/66 the distribution was 36.6 percent for food, textiles, and clothing; 12.1 percent for building materials; 31.9 percent for machinery, etc.; 4.9 percent for chemical products; and 14.5 percent miscellaneous. Since that year the percent distribution has remained essentially the same. The changes in the composition of imports in favor of building materials and machinery suggests that the government's efforts to direct resources away from consumption and toward industrial goods needed for development has met with some success. It is significant that following the huge increases in revenues resulting from increases in oil, prices have not shifted the composition of imports back to a larger share of consumption goods.

The Geographic Distribution of Foreign Trade

During the 11-year period from 1960/61 to 1972 total exports rose more than fivefold, from S.R. 3.9 billion to S.R. 24.1 billion, at an annual rate of growth of 18 percent (see Table 6.17). During the same time imports rose more than 300 percent, from S.R. 1.1

TABLE 6.16

Composition of Imports, 1958/59 to 1971
(S.R. million)

	1958/59	1962/63	1963/64	1964/65	1965/66	1966/67	1967/68	1968/69	1969/70	1970[b]	1971	1972
Foodstuffs	317	396	432	496	600	693	666	894	865	1,011	1,097	1,222
Building materials	89[a]	152	154	183	248	305	199	430	413	389	463	480
Wood, timber, and so on	17	25	30	44	58	53	45	52	68	62	78	75
Cement	23	23	20	27	32	37	25	48	67	48	58	35
Iron bars, sheets	15 }	69 }	77	42	51	61	48	78	92	107	82	131
Pipes and parts	25 }			29	51	43	40	100	79	83	149	155
Textiles and clothing	106	103	131	167	154	148	147	154	157	142	203	344
Machinery, and so on	256	320	353	452	656	708	709	880	1,022	1,018	1,099	1,686
Cars (including buses, trucks, tractors)	50	108	150	183	262	219	220	222	293	273	255	392
Machinery	30			96	140	184	150	213	199	231	304	500
Agricultural machinery	8	88	92	9	10	23	46	46	64	59	53	89
Air conditioners and refrigerators	5			20	23	26	24	45	51	46	47	49
Batteries	5	6	6	7	7	9	10	9	8	5	8	9
Parts of cars, trucks, tractors	38	35	40	54	70	75	74	76	84	61	63	80
Radio, household electrical appliances	8	15 }	29	22	22	29	22	40	49	31	33	79
Electric machinery (including parts)	41	9 }		5	9	22	26	6	5	3	3	8
Railroad equipment	1	1	1	1	1	2	12	2	2	2	5	3
Aircraft	8	15	7	9	12	34	67	52	62	63	64	166
Ships, boats, and so on	1	1	4	3	19	8	6	12	32	6	11	18
Chemical products	57	73	68	85	101	118	111	159	238	180	240	244
Medicine, drugs	18	23	26	36	43	52	42	63	65	69	109	102
Soaps, and so on	7	11	12	9	7	6	5	6	7	5	7	14
Perfumes, and so on	4	4	4	4	5	6	6	10	13	13	16	22
Miscellaneous	140	222	220	310	299	286	380	287	518	462	565	732
Total imports	965	1,266	1,353	1,693	2,058	2,258	2,212	2,804	3,213	3,197	3,667	4,708

[a]The detail does not add up to the various subtotals because only selected items are listed.

[b]A slight double counting with the year 1969/70 is unavoidable because of the overlapping relationship between the Hijra and the Gregorian calendars.

Source: SAMA, Annual Report, various years.

billion to S.R. 4.7 billion, at an annual rate of 14.1 percent. As would be expected, Western Europe and Asia accounted for about 80 percent of the exports, and Western Europe, Asia, the Middle East, and North America accounted for more than 90 percent of total imports.

By far the largest portion of the nation's international trade takes place with Western Europe. In 1960/61 exports to Western Europe amounted to S.R. 1.4 billion (35.6 percent of total exports). This share rose consistently at an annual rate of 21.1 percent, reaching S.R. 12.6 billion, or about 55.5 percent, in 1972. There has been a slight shift in the ranking of the three most important European buyers of Saudi oil. In 1960/61 Italy, West Germany, and the Netherlands were the most important recipients with 8.4, 7, and 6.3 percent of total exports, respectively. In 1972 the Netherlands stood in first place, with 11.9 percent, followed by Italy with 11.2 percent, and France, with 9.3 percent of total exports.

Western Europe was also the largest source of imports, which rose from S.R. 0.4 billion (35.6 percent) in 1960/61 to S.R. 1.3 billion (28.6 percent) in 1972. At the beginning of the period the United Kingdom was the largest supplier of goods, with S.R. 0.9 billion (8.6 percent of all imports), followed by West Germany (6.6 percent), and the Netherlands (6.1 percent). By 1972 the United Kingdom and West Germany still stood in first and second place, with 7.3 and 6.2 percent of total imports, respectively, followed by the Netherlands and Italy with 4 percent of imports apiece.

The second largest destination of Saudi exports is Asia, which absorbed 17.3 percent of total exports in 1960/61 and 24.3 percent in 1972. Of course, Japan received the lion's share of the nation's exports (11.2 percent of total 1960/61 exports), followed by India (2.9 percent). In 1972 Japan bought S.R. 3.4 billion (15.1 percent) of exports, and India and Pakistan each absorbed about 1 percent. The effect of the recent price increases of crude oil is reflected in the small increase in exports to India. In 1971 India bought S.R. 222.1 million of the Kingdom's oil exports, and in 1972 S.R. 230.5 million. This very small increase of 3.8 percent (S.R. 8.4 million) compares with an S.R. 91.2 million (69.7 percent) for the period 1970-71. Clearly, the increases in the price of oil have severely damaged India's ability to acquire the needed energy imports to guarantee its economic development. Imports from Asia have risen consistently during the period under discussion. In 1972 they amounted to S.R. 1 billion, or 22 percent of total imports.

The most drastic effect of the oil-price increases can be seen in exports to Africa, which fell more than 50 percent from 1971 to 1972. However, even with that drastic reduction in oil imports, the African nations were unable to eliminate the deficit they had with

TABLE 6.17

Geographic Origin of Exports and Imports, Selected Years

	1960/61		1964/65		1968/69	
	S.R. Million	Per-cent	S.R. Million	Per-cent	S.R. Million	Per-cent
Exports						
North America	475.1	12.2	569.6	9.5	383.3	4.3
Western Europe	1,382.2	35.6	2,233.3	37.3	3,794.4	42.4
Eastern Europe	—	—	—	—	—	—
Middle East	647.5	16.8	649.7	10.9	569.4	6.3
Africa	64.1	1.2	131.1	2.2	312.8	3.5
Asia	678.1	17.3	1,539.6	25.7	2,690.0	30.0
South America	217.7	5.6	222.9	3.7	249.1	2.8
Oceanea	126.1	3.2	257.4	4.3	258.0	2.9
Total	3,888.4[a]	100.0	5,984.4[b]	100.0	8,952.9[c]	100.0
Imports						
North America	217.3	20.6	347.4	20.5	577.6	20.6
Western Europe	375.1	35.6	586.0	34.6	866.5	30.9
Eastern Europe	13.7	1.3	35.4	2.1	43.3	1.5
Middle East	253.9	24.1	365.0	21.6	556.3	19.9
Africa	49.1	4.7	83.6	4.9	166.0	5.9
Asia	149.5	14.2	252.6	14.9	545.1	19.4
South America	—	—	1.2	0.1	1.6	0.1
Oceanea	8.0	0.8	21.5	1.3	40.0	1.4
Total	1,052.9	100.0	1,692.7	100.0	2,804.0	100.0

1969		1970		1971		1972	
S.R. Million	Per-cent	S.R. Million	Per-cent	S.R. Million	Per-cent	S.R. Million	Per-cent
320.3	3.4	146.4	1.3	733.3	4.2	1,313.6	5.8
4,084.7	43.0	4,820.3	44.2	8,386.1	48.5	12,622.4	55.5
4.9	0.1	—	—	—	—	—	—
594.3	6.2	608.6	5.6	805.7	4.7	858.8	3.8
409.5	4.3	473.7	4.3	758.9	4.4	357.4	1.6
2,825.2	29.8	3,339.4	30.6	4,413.7	25.5	5,536.9	24.3
292.0	3.1	445.0	4.1	973.9	5.6	1,207.2	5.3
270.4	2.8	308.1	2.8	254.1	1.5	150.0	0.6
9,496.2[c]	100.0	10,907.2[e]	100.0	17,302.7[f]	100.0	24,120.7[g]	100.0
626.9	18.6	575.6	18.0	629.2	17.2	924.9	19.7
1,228.6	36.4	1,080.8	33.8	1,218.3	33.2	1,345.5	28.6
52.4	1.6	69.3	2.2	77.1	2.1	93.1	2.0
629.7	18.6	636.2	19.9	810.0	22.1	1,036.6	22.0
152.0	4.5	127.4	4.0	152.4	4.2	180.2	3.7
625.1	18.5	610.8	19.1	711.9	19.4	1,033.1	22.0
0.2	0.1	1.0	0.1	1.0	0.1	9.0	0.2
62.1	1.8	94.6	3.0	65.9	1.8	85.7	1.8
3,377.0	100.0	3,197.2[h]	100.0	3,667.5[i]	100.0	4,708.3	100.0

[a]Includes S.R. 297.6 million various exports.
[b]Includes S.R. 380.8 million various exports.
[c]Includes S.R. 693.2 million various exports.
[d]Includes S.R. 694.9 million various exports.
[e]Includes S.R. 405.6 million bunker fuel.
[f]Includes S.R. 592 million bunker fuel.
[g]Includes S.R. 1.5 million others.
[h]Includes S.R. 1.7 million others.
[i]Includes S.R. 1,359.5 million others.

Source: SAMA, Annual Report, various years.

Saudi Arabia. In 1972 exports from Saudi Arabia to Africa amounted to S.R. 357.4 million, and imports from Africa amounted to only S.R. 180.2 million: a gap of S.R. 177 million.

In view of the current (October 1974) domestic developments in the United States, it is important to take a closer look at the Kingdom's trade statistics to show how important the price increases since 1971 in Saudi oil have been to the United States. In 1970 the United States imported S.R. 97.8 million ($21.7 million) and exported to Saudi Arabia goods valued at S.R. 568.5 million ($126.3 million); that is, Saudi Arabia's purchases of U.S. goods exceeded receipts by S.R. 471 million ($104.6 million). In 1971 exports to the United States amounted to S.R. 589 million and imports to S.R. 615.1 million. Again, Saudi Arabia purchased more from the United States than the United States did from Saudi Arabia. By 1972 exports to the United States almost doubled, and imports increased by nearly 50 percent. Thus, 1972 was the first year that the United States paid more to Saudi Arabia than the Kingdom paid to the United States in the form of imports. This trend has continued since 1972. Nevertheless, the figures until 1972 do not justify the U.S. claim that oil imports from Saudi Arabia constituted a significant factor in recent U.S. price trends; so long as the United States imports the relatively small quantities of oil reflected in the above statistics, it is unreasonable to blame the U.S. inflation on the rising price of Arab oil. Furthermore, it must be remembered that a good deal of the outflow of dollars is offset by the value of the substantial U.S. exports to Saudi Arabia.

NOTES

1. CDS, Statistical Yearbook, 1386 A.H., vol. 2 (Riyadh, 1966), p. 119.
2. CPO, Development Plan, 1390 A.H. (Riyadh, n.d.), p. 249.
3. Author's private information.
4. CDS, Statistical Yearbook, 1386 A.H., p. 126.
5. Ibid., p. 127.
6. For additional information see "A Dam in Saudi Arabia," Aramco World Magazine 25, no. 2 (March-April 1974): 4 ff.
7. CDS, Statistical Yearbook, 1386 A.H., p. 130.
8. Ibid., p. 121.
9. SAMA, Annual Report, 1392/93 A.H. (Jedda, 1974), p. 53.
10. Edmond Y. Asfour, Saudi Arabia: Long Term Projections of Supply of and Demand for Agricultural Products (Beirut: American University of Beirut, 1965), p. 64.
11. Ibid.
12. SAMA, Annual Report, 1387/88 A.H. (Jedda, 1969), pp. 28-29.

13. This summary is based on K. S. Twitchel, Saudi Arabia, 3d ed. (Princeton, N.J.: Princeton University Press, 1958), pp. 29-33.

14. SAMA, Annual Report, 1390/91 A.H. (Jedda, 1972), p. 26.

15. Ibid., pp. 181, 183.

16. Ibid., p. 182.

17. SAMA, Annual Report, 1391/92 A.H. (Jedda, 1973), p. 62.

18. Said H. Hitti and Georg T. Abeel, "The Economy and Finances of Saudi Arabia," International Monetary Fund Staff Papers 21, no. 2 (July 1974): 266.

19. Ibid.

20. SAMA, Annual Report, p. 105.

21. Ahmed Zaki Yamani, in Petromin Progress Report 1968, p. 5.

22. Ibid., p. 9.

23. Ibid.

CHAPTER 7
THE GOVERNMENT AND THE ARABIAN AMERICAN OIL COMPANY

The relationship between government and the oil companies is determined by agreements defining the privileges granted to the companies and establishing the obligations under which the companies are permitted to operate in the Kingdom. Until 1965 three companies held exploration and exploitation licenses: the Arabian American Oil Company (Aramco), granted in 1933; the Getty Oil Company, 1949; and the Arabian Oil Company (Japan) (AOC), 1957. The nature of these agreements differed from company to company, depending on the year the basic agreement was written and the geographic area of the company's operation. The Aramco agreement was a concession in which the concessor, the government, grants the concessionaire the right to exploit the Kingdom's oil resources. The government received compensation for this concession but had no right to a portion of company profits and no influence on its policy. The Getty agreement and those following departed from the concession principle in that they provide, among other things, for a share of the company's net profits.

The contracts written between 1933 and 1957 can be divided into six parts, dealing with the following aspects of government-company relations: the size of the original concession area and the relinquishment of unexplored regions of this area; length of contract and termination; types of compensation to be made to the government, the amounts and methods of payment; the time at which the various payments must begin following the discovery of oil in commercial quantities; provisions limiting the impact of the company and the company's non-Saudi employees on Saudi society; and the disposition of company property at the time of agreement termination.

The first agreement was entered into at a time when the government officials were relatively inexperienced in dealing with the international oil companies, so it was to be expected that the government would demand revisions in the agreements. Until 1960 this meant primarily changes in the Aramco agreements. With the relinquishment of parts of Aramco's concessions, new agreements were written with other oil companies, and the government relinquished its role as landlord and became an active partner in the exploration for and the exploitation of oil.

In 1965 an exploration license was issued to the Societe Auxiliaire de la Regie Autonome des Petroles (Auxirap), ushering in a new phase in the government-company relationship. Two years later the General Petroleum and Mineral Organization (Petromin), a Saudi government corporation, was granted exclusive licenses for exploration and exploitation in two areas: the Rub al-Khali (the Empty Quarter) and along the coast of the Red Sea. Petromin in turn entered into agreements with several oil companies, assigning all rights granted to it under these licenses to them.

In this chapter we will trade the development of the Aramco-government agreement. The other agreements will be discussed in Chapter 8. To maintain historical continuity, however, brief mention must be made of the short-lived agreement of 1923 between the Eastern and General Syndicate and Abd al-Aziz al Saud.

THE EASTERN AND GENERAL SYNDICATE

In 1922 Major Frank Holmes, a representative of a British group of investors, entered into negotiations with Abd al-Aziz al Saud for an exploration license in the al-Hasa region of eastern Arabia. Encouraged by discoveries on Baharain Island, 12 miles offshore, Holmes believed that oil might be found in al-Hasa. One year later the Syndicate was granted a concession covering more than 30,000 square miles. The agreement provided for an annual payment of £2,000 for exploration rights and obligated the Syndicate to arrange for exploitation as soon as oil was found in commercial quantities. The government reserved cancellation rights of the concession in case of default on the rental payments or an interruption of exploration of more than 18 months.

The Syndicate was not an oil company but a group of entrepreneurs who hoped to interest British companies in the exploitation of Eastern Arabian oil resources. They failed to attract support and ceased exploration in 1925. The concession was formally declared void in 1928.

THE ARABIAN AMERICAN OIL COMPANY

The contractual relationship between the Saudi Arabian government and Aramco has changed considerably in the course of time. As the company's activities expanded, it became apparent that the Original Concession Agreement did not protect and advance the government's interests properly. Continuous negotiations ensued, with the government demanding changes in the agreements and Aramco defending its position but eventually yielding to government demands. From 1933 to 1960 these negotiations were carried out between the government and the company. Since 1960 the negotiations have taken place within the framework of the Organization of Petroleum Exporting Countries (OPEC), which was founded by the oil-producing states in an effort to strengthen their bargaining position with the international oil companies.

The Original Concession Agreement was executed with the Standard Oil Company of California (Socal). Several months later the franchise was transferred to the California Arabian Standard Oil Company (Casoc), a wholly owned subsidiary of Socal. In 1936 the Texas Company (Texaco) acquired a one-half interest in Casoc, and in 1944 the company name was changed to Arabian American Oil Company (Aramco).

By the end of World War II the enormous extent of the Saudi oil reserves had been recognized. It became apparent that large amounts of investment capital as well as an extensive network of market outlets would be needed for the most efficient exploitation of Saudi oil. Negotiations initiated in 1946 with a number of oil companies culminated in 1947 when Standard Oil of New Jersey (Exxon) and the Socony-Vacuum Oil Company (Mobil) each bought shares in Aramco. From 1948 to 1972 ownership of Aramco was distributed as follows: Socal, 30 percent; Texaco, 30 percent; Exxon, 30 percent; and Mobil, 10 percent. In 1972 the government demanded a share in Aramco's ownership. Following the Participation Agreement of December 20, 1972, Petromin owned 25 percent of Aramco; Socal, Texaco, and Exxon held 22.5 percent each, and Mobil's share was 7.5 percent. The Participation Agreement was the first step in the government's takeover of Aramco's ownership.

The changing relationship between the government and the company can be divided into three periods. From 1933 to 1949 the basic compensation (royalties) was laid down, and the government's basic share from oil production was fixed. Also determined during this period was the largest extent of the concession area and the eventual relinquishments of those parts of the area in which the company did not intend to explore. A number of minor adjustments owing to war conditions occurred. From 1950 to 1971 numerous important agreement revisions and amendments were made. Beginning with the so-called fifty-fifty principle of profit sharing, the government's aim was to establish a precise definition of taxable net income and a stable starting point for tax liability calculations. Among the major changes were the use of posted prices in billings to offtakers, capitalization of exploration and intangible development costs, expensing of royalties, the elimination of third-party sales, and OPEC allowances.*

With the Teheran Agreement on February 2, 1971, a new era began in the relationship between the company and the government. Until that time control over production and marketing policies rested exclusively with Aramco and, thus, with the international oil companies. Posted prices and output were determined by the oil companies based upon their evaluation of the demand and supply conditions in the international oil market. In 1971 the oil producing countries wrested control over posted prices from the international oil companies, and about two years later the Participation Agreement between Aramco and Petromin opened the door to extensive Saudi marketing of Saudi oil.

The Original Concession Agreement

On May 29, 1933, Socal and the government of Saudi Arabia signed an agreement[1] granting the company "the exclusive right, for a period of 60 years, to explore, prospect, drill for, extract, treat, manufacture, transport, deal with, carry away, and export" oil and oil products, and to create the facilities to carry out these activities. The company was granted an "exclusive" exploration area of more than 400,000 square miles, covering almost all of eastern Saudi Arabia. It also provided for a "preference right" to acquire additional concessions in the remaining area of eastern Saudi Arabia, as well as any rights that the government might acquire in the so-called Neutral Zone south of Kuwait (see Map 6).

---

*Posted (published) prices are prices at which a supplier will sell oil to purchasers in cargo lots f.o.b. the supplier's terminal. They may differ from realized prices, and since 1960 they have primarily been used as tax-reference prices for the calculation of tax liabilities due the host countries' governments.

MAP 6

Areas of Aramco Concessions, 1933-63

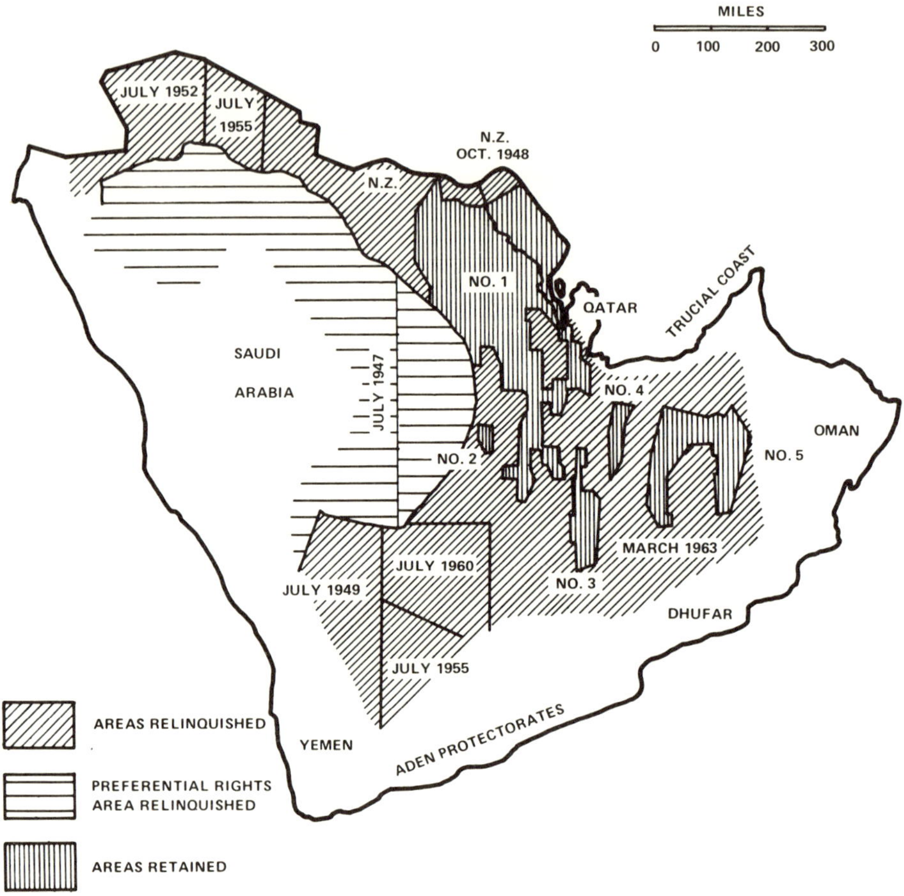

Source: Arabian American Oil Co., Aramco 1963, p. 12.

In return for these concessions the company agreed to meet the following conditions:

1. A loan of £30,000 gold or its equivalent, was to be payable within 15 days of the effective date of the agreement. An additional loan of £20,000 gold after 18 months, if the agreement was still in force. Repayment of those loans was to be made by deductions from one-half of the anticipated royalties owing to the government.

2. An "annual rental" payment of £5,000 gold, was to be payable in advance until the discovery of commercial quantities of oil.

3. Upon discovery of oil in commercial quantities the company was to make an immediate advance royalty payment of £50,000 and another payment of the same amount one year later. Repayment was to be made out of anticipated royalties. Furthermore, the company agreed to begin relinquishment of areas it chose not to explore, within 90 days of the discovery of oil in commercial quantities.

4. Once oil had been discovered the government was to receive a royalty on all net crude produced, sold, and run from field storage:

> . . . after first deducting:
> (a) Water and foreign substances; and
> (b) Oil required for the customary operations of the company's installations within Saudi Arabia; and
> (c) The oil required for manufacturing the amounts of gasoline and kerosene to be provided free each year to the government. . . .

The rate of royalty was to be four shillings, gold, or its equivalent per ton. In addition, a royalty payment was stipulated "equal to one-eighth of the proceeds of the sale" of natural gas produced, saved, and sold.

5. The company agreed to build a refinery as soon as practicable after oil discovery and to supply 200,000 gallons (U.S.) of gasoline and 100,000 gallons (U.S.) of kerosene to the government without charge.

6. The government agreed that "the company and enterprise shall be exempt from all direct and indirect taxes, imports, charges, fees and duties (including, of course, import and export duties). . . ."

The Original Agreement could have been more favorable to the Kingdom. Although it provided for loans totaling £50,000 and an annual rental of £5,000, the government's share from any possible future lifting of oil was relatively small. The agreement accurately reflects the relative bargaining positions of the two parties. When the government signed the agreement it had no experience in the oil business. The King's major objective was to gain relief from severe fiscal difficulties caused by the decline in the number of pilgrims coming to Mecca. As long as the presence of oil was only a gleam in thc geologist's eye, the question of total compensation for the privilege of depleting the Kingdom's resources was given less attention than it deserved. Instead, the government's effort was directed toward the immediate fiscal benefits to be gained in the form of "rentals" and loans. The company supplied the know-how and funds to develop the Kingdom's potential resources, and the government decided to collect a rent for the use of the land.

Royalty payments as the government's basic compensation for the exploitation of oil resources shows the influence of U.S. legal practice. In the United States, ownership of subsurface minerals rests with the owner of the land. If the owner of the land grants the right of exploitation to another party, he is entitled to a royalty. In crude-oil production this means that the concessionaire must deliver one-eighth of the oil extracted to the landowner. Cash payments in lieu of delivery of oil are often arranged. The one-eighth share of the concessor is a minimum. Other factors, such as quality of the crude, duration of concession, and so on, may lead to higher payments. For taxation purposes the receipt of a royalty is income to the concessor and a deductible business expense to the concessionaire.

The Original Concession Agreement followed this practice but did not take into account one important point: The owner of the oil is a sovereign government. This means that the Saudi government should have received two types of payments: the royalty payment owing the landlord and a share of the income from the sale of oil owing to the fiscal authority. Thus Article 21, exempting the company from "all direct and indirect taxes," deprived the Kingdom of an important source of revenue and gave the company potentially enormous returns on its investment. It might be argued that considering the government solely as an owner of resources and compensating it under this assumption is unfair, because the company is subject to income taxes in its home country, but that consideration is irrelevant. Business firms operating in a foreign country have always been subject to the payment of taxes on the income earned in the host country. Furthermore, the first oil concession agreement signed in the Middle East recognized that the concessionaire was subject to two kinds of financial obligations: royalty and income tax.

Supplemental Concession Agreement of May 31, 1939

On October 16, 1938, the company announced the discovery of oil in commercial quantities, and on May 1, 1939, the first cargo of Saudi Arabian crude oil was shipped from Ras Tanura. Encouraged by these events, the government agreed to enlarge the original concession area in the northern and southern regions of eastern Arabia, and to grant the company the right of exploration in the Saudi portions of the Neutral Zones between Saudi Arabia and Iraq and between Saudi Arabia and Kuwait. This raised the size of the exclusive area to approximately 495,000 square miles, of which 484,000 square miles were onshore and 11,000 miles offshore. The new concession was granted for a period of 60 years, and the period of the Original Agreement was extended by six years. The company was granted a ten-year moratorium on the relinquishment of any portion of the exclusive area. In return for those additional privileges the company agreed to meet the following conditions:

1. Upon completion of the ten-year moratorium on relinquishment, the company would give up from time to time those areas of the exclusive area it no longer wished to explore.
2. An immediate payment of £140,000 gold and an additional £100,000 gold upon discovery of oil in commercial quantities.
3. An annual rental of £20,000 for the additional area payable until oil was found in commercial quantities.
4. An increase in the amount of free gasoline and kerosene to 1.3 million and 100,000 gallons, respectively.

The Agreement of October 10, 1948

The search for oil led eventually to the offshore areas. The right to explore offshore had been fixed in previous agreements, without distinction in the payments to be made for oil lifted in these areas. In October 1948 an agreement was signed covering royalty payments from offshore operations. The company agreed to pay the same amount of royalty as provided in the Original Concession Agreement plus five cents (U.S.) on each barrel recovered offshore. Furthermore, Aramco guaranteed a minimum annual royalty from offshore oil of $2 million payable in advance. If Aramco elected to pay the royalty in gold pounds, the conversion was to take place at $35 per ounce of gold. The additional five cents per barrel, however, was always to be calculated in U.S. currency. Aramco gave up its rights to the Saudi portion of the Kuwait Neutral Zone and set out a 22-year schedule of periodical relinquishment of those parts of the "exclusive" area in which it did not want to carry out further exploration.

The 50-50 Profit Sharing Agreement

Between 1948 and 1950 Aramco exploration teams substantiated the existence of huge oil deposits. Numerous producing wells were drilled and the true magnitude of the Kingdom's oil deposits was established. Encouraged by the Venezuelan example, Saudi Arabia asked for a more equitable division of the enormous profits realized by the company. Following a period of intensive negotiations and strained relations an agreement was concluded on December 30, 1950, providing for income-tax payments on the profits of oil sales.* With this agreement a new era began in the relationship between the government and Aramco. From now on the most important questions between the two parties became: What is net income, and who controls posted prices?

In the Agreement of December 30, 1950, Aramco submitted to payment of income taxes called for in the Royal Decrees of November 4, 1950, and December 27, 1950, provided that:

> in no case shall the total of such taxes and all other taxes, royalties, rentals and exactions of the Government for any year exceed fifty percent (50%) of the gross income of Aramco, after such gross income has been reduced by Aramco's cost of operation, including losses and depreciation, and by income taxes, if any, payable to any foreign country, but not reduced by taxes, royalties, rentals, or other exactions of the Government for such a year.

The agreement also called for an increase in the annual free deliveries of gasoline and kerosene for government use to 2.6 million and 200,000 gallons, respectively, and the delivery of 7,500 tons of road asphalt. Furthermore, Aramco agreed to pay $700,000 "per annum towards expenses, support and maintenance of representatives of the Government concerned with the administration of Aramco operations." The agreement was supplemented by a letter from Aramco assuring the government that there would be no reduction in royalty

---

*Technically, this levy should not be called an "income tax." Income taxes are generally paid on actual receipt after subtraction of all costs. The new tax was simply a per-barrel tax based on posted prices.

and rental payments in the event that Aramco should suffer an operating loss.

The agreement was a considerable advance. Oil revenues nearly doubled from 1950 to 1957, and the Kingdom now received compensation from all aspects of the earnings from oil exploitation. It guaranteed the government royalty and income-tax payments; it raised the amount of free deliveries, and it contributed something to defray the government's cost of protecting the oil installations. Nevertheless, it was unsatisfactory, because it allowed the deduction of royalties paid to Saudi Arabia and taxes paid to foreign governments from gross income, considerably reducing the amount of profit to be divided. The first of these inequities was removed on February 13, 1952, when Aramco agreed to submit to a Royal Decree deleting that part of Article 1, paragraph (a), of the December 1950 Agreement, which allowed the deduction of income taxes paid to foreign governments from gross income.

The government's attempts to capture a larger share of the profits continued. In October 1954 Aramco agreed to increase its offtake prices by 26.4 cents per barrel, retroactive to December 31, 1951, and to bill the offtakers for the additional amounts due. The company in turn was to file amended income tax returns for 1952 and 1953, showing an additional tax liability of $39.4 million for 1952 and $30.6 million for 1953.

Settlement of the government's claims for additional income tax payments on the basis of higher published prices was the first step in the solution of the controversy surrounding the company's method of calculating its income-tax liability. Aramco had used the realized price as its tax base price, while the government insisted that the proper price was the company's published prices. These prices were published by the offtakers (the buyers of Saudi-produced oil) and constituted the prices at which Aramco-produced oil was available to any buyer in the world.

The company's realized price was not equal to the posted price. Aramco is a producing company. The parent companies set the posted price at which <u>they</u> were willing to sell Saudi Arabian oil to all buyers. Aramco did not receive this price from its owners. Its realized price was considerably lower, because Aramco granted the owners a series of discounts. Thus, the base price upon which the income-tax liability was calculated was substantially below the posted price.

Use of posted prices as a basis for tax liability calculation is important to the government. Realized prices change with market conditions, causing tax receipts to fluctuate. Posted prices can be held stable, allowing more accurate revenue estimates. As long as the major consumers have few—if any—alternative sources of supply, the host countries can force the producing companies to pay larger amounts in taxes by maintaining posted prices at a higher level than market prices.

Aramco defended the use of discounts off posted price and the use of realized prices as the proper basis for income-tax liabilities, because the sellers of Aramco oil (i.e., the four owners) had to market their product below the posted price. On October 12, 1955, however, the company agreed in principle to bill its offtakers "at prices published by them for deliveries ex-Ras Tanura, with certain adjustments." Additional billings for the period October 6, 1953, through September 30, 1955, at published prices less the following deductions were issued:

1. A five-cent stabilization differential for each barrel of unstablized crude oil sold to offtakers or used in the making of refined products sold to them;
2. A 2-percent marketing allowance off published price for stabilized crude and off adjusted published price for unstabilized crude;
3. A "refining fee of eight cents per barrel of crude oil used to manufacture refined products sold to the offtakers"; and
4. A volume discount off published price or adjusted published price as follows:

Annual sales of not more than 750,000 barrels per day (BPD)	—
Annual sales of more than 750,000 BPD but of not more than 1 million BPD	5.0%
Annual sales of more than 1 million BPD but of not more than 1.2 million BPD	7.5%
Annual sales of more than 1.2 million BPD	10.0%

This method of calculating income-tax liabilities had several advantages for the government: It yielded back taxes of about $65 million; it specified precisely what price and discounts were to be used in arriving at taxable income; it made the implementation of the 50-50 principle comparable with general Middle Eastern practice.

The government had taken another small step forward in its attempts to capture what it considered a fair share of oil profits. Nevertheless, the discounts and deductions taken off posted price reduced the tax liability, causing considerable revenue losses to the Kingdom. The government, therefore, demanded the abolition of the 2-percent marketing allowance, the volume discounts, the stabilization charge, and the refinery fee. On June 25, 1956, Aramco submitted to these demands. Refinery fees and volume discounts were eliminated; actual audited marketing expenses were substituted for the fixed 2-percent marketing allowance, and a mutually acceptable stabilization formula was worked out for the period after October 6, 1953. Again, the company agreed to revise its billings to the offtakers and to submit amended income-tax returns retroactive to 1953.

It appears that Aramco did not suspend the practice of granting volume discounts and a fixed 2-percent marketing allowance. In a letter dated December 13, 1958, Aramco submitted to a recalculation of its 1956, 1957, and 1958 income-tax liability, eliminating the volume discounts and fixed marketing allowance; to use actual audited marketing expenses; to account for income-tax payments on sales ex-Ras Tanura and Sidon at Ras Tanura posted prices for those years and to use actual sales realizations on the sale of refined products. Furthermore, Aramco promised to "make all future sales for export of crude and refined products, at Ras Tanura published prices," and to "limit marketing expenses to actual expenses accepted by Aramco as having been incurred by the offtakers as determined by independent audit." The letter also stipulated that "the foregoing price arrangements effective January 1, 1959 shall be effective for 1959 and shall thereafter automatically extend yearly unless the Government upon ninety days notice requests some change in arrangements for the succeeding calendar years." With this stipulation the company appears to have accepted the principle of continuous review of its relationship with the government.

The Organization of Oil-Exporting Countries

It is now necessary to interrupt the examination of the government-Aramco relationship to recount briefly the formation of OPEC. Despite the fact that the government was fairly satisfied with the existing conditions, it realized that the international oil companies received larger benefits by far from oil exploitation than did Saudi Arabia. Since its inception the Arab League had agitated for an association of Arab oil-producing countries to strengthen the host countries' bargaining position vis-a-vis the oil companies. In April 1959 the first Arab Petroleum Congress was convened. Although it was to consider only matters affecting Arab interests, the conferees invited all oil-exporting countries to send observers, realizing that the final success of their actions depended on cooperation among all oil-exporting states.

A particularly worrisome development to the oil-exporting countries had been the successive reduction of posted prices. Owing to excess capacity and large oil reserves, the price of oil fell in the world markets, and the oil companies lowered their prices from a high of $2.12 (f.o.b. Ras Tanura) in June of 1957 to $1.84 in August 1960.[2] Faced with possible additional cuts in prices, representatives of Iran, Iraq, Kuwait, Saudi Arabia, and Venezuela met in Baghdad on September 14, 1960, and established OPEC, whose main objectives were to restore crude oil prices to 1957 levels; to ensure maintenance of crude-oil price levels; to achieve consultation between host countries and companies whenever a change in prices is needed; to ensure price stability, even if it requires production controls; to conduct studies designed to find a means to guarantee stable revenues for the producing countries, adequate supplies of oil to consumers, and fair returns to investors; and to meet regularly and maintain common policies to advance the members' interests. OPEC succeeded beyond anyone's expectations: By 1971 it had wrested control of product prices and production policies from the companies.

The Sidon Agreement

Until 1951 Saudi Arabian oil was shipped to its major markets in northern Europe via tankers from Ras Tanura in the Arabian Gulf, a jounrey of more than 6,200 miles. Following World War II, it became apparent that a pipeline from the Saudi oil fields to the Mediterranean coast of Lebanon would cut transport costs to northern Europe by between one-third and one-half of tanker costs.[3] Based on this estimate it was decided to construct a 30-inch pipeline from the Abquaiq oil fields in Saudi Arabia to Zahrani, a few miles south of Sidon, Lebanon. Its designed throughput with seven pumping stations, about 15 million tons of crude per year, has been raised today to about 25 million tons.

Almost from the first day of operation a disagreement developed over the calculation of tax liabilities on Sidon sales. The company used the Ras Tanura posted price rather than the higher Sidon price, contending that the differential was due to transportation cost earned by Tapline and not by Aramco. The government claimed that it had a share in the profits at Sidon rather than at Ras Tanura and contested Aramco's income-tax returns, saying that the company's tax liability should be calculated on Sidon posted prices for crude delivered there, rather than those at Ras Tanura. The dispute dragged on until 1963 when, on March 23, the company agreed to raise its price for each barrel delivered at Sidon retroactive to October 6, 1953, and to pay income taxes on the additional income. As far as the government was concerned, prior to December 13, 1962, Sidon sales were billed at Ras Tanura prices with offtakers paying Tapline costs. After this agreement a clear distinction was made between

Ras Tanura and Sidon sales, leading to an increase of income tax per barrel on the Sidon portion of crude sold from $0.681 to $0.778.

The Sidon Agreement contained two additional changes. Prior to 1963 the company wrote off its exploration and intangible development costs in the years during which they were incurred. Because those two cost items are often quite high, complete deduction in the year in which they are incurred reduces taxable income considerably. Beginning with the taxable year 1963, the company agreed to capitalize its exploration and intangible development cost and to write them off at 5 percent for exploration cost and 10 percent of intangible development cost or to divide the amount of such costs by the number of years remaining in the concession agreement and take the higher of the two amounts.[4] Cost of dry holes and abandoned wells or of wells in a relinquished area was to be deducted in the year the hole was found dry or in which the area was relinquished. Finally, the company agreed to relinquish additional portions of the exclusive area.

A minor adjustment in Aramco's obligations was made on April 27, 1963, when the company agreed to pay the government for the free products that it had not used during 1959, 1961, and 1963. In the future undelivered portions of the free goods were to be paid by the company in cash in lieu of product.

Also in April 1963 the government and Aramco came to an agreement regarding the marketing allowance. In place of actual audited marketing expenses deducted from income, the company substituted a fixed one-half cent per barrel charge on all crude oil, refined products, and liquefied petroleum gas sold for export. This change covered 1962 and any future billings.

The Royalty-Expensing Agreement

Among the unresolved major issues regarding the calculation of income-tax liabilities was the treatment of royalties. The Agreement of December 1950 provided that royalties were to be subtracted from the income-tax liability and that the remainder constituted income tax payable per barrel. For some time OPEC had been demanding a change in this provision. It was argued that under the existing practice:

> the state receives no royalty whatever from the concessionaire in consideration of having placed its oil deposits at his disposal, or, if the basis of the relationship is sale of crude oil, then the state receives nothing representing the price of the sale. The state receives income tax that is

normally applicable to any commercial enterprise, but receives nothing for providing the raw material.[5]

In effect the provisions of the 1950 agreement did not distinguish between the state as the owner of the land (the concessor) and the state as the fiscal authority. On January 25, 1965, the government and Aramco signed an agreement in which the company accepted the principle of expensing of royalties, subject to certain conditions. Basically, the change provided that "royalties shall be treated as an expense deductible from gross income" in computing the income tax due, "rather than as a subtraction from said [income] tax." The agreement fixed royalties to be expensed at 12.5 percent of the posted price; any royalties paid in excess of the amount expensed were still subtracted from income taxes payable by Aramco. To ease the burden of the Royalty-Expensing Agreement on parent companies' profits, it was agreed that Aramco should be permitted to sell crude oil to the parent companies at a discount off the posted price (called OPEC Allowances). This discount consisted of two parts: the Percentage Allowance and the Gravity Allowance, set at 8.5 percent for 1965 and to 6.5 percent for 1966 and the years following.* It was further agreed that if the market price (realized price) of crude oil improved, or if Aramco's unit operating costs declined relative to 1964, the discounts from posted price would be reduced (for the effect of this change on government receipts, see Table 13.9, p. 474.

The government's attempts to capture all possible advantages from the sale of crude oil for itself continued and the next change concerned "arm's length" sales. Until September 1966 Aramco made a distinction between sales to owner-company affiliates and nonaffiliates (third-party sales). Offtakers affiliated with Aramco's owners were billed at posted prices and nonaffiliates at market price, which had been as much as $0.20 to $0.30 below posted price. By 1966 third-party sales had grown to about 30 percent of total sales.

The income received on arm's length sales was considerably lower than that from other sales because the starting point for liability calculations was well below the posted price. Therefore, Aramco was asked to stop third-party sales, and to bill offtakers at posted prices. On September 30, 1966, the dispute was settled when the company agreed to end all arm's length sales and to increase its billings to nonaffiliated offtakers for crude and refined products retro-

---

*1965: Percentage Allowance 7.5 percent off posted price, plus $0.0013235 per barrel for each full degree of API gravity above 27°. 1966: Percentage Allowance 6.5 percent, plus $0.0026470 per barrel gravity allowance.

actively to January 1, 1961 eliminating market prices as the basis for billings. The company also agreed to pay additional income taxes on the revised billings.

The final step in the use of full posted prices as the basis of income-tax payments was the elimination of the OPEC Allowances. On September 15, 1967, Aramco eliminated the OPEC Allowances on Sidon sales and entered into negotiations regarding the elimination of Allowances on all sales. In January 1968 the government and Aramco agreed on a fixed schedule leading to the gradual elimination of OPEC Allowances, beginning in that year (see Table 7.1). The Percentage Allowance was to be eliminated by the end of 1971. The Gravity Allowance was to rise slightly until 1972; thereafter, it was to be eliminated in two steps by the end of 1974. The elimination of the Percentage Allowance was the more important of the two, because its rapid elimination more than offset the small increases in the Gravity Allowance. The government's goal of the use of full posted prices as the starting point for the calculation of Aramco's income tax calculations was to be realized by 1974.

The Teheran Agreement

In September 1969 Saudi Arabia announced a five-year development plan for 1970/71 to 1975/76. Designed to raise the Kingdom's rate of economic growth, it aimed at the diversification of the economy. A year later Hisham Naser, the head of CPO, held a news conference in which he discussed the Kingdom's future economic development. Among other things he said:

> The success of the plan depended on a number of factors, one of which was the oil companies' appreciation of the Government's need for greater financial capability, necessitating an increase in oil company payments to it, and called on them to "redouble their efforts" in this regard.[6]

In a speech delivered before a conference of OPEC in July 1970 the president of the People's Democratic Republic of Algeria, Houari Boumedienne, called on the members to seize control over the pricing mechanism in the international oil markets. While Saudi Arabia and Algeria talked, Colonel Qadhafi, the president of Libya's Revolutionary Command, forced major concessions from the oil companies operating in his country. Kuwait and Iran also gained important concessions that raised the tax rate from 50 percent of profits to 55 percent. Libya's increased militancy and obvious success caused Saudi

TABLE 7.1

Schedule for the Elimination of Percentage and Gravity Allowances

		Gravity Allowance	
Year	Percentage Allowance	A (cents per barrel)	B (cents per barrel)
1968	5.5	.2647	.059559
1969	4.5	.2647	.119118
1970	3.5	.2647	.178677
1971	2.0	.2647	.238236
1972	0	.2647	.297795
1973	0	.176467	.297795
1974	0	.088233	.099265
1975	0	0	0

Note: Gravity Allowance is the sum of A and B, each to be applied to different gravity ranges not noted in the following. Column A is the amount per barrel for each full degree of API gravity by which the API gravity of such crude oil or crude equivalent exceeds 27°. Column B is the amount per barrel for each full degree of API gravity by which the API gravity of such crude oil or crude equivalent exceeds 27°, provided that all crudes with API gravity in excess of 37° API will for the purpose of column "B" be treated as if they were 37° API gravity.

Source: Aramco, The Saudi Arab Government and Arabian American Oil Company, Basic Agreement and Selected Documents Pertaining Thereto, n.d., p. 189.

Arabia to reopen its demands for an increase of Ras Tanura posted prices. On November 13, 1970, Ahmad Zaki Yamani declared that Saudi Arabia had renewed its claim for an upward adjustment of Ras Tanura posted prices. OPEC followed suit and on December 28, 1970, announced a new strategy with respect to crude oil prices. Intense negotiations ensued and on February 14, 1971, an historic agreement was signed between the six Arabian Gulf members of OPEC and the international oil companies operating in the Gulf, transferring control of posted prices from the companies to the oil-producing states—Abu Dhabi, Iran, Iraq, Kuwait, Quatar, and Saudi Arabia. The agreement contained the following major provisions:

1. An increase of the tax rate to 55 percent;

2. A uniform increase of posted prices by 33 percent per barrel plus a two-cent-per-barrel increase "in satisfaction of claims to freight disparities";

3. Additional increases in posted prices of five cents effective June 1, and thereafter on each January 1 from 1973 to 1975;

4. An adjustment of 2.5 percent of each price on June 1, 1971, and thereafter on each January 1 from 1973 to 1975, as guard against loss of purchasing power through inflation;

5. Reduction of the two-cent-per-barrel degree differential to 1.5 cents and gravity escalation of 0.5 cents per barrel of crude between 30.0° and 39.9° API for each degree below 40°;

6. Elimination of the existing percent allowance and marketing allowance; and

7. The remaining in force of the agreement for five years ("leapfrogging" of financial terms based on events elsewhere and embargos were prohibited).

Three benefits were gained: a substantial increase in revenue payments to the government, partial protection from purchasing power losses owing to worldwide inflation, and establishment of a floor to posted prices, preventing possible declines like those of the late 1950s.

The Geneva Agreement

With the signing of the Teheran Agreement OPEC had accomplished one of the goals established in 1960. There remained, however, the participation issue that had been made an OPEC concern in June 1968. As early as 1964 King Faisal had announced that he was determined to achieve direct participation in the production and marketing of Saudi oil. This was a clear indication that the government would not be satisfied as a collector of revenue until the expiration of the Aramco concession. Whereas the previous changes in the concession agreement were largely modifications and additions to the concession agreement, the call for participation implied a fundamental change.

Before the participation issue could be resolved the devaluation of the dollar forced a reopening of the Teheran Agreement. This agreement did not include a provision for changes in receipts resulting from changes in the parity rates between the U.S. dollar and the other major currencies. In December 1971 the U.S. dollar was devalued by about 12 percent. Shortly thereafter, OPEC called a meeting in Geneva and negotiated an adjustment of the Teheran Agreement.

The Geneva Agreement was "supplemental to and incorporated in existing arrangements between each of the Gulf States and each of the companies."[7] It raised the posted prices of crude in the Gulf area by 8.49 percent. It also settled on a formula that would raise or lower posted prices in accordance with exchange-rate movements. For the Gulf terminals adjustments of posted prices were to be calculated as follows:

1. The arithmetic average of exchange-rate changes of nine major currencies against the U.S. dollar in terms of IMF parities as of April 30, 1971, was calculated as 11.02 percent. This was called the "Starting Average."

2. On the first day of March, June, September, and December of each year the arithmetic average of rate change was to be recalculated against IMF parity rates of April 30, 1971. If the recalculation varied more than plus or minus two points from the Starting Average, the new average, called the Effective Average, would become the ruling average, effective the following quarter.

3. Once the new Effective Average had been established posted prices were to be adjusted by the following formula:

$$\text{Posted price} + .0849\frac{T \times B - A}{11.02}$$

where T = "posted price as of the day before the effective date of" the Teheran or other related agreements; A = "the most recent prior Effective Average preceding the currency change"; and B = the new Effective Average.[8]

The Participation Agreement

The Teheran Agreement and the Geneva supplement satisfied the immediate demands with respect to compensation. On January 21, 1972, OPEC and the oil companies began talks on the participation question.

The government had three options for changing the concession agreement: reduction of the length of the Original Concession Agreement; full nationalization; or renegotiation of the existing concession to include at least partial participation at once, leading to eventual ownership of the oil industry. It is unlikely that the government would have chosen nationalization. King Faisal is committed to private enterprise, private property, and just compensation to the owners of Aramco. As long as the King holds that position immediate, full nationalization with or without compensation seems unlikely, and according to the Saudi Oil Minister Ahmad Zaki Yamani, "Participation is . . . a substitute for nationalization in satisfying the politico-economic aspirations of the producing countries for control over their natural resources."[9] The first alternative does not solve the problem, because the state would have to wait until expiration of the new concession before it could gain control over its oil resources. Thus, the third option was chosen.

OPEC named the Saudi oil minister as its chief representative in the negotiations with the oil companies. Following months of difficult negotiations, an agreement was worked out between OPEC and the international oil companies. The main features were:

1. Following an initial participation of 25 percent, the state's additional interests will rise by 5 percent on January 1, for each year from 1979 to 1982, and reach 51 percent on January 1, 1983.

2. The companies are to be compensated on the updated book value of the assets adjusted for inflation, with an initial payment of $500 million for the 25-percent participation in Aramco. The increments in participation are to be paid on the same basis.

3. The government has the right to a percentage of crude equal to the participation level of that year. To insure the company's contractual arguments the government will resell 75, 50, and 25 percent of its share for the years 1973, 1974, and 1975, respectively. Other provisions were made to insure a smooth phase-in of the national oil companies into the market.

THE TRANS ARABIAN PIPE LINE COMPANY

Almost from the beginning of crude oil shipments from Ras Tanura it became apparent that a pipeline from Saudi Arabia to the Mediterranean Sea would be an excellent supplement to sea transportation. The advantage is all too obvious: The distance from Ras Tanura to Europe around Africa is 11,000 miles; through the Suez Canal, 3,350 miles; while the total distance from Ras Tanura to Sidon is only 1,068 miles. Tapline was completed in 1951. From the beginning an argument arose about the payments due to various countries. Outside Saudi Arabia the problem was to determine a fair transit fee for the concession to transport oil across several sovereign states. Following several years of negotiations between Lebanon, Jordan, and Iraq, an agreement was reached regarding the payments due to those governments from the Tapline company.

The problem between the government and Aramco was more complicated and was not completely settled until 1963. From the beginning Saudi Arabia demanded a 50 percent share of profits. Aramco refused, contending that the 50-50 profit distribution applied only to oil production and that because the Tapline was engaged in transportation that agreement was inapplicable. The dispute dragged on for some time and was at one time submitted to arbitration. However, both parties decided to recall their arbitration offer and reached a negotiated settlement.

SUMMARY

From the beginning of the shipment of crude from Saudi Arabia two major problems dominated the relationship between the government and Aramco: the size of the concession area and the relinquishment of unexplored regions and the division of profits derived from crude-oil exploitation. The second of these problems was by far the most important. Until 1960 negotiations regarding the contracts and agreements took place on a bilateral basis. Since 1960 contract changes have been negotiated within the framework of OPEC.

Until 1950 Saudi Arabia derived its its share of the oil profits from a fixed royalty per barrel of crude produced. In 1951 a second source of revenues for the government was agreed upon with the introduction of an income tax on Aramco profits. During the 1950s and 1960s the discussions revolved about the determination of the tax base upon which income-tax calculations are to be made.

During the two decades since 1950 the oil companies controlled the price mechanism in the market for crude oil. Posted prices were set by the companies and output was based on the companies' interpretation of world market conditions. Since the end of 1970 the producer countries have nearly eliminated company influence in price and production of crude oil.

POSTSCRIPT

Events have moved swiftly since this chapter was completed. The most important change with respect to the relationship between Aramco and the government has been the participation question. The question of full Saudi Arabian ownership of Aramco has been settled in principle. At a meeting between the owners and representatives of the government in London on December 10, 1974, a Saudi official stated: "[W]e are optimistic and feel that the chances of reaching an agreement are high."[10]

According to news releases, the takeover by the Saudi government of Aramco will take the following shape:

1. The government will take over complete operation of the company, and the owners will be paid according to the net book value of the company.

2. The former owners will be guaranteed a certain amount of crude oil at the going market price. The precise amount will be specified in future discussions.

3. The previous owners will continue to supply management and other services as required, for which they will be paid in accordance with the value of services rendered.

4. The former owners will continue to explore for oil under a separate arrangement.[11]

Furthermore, Saudi Arabia adopted new royalty and tax rates, as agreed upon by OPEC in July and October 1974: The Saudi government raised the royalty rate to 16.67 percent and the tax rate to 65.75 percent. (The OPEC proposals were announced in two steps; OPEC raised the royalty rate to 14.5 percent, beginning July 1, 1974, and effective October 1, 1974, the aforementioned rates became the ruling rates.)

NOTES

1. All quotations from contracts in this and following sections are based on Kingdom of Saudi Arabia, Agreements Between the Saudi Arab Government and the Arabian American Oil Company (Mecca: Government Press, 1964); Aramco, The Saudi Arab Government and Arabian American Oil Company Basic Agreements and Selected Documents Pertaining Thereto (no place or date of publication).

2. Fuad Rouhani, A History of OPEC (New York: Praeger, 1971), p. 190.

3. Stephen H. Longrigg, Oil in the Middle East, 3d ed. (London: Oxford University Press, 1968), p. 206.

4. For a general discussion of accounting theory and practice in the international oil industry see Abdulhady H. Taher, Income Determination in the International Petroleum Industry (Oxford: Pergamon Press, 1966).

5. OPEC, "Explanatory Memorandum on Royalties," cited in Rouhani, A History of OPEC, p. 223.

6. Middle East Economic Survey (MEES) 12, no. 47 (September 18, 1970): 1.

7. "Agreement" as published in MEES, suppl. to vol. 15, no. 13 (January 21, 1972): 6.

8. Ibid., pp. 6-7.

9. MEES 15, no. 48 (September 22, 1972): 1.

10. MEES 28, no. 8 (December 13, 1974): 1.
11. MEES 28, no. 7 (December 6, 1974): 1-2.

CHAPTER

8

THE GOVERNMENT AND THE OTHER OIL COMPANIES

The Original Concession Agreement of 1933 and its amendment of 1939 gave Aramco preference rights for exploration and exploitation over virtually all of the eastern and central part of the Kingdom as well as over the government's one-half share of the oil resources in the Neutral Zone. As Aramco concentrated its efforts in the Eastern Province it relinquished large sections of the unexplored concession, offering the government an opportunity to enter new agreements with different concessionaires.

In many ways the Saudis considered the Aramco agreement an insult. Neither the government nor any private Saudi citizens owned a portion of Aramco or had the right to be heard in its management. The Saudis resented exclusion from the whole process, "downstream" and "upstream," and considered themselves cheated out of a large portion of the profits.* They resented the exclusion from management as a slur on their ability. This attitude was especially strong among the young, foreign-educated men. Even the fact that only the English version of the Original Concession Agreement was regarded as legally binding was objectionable to them as an affront to Arab culture.

Thus, when the relinquished areas were offered for exploration an opportunity arose to rectify the injustices of the past. Instead of dealing with the seven major international companies, the government turned to smaller independent or newly formed private or gov-

---

*"Downstream operations" are those operations that take place after crude oil has been lifted, including transportation, refining, and marketing. "Upstream operations" include the lifting of crude oil and transportation to field storage.

ernment-owned companies. Eager to enter into the market, the newcomers were more aggressive and willing to offer more advantages than the established majors. From the Getty agreement in 1949 to the Petromin concession in 1967 the agreements departed ever more radically from the old concession agreements. Each contract broke new ground, until complete control over all "upstream" and partial influence over "downstream" operations was achieved.

THE GETTY OIL COMPANY

In September 1945 President Truman issued a declaration affirming the federal government's right to the natural resources of the subsoil and seabed off the continental shelf. Designed by Truman to bar extension of state claims past the three-mile limit, it was the legal basis upon which the Saudi Arabian government extended its claim to the oil resources in the Arabian Gulf area from 3 to 12 miles offshore.

Aramco had refrained from operations in the Neutral Zone south of Kuwait and concentrated its activities in the al Hasa region. In 1948 the company surrendered its rights in the Neutral Zone in exchange for the Saudi portions of the continental shelf off al Hasa. The relinquishment was prompted in part at least by the extremely advantageous agreement concluded between the ruler of Kuwait, Ahmad al-Subah, and the American Independent Oil Company (Amin Oil), which Aramco preferred not to match.

In 1949 a concession for a period of 60 years was granted to the Pacific Western Oil Corporation (later renamed Getty Oil Company). In return for the right to explore for and exploit hydrocarbon resources in the Saudi undivided one-half share of the Neutral Zone the company agreed to meet the following obligations:

1. There would be a one-time payment of $9.5 million.

2. The company would pay a royalty of 55 cents for each barrel of crude it obtained and a 12.5-percent royalty from the sale of natural gas or gas products produced, and it would make an advance payment of $1 million against royalty payable. If the total royalty due amounted to less than that sum, the government was not obliged to return the advance payment.

3. The company agreed to pay 25 percent of the net profits on the "sale of products and by-products, including gas and gas by-products . . . not refined by the company at any refinery built by the company in said Neutral Zone," and 20 percent of the net profits from refinery operation in the zone.

4. In the event the company sold or assigned the concession to a third party, the government would be entitled to 25 percent of

the net capital gain resulting from the sale. Furthermore, if the company organized a subsidiary to carry out its activities in the Neutral Zone, Saudi Arabia would be entitled to subscribe to 25 percent of the stock issue.

5. The company agreed to deliver free of charge at Jedda and Riyadh specific amounts of petroleum products and to construct a refinery with a 12,000-barrel-per-day throughput.

6. In the event of abandonment of the concession by the company, all immovable assets would become government property. Upon expiration of the concession period, ownership of all assets, movable or immovable, falls to the government.

7. Finally, the company agreed to give Saudi citizens priority in hiring, to train Saudi employees for responsible positions, to establish schools in the zone, to set up a scholarship program for advanced training of gifted students, and to provide free medical care for its employees.

Clearly, this agreement was a considerable advance over the Aramco concession. It provided for higher royalties per barrel of crude, called for a share of net profits of the company's refining operations of Saudi crude outside the Neutral Zone, and offered a chance for participation if the concessionaire created an operating company. The government's share in company profits was defined as that amount left after subtracting the <u>total</u> amount of expenses, including <u>all</u> capital outlays made during the year.

THE ARABIAN OIL COMPANY (JAPAN)

In 1957 Japan entered the world oil markets and became an active challenger to the existing arrangements. Entirely dependent on oil imports, the Japanese approached the Saudi Arabian government for exploration rights to offshore oil resources in the Neutral Zone. The agreement with the AOC signed on December 10, 1957, was a logical extension of conditions laid down in the Getty agreement of 1949.

The Arabian Oil Company was granted "an exclusive petroleum exploration and prospecting license for a period not exceeding two years," subject to extension. Upon the discovery of crude oil in commercial quantities the government would "grant to the Company . . . an exploitation concession lease for a period of forty years," for its undivided one-half interest in the Neutral Zone. For these privileges AOC agreed to meet the following conditions:

MAP 7

Other Oil Company Concession Areas

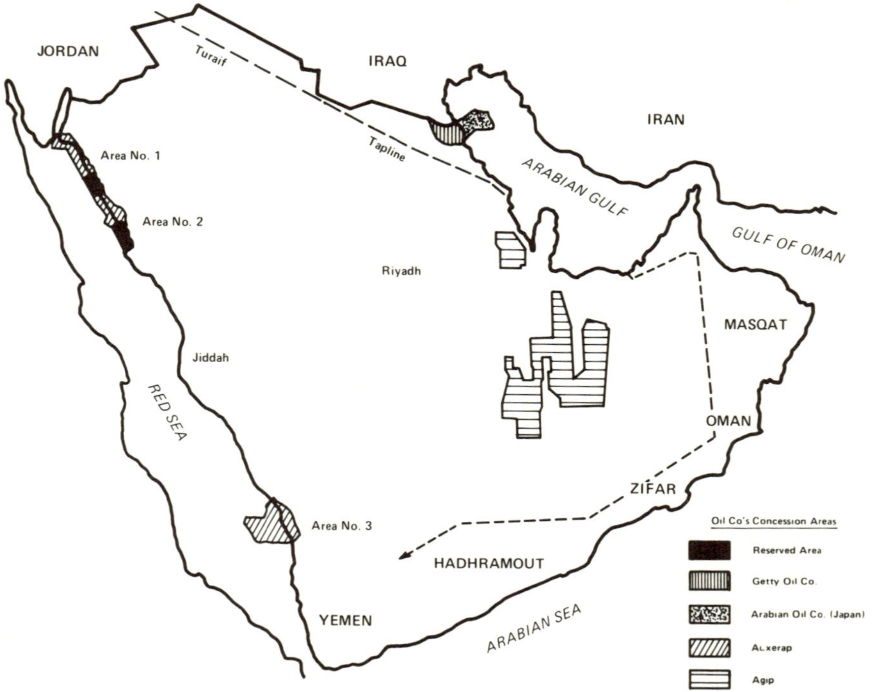

Source: Central Department of Statistics, Statistical Yearbook 1392 A.H., p. 212.

1. There would be an annual rental of $1.5 million until discovery of oil in commercial quantities. Upon discovery of oil the company would pay an additional $1 million per annum, retroactive from the date of the agreement to the date of discovery.

2. Beginning with the production of oil, a royalty of 20 percent of the crude oil produced, 20 percent on the natural asphalt extracted, and 20 percent of the natural gas alienated or used would be due, either in cash or in kind. If the royalty payable under these headings should amount to less than $2.5 million, the government would be entitled to that amount as a minimum royalty. The calculation of royalty value of the products would be based on prevailing posted prices.

3. The concessionaire was required to establish an integrated company from the production of crude to the marketing of finished products.

4. The company was subject to income-tax payments "on all the operations of the Company inside and outside Saudi Arabia, including sale of crude oil, refining, transportation and marketing."

5. If the government's share of royalties and taxes should not amount to 56 percent of the company's net income from all operations an additional payment would have to be made to bring the government's share up to 56 percent during the taxable year. (The government's share was raised to 57 percent on September 12, 1963.)

6. Seventy percent of the labor force inside the Neutral Zone and 30 percent outside the zone would consist of Saudi nationals.

7. As soon as production reached 30,000 barrels per day for 90 days, the company would construct a refinery with 75,000 BPD throughput. The refinery would be completed within two years of the above event.

8. If, after the discovery of crude in commercial quantities, a newly formed production company should undertake the venture, "the Government [would] have the right . . . to subscribe for itself and/or for Saudi Arabian subjects to ten percent (10%) of the shares issued." The 10-percent-share offer applied, if the company acquired a concession from the Sheikh of Kuwait; "otherwise the said percentage [would] be twenty percent (20%)."

9. Three years after the original discovery of oil and every five years thereafter the company would relinquish 20 percent of the unexploited area.

Although the rental and bonuses exacted for the period before discovery of oil in commercial quantities were rather modest, the AOC agreement was a radical departure from existing concession agreements. It heralded a new era in the relationship between oil companies and producing countries, with more and more of the benefits from oil exploitation accruing to the host countries. Three aspects were particularly important: The government was to receive 56 instead of 50 percent of net income; the 56 percentage was to apply to all activities of an integrated company inside and outside of Saudi Arabia, including transport, refining, and sale of crude; the government was entitled to one-third of the seats of the company's board of directors. The new agreement was not well received by the international oil companies, because they realized that sooner or later the oil-producing countries would demand changes in the existing agreements based on the AOC contract.

SOCIETE AUXILIAIRE DE LA REGIE AUTONOME DES PETROLES

In April 1965 an agreement was concluded with Auxirap, in which the company was granted a petroleum-exploration and prospecting license covering certain areas onshore and offshore in the Red Sea.* Following the completion of seismic surveys three areas, covering 10,000 square miles, were agreed upon: two north of Yanbu and one between Jedda and Jizan. The license was granted for two years, subject to renewal for three years provided the company met certain specified conditions. Upon discovery of crude in commercial quantities an exploitation license for a period of 30 years was to be issued. Following the granting of this license, "a Saudi company [would] be created in which a participation of forty percent [would] be offered for subscription to the Government, to be subscribed either for itself and/or for any of its agencies, organizations or for Saudi Arabian subjects." Saudi and French interests had equal voting rights on the board of directors, and the Saudis had a voice in the management of the operating company. Auxirap was entitled to relinquish any part of the unexploited area at any time but was required to relinquish 20 percent of the unexplored area on the third anniversary of the agreement and a similar portion every five years thereafter.

As was the case in the AOC agreement the Auxirap contract was an important step in the changing relationship between host country and company. The contract separated the exploration and exploitation phase; it specified the expenditure of $5 million on exploration and prospecting by the company without any Saudi obligation. For the first time Saudis would participate in the production company, have equal voting rights on the board of directors and a word in the man-

---

*In May 1968 a U.S. oil company, Tenneco, acquired a one-third interest in the concession.

agement. Participation in management was an important advance, because it offered young Saudis with advanced education suitable outlets for their talents.

The agreement provided for bonuses, rental, and royalty and income-tax payments as follows:

1. Within one month of the effective date of the agreement Auxirap was required to pay $500,000 and an additional $1 million within two months of that date; $4 million were due when crude oil production reached 70,000 BPD for 90 days.

2. There would be surface rentals payable in cash according to the following schedule:

Years from Effective Date of Agreement	Payment per km^2 (U.S.$)
0 to 5	5
6 to 10	50
11 to 15	250
16 to 20	300
21 to 25	400
26 to end of concession	500

3. Royalties would be as follows:
   a. There would be a sliding-scale, fully expensed royalty beginning at 15 percent for average crude oil production of less than 60,000 BPD, rising to 17 percent on the entire production if average production should fall between 60,000 and 80,000 BPD, and to 20 percent for average production levels of more than 80,000 BPD.
   b. There would be a 20 percent royalty on the natural asphalt extracted.
   c. There would be a 12.5 percent royalty on natural gas alienated or used as fuel each year.
   d. There would be a minimum royalty payment of $1.5 million.

4. There would be income taxes payable on all integrated operations "imposed by the relevant Saudi Laws and Decrees now existing or which may later exist at any time during the life of this agreement."

The Auxirap contract was a pathbreaking document, reflecting many ideas suggested by OPEC for "new" oil contracts. The sliding-scale, fully expensed royalty rising from 15 to 20 percent instead of the flat 12.5 percent of posted prices guaranteed the government an increasing share of profits as production increased. Relatively small bonus payments before discovery of commercial quantities of crude oil in the concession areas were required, but more important than the size of the bonus payments was the imposition of surface rentals throughout the life of the agreement, rather than until the discovery of oil. The most important advance was the payment of income taxes existing or imposed at a later time, eliminating the "freezing" of income taxes to a specific rate for the life of the contract as in all previous agreements. In calculating income-tax liabilities, exploration costs would be capitalized.

In the event that Auxirap should discover oil in commercial quantities, Petromin's 40 percent equity participation plus the provision requiring the joint company to "carry out all those operations of an integrated oil enterprise including production, refining, transportation and marketing of crude oil" assured Petromin's entry into the international oil business. The joint company's refining capacity was limited to 50 percent of annual production. All c.i.f. sales of crude would be shipped on company-owned, Saudi Arab private, or government-owned tankers. Furthermore, the company agreed that 50 percent of the annual crude production would be marketed by the company itself.

The agreement insured that marketing of the production of crude would not interrupt the existing oil price structure, by calculation of royalties and taxes on the basis of posted prices. The price at which Petromin and Auxirap take their share of crude production would be fixed by the joint company's board of directors. If Petromin were unable to market its 40 percent share of production, Auxirap would be required to market all or part of that share.

When crude-oil production should reach an average level of 100,000 BPD, Auxirap would be obliged to build in Saudi Arabia a refinery with a minimum daily throughput of 30,000 BPD. Auxirap agreed to use at least 75 percent Saudi labor inside the country and 30 percent outside. A training program for Saudi employees was to be instituted covering "various aspects of the oil industry including supervisory and management training, as well as free medical care to all employees and Government officials working in the concession area."

Upon termination of the agreement ownership of all fixed or movable company property within the concession area would be transferred to Saudi Arabia.

THE GENERAL PETROLEUM AND MINERAL ORGANIZATION

Each of the "new" agreements discussed so far led to increasing Saudi participation in all phases of the oil industry. The final step was taken in December 1967 when the government granted Petromin two exclusive prospecting and exploration licenses covering an area of about 86,000 square km. in the Rub al-Khali and a 25,000-square-km. area on the Red Sea coast. The licenses provided that Petromin would prospect and explore within six months of the effective day for hydrocarbons, either on its own account or through others.

The licenses granted to Petromin reflect the precedent set by the Auxirap agreement. Petromin was obliged to drill, within three years of the effective date, at least one well in the Rub al-Khali and at least two wells in the Red Sea area and to spend during the same period at least $5 million in each of the areas. If the company fulfilled its obligations, the license would be renewed for three years for the Rub al-Khail area and for two years on the Red Sea coast. Petromin was expected to relinquish 20 percent of the unexplored portion of the unexplored areas prior to or upon the end of three years and a similar amount every five years thereafter.

Upon discovery of oil in commercial quantities Petromin would be issued an exploitation license for a duration of 30 years. The company was to conserve natural gas to the greatest extent possible.

Petromin agreed to the following bonus payments: $2 million within one month of the effective date; $3 million within two months of the granting of the exploitation concession; $8 million when crude oil production should average 300,000 BPD. Surface rentals were to be due as follows:

Years from Effective Date of Agreement	Payment per km^2 (U.S.$)
0 to 5	10
6 to 10	60
11 to 15	250
16 to 20	375
21 to 25	500
26 to 30	625

The company was to be subject to royalty and income-tax payments. Royalties were to be due on a sliding-scale designed to produce a greater take as production should expand: 12.5 percent on the entire production so long as it should not exceed an average level of 60,000 BPD; 13 percent on the entire production for an average output of 60,000 BPD but less than 80,000 BPD; 14 percent of the entire output, if in a calendar year production should reach more than 80,000 BPD. In any case a minimum royalty payment of $5 million was stipulated three years after issuance of the exploitation license. The agreement also provided that Petromin would publish posted prices for crude and refined products at each export point in the

Kingdom, taking into account prevailing Arabian Gulf and Mediterranean posted prices. An income tax of 50 percent "of such higher rate of income tax as may be imposed by the relevant Saudi Laws and Decrees which may later exist during the life of this Agreement" would be due on the net income from the sale of crude oil, refining, transportation, and marketing, both inside and outside the Kingdom.

Petromin would carry out its exploitation rights as a fully integrated company subject to the following conditions. When crude oil production should average 200,000 BPD for 90 days, Petromin would begin construction of a refinery (or refineries) with a minimum throughput of 30,000 BPD. C.i.f. sales of Petromin crude would be shipped in company-owned, Saudi government, or private-Saudi-owned tankers. In addition to investments made in refineries, Petromin agreed to invest at least 30 percent of its cumulative net income from production in integrated operations.

Furthermore, the agreement contained stipulations regarding employment of Saudi citizens, special training programs for employees, social and medical benefits, and contributions to the College of Petroleum and Minerals.

The Petromin Agip Agreement

To carry out its obligations Petromin assigned its prospecting and exploration rights—except for legal title to the license—in the Rub al-Khali area to Agip Saudi Arabia, a subsidiary of the Italian corporation ENI. Agip in turn decided to assign 50 percent of its interest to Phillips Saudi Arabian Company, a subsidiary of the American Phillips Oil Corporation. It was agreed that when crude oil in commercial quantities should be found, Petromin would apply for an exploitation license. Upon receipt of the concession, Petromin agreed to assign to Agip all of the rights associated with the exploitation license, unless Petromin should choose to retain a 30-percent participation. In the event that Petromin should decide to exercise the option, it would be obliged to pay Agip 30 percent of the initial prospecting and exploration costs, and if production should reach 300,000 BPD for a period of 90 days, Petromin would have the right to acquire an additional 10 percent of the license rights, raising its total participation to 40 percent.

In addition, the agreement called for the formation of a joint Saudi Arabian corporation to carry out the activities of the exploitation concession, including marketing of produced oil. Petromin retained the right to market all or part of its share of the crude oil on its own account.

When the average production in the concession area should attain 200,000 BPD, the joint company would be obliged to consider the formation of an integrated petroleum enterprise, including the construction of refineries in Saudi Arabia with a minimum throughput of 30,000 BPD and the formation of sales and marketing organizations.

As in the AOC and Auxirap contracts, the agreement laid down conditions with respect to the employment and training of Saudi citizens, as well as provisions regarding the company's medical and social obligations. Furthermore, the contract provided that Agip utilize as far as possible Saudi Arabian contractors and goods in its day-to-day operations.

Finally, in an appendix to the agreement between Petromin and ANIC, another subsidiary of ENI, the groundwork was laid for the creation of a petrochemical industry.

An interesting feature of the Auxirap and Agip agreements, as well as all subsequent others, is the arbitration clause. Prior to these contracts any unresolved dispute leading to arbitration had to be submitted to an international board of arbitrators chosen by both parties. Under the last two agreements arbitration of disputes was subject to a Saudi Arabian tribunal, constituted in accordance with Article 50 of the Saudi Arabian Mining Code.

The Natomas-Sinclair-Pakistan Agreement

On December 23, 1967, Petromin assigned its rights covering the area on the Red Sea Coast to the Natomas-Sinclair-Pakistan group, a venture between the Natomas International Corporation, the Sinclair Arabian Oil Company, and the Pakistan government. The agreement follows in form and content that made between Petromin and Agip with one difference: If Petromin decides to retain 50 percent of the exploitation rights upon issuance of such a license, Petromin must pay 50 percent of exploration costs to the group.

The group has undergone a number of changes and is now constituted as follows: Arabian Sun Oil Company, Natomas Arabian Oil, Dillingham Arabian Oil Inc., Santa Fe International Corporation, Ti Arabian Exploration Corporation, and Oil and Gas Development Corporation of Pakistan.

SUMMARY

As soon as the government had a chance to loosen its ties with Aramco, it entered into concession agreements with several oil companies for areas along the Red Sea, the Rub al-Khali, and in Al Hassa. Beginning with the Getty contract and continuing with Auxirap and the others, the government secured more control over the concessionaires by gaining a greater voice in management, a greater share of income from all operations of an integral company upon discovery of crude oil in commercial quantities, and a larger percentage of ownership. The interposition of Petromin reduced the need for the government itself to deal with private non-Saudi corporations. In fact, control over Saudi crude oil sources passed from the oil companies to the government.

CHAPTER 9
THE OIL INDUSTRY

Because the oil sector affects every aspect of the Kingdom's economy, it has been discussed under various headings in this study. To round out the presentation this chapter is concerned with the objective facts of the oil industry: production of crude and refined products, prices, and so on. Unfortunately, there is a considerable dearth of reliable, up-to-date data in the petroleum industry; this is particularly true for information on investment, profits, and costs. To give the reader an insight into the question of profits, however, some information for the period prior to 1962 is given at the end of this chapter. The rest of this chapter will be used to sketch the basic outline of the oil sector in the Kingdom.

THE SUPPLY OF CRUDE OIL

Table 9.1 gives the estimated supply of crude oil in Saudi Arabia since 1955. Estimated years of supply fell 68.1 percent, from 113.6 years in 1955 to 36.2 years in 1973. It reached its highest point in 1957 when supplies stood at 124.3 years and has declined ever since that time. The data given in Table 9.1 clearly illustrate the fact that oil reserves are a wasting asset. Despite the most intensive exploration efforts, the crude oil has been pumped out of the ground faster than new pools have been discovered. Thus, it follows that production controls—i.e., reduction in output—are advantageous to Saudi Arabia. Current oil revenues exceed the economy's absorptive capacity and, given the problems of finding sound investments for the accumulated excess revenues as well as for unstable international economic conditions, it is to the Kingdom's advantage to leave the oil in the ground rather than lift it for current consumption. As

TABLE 9.1

Estimated Years of Supply of Crude Oil, 1955-73

Year	Year's Supply
1955	113.6
1956	116.4
1957	124.3
1958	121.5
1959	120.1
1960	111.7
1961	104.3
1962	107.7
1963	97.2
1964	93.0
1965	86.2
1966	69.5
1967	72.9
1968	79.0
1969	78.7
1970	68.0
1971	54.9
1972	44.3
1973	36.2

Note: Proved reserves are divided by production.

Sources: 1955-63: CDS, Statistical Yearbook, 1385 A.H., vol. 1 (Riyadh, 1965), p. 89; 1964-68: Ibid., 1389 A.H., vol. 5 (Riyadh, 1969), p. 226; 1969-73: Aramco, Aramco 1973, pp. 7, 8.

long as the industrial nations suffer from rates of inflation of 12 percent and more, the value of revenues received from current sales will be reduced while the value of crude in the ground will rise in harmony with the rising international prices.

PRODUCTION OF CRUDE OIL

Aramco began lifting crude oil in 1938, but it produced a total of only 31 million barrels until the end of World War II (see Table

9.2). From 1944 to 1945 output rose almost threefold, from 7.8 million barrels to 21.3 million barrels, and it reached 89.9 million barrels by 1947. The next significant increase in output took place in 1948, when crude output rose by nearly 60 percent over the previous year.

The rapid increase of output following the end of World War II reflects the expansion of Aramco's ownership by the inclusion of the Standard Oil Company (New Jersey) and the Mobil Oil Company. The recognition that the Saudi Arabian oil fields were the largest oil deposits ever discovered forced Aramco's original owners, Standard Oil of California and Texaco, to search for additional partners, because their own marketing facilities and investment funds were inadequate for full development of this bonanza.

Expanding world demand for oil, especially from the rebuilt European industries, as well as Saudi demands for greater revenues, led to rapid expansion of output. Annual output rose to nearly 200 million barrels by 1950 and to about 350 million barrels in 1954, the first year the Getty Oil Company produced a significant amount of crude in the Neutral Zone.

Despite the addition of output by the Getty Oil Company, crude-oil production expanded very slowly during the second half of the 1950s. The rate of expansion of total output fell from 16 percent for the period 1948-54 to about 3 percent for the years 1955-59. The opening of the Getty facilities in the Neutral Zone actually prevented an even greater decline in the rate of crude output. For the period 1955-59 Aramco's output of crude rose only 2 percent per annum.

In 1961 AOC went on stream with production from the Neutral Zone. In that year Aramco accounted for 94 percent, Getty for 5.3 percent, and AOC for 0.7 percent of total output. From 1961 to 1966 total output expanded at an annual rate of 11.9 percent; Aramco's output rose by 11.4 percent per annum, while Getty's and AOC's outputs rose by 1 and 65 percent, respectively. The rather large annual increment in AOC's output is explained by the low base from which the growth rate was calculated.

While Aramco and AOC registered substantial increases in crude oil production during the second half of the 1960s, output by the Getty Oil Company fell from a high of 34.4 million barrels in 1964 to a low of 22.7 million barrels in 1969. The decline in output reflects the shift in demand away from sour, high-sulfur-content crude to sweeter, low-sulfur crude that characterized the late 1960s. Aramco experienced a decline in the rate of increase in crude output from 1967 to 1969, owing to the Arab-Israeli war of 1967 and the repeated cutting of the Tapline in Syria. From 1970 to 1973 total output doubled, from 1.4 billion barrels to 2.8 billion barrels.

There appears to be no pattern of exploitation of the various oilfields (see Table 9.3). By far the largest amount of crude oil was

TABLE 9.2

Annual Production of Crude Oil by Producing Company, 1938-73
(million barrels)

Year	Aramco	Getty Oil	AOC	Total
1938	0.5	—	—	0.5
1939	3.9	—	—	3.9
1940	5.1	—	—	5.1
1941	4.3	—	—	4.3
1942	4.5	—	—	4.5
1943	4.9	—	—	4.9
1944	7.8	—	—	7.8
1945	21.3	—	—	21.3
1946	59.9	—	—	59.9
1947	89.9	—	—	89.9
1948	142.9	—	—	142.9
1949	174.0	—	—	174.0
1950	199.5	—	—	199.5
1951	278.0	—	—	278.0
1952	301.9	—	—	301.9
1953	308.3	—	—	308.3
1954	347.8	3.0	—	350.8
1955	352.2	4.4	—	356.6
1956	360.9	5.8	—	366.8
1957	362.1	11.6	—	373.7
1958	370.5	14.7	—	385.2
1959	399.8	21.2	—	421.0
1960	456.5	24.9	—	481.4
1961	508.3	28.7	3.8	540.7
1962	555.1	33.7	11.0	599.7
1963	594.6	33.1	24.1	651.9
1964	628.1	34.4	31.8	694.3
1965	739.1	32.6	33.1	804.8
1966	873.3	30.2	46.5	950.0
1967	948.1	25.1	50.6	1,023.8
1968	1,035.8	23.2	55.0	1,114.0
1969	1,092.4	22.7	58.8	1,173.9
1970	1,295.3	28.3	62.7	1,386.3
1971	1,641.6	33.7	65.5	1,740.8
1972	2,098.5	28.3	75.0	2,201.8
1973	2,677.4	23.4	71.9	2,772.7

Sources: 1938-53: SAMA, Annual Report, 1380 A.H. (Jedda, n.d.), p. 49; 1954-64: CDS, Statistical Yearbook, 1385 A.H., vol. 1 (Riyadh, 1965), p. 90; 1965-73: SAMA, Statistical Summary, 2nd Issue, 1393/94 (Jedda, 1974), p. 46.

TABLE 9.3

Aramco Crude Oil Production by Field, 1954-72
(million barrels)

Year	Berri (L)	Abu Safah (L)	Manifa (M)	Fadhilli (L)	Khursaniyah (H)	Safaniyah (H)	Khurais (M)	Abu Hadriyah (L)	Ghawar (L)	Quateef (L)	Dammam (L)	Abquaiq (L)	Total
1954	—	—	—	—	—	—	—	—	207.5	12.6	21.4	106.4	347.8
1955	—	—	—	—	—	—	—	—	227.7	10.6	18.2	95.8	352.2
1956	—	—	—	—	—	—	—	—	227.1	11.6	17.2	105.0	360.9
1957	—	—	—	—	—	20.5	—	—	214.0	9.1	14.5	104.0	362.1
1958	—	—	—	—	—	13.9	—	—	247.5	6.7	13.6	88.8	370.5
1959	—	—	—	—	—	27.8	a	—	256.1	5.8	12.4	97.6	399.8
1960	—	—	—	—	0.5	66.2	a	—	261.4	5.9	12.7	109.7	456.5
1961	—	—	—	—	15.6	88.1	—	—	257.5	7.4	11.8	127.9	508.3
1962	—	—	—	—	29.1	107.1	—	a	261.3	10.2	11.8	135.4	555.1
1963	—	—	—	a	26.0	111.4	a	15.1	281.0	9.3	11.6	139.9	594.6
1964	—	—	0.3	8.2	39.2	142.2	0.2	9.1	268.5	10.3	12.3	137.8	627.8
1965	—	—	—	7.2	47.3	172.4	0.3	14.6	324.8	11.8	9.4	149.5	739.1[b]
1966	—	11.8	18.6	11.3	47.5	198.7	0.4	22.0	351.0	26.6	9.5	175.9	873.3
1967	—	14.6	19.9	14.9	32.6	160.3	0.5	23.9	454.1	22.1	8.7	188.0	939.6
1968	7.1	22.1	16.4	18.6	11.4	149.3	0.9	29.9	556.2	19.9	8.3	195.8	1,035.8
1969	10.3	23.9	14.6	11.6	37.1	155.0	5.3	20.8	543.4	30.9	8.2	231.1	1,092.3
1970	15.0	27.3	6.3	11.6	30.5	281.5	10.4	19.4	575.1	33.5	8.3	277.3	1,295.3[c]
1971	67.7	31.6	4.1	18.9	31.3	280.9	5.9	38.4	787.9	38.5	7.7	328.7	1,641.6
1972	163.7	33.7	18.0	19.5	45.1	350.0	7.9	35.8	999.4	47.1	8.6	369.6	2,098.3

[a]Fewer than 100,000 barrels.

[b]Total should be 737.3 million barrels; the original source contains an error.

[c]Total should be 1,296.2 million barrels; the original source contains an error.

Note: L: Arabian Light; M: Arabian Medium: H: Arabian Heavy.

Sources: 1954-64: CDS, Statistical Yearbook, 1385 A.H., vol. 1 (Riyadh, 1965), p. 92; 1965-72: Ibid., 1393 A.H., vol. 9 (Riyadh, 1973), p. 237.

taken from the giant Ghawar field whose output has risen nearly fivefold, from 207.5 million barrels in 1954 to 999.4 million barrels in 1972. The second- and third-largest producing fields have been the Dammam field, whose output rose 335 percent from 1954 to 1972, and the Safaniyah field, where output rose from 20.5 million barrels in 1957 to 350 million barrels in 1972. The Berri field is the fourth-largest producer; it came on stream in 1968 with an output of 7.1 million barrels and reached 163.7 million barrels in 1972. Those four fields have been the most important producers of crude oil; in 1972 they accounted for almost 90 percent of crude output.

In terms of API gravity, output has always favored the Arabian Light crude. Since 1954 production of 34° API crude has accounted for the largest proportion of output. In 1960 Arabian Light crude oil supplied 85.4 percent of total output, and the remaining two grades, 14.6 percent. In 1972 Arabian Light still constituted the largest proportion of crude oil lifted, with 78.3 percent of total output, while Arabian Medium and Arabian Heavy accounted for 5 and 16.7 percent, respectively.

OUTPUT OF REFINED PRODUCTS

The first refinery was built at Ras Tanura about 30 miles north of Damman on the shore of the Arabian Gulf. It was placed in full operation in December 1945, with a daily capacity of 50,000 barrels. In addition to the refinery itself, storage facilities and a T-shaped pier able to accommodate two tankers at the same time were built. Since that date the refinery has been enlarged to several times its original size. Refining capacity has risen to 325,000 barrels per day. In 1967 two piers could accommodate ten tankers simultaneously. To expand loading capacity the company constructed a sea island about one mile offshore from the terminal designed to accommodate five tankers, up to 200,000 deadweight tons. The sixth berth will accept a tanker of up to 400,000 deadweight tons.

In 1954 the Ras Tanura refinery produced 75.3 million barrels of refined products, of which 48.1 percent was fuel oil; 23.3 percent, diesel oil; 7.6 percent, kerosene; 3.7 percent, jet fuel; 16.9 percent, motor gasoline and naptha; and 0.4 percent, miscellaneous products (see Table 9.4). Output expanded, and in 1958 asphalt and liquefied petroleum gas (LPG) were added to the product mix. By 1972 output stood at 199.4 million barrels distributed among the various products as follows: fuel oil, 52.7 percent; motor gasoline and naptha, 17 percent; diesel fuel, 11.3 percent; jet fuel, 8.2 percent; LPG, 7.9 percent; kerosene, 2.5 percent; and the remainder, asphalt.

TABLE 9.4

Output of Refined Products, Ras Tanura (Aramco), 1954-72
(million barrels)

Year	Asphalt	LPG	Fuel Oil	Diesel Oil	Kero-sene	Jet Fuel	Motor Gasoline, Naptha	Aviation Gaso-line, Other
1954	—	—	36.2	17.6	5.7	2.8	12.7	0.3[a]
1955	—	—	35.4	15.2	5.4	2.3	11.1	0.2
1956	—	—	35.4	15.1	4.0	2.0	10.7	0.3
1957	—	—	38.1[b]	11.0	3.9	3.1	8.9	0.4
1958	0.3	[a]	25.6	14.7	4.3	4.2	7.5	—
1959	0.3	[a]	31.6	10.5	4.9	3.1	8.1	—
1960	0.2	0.2	45.6	10.6	5.9	2.6	9.3	0.1
1961	0.4	0.1	49.9	13.1	5.8	3.4	9.0	0.4
1962	0.4	1.1	52.2	12.3	3.8	4.4	8.3	0.3
1963	0.3	2.1	53.5	15.2	3.8	4.5	10.6	—
1964	0.4	4.0	56.7	13.8	3.2	6.1	13.2	—
1965	0.3	5.1	63.8	12.8	2.1	8.4	16.9	—
1966	0.6	5.7	60.3	15.9	1.9	10.4	17.7	—
1967	0.8	6.7	64.6	16.3	3.0	9.4	20.4	—
1968	0.8	10.6	76.4	18.8	3.0	13.2	24.4	—
1969	0.9	13.2	80.7	18.3	3.2	14.1	25.4	—
1970	0.9	17.0	113.6	20.9	6.9	13.7	34.3	—
1971	1.0	17.9	108.3	22.1	5.3	13.3	30.5	—
1972	0.9	15.8	105.0	22.5	5.0	16.3	33.9	—

[a]From 1954 to 1958 this category contains only other products.

[b]The source gives 380,145 barrels, but the figure is too high. We assumed a figure of 38.1 million barrels.

Sources: 1954-62: CDS, Statistical Yearbook, 1386 A.H., vol. 2 (Riyadh), p. 154; 1963-72: Ibid., 1393 A.H., vol. 9 (Riyadh), pp. 240-41.

TABLE 9.5

Output of Refined Products, Jedda Refinery, 1968-72
(million barrels)

	1968	1969	1970	1971	1972
Intermediate products	—	*	*	*	0.1
Asphalt	—	—	*	*	*
LPG	*	*	*	36.6	*
Fuel oil	0.5	1.2	0.6	0.5	0.7
Diesel oil	0.2	0.6	0.6	0.6	0.6
Motor gasoline	0.2	0.5	0.6	0.7	0.8

*Fewer than 100,000 barrels.

Source: CDS, Statistical Yearbook, 1393 A.H., vol. 9 (Riyadh, 1973), pp. 240-41.

Two additional refineries have been constructed. The Jedda refinery went on stream in 1968 with a rated capacity of 15,000 BPD (See Table 9.5). In 1970 output was 2 million barrels, meeting about 30 percent of demand for refined products. To meet even more of the demand for refined products in the western part of the country capacity of the refinery was enlarged to 45,000 BPD. This project was to be completed by the end of 1974. An additional 15,000 BPD capacity is planned to be added by 1978. With this expansion it is expected that the Jedda refinery will meet total demand for refined products in the western regions.

The other refinery with a capacity of 15,000 BPD is under construction in Riyadh. Designed to meet the needs of the Central Province, the first construction stage was expected to be completed by the end of 1974. An additional 5,000 BPD capacity is planned to be added by 1977.

Table 9.6 gives the production statistics for the refineries built by Getty Oil and AOC. Although located outside the Kingdom in the Neutral Zone between Saudi Arabia and Kuwait, these installations must be considered part of the nation's petroleum sector. The Mina Saud refinery went on stream in 1958, and the Al Khafji refinery (built by AOC) in 1966. Both installations are relatively small. In its first year of operations the Getty refinery produced 5 million

TABLE 9.6

Output of Refined Products in the Neutral Zone, by Refinery, 1958-72
(million barrels)

	Al Khafji (AOC)			Mina Saud (Getty Oil)			
Year	Diesel Oil	Bunker Oil	Naphtha	Exhaust Gas	Topped Crude Oil	Naphtha	Fuel Oil
1958	—	—	—	0.1	2.4	0.3	2.2
1959	—	—	—	—	—	0.5	3.5
1960	—	—	—	0.3	9.8	0.4	2.4
1961	—	—	—	0.3	7.1	0.4	2.8
1962	—	—	—	0.3	6.0	0.7	5.0
1963	—	—	—	—	6.3	0.3	2.8
1964	—	—	—	—	4.3	0.5	4.6
1965	—	—	—	—	2.9	0.8	7.5
1966	*	0.3	0.1	—	0.7	0.8	8.2
1967	*	2.7	0.9	—	0.2	0.8	7.4
1968	0.2	4.8	1.4	—	1.1	0.7	6.6
1969	*	2.2	0.7	—	2.9	0.8	4.6
1970	0.2	5.3	1.7	—	0.7	0.9	7.3
1971	0.3	6.1	1.9	—	*	1.2	9.5
1972	0.3	6.6	2.1	—	*	1.5	10.3

*Fewer than 100,000 barrels.

Sources: 1958: CDS, Statistical Yearbook, 1385 A.H., vol. 1 (Riyadh, 1965), p. 94; 1959-62: Ibid., 1389 A.H., vol. 5 (Riyadh, 1969), p. 232; 1963/72: Ibid., 1393 A.H., vol. 9 (Riyadh, 1973), pp. 240-41.

barrels of products, and in 1972 production was 11.8 million barrels of refined products. The Al Khafji refinery began operations with about 400,000 barrels of product and reached 9 million barrels of refined products in 1972.

PRODUCT EXPORTS, BY COMPANY AND DESTINATION

Crude Oil Exports

By far the largest percentage of crude oil exported by Aramco went to Europe, Asia, and Australia (see Table 9.7). In 1955, 42.9 percent of crude oil exported was shipped to Europe, 38 percent to Asia and Australia, 13.5 percent to North America, and 3.5 percent to Africa. From 1955 to 1957 the shipments to Europe rose 29.6 percent, from 118.6 million barrels to 153.7 million barrels, declined to 144.8 million barrels in 1958, increased to 161.4 million barrels in 1959, and rose by only 10.6 percent from 1959 to 1961. From 1955 to 1964 exports of crude oil to Europe by Aramco fluctuated between about 43 and 46 percent of total shipments. Beginning in 1967, crude shipments to Europe rose steadily as a percent of total shipments, from 51.2 percent to 59.2 percent in 1972. Shipments to Asia and Australia declined from 38 percent of total in 1955 to 27.4 percent in 1972. Thus, it appears that the increased shipments to Europe were made by a decline of Aramco shipments to Asia and Australia.

As shown, too, in Table 9.7, exports of crude to North America during the period under discussion were not important. In 1955 Saudi Arabia shipped 37.4 million barrels, or 13.5 percent of total output, to North America. In the subsequent years the amount of crude exported in that direction rose slightly, while the relative share of total exports to the North American continent declined to 7.9 percent in 1964. In 1970 exports of crude to North America reached their low point, with 12.2 million barrels, or 1.1 percent of total shipments. During the next two years, crude exports shot up to 84.2 million barrels, or 4.4 percent of total exports, and it appears that this trend of increasing exports to North America has continued.

Aramco's exports to the rest of the world have been relatively unimportant. It is interesting to note, however, that the effect of the recent price increases in Africa is already reflected in exports to Africa. From 1967 to 1971 exports of crude to Africa rose from 40.9 million barrels, or 5 percent of total exports, to 67.4 barrels, or 4.7 percent of total exports. In 1972 these exports declined to

TABLE 9.7

Exports of Crude Oil and Refined Products, by Company and Destination, Selected Years, 1955-72
(million barrels)

	1955				1958			
	Crude Oil		Refined Products		Crude Oil		Refined Products	
	Barrels	Percent	Barrels	Percent	Barrels	Percent	Barrels	Percent
Aramco								
Europe	118.6	42.9	5.4	8.2	144.8	47.2	5.9	11.2
North America	37.4	13.5	—	—	39.9	13.0	—	—
South America	5.8	2.1	—	—	12.0	3.9	—	—
Asia and Australia	104.9	38.0	18.3	27.6	109.2	35.5	13.1	24.8
Africa	9.7	3.5	10.0	15.1	1.3	0.4	6.5	12.3
Other	—	—	32.5	49.1	—	—	27.4	51.7
Total	276.4	100.0	66.1	100.0	307.2	100.0	52.9	100.0
Getty Oil								
Europe	1.1	27.5	—	—	0.4	2.8	—	—
North America	1.4	35.0	—	—	13.2	92.3	1.5	93.7
South America	1.5	37.5	—	—	0.7	4.9	—	—
Asia and Australia	—	—	—	—	—	—	—	—
Africa	—	—	—	—	—	—	—	—
Other	—	—	—	—	—	—	0.1	6.3
Total	4.0	100.0	—	—	14.3	100.0	1.6	100.0
AOC								
Europe	—	—	—	—	—	—	—	—
Asia and Australia	—	—	—	—	—	—	—	—
Other	—	—	—	—	—	—	—	—
Total	—	—	—	—	—	—	—	—
All companies	280.4	—	66.1	—	321.5	—	54.5	—

(continued)

TABLE 9.7 (continued)

	1961				1964			
	Crude Oil		Refined Products		Crude Oil		Refined Products	
	Barrels	Percent	Barrels	Percent	Barrels	Percent	Barrels	Percent
Aramco								
Europe	178.5	42.8	1.7	2.2	242.8	46.0	1.4	1.5
North America	42.0	10.1	0.2	0.3	41.4	7.8	0.8	0.9
South America	42.5	10.2	*	—	38.0	7.2	0.1	0.1
Asia and Australia	150.0	36.0	29.2	38.0	193.3	36.7	35.6	38.9
Africa	3.9	0.9	9.0	11.7	11.5	2.2	12.9	14.1
Other	—	—	36.7	47.8	—	—	40.7	44.5
Total	416.8	100.0	76.8	100.0	527.0	100.0	91.6	100.0
Getty Oil								
Europe	2.2	8.2	0.1	5.6	4.9	17.1	0.3	7.3
North America	17.7	66.3	0.4	22.2	17.3	60.5	0.3	12.2
South America	6.8	25.5	—	—	—	—	—	—
Asia and Australia	—	—	0.2	11.1	6.2	21.7	2.4	58.5
Africa	—	—	—	—	—	—	—	—
Other	—	—	1.1	61.1	0.2	0.7	0.9	22.0
Total	26.7	100.0	1.8	100.0	28.6	100.0	4.2	100.0
AOC								
Europe	—	—	—	—	—	—	—	—
Asia and Australia	—	—	—	—	31.6	100.0	—	—
Other	3.5	100.0	—	—	—	—	—	—
Total	3.5	100.0	—	—	31.6	100.0	—	—
All companies	447.1	—	78.7	—	587.6	—	95.2	—

	1967				1970			
	Crude Oil		Refined Products		Crude Oil		Refined Products	
	Barrels	Percent	Barrels	Percent	Barrels	Percent	Barrels	Percent
Aramco								
Europe	421.9	51.2	3.7	3.3	606.8	55.4	5.8	3.0
North America	38.4	4.7	—	—	12.2	1.1	0.1	0.1
South America	32.6	4.0	1.5	1.3	50.6	4.6	6.1	3.2
Asia and Australia	288.2	35.1	42.7	38.2	376.5	34.3	92.3	47.9
Africa	40.9	5.0	3.9	3.5	50.6	4.6	7.9	4.1
Other	—	—	59.9	53.5	—	—	80.4	41.7
Total	822.0	100.0	111.7	100.0	1,096.7	100.0	192.6	100.0
Getty Oil								
Europe	3.2	19.8	0.3	4.2	1.0	5.3	0.9	11.1
North America	3.3	20.4	0.9	12.7	8.6	45.7	0.6	7.4
South America	—	—	—	—	—	—	—	—
Asia and Australia	9.5	58.6	5.0	70.4	9.2	49.0	6.6	81.5
Africa	—	—	—	—	—	—	—	—
Other	0.2	1.2	0.9	12.7	—	—	—	—
Total	16.2	100.0	7.1	100.0	18.8	100.0	8.1	100.0
AOC								
Europe	—	—	—	—	0.2	0.3	—	—
Asia and Australia	46.6	100.0	2.0	100.0	58.4	99.7	7.1	100.0
Other	—	—	—	—	—	—	—	—
Total	46.6	100.0	2.0	100.0	58.6	100.0	7.1	100.0
All companies	884.8	—	120.8	—	1,174.1	—	207.9	—

(continued)

TABLE 9.7 (continued)

	1971				1972			
	Crude Oil		Refined Products		Crude Oil		Refined Products	
	Barrels	Percent	Barrels	Percent	Barrels	Percent	Barrels	Percent
Aramco								
Europe	809.8	56.2	7.6	8.1	1,125.5	59.2	7.1	3.8
North America	58.4	4.0	2.6	2.8	84.2	4.4	5.4	2.9
South America	91.3	6.3	7.5	8.0	114.4	6.0	5.3	2.8
Asia and Australia	416.4	28.8	69.6	74.4	522.6	27.4	74.8	39.8
Africa	67.4	4.7	6.3	6.7	57.9	3.0	7.9	4.2
Other	—	—	—	—	—	—	87.1	46.5
Total	1,443.4	100.0	93.4	100.0	1,904.6	100.0	187.8	100.0
Getty Oil								
Europe	1.2	5.1	1.6	15.8	—	—	—	—
North America	11.9	50.4	1.3	12.9	5.7	33.5	0.4	3.6
South America	—	—	—	—	—	—	—	—
Asia and Australia	10.5	44.5	7.0	69.3	11.3	66.5	9.9	88.4
Africa	—	—	—	—	—	—	—	—
Other	—	—	0.2	2.0	—	—	0.9	8.0
Total	23.6	100.0	10.1	100.0	17.0	100.0	11.2	100.0
AOC								
Europe	2.9	4.8	—	—	4.8	6.8	—	—
Asia and Australia	58.1	95.2	5.6	67.5	65.0	91.5	6.1	67.0
Other	—	—	2.7	32.5	1.2	1.7	3.0	33.0
Total	61.0	100.0	8.3	100.0	71.0	100.0	9.1	100.0
All companies	1,528.3	—	111.3	—	1,992.5	—	208.2	—

*Fewer than 100,000 barrels.

Sources: 1955, 1958, 1961: CDS, Statistical Yearbook, 1385 A.H., vol. 1 (Riyadh, 1965), pp. 99-100; 1964: Ibid., 1389 A.H., vol. 5 (Riyadh, 1969), p. 233; 1967, 1970-72: Ibid., 1393 A.H., vol. 9 (Riyadh, 1973), p. 242.

57.9 million barrels, or 3 percent of total exports. In view of the steady increase of crude exports to Africa prior to 1972 and the known acceleration of African economic development in recent years, it can only be concluded that the decline in crude shipments to Africa is the result of the increase in crude oil prices.

From 1955 to 1961 shipments of crude produced by the Getty Oil Company went to Europe and North America. In 1955 Europe received 27.5 percent of Getty crude shipments, and North and South America accounted for 35 and 37.5 percent of shipments, respectively. Beginning in 1962 the Getty Oil Company stopped shipments to Latin America and lowered shipments to Europe until it stopped these shipments altogether in favor of North America and Asia and Australia. Crude shipments to North America fluctuated considerably between 1962 and 1972, with a high of 50.4 percent in 1971. In 1972, one-third of Getty crude shipments went to North America and two-thirds to Asia and Australia.

Shipments by the AOC began in 1961. Since its beginning, AOC has exported more than 90 percent of its crude to Japan; the remainder has gone to Europe or other destinations.

Refined Oil

Table 9.7 gives the picture for the export of refined oil by Aramco, Getty Oil, and AOC. It is somewhat difficult to determine the geographic distribution of Aramco-produced refined oil, because nearly 50 percent of those shipments have been classified under the "other" category: In 1955, 53.5 percent of total refined oil shipped by Aramco is listed in the "other" category; the proportion of total refined oil registered under that category fluctuated considerably in the subsequent years, reaching a low in 1970, with 80.4 million barrels, or 41.7 percent of total shipments, and a high of 53.5 percent of total shipments, or 59.9 million barrels, in 1967. Of course, the change in the proportional share of the shipment of refined oil is affected by changes in total production, but the overall conclusion holds: Most of Aramco's output of refined oil has not been classified among the four major geographical areas. It is impossible to explain why such a large portion was reported in a catch-all classification for the period 1955-67. However, it is possible that since 1968 the largest portion of this oil went to the U.S. military fighting in South Vietnam. Europe absorbed a declining share of refined oil output until 1966, and since that year it rose slowly until it reached 3.8 percent of total output in 1972. Refined oil was first exported to North America in 1960; until 1970 the proportion was less than 1 percent in most years, but in 1971 and 1972 it rose to nearly 3 percent of total refined oil products. Africa and Asia and Australia accounted for most of the refined oil recorded in the remaining categories except those listed under "other."

Shipments of refined oil by the Getty Oil Company have been primarily destined for Asia and Australia. Shipments of refined oil to these continents by this company began in 1961, when 11.1 percent of refined oil was shipped in that direction. In 1972 the percentage of total refined shipments by Getty Oil reached 88.4 percent. Refined oil shipped from the Al-Khafji refinery operated by AOC was destined for Asia and Australia until 1970. In 1971 and 1972 there was a shift away from Asia and Australia, and in the latter year the geographic distribution of refined oil shipments was 67 percent to Asia and Australia and 33 percent "other" destinations.

EMPLOYMENT

By far the largest single employer of Saudi workers in the private sector is Aramco. The company's employment record is a textbook illustration of the small number of employment opportunities created when the leading sector is a capital intensive industry. Total employment by Aramco fluctuated between 24,160 in 1952 and 10,865 in 1969 (see Table 9.8). Total employment declined steadily between 1952 and 1972. While overall employment declined throughout the period shown in Table 9.8, the percentage of Saudi employees in the Aramco workforce rose from 61 percent in 1952 to 83 percent in 1969. The increase in the workforce from 11,282 in 1972 to 13,001 in 1973 is associated with the increase in output beginning in 1971, following the Teheran Agreement.

Although the total number of Saudi employees of Aramco is small relative to the nation's labor force, the men employed by the company have reached a high degree of skill in their various jobs. Aramco's workforce is by far the most highly trained group of workers in the economy. Over the years more and more Saudi nationals have been promoted into professional and management positions. In 1963 Saudi Arabs held 75 percent of the first-line supervisory positions, 42 percent of the technical positions, and 8 percent of the professional positions.[1] In 1969, 37 percent of the 573 supervisory and management positions were held by Saudi Arabs,[2] and by 1973 this proportion had risen to 40 percent.[3]

Aramco has contributed greatly to the skill level of the Saudi labor force. It has an active training program that has turned out numerous skilled workers. Unfortunately, the spread effect from this training effort has been low because of the wage structure prevailing in the industry. On the average, Aramco employees receive a higher

TABLE 9.8

Employment in the Oil Sector, Aramco, Selected Years, 1948-73

Year	Total Employment	Number of Saudis in Workforce	Saudi Employees as Percent of Workforce
1948	18,637	12,226	66
1949	15,314	10,026	65
1952	24,160	14,819	61
1955	20,397	13,371	66
1957	18,325	12,729	69
1959	16,257	11,682	72
1962	13,573	10,582	78
1964	12,880	10,304	80
1966	12,664	10,258	81
1968	11,525	9,451	82
1969	10,865	9,018	83
1972	11,282	9,211	82
1973	13,001	10,238	79

Sources: 1948-59: Aramco, Aramco Handbook (1960), p. 161; 1962-73: Aramco, annual reports, various issues.

wage for any given job than do those in the rest of the economy. As has been shown, employment by the company declined between 1952 and 1972, freeing a number of skilled workers for employment in the nonoil sectors. However, the movement of skilled workers from Aramco to other sectors of the economy did not take place, because of the high wage levels and relatively pleasant working conditions prevailing in the oil industry. Instead of moving out and seeking jobs elsewhere, skilled workers have been "bumping" less skilled workers out of their positions. Thus, it is not unusual to find low-skill jobs, such as tea boy, cafeteria helper, and so on, filled by heavy-equipment operators. The recent dramatic increase in production may have reversed this trend. However, it is too soon to draw a firm conclusion.

A similar trend in the employment pattern is apparent in the activities of AOC. In 1967, about 45 percent of all employees were Saudi nationals, and in 1969 about 46 percent of the jobs were held by Saudis. The lower number of Saudi nationals employed by AOC results from its location in the Neutral Zone, where the employment of

Kuwaities and other Arabs compares favorably with the employment pattern of Aramco. In 1967, 86.4 percent of all AOC employees were Arabs, and in 1969 Arabs constituted 87.6 percent. As in the case with Aramco, AOC has spared no effort to train Arabs and prepare them for professional or management positions.[4]

OIL PRICES

It is difficult to conceive of markets for any commodity where the pricing mechanism is more complicated and information on actual prices more jealously guarded than those in the oil market. Two types of price prevail in the oil industry: realized prices and posted prices. Realized prices are those actually paid by the buyers of oil and oil products; posted prices are those that are announced publicly and at which the seller of crude is willing to sell his product to an offtaker f.o.b. the seller's terminal. From an economist's view, posted prices are "nonprices" that are "merely a means of roundabout calculation of what comes close to a per-barrel tax on production."[5] Except for mid-year 1957, discounts of various types reduced realized prices below posted prices.[6]

Despite their unimportance to an economic analysis of the oil industry, posted prices are significant to our analysis of the Saudi economy because they determine the revenue received by the government. Table 9.9 gives the posted prices for crude exports from Ras Tanura since 1948. In 1948 posted prices fluctuated between $2.03 and $2.08 for an average price of $2.05.* The following years posted prices fell to $1.75 and remained at that level until July 1953, when they were raised by 12.6 percent to $1.97. A second increase took place in 1957, when 36.0° crude was raised to $2.12, and that for 34.0° crude to $2.08. Also in that year a posted price of $1.79 was announced for Arabian Heavy crude. Those increases amounted to 7.6 percent of posted prices for 36.0° crude and 7.8 percent of 34.0° crude.

The 1957 increases were maintained for a short time only. In September 1958 the posted price of Arabian Heavy crude oil was lowered to $1.65; there was an additional reduction to $1.50 in February. At the same time the posted price for Arabian Light (34.0 API) was lowered to $1.90 per barrel. By the end of 1960 posted prices had settled at $1.80, $1.59, and $1.47 for Arabian Light, Medium, and Heavy, respectively. With minor adjustments these prices

---

*This is for Arabian Light. Sales of the grade of crude oil were stopped in July 1953.

TABLE 9.9

Posted Crude Oil Prices f.o.b. Ras Tanura, May 1948 to January 1974
(dollars per barrel)

	Arabian Light (36.0° to 36.9°)	Arabian Light (34.0° to 34.9°)	Arabian Medium (31.0° to 31.9°)	Arabian Heavy (27.0° to 27.9°)
1948				
May 18	2.03	—	—	—
June 15	2.08	—	—	—
July 1	2.07	—	—	—
October 15	2.03	—	—	—
1949				
April 1	1.88	—	—	—
September 7	1.75	—	—	—
1950				
November 1	1.75[a]	—	—	—
1953				
July 17	1.97	—	—	—
July 21	—	1.93	—	—
1957				
April 29	—	—	—	1.68
June 7	2.12	2.08	—	1.79
1958				
September 8	—	—	—	1.65
1959				
February 13	—	1.90	—	1.50
1960				
August 9	—	1.80	—	1.47
October 1	—	—	1.59	—
1970				
August 31	—	1.80	1.68	1.56
Terheran Agreement				
February 15, 1971	—	2.180	2.085	1.960
Follow-up, January 1, 1973[b]	—	2.591	2.482	2.345
Geneva Agreement				
January 20, 1972	—	2.479	2.373	2.239
Revised, June 1, 1973	—	2.898	2.776	2.623
First Gulf States Price Declaration				
October 16, 1973	—	5.119	4.903	4.633
Second Gulf States Price Declaration				
January 1, 1974	—	11.651	11.561	11.441
Percent Change				
August 1970 to January 1974	—	547.3	588.2	633.4

[a]First public posting.
[b]An increase of 2.5 percent +5 cents over the previous price.

Sources: 1948-1960: Aramco, Folio of Background Petroleum Data (January 1969), p. 68; 1970-1974: SAMA, Annual Report, 1392/93 A.H. (Jedda, 1974), p. 26.

prevailed until the Teheran Agreement between OPEC and the international oil companies.

The next round of posted price changes began in 1971, following the successful takeover of the pricing mechanism, by the oil-producing nations. As a result of a series of negotiations between OPEC and the oil companies, posted prices for Arabian Light rose nearly 550 percent, from $1.80 per barrel in August 1970 to $11.651; those for Arabian Medium rose 588 percent, from $1.68 to $11.561; those for Arabian Heavy rose 633 percent, from $1.56 to $11.441.

Since the body of this chapter was written further changes have taken place. Saudi Arabia and the three Gulf states decided to lower the posted price by $0.40 while at the same time adjusting royalty and income-tax rates. The new posted prices as of November 1, 1974, are:

Arabian Light	$11.251
Arabian Medium	$11.161
Arabian Heavy	$11.041

At the beginning of December 1974 OPEC members met in Vienna and decided to adopt a new price for Arabian Light crude (the benchmark for setting the prices for all other types of crude) at $10.12 per barrel. That price will prevail from January 1, 1975, to September 30, 1975, at which time new prices may be announced. The method of pricing by the oil cartel appears to signal the end of the posted-price tax-reference price mechanism.

A NOTE ON ARAMCO'S PROFITS

As was the case with actual market prices, information on the profitability of oil company operations is not available. Only one study has been published that attempts to lift the curtain of secrecy surrounding oil company profits: Zuhayr Mikdashi's.[7] Mikdashi reproduces two sets of accounting rates of return on invested capital that yield an average rate of return for the ten-year period 1952-61 of 57.6 percent and an average rate of 61 percent for the period 1956-60.[8] He concludes that the rates are too high, because they "are quoted for recent years only when Aramco's profitability was relatively high, and do not account for earlier years of little or no return."[9] To derive a better estimate of Aramco's profitability he applied the discounted-cash-flow method to the problem and concluded that Aramco's owners' DCF rates for the period 1934-64 were between 21 and 28 percent, considerably lower than the accounting rates of return. (The DCF is a better method of estimating rates of return, because it takes into account all investment, including those early years when Aramco's return on investment was nonexistent.)

NOTES

1. Aramco, Aramco 1963, annual report, p. 21.
2. Ibid., 1969, p. 14.
3. Ibid., 1973, p. 11.
4. AOC, Annual Review of Operations, 1969, p. 24.
5. Morris A. Adelman, The World Petroleum Market (Washington, D.C.: Resources for the Future, Inc., 1973), p. 161.
6. Ibid.
7. Zuhayr Mikdashi, A Financial Analysis of Middle Eastern Oil Companies: 1901-65 (New York: Praeger, 1966).
8. Ibid., p. 182.
9. Ibid., p. 183.

PART III

THE ECONOMY: THE PUBLIC SECTOR

CHAPTER

10

THE SOCIAL INFRASTRUCTURE

As in all other phases of Saudi life the development of sound and modern education and health-care systems had to begin from scratch. The existing traditional educational system with its religious orientation was not suitable for a modern economy. Except for one or two small institutions providing a secular education, Saudi Arabia's educational system was oriented toward religious schooling that stressed knowledge of the Koran and the Hadith, with special emphasis on memorization of the Koran. Secular subjects, except for basic arithmetic, reading, and writing, were not taught in the traditional schools. Thus, an important problem facing the economic planners was the creation of a modern, secular school system, from kindergarten to postgraduate university level.

The national health-care system was as primitive as the education system. Except for the medical care provided in the Eastern Province by Aramco and a few physicians trained in Western medical practice who worked in the major population centers, good health care was only available to those individuals who could go to England, Switzerland, or other European countries for treatment. Superstition and fear among the lower classes of Saudis prevented many of them from taking advantage of the rudimentary medical facilities.

In this chapter we will discuss the development of modern educational and health-care systems and pay brief attention to the cooperative movement and the facilities built to accommodate the pilgrims.

EDUCATION

Until the mid-1950s education consisted primarily of the teaching of Moslem doctrine and memorization of the Koran to boys; education of girls was practically nonexistent and took place, if at all, in the home. By and large the people accepted this state of affairs without complaint, because with very few exceptions Bedouin life—and even life among the sedentary—did not require much formal education. The resistance to education among the population is illustrated by the example of a driver in the employ of the agency for which the author worked: Again and again the Western-educated members of the team urged the man to go to school, but he refused because his grandfather had forbidden it. Clearly, raising the educational level of the population involves more than building the necessary schools; before that task can be accomplished attitudes toward education must be changed.

Table 10.1 gives the government's outlay on education. Total expenditures for education in 1959 amounted to S.R. 118 million, or 10.6 percent of the total government budget. From 1959 to 1973/74 total expenditures for education rose at an annual rate of 92.7 percent, to S.R. 1.7 billion in 1973/74. During that period, total education allocation as a percentage of total budget fluctuated between 9.2 and 12.2 percent, while allocations for educational purposes in the projects budget fluctuated between 2.3 and 6.5 percent.

What have these outlays achieved? As Table 10.2 shows, in terms of the number of students enrolled the achievement has been impressive: Total enrollment rose more than fourfold, from 143,000 pupils in 1960/61 to 739,300 in 1972/73, at an annual rate of 24.9 percent. Throughout the period under discussion the enrollment of boys rose about 280 percent, from 131,300 to 497,700. The most significant change, however, concerns the education of girls, whose enrollment rose from 5,200 in 1960/61 to 200,800 in 1972/73. This tremendous increase in female enrollment foreshadows important social changes. As long as women are held in ignorance and considered inferior to men, many of the social changes required to advance the nation's economic development will not take place, but the better educated the mothers of the coming generations are, the more substantial will be their influence in the breaking up of many conservative social constraints.

The number of students graduating on the elementary, intermediate, and secondary level has increased substantially (Table 10.3). The total number of male graduates rose 306.9 percent, from 10,020 in 1960/61 to 40,773 in 1971/72. In 1960/61 about 80 percent of the number of all male students graduated from elementary schools, 14.5 percent from intermediate schools, and 5.4 percent from secondary schools. By 1971/72 the percentage distribution had changed considerably: 66.5 percent of graduates came from the elementary level, 25.5 percent from the intermediate level, and 7.7 percent from the secondary level. Analysis of the statistics in Table 10.3 and an ex-

TABLE 10.1

General Budget Allocations for Education, Selected Years, 1959 to 1973/74
(S.R. million)

Year	Education in the General Budget	Percent of General Budget	Education in the Projects Budget	Percent of Projects Budget	Total Allocations as Percent of Total Budget
1959	118	10.6	—	—	10.6
1960/61	149	10.4	15.2	5.2	11.5
1962/63	223	9.8	35.4	6.4	11.3
1964/65	305	9.8	74.0	6.1	12.2
1966/67	399	7.9	113.4	6.5	10.2
1968/69	483	8.7	60.1	2.3	9.2
1970/71	646	10.1	72.9	2.7	11.0
1972/73	1,300	9.8	298.4	4.4	11.7
1973/74	1,677	7.4	565.5	4.0	9.3

Sources: General budget: see Appendix Table C.7; projects budget: see Appendix Table C.8.

TABLE 10.2

Number of Students, by Sex, in Public and Private Schools, Selected Years, 1960/61 to 1972/73
(thousand)

Year	Government Schools Boys	Government Schools Girls	Private Schools	Total
1960/61	131.3	5.2	6.6	143.0
1962/63	188.7	19.1	6.0	213.9
1964/65	244.3	42.2	13.0	299.5
1966/67	296.8	71.2	17.6	385.6
1968/69	352.9	105.4	27.1	485.4
1970/71	418.1	143.6	30.9	592.6
1972/73	497.7	200.8	40.8	739.3

Sources: 1960/61 to 1962/63: CDS, Statistical Yearbook, 1391 A.H., vol. 7 (Riyadh, 1971), p. 36; 1964/65 to 1972/73: Ibid., 1393 A.H., vol. 9 (Riyadh, 1973), p. 36.

amination of the allocation of funds to various aspects of education reveals an interesting fact: Although, according to Blaug, underinvestment in primary education in favor of higher education has been an important trend in most developing countries,[1] the trend has been reversed in Saudi Arabia. In 1963/64 almost 88 percent of general-budget funds and 96.7 percent of projects-budget funds were allocated by the Ministry of Education to primary education, 5.6 percent to college and university education, and 6.8 percent to religious education.* Those proportions stayed approximately the same with respect to the general budget. As far as the projects budget is concerned, the allocations for 1967/68 and 1972/73 show that higher education received an increasing share of the budget in those years. The growing share of the projects budget resulted from the need to build campuses for

*The division of the Ministry budget was made under the assumption that all funds not directly allocated to higher education or religious institutions are used to advance primary, intermediate, and secondary education. Furthermore, this broad classification of Ministry of Education budget allocations includes evening schools, most of which are concerned with the teaching of the basic skills.

TABLE 10.3

Male Students Graduated, by Level of Education, Selected Years, 1960/61 to 1971/72

Level and Major Subject	1960/61	1962/63	1964/65	1966/67	1968/69	1970/71	1971/72
Elementary	8,027	11,535	12,001	20,073	18,114	24,657	27,109
Intermediate							
General	1,390	2,443	2,653	4,632	5,829	6,867	10,069
Commercial	—	72	131	118	85	—	—
Agricultural	—	—	82	151	36	—	—
Industrial	—	168	231	305	4	—	—
Theology	59	65	95	98	146	110	118
Other	—	—	—	2	7	104	171
Secondary							
Arts	160	206	351	605	738	1,344	1,470
Sciences	351	477	459	592	1,012	1,187	1,469
Theology	33	—	68	78	77	180	163
Industrial	—	21	20	20	—	—	—
Professional	—	—	—	—	42	207	152
Other	—	—	17	22	19	23	25
Total	10,020	14,987	16,061	26,696	26,109	34,679	40, 773

Sources: 1960/61: CDS, Statistical Yearbook, 1391 A.H., vol. 7 (Riyadh, 1971), p. 60; 1962/63 to 1971/72: Ibid., 1393 A.H., vol. 9 (Riyadh, 1973), p. 61.

the country's colleges and universities. Our conclusion about budgetary priorities is further strengthened by the large number of primary-level students graduating from year to year.

Another interesting trend is the relatively small number of primary-level graduates who continue their education. Since 1966/67 the number of male elementary-school graduates has been close to 20,000 annually. Yet intermediate- and secondary-school graduates amounted to less than 50 percent of those receiving a primary-school diploma except for the year 1971/72. The relatively small number of advanced graduates is a direct effect of the government salary schedule. Salary scales for government employees are relatively high on all levels as compared with similar jobs in the private sector. Furthermore, the government needs many employees for which a primary-school education is sufficient. Given the fact that there are many openings on the lower levels of civil service at wage rates above those prevailing in the private sector, there is no incentive to acquire more advanced education. The inclusion of female graduates does not affect the outcome of the analysis.

An additional reason for the relatively small number of students continuing to more advanced education lies in the nature of Saudi society. The number of liberals is very small, and it cannot be stressed often enough that the majority of the population supports the conservative aspects of Wahhabism. Even many of those who have spent years abroad still subscribe to the conservative customs. Given the strong conservatism of the population, it is only natural that they neglect more advanced secular education. The Koran, shariah, and Hadith contain all the rules that should govern a Moslem's life. Once a youngster has studied those subjects and has acquired a minimum knowledge of reading, writing, and arithmetic there is no incentive to continue his education, because everything else is irrelevant to a good Moslem's life.

Postsecondary education is offered in two universities, one college, and three institutions dedicated to religious instruction (see Table 10.4). By far the largest institution of higher learning is Riyadh University. Established in 1957, it has grown into an institution with eight faculties and colleges and an enrollment of 4,369 students. Since 1960/61 enrollment has risen 88 percent, and the number of graduates rose from 15 in 1960/61 to 349 in 1970/71. The second largest secular university is King Abdul Aziz University in Jedda. Originally founded as a private institution, it has been taken over by the government and expanded considerably. Enrollment rose from 148 in 1968/69 to 2,480 in 1972/73, an increase of more than 1,500 percent. In 1970/71 the first class of 116 students graduated. In the third place stands the College of Petroleum and Minerals. Established as a training center for petroleum engineers, its student body

TABLE 10.4

University Education: Students and Graduates, by University, Selected Years, 1960/61 to 1972/73

	1960/61	1962/63	1964/65	1966/67	1968/69	1970/71	1972/73
University of Riyadh							
Students	541	1,005	1,194	1,352	2,202	3,607	4,369
Graduates	15	102	133	135	204	349	n.a.
King Abdul Aziz University							
Students	—	—	—	—	148	491	2,480
Graduates	—	—	—	—	—	116	—
College of Petroleum and Minerals							
Students	—	—	67	142	279	506	894
Graduates	—	—	—	—	—	—	—
Islamic University (Medina)							
Students	—	—	277	450	572	551	660
Graduates	—	—	—	—	108	135	—
Religious colleges and institutes							
Students	2,179	3,187	4,740	7,364	9,328	10,942	—
Graduates	261	390	477	511	870	452	—
Higher Institute of Islamic Law							
Students	—	—	—	67	67	75	68
Graduates	—	—	—	—	22	12	—

Source: CDS, Statistical Yearbook, various years.

has grown 123 percent, from 67 in 1964/65 to 894 in 1972/73. The three types of religious institution enrolled 11,568 students in 1970/71 (the last year for which reliable statistics are available). In that year they graduated nearly 600 students. The relative importance of religious schooling in Saudi Arabia is again underscored by those statistics.

Secular post secondary education has been considerably diversified since 1960/61 (see Table 10.5). In 1960/61 Riyadh University was the only institution with degree programs. In that year the university consisted of three colleges (faculties): liberal arts, science, and pharmacy, with enrollments of 189, 65, and 17 students, respectively; the Liberal Arts College graduated 15 students. By 1972/73 the university had grown to eight colleges with a total enrollment of 4,369 students of whom 825 (18.9 percent) attended the liberal arts college; 831 (19 percent), the faculty of commerce; 761 (17.4 percent), the college of science; 204 (4.7 percent), the college of pharmacy; 258 (5.9 percent), the college of agriculture; 590 (13.5 percent), the engineering college; 756 (17.3 percent), the school of education; and 138 (3.2 percent), the Faculty of Medicine.

The distribution of enrollments by college shows that the Kingdom's higher education is geared to the development effort. There can be no doubt that commerce, science, engineering, and education are crucial areas in which manpower requirements have to be met. Even the relatively high percentage of liberal-arts enrollments is designed to advance the development process, because these persons become the generalists needed to coordinate the separate efforts of the various governmental departments. In Saudi eyes the training of Saudi nationals as teachers has as much urgency as, if not more than, the education of engineers and scientists, because it is felt that non-Saudi Arabian teachers do not educate the nation's children sufficiently in the traditional ways of Islam.

To supplement the output of Saudi-trained experts and technicians from local institutions of higher learning the government supports a large program of scholarships for study abroad. In the year 1972/73 about 2,800 persons were studying in various countries under the direct sponsorship of the government. In addition to those students there is an unknown number of persons enrolled abroad who maintain themselves by private means. Of those students known to be abroad the majority are enrolled in engineering, public and business administration, and various medical fields.[2]

Education for the handicapped has not been neglected (see Table 10.6). In 1963/64 a total of 492 handicapped students received instruction in 34 classes; the number of individuals instructed in schools for the handicapped had grown to 1,572 by 1972/73. Instructed in 190 classes, 75.1 percent of those students received instruction on the

TABLE 10.5

Enrollment and Graduates, Riyadh University, by Faculty, Selected Years, 1960/61 to 1972/73

Faculty or College	1960/61	1964/65	1968/69	1970/71	1971/72	1972/73
Liberal arts						
Students	189	458	777	1,118	971	825
Graduates	15	50	75	120	143	—
Commerce						
Students	270	510	629	817	730	831
Graduates	—	48	51	79	111	—
Science						
Students	65	196	275	613	707	761
Graduates	—	24	30	60	73	—
Pharmacy						
Students	17	30	89	107	168	204
Graduates	—	11	4	15	18	—
Agriculture						
Students	—	—	95	161	200	258
Graduates	—	—	18	16	14	—
Engineering						
Students	—	125	294	410	425	590
Graduates	—	—	26	34	36	—
Education						
Students	—	—	43	312	481	756
Graduates	—	—	—	25	44	—
Medicine						
Students	—	—	—	69	100	138
Graduates	—	—	—	—	—	—

Sources: 1960/61 to 1968/69: CDS, Statistical Yearbook, 1390 A.H., vol. 6 (Riyadh, 1970), pp. 57-59; 1970/71 to 1972/73: Ibid., 1393 A.H., vol. 9 (Riyadh, 1973), pp. 49-51.

TABLE 10.6

Education of the Handicapped, Selected Years, 1963/64 to 1972/73

Level	1963/64	1965/66	1967/68	1969/70	1971/72	1972/73
Primary						
Students	—	—	859	1,052	1,056	1,180
Classes	—	—	73	106	120	145
Intermediate						
Students	—	—	40	81	89	137
Classes	—	—	4	11	15	19
Secondary						
Students	—	—	5	21	47	55
Classes	—	—	1	3	5	8
Total						
Students	492	722	990	1,248*	1,287*	1,572*
Classes	34	64	88	128*	151*	190*

*Excludes preparatory and nursing education.

Source: CDS, Statistical Yearbook, 1393 A.H., vol. 9 (Riyadh, 1973), p. 45.

primary level, 8.7 percent on the intermediate, and 3.5 percent on the secondary level. The remainder was enrolled in nursery and preparatory classes.

The first vocational school was established in 1949, but it appears that that sector of education has not grown as rapidly as the general education sector (see Table 10.7). In 1972/73 enrollment in industrial-training schools amounted to 58 in the higher levels and 977 on the secondary level. In addition, 363 students were enrolled in the Institutes of Physical and Technical Education of Riyadh; of those, 178 attended the Institute of Technical Education (see Table 10.8). An additional source of technically trained manpower is provided by the centers for complementary studies, which offer persons employed in various trades a chance to broaden their education or to keep themselves informed in the latest advances of their trade. Finally, there are the technical training centers supervised by the Ministry of Labor. Located in Dammam, Riyadh, Jedda, and the Qaseem they were established to alleviate local shortages of craftsmen. In 1972/73 they offered instruction in 14 different trades and graduated 2,466 persons, with the majority of graduates concentrated in automotive repair and maintenance (410), electricity (428), building trades (344), carpentry (332), and general mechanics (285).[3]

As has been mentioned before, one of the major concerns of the educational authorities is the nation's reliance on non-Saudi teachers. Table 10.9 offers an insight into this problem. In 1961/62, 7,431 teachers were employed in the school system. Of those teachers nearly 90 percent were engaged on the primary level, 10 percent on the intermediate and secondary levels, and the remainder were employed in higher education. Of the elementary teachers 46.1 percent were Saudi nationals, and 53.9 percent were non-Saudis. By 1972/73 the total number of elementary teachers had risen to 15,380, of whom 54.6 percent were Saudi nationals and the rest non-Saudis. That change in the proportion of Saudi versus non-Saudi elementary-school-teachers was achieved by the rapid expansion of elementary-school-teacher training. In 1966/67 there were seven institutes for the training of primary teachers, with an enrollment of 488 students.[4] By 1972/73 the number of institutes for elementary teacher training had been increased to 14, with an enrollment of 7,116 students.

On the intermediate, secondary, and university levels the instructional staff is predominantly non-Saudi. The total number of teachers on these levels rose more than fivefold from 848 in 1961/62 to 5,571 in 1972/73. While the number of Saudi teachers rose twelvefold, from 129 in 1961/62 to 1,746 in 1972/73, the number of non-Saudi teachers increased by more than 430 percent. However, the gap between Saudi and non-Saudi teachers has been narrowed: In 1961/62 Saudi teachers accounted for about 15 percent of all teachers

TABLE 10.7

Industrial Education, by Level, Selected Years, 1963/64 to 1972/73

Level	1963/64	1965/66	1967/68	1969/70	1971/72	1972/73
Higher technical institute						
Students	—	—	—	—	—	58
Classes	—	—	—	—	—	3
Secondary						
Students	—	—	543	692	765	977
Classes	—	—	34	26	43	52
Intermediate						
Students	2,305	1,445	182	2	—	—
Classes	80	72	15	1	—	—

Source: CDS, Statistical Yearbook, 1393 A.H., vol. 9 (Riyadh, 1973), p. 43.

TABLE 10.8

Various Educational Institutions, Selected Years, 1966/67 to 1972/73

	1966/67	1968/69	1970/71	1972/73
Physical and technical education institutes				
Students	118	233	310	363
Classes	6	11	17	17
Centers of complementary studies				
Students	940	867	989	995
Classes	30	30	31	31

Source: CDS, Statistical Yearbook, 1393 A.H., vol. 9 (Riyadh, 1973), pp. 43, 44.

employed on the postprimary levels; in 1972/73 the proportion of Saudi teachers was about 30 percent.

In the preceding discussion we have taken a look at the growth of Saudi Arabia's educational system. We will now briefly examine the quality and content of that system. Unfortunately, there is no adequate statistical description of the population and, therefore, it is impossible to derive the various quantitative measures usually employed to evaluate the effectiveness of the educational system. The only available statistics giving some insight into the quality of education concern the relationships between numbers of students, classes, and teachers. In 1960/61 there were 24 students per elementary class and 21 pupils per instructor. On the intermediate level there were 23 students per classroom and 15 per teacher; on the secondary level the relationship was 25 and 12 students per classroom and teacher, respectively (see Table 10.10). By 1972/73 the ratios had changed slightly: On the elementary level the number of students per classroom remained the same, but the student teacher ratio rose to 22; on the intermediate level the student-classroom ratio rose to 28.1, and the student-teacher ratio stayed the same; on the secondary level the ratios rose slightly, to 27:1 and 15:1. The ratios show that the expansion of the education sector since 1960/61 has been well thought through and has been implemented without any significant increase in classroom size or student-teacher ratios. It is important

TABLE 10.9

Number of Teachers, by Level and Nationality, Selected Years, 1961/62 to 1972/73

Level	1961/62	1963/64	1965/66	1967/68	1969/70	1971/72	1972/73
Elementary							
Saudi	3,037	4,472	4,551	6,175	6,786	7,504	8,391
Non-Saudi	3,546	3,829	4,151	4,658	5,441	6,283	6,989
Intermediate							
Saudi	105	194	326	601	778	1,106	1,265
Non-Saudi	514	591	813	1,423	1,896	1,851	2,409
Secondary							
Saudi	9	29	33	43	69	146	139
Non-Saudi	128	100	143	243	425	655	799
University							
Saudi	15	26	31	46	119	266	311
Non-Saudi	77	80	127	212	281	557	608

Sources: 1961/62: CDS, Statistical Yearbook, 1391 A.H., vol. 7 (Riyadh, 1971), pp. 39-41, 51, 52, 54; 1963/64 to 1972/73: Ibid., 1393 A.H., vol. 9 (Riyadh), pp. 39-41, 51, 52, 54.

TABLE 10.10

Number of Classes and Students, by Educational Level, Selected Years, 1960/61 to 1972/73

	1960/61	1962/63	1964/65	1966/67	1968/69	1970/71	1972/73
Kindergarten							
Classes	—	—	—	—	—	174	219
Students	—	—	—	—	—	5,694	7,679
Elementary							
Classes	4,406	5,991	7,374	9,038	10,414	11,740	13,950
Students	104,203	139,338	174,514	212,674	252,207	286,149	332,352
Intermediate							
Classes	341	414	487	728	1,203	1,515	2,041
Students	7,875	11,148	14,832	20,279	33,134	43,016	57,092
University							
Classes	45	68	76	117	263	395	517
Students	1,136	1,997	2,484	3,428	6,913	11,566	14,170

Sources: Kingergarten: CDS, Statistical Yearbook, various years; 1960/61: Ibid., 1390 A.H., vol. 6 (Riyadh, 1970), pp. 45-47; 1962/63: Ibid., 1391 A.H., vol. 7 (Riyadh, 1971), pp. 39-41; 1964/65 to 1972/73: Ibid., 1393 A.H., vol. 8 (Riyadh, 1972), pp. 39-41.

to stress that the gains in the educational level of the population were begun by the creation of a large pool of primary-school graduates, some of which are now moving into the intermediate and secondary levels.

It has been observed on several occasions that the Saudi Arabian school system is biased in favor of the traditional Moslem education. Although considerable changes have been made toward liberalization, many steps need to be taken before Saudi students are well prepared to contribute to the growth of a modern Saudi Arabia. The best illustration of the emphasis on religion in education is found in the time allocation of subject matter in the first six grades. In the first grade 75 percent of the school day is devoted to Arabic and writing and 14 percent to religion and Moslem Law.[5] In the second, third, and fourth grades the emphasis shifts to religious education: 57, 53, and 35 percent of class time in those grades, respectively, are devoted to religious subjects. Science is not taught, and about 10 percent of class hours is given over to the teaching of arithmetic.

PUBLIC HEALTH

Public Health and medical care appear to have had a relatively low priority in the allocation of the Kingdom's revenues. In 1960/61 S.R. 58 million, or 4.1 percent of general budget appropriations, were allocated to health-related activities. In the same year 3.8 percent of the projects budget (S.R. 11 million) was appropriated to medical facilities. By 1973/74 general-budget appropriations for the Ministry of Health amounted to S.R. 499 million, and projects budget appropriations stood at S.R. 842 million. However, while the absolute amounts allocated rose 760 and 665 percent, respectively, the relative share of total appropriations declined to 2.2 percent of general budget funds and to 0.6 percent of projects budget appropriations (see Table 10.11).

Given those trends, it appears that the government has been neglecting the health of the population. Furthermore, the relatively low priority assigned to public health care suggests that the government has missed a chance to redistribute income from oil, which would occur if the population were provided with high-standard, low-cost (or even free) medical services. Condemnation of government policy on this count is premature. The real reason for the relatively slow growth of outlays for health purposes is the low absorptive capacity of the economy for these expenditures. Modern medical science is highly capital intensive and requires well-trained professional and technical manpower that is unavailable in the Kingdom. In Saudi Arabia even the lowliest janitor must first be trained to appre-

TABLE 10.11

Budget Appropriations for Health, Selected Years, 1960/61 to 1973/74
(S.R. million)

	1960/61	1963/64	1966/67	1969/70	1972/73	1973/74
General budget						
Amount	58.0	103.0	154.0	155.0	375.0	499.0
Percent of total	4.1	3.8	3.1	2.6	2.7	2.2
Projects budget						
Amount	11.0	16.0	28.3	13.9	47.0	84.2
Percent of total	3.8	2.3	1.6	0.5	0.7	0.6

Source: See Appendix Tables C.7 and C.8.

ciate the need for absolute cleanliness before he can be trusted to perform his job well. Thus, the real reason for the relatively slow growth of public-health services is a reflection of the constraints to which that sector of the economy is subject—constraints that cannot be changed without prior social change. Given that factor, how much medical and health care is available to the population?

Table 10.12 gives the expansion of medical facilities in the nation. From 1960/61 to 1973 the total number of medical facilities rose about 320 percent, from 147 to 620. The number of hospitals grew from 40 to 54; the number of dispensaries grew 329.2 percent, from 48 to 206; the number of health centers grew more than fivefold, from 59 to 360 during that 14-year period. A look at the geographic distributions of the health care facilities shows that they are placed in the major population centers, and it appears that most of the people have access to them. In addition to the facilities mentioned in Table 10.12, a number of medical stations are maintained by the Tapline along the right of way of its pipeline. Finally, there exists a small number of private hospitals and physicians in private practice who supply medical care in the larger cities. Very little is known about the quality of those facilities, but the author's experience suggests that most of the dispensaries and health centers are well maintained and that staffing is adequate for treatment of minor illnesses and complaints. The quality of the hospitals varies with age, but most of them are well equipped for all but the most sophisticated procedures. The decline in the number of hospitals from 1966/67 to

TABLE 10.12

Number of Hospitals, Dispensaries, and Health Centers, Selected Years, 1960/61 to 1972

	Hospitals	Dispensaries	Health Centers
1960/61	40	48	59
1963/64	44	113	97
1966/67	51	179	209
1969	47	191	301
1972	51	190	343
1973	54	206	360

Sources: 1960/61: CDS, Statistical Yearbook, 1388 A.H., vol. 4 (Riyadh, 1968), p. 80; 1963/64 to 1972: Ibid., 1393 A.H., vol. 9 (Riyadh, 1973), p. 87; 1973: SAMA, Annual Report, 1393 A.H. (Jedda, 1974), p. 63.

1969 reflects the closing of several old, inadequate facilities and the consolidation of a number of smaller hospitals into larger, more efficient units.

The number of physicians and allied medical personnel rose considerably during the 13-year period beginning in 1960/61 (see Table 10.13). In that year 1,186 people provided various types of medical service. By 1972 this number had risen nearly fourfold, to 5,823 persons. In 1960/61 nurses (including midwives) accounted for 63.2 percent of medical workers, and physicians for 23.6 percent. In 1973 there were 1,268 physicians and 685 nurses (including midwives) employed in the Kingdom, increases of more than 350 and 324.4 percent, respectively.*

The data given in Table 10.14 suggest that there has been some improvement in the quality of medical care as reflected in the ratio of hospital beds per physician. The ratio declined 58 percent, from 16.7 in 1966/67 to seven in 1973, while the ratio of technical personnel to physicians stayed about the same. Furthermore, the ratio of in-patients to physicians in government-operated hospitals in 1972 was 200:1. On the average that amounts to less than one patient per day, implying that those sufficiently seriously ill to require hospitalization received adequate care from physicians.

The numerical relationship between physicians and medical technicians suggests that short-run improvements in medical care can be attained by greater emphasis on the training of medical technicians and assistants. One physician can easily supervise and direct more nurses than are currently available to him. Therefore, the employment of additional technicians to support available physicians would increase the productivity of the more costly factor, and because it is faster and less expensive to train assistants and technicians, it would help to bridge the longer time span required to train additional physicians.

The government carries on an extensive public-health program. Simple hygiene, prenatal advice to pregnant mothers, child care, and other education programs have been instituted in all parts of the country. Mass inoculation programs to combat smallpox, yellow fever, and many other diseases are being carried out. In 1971 about 1.6

*An interesting side issue is illuminated by the distribution of nurses by nationality. Of the 317 female recorded nurses and midwives only 12, or 3.8 percent, were Saudi nationals, and of the 634 male nurses 198, or 31.2 percent, were Saudi nationals. The distribution clearly illustrates the limited role of women in Saudi society. Yet it also suggests that despite all obstacles some Saudi women are discarding obeya and veil; the social order is changing. It may be slow, but the process has begun.

TABLE 10.13

Physicians and Allied Medical Personnel, Selected Years, 1960/61 to 1972

	1960/61		1963/64		1966/67		1969		1972		1973	
	Number	Percent	Number	Percent	Number	Percent	Number	Percent	Number	Percent	Number	Percent
Physicians	280	23.6	489	29.3	640	22.6	770	18.2	1,081	18.6	1,268	24.7
Pharmacists	21	1.8	23	1.4	41	1.4	50	1.2	78	1.3	685	13.3
Pharmacy assistants	86	6.7	127	7.6	329	11.6	447	10.6	513	8.8		
Nurses*	749	63.2	908	54.5	1,614	57.0	2,057	48.6	2,962	50.8	3,179	61.9
Laboratory assistants	32	2.7	76	4.6	137	4.8	184	4.3	253	4.3	n.a.	n.a.
X-ray assistants	24	2.0	44	2.6	71	2.5	98	2.3	138	2.4	n.a.	n.a.
Anesthesia assistants	—	—	—	—	—	—	50	1.2	65	1.1	n.a.	n.a.
Sanitary inspectors	—	—	—	—	—	—	303	7.2	440	7.6	n.a.	n.a.
Other technicians	—	—	—	—	—	—	275	6.5	293	5.0	n.a.	n.a.
Total	1,186	100.0	1,667	100.0	2,832	100.0	4,234	100.0	5,823	100.0	5,132	100.0

*Male and female nurses including midwives.

Sources: 1960/61: CDS, Statistical Yearbook, 1388 A.H., vol. 4 (Riyadh, 1968), p. 81; 1963/64 to 1972: Ibid., 1393 A.H., vol. 9 (Riyadh, 1973), p. 86; 1973: SAMA, Annual Report, 1393 A.H. (Jedda, 1974), p. 63.

TABLE 10.14

Hospital Beds and Technicians per Physician, Selected Years, 1966/67 to 1972

Number per Physician	1966/67	1969	1972	1973
Beds	16.7	13.4	10.1	7.0
Nurses	2.5	2.4	2.5	2.5
Health assistants	1.0	0.9	0.8	n.a.
Other technicians	0.2	0.3	0.3	n.a.

Sources: 1966/67: CDS, Statistical Yearbook, 1387 A.H., vol. 3 (Riyadh, 1968), p. 88; 1969: Ibid., 1390 A.H., vol. 6 (Riyadh, 1970), p. 91; 1972: Ibid., 1393 A.H., vol. 9 (Riyadh, 1973), p. 89; 1973: SAMA, Annual Report, 1393 A.H. (Jedda, 1974), p. 63.

million vaccinations and inoculations were administered, and in 1972 the number was almost twice that of the previous year.

Government medical care is augmented by physicians and hospitals in private practice (see Table 10.15). In 1969, 18 private hospitals with 917 beds offered medical services; in 1972 the numbers stood at 20 hospitals and 1,004 beds. On the whole the quality of care in private medical facilities is better than that found in public facilities. This evaluation is based on the author's personal experience, as well as on the relationship between physicians and technical personnel. In 1969 there were six beds per physician, and the ratio of nurses to physician stood at 4.1:1. By 1972 the ratio of beds to physician was 5.2:1 and that of nurses to physicians 3.6:1. Although the ratio of nurses to physicians declined between 1969 and 1972, it is interesting that it was almost twice as high as that found in government hospitals in 1969 and 40 percent higher in 1972. The relationship between health assistants and other technicians was about the same in both sectors.

In addition to education and health services there are two other aspects of the social infrastructure: cooperative societies and pilgrims. Both of these activities are supported and encouraged by the government and because they are related to social affairs we will cover them under the social-infrastructure classification.

TABLE 10.15

Private Medical Care, 1969 and 1972

Year	Hospitals	Beds	Physicians	Nurses	Other Technicians
1969	18	917	154	630	284
1972	20	1,004	192	695	211

Source: 1969: CDS, Statistical Report, 1390 A.H., vol. 6 (Riyadh, 1970), p. 121; 1972: Ibid., 1393 A.H., vol. 9 (Riyadh, 1973), pp. 118-19.

COOPERATIVE SOCIETIES

The cooperative movement was started in 1962 as part of the government's social-affairs program. Designed to give the members the advantages to be derived from joint action, the societies have been supported by the government, which has actively encouraged their formation with financial grants at start-up time, subsidies for current operations, and training in the bookkeeping and other skills needed to administer them.

In January 1973, 80 cooperatives with 25,828 members provided services. Five types of cooperative are currently active throughout the country. Multipurpose societies make up the largest number (29) of them: They build power stations and medical-care facilities; they have set up supply stations for consumer goods and have purchased well-digging equipment. The next largest number of cooperatives (22) were established for agricultural purposes, producing, storing, and selling produce. In third place stood consumer cooperatives (17) that specialize in the wholesale purchase of consumer goods for its membership. Service societies (10) and professional societies (2) account for the remaining number.[6]

By January 1973 the government had spent about S.R. 750,000 in its effort to encourage the growth of cooperative societies. It is impossible to evaluate the performance record of the societies because of lack of data. One set of statistics, however, offers some insight into their activities: Up to January 1973, 70 percent of the societies reported net profits totaling S.R. 627,769, which amounts to S.R. 11,120 per society and S.R. 27.5 per member of those units reporting a profit.[7] (Net profit is defined as total profit less transfers to reserves.) The value of total transactions undertaken amounted to

S.R. 9.2 million (S.R. 115,000 per society), and the value of social services performed amounted to S.R. 155,347. Measured in monetary terms, the effectiveness of the societies appears to be rather low. However, the real contribution of the cooperatives is not the profit returned to the members. Their contribution is that they provide services—for example, power stations—that the government would not have provided.

PILGRIMS

Until the discovery and exploitation of oil the receipts from payments made by pilgrims to Mecca were by far the largest item in the Kingdom's budget. Saudi Arabia's future rode on these receipts, and even the slightest decline or slowdown caused serious difficulties. Today, of course, taxes paid by pilgrims are of small consequence in the annual revenues. However, the facilities built to assure the pilgrims' arrival in Mecca and their comfort have increased from a few shacks to modern dormitories. At the Jedda airport and in the harbor the government has erected modern facilities to accommodate the ever-increasing flood of pilgrims. Those buildings are used only during the pilgrimage season.

Between 1956/67 (1376 A.H.) and 1973 (1393 A.H.) the number of pilgrims rose 182 percent, from 215,565 to 607,755. In 1972, 60,756 vehicles were used to move this mass of humanity in the performance of their religious duties. The government views the protection and care of the pilgrims as one of its most important obligations. To that end the facilities required have been constantly enlarged and improved, despite the fact that they are only fully utilized during the season of the Hadj.

NOTES

1. Mark Blaug, Education and the Employment Problem in the Developing Countries (Geneva: ILO, 1973), Ch. 2.
2. CDS, Statistical Yearbook, 1393 A.H., vol. 9 (Riyadh, 1973), pp. 68-69, 72-73.
3. Ibid., p. 145.
4. Ibid., p. 42.
5. George A. Lipsky, Saudi Arabia (New Haven, Conn.: HRAF Press, 1959), p. 328.
6. CDS, Statistical Yearbook, 1393 A.H., p. 152.
7. Ibid., pp. 149-51.

CHAPTER

11

THE MONETARY SYSTEM

A viable economy must have a well-developed, efficient financial system. This means that it must develop a money market, a capital market, and a banking system that facilitates the operation of these markets. The Kingdom has a fairly well-developed money market and an adequate commercial-banking system, but it lacks a capital market. SAMA, the central bank, controls the commercial banks, issues currency and coin, and administers the investment of the country's excess oil revenues, which the economy cannot absorb.

SAMA AND THE HISTORY OF MONETARY POLICY

Prior to 1948 the Kingdom did not have a financial system. Only one commercial bank, the Netherlands Trading Society, operated in the economy. Located in Jedda, the bank concentrated its activities in the import and export business through that port city. The money supply consisted of full-bodied coin, and the state's income was considered the King's personal income.

By the early 1950s the government realized that the increasing oil revenues provided a unique opportunity to accelerate the country's economic development. To achieve that end it was decided in the summer of 1951 to invite a group of U.S. financial experts into the country. The U.S. government formed a group of experts for this purpose and sent them to Saudi Arabia under the auspices of the Point Four Program. In October 1952 the main aspects of the reform program recommended by the experts were implemented. The government established a modified central bank called the Saudi Arabian Monetary Agency, with the following functions: (1) stabilizing the internal and external values of the riyal; (2) holding the country's monetary reserves; (3) selling gold and silver for the government; (4) assisting the Ministry of Finance and National Economy in holding the government's expenditures within the annual budgets; and (5) regulating the commercial banks. The following activities were expressly prohibited: (1) the granting of loans to the government or private individuals; (2) the taking or giving of interest; and (3) the issuing of paper money.

The agency was operated by a governing body headed by the minister of Finance and National Economy. Day-to-day operations were carried out by a U.S. financial expert, but control of the agency rested with the Ministry of Finance. Until 1958 SAMA had little independence, and by and large its activities were limited to the execution of the government's policy.

The Royal Decree establishing SAMA did not specify the extent of the agency's control over the commercial banks. That oversight was remedied on June 11, 1966, with the issuance of the Banking Control Law of 1966. Article 16 of that law provided:

> The Agency may, with the approval of the Minister of Finance and National Economy, issue general rules regarding the following matters:
>
> 1. The maximum limits of total loans that can be extended by a bank or banks.
> 2. The prohibition or limitation of specific categories of loans or other transactions.
> 3. Fixing the terms and conditions which banks should take into consideration when carrying out certain types of transactions for their customers.
> 4. The cash margins to be obtained by banks against specified categories of credits or guarantees.
> 5. The minimum ratio to be observed between the limits for loans and the collateral for such loans.
> 6. Fixing the assets to be maintained by each bank within the Kingdom. Such assets should not fall below a certain percentage of the bank's deposit liabilities [sic] which shall be fixed by the Agency from time to time.

The agency may vary the commercial-bank reserve requirement between 10 percent and 17.5 percent, "if it deems it to be in the public interest." If the need arises, the agency may alter these limits with the approval of the minister of Finance and National Economy. Finally, the agency has the usual supervisory powers to protect the public against fraud and mismanagement.

Until the end of the 1940s consumption by all sections of the population was constrained by the limited resources available. During most of his reign King Abd al-Aziz had scarcely enough funds to meet his current needs. It was not unusual that salary and wages of government employees were several months behind in payment. All that changed with the beginning of the oil revenue bonanza. As long as the Old King reigned the excessive spending did not affect the economy adversely, because he continued the frugal lifestyle of the desert. Following his death in November 1953, the restraints on spending loosened and the nation was plunged into debt.

In July 1955 two important constraints on monetary expansion through SAMA were eliminated. Owing to the successful introduction of "pilgrim receipts" (see p. 244), the injunction against the issue of paper currency and the granting of loans to the government was removed. Profligate spending, especially by the members of the royal family, triggered an unwarranted expansion of the money supply. To meet the government's increasing demand for funds 100 percent backing in full-bodied silver riyals of pilgrim receipts was abandoned. Although irresponsible expansion of the money supply was an important factor in the developing inflation, the primary cause of the 1957-60 monetary crisis was the sudden decline and leveling off of oil revenues, beginning in 1956. Oil revenues fell from $340.8 million to $290.2 million, a decline of about 15 percent, and by 1960 oil revenues had almost reached the level of 1955. The government's failure to adjust its expenditures on economic-development projects as well as on the King's private use, led to a considerable increase in the public debt. Those deficits were financed by loans from SAMA and from external sources: "At its peak, total government indebtedness had reached a figure somewhat exceeding one year's revenue receipts. Net indebtedness to the Monetary Agency alone amounted to about Rls 700 million by the middle of 1377 [December 1957]."[1]

The large deficits created balance-of-payments difficulties, because imports exceeded the available foreign exchange. Since Saudi Arabia must import nearly all its needs, it was not surprising that the domestic problems caused a large balance-of-payments deficit. In July 1957 foreign-exchange controls were introduced to correct the unfavorable balance of trade. The controls were ineffective, and the value of the Saudi Riyal declined on the international exchange markets to a low of S.R. 6.25 per U.S. dollar. By the end of January 1958 the agency's gold, silver, and foreign-exchange reserves had declined to 14 percent of the note issue. Import restrictions and the falling exchange rate increased the upward pressures on the price level, and a crisis of confidence ensued. That, in turn, resulted in a flight of capital from the Kingdom.

To limit the worsening crisis, Crown Prince Faisal engaged a team of IMF experts under the leadership of the late Anwar Ali, the funds director of the Middle East Department, and charged them to implement a reform program designed "to balance spending and income, pay off the national debt, curb inflation, and above all stabilize the riyal without disrupting business."[2]

The first phase of the program called for the elimination of budget deficits, and budget surpluses were planned to allow quick repayment of the outstanding debt. To prevent further declines in the international value of the riyal a dual-exchange system was introduced. Foreign exchange was made available at the official rate of S.R. 3.75 per U.S. dollar for the importing of basic necessities, such as textiles, milk, food grains, cattle, sheep, and so on, and of capital goods. For other imports the required foreign exchange was made available at the depreciated free-market exchange rate. The importing of automobiles was prohibited.

The program was an unqualified success. Two years after its implementation the government's debt to SAMA had been almost repaid. Owing to the elimination of budget deficits, the nation's foreign exchange position improved, and SAMA's gold and foreign-exchange holdings rose by about S.R. 644 million by December 1959. During the same time the free-market exchange rate of the riyal rose from S.R. 5.50 to S.R. 4.75 per U.S. dollar. The stabilization of the riyal's external value and the availability of increasing amounts of foreign exchange led to downward pressure in the domestic price level of consumer goods, "which stabilized after registering declines ranging between 15 percent and 20 percent during the period."[3]

The second phase of the reform began in December 1959 with the elimination of the dual-exchange-rate system and all import and export controls. The international exchange rate of the riyal was fixed at a par value of 0.197482 grams of gold, or equal to S.R. 4.50 per U.S. dollar. Two reasons are given for the choice of this exchange rate: First, it was felt that an increase to the old par value of S.R. 3.75 to the dollar would cause further deflation of the price level; second, an additional appreciation of the exchange value would have deprived the government of the source of income that had been used to repay the national debt.[4]

An important consideration in the establishment of the dual exchange rate was the desire to prevent losses to those businessmen who had made investments at the time of the riyal's lowest value. To achieve this an exchange-stabilization fund was established and used to meet importers' demand for foreign exchange. Furthermore, to prevent increases in domestic prices of essential goods the subsidy payments on imports of drugs and medicine, sheep, foodgrains, vegetable oil, and other critical items were continued. The subsidy payments were made in cash to importers for the amount of the difference between the old and new exchange rates.

THE CREATION OF A SYSTEM OF COINS AND CURRENCY

The creation of a system of coinage and paper currency is one of the government's outstanding achievements.[5] For hundreds of years numerous coins, minted in many parts of the world, circulated side by side in Arabia. Introduced by the Hadjis, British pounds, Dutch guilders, Indian rupees, and Maria Theresa thalers served as the medium of exchange. The circulation of paper money was limited to the areas around the major ports and coastal trading centers.

The establishment of a modern system of coinage was complicated by the government's adherence to the Koranic injunction that "things exchanged shall be of equal value." It led to several attempts to issue full-bodied silver coins that, in accordance with Gresham's Law, soon disappeared from circulation. That is, the coin's silver content became more valuable than its value as a coin. As a result, money changers and other holders of silver coins collected them, melted them down, and sold them on the international silver markets.

The first step in the creation of a national coinage was taken in 1925. Abd al-Aziz issued a copper-and-nickel coin called the quirsh. In January 1928 the silver riyal was issued, and it became the basis of the Kingdom's coinage. That riyal contained 22 quirsh, and its exchange value was fixed at 10 riyals for each British gold sovereign. As long as the relationship between gold and silver coins continued as it was at the time of issue, the silver riyal circulated freely. But the price of silver rose during the 1930s; the silver riyal became undervalued in terms of the price of silver, and it disappeared from circulation.

In 1936 a new silver coin was issued. It weighed 11.66 grams of silver, and its exchange rate was fixed about 3.75 silver riyals to the U.S. dollar. At the same time new half and quarter riyals and one, one-half, and one-quarter quirsh coins were issued.

As the economy grew, so did the demand for cash. In keeping with its policy that only full-bodied coins were acceptable as the basis of its coinage, the government placed additional gold and silver coins in circulation. In 1944 the government ordered large quantities of full-bodied silver riyals from the U.S. mint. The value of these coins was fixed at 30 U.S. cents, equal to the price the government paid to the U.S. mint. In 1948 and 1949 Aramco was asked to pay its oil revenue in foreign gold coins.

The Kingdom's first modern budget was issued in 1948, and it revealed the fact that the existing system of coinage was unsuited to meet the requirements of a growing economy. It proved unworkable, because the silver riyal, in which the budget items were expressed, fluctuated from day to day as the riyal changed in value in terms of the foreign coins still circulating in the country. Furthermore, the government's internal obligations were paid in silver riyals that became scarce as the price of silver rose in the world market.

The disappearance of silver coins owing to overvaluation was not the only problem resulting from the insistence on full-bodied coins in a world where such coins had long fallen into disuse. The "Gold Clause" controversy arose out of the provision that royalty had to be paid in gold. The agreements of 1933 and 1939 called for the payment of royalties at the rate of four gold shillings or its equivalent per ton. Following the outbreak of World War II, the price of gold sovereigns in Saudi Arabia rose far above that of New York or London official rates. The government demanded that royalty payments were to be made at the higher exchange rate prevailing in Saudi Arabia. The company refused and continued to calculate the sterling and dollar equivalents of its royalty payments on the basis of the prices prevailing in New York and London. Relations between the government and Aramco became strained and several attempts were made to resolve the dispute. In March 1948 a solution to the "Gold Clause" controversy was reached: The company agreed to calculate royalties due when paying in dollars at the rate of $12 per gold pound. In addition to acceptance of this new arrangement, Aramco agreed to pay $20.3 million in settlement of all past claims arising from this matter.

In 1952 SAMA issued a Saudi gold sovereign of the same weight and fineness as the British gold sovereign, with a par value of 40 Saudi riyals equal one British gold sovereign.

In addition to the government, Aramco became an important source of circulating coin. In the early 1950s Aramco met its payroll with silver riyals purchased from the government:

> With only one denomination of silver coin available a month's wages for a typical worker would weigh about 10 pounds. To meet the entire payroll the company had to transport, store, guard and count out 60 tons of silver each month. It also had to find extra storage space, provide a fleet of trucks and dozens of laborers to load and unload the sacks of coins plus a large staff of sorters and counters.[6]

By the end of the 1950s the silver coins had again become more valuable as a commodity than as currency. The Saudi government stood ready to redeem silver riyals at 27 U.S. cents, but the value of its silver content rose to more than 30 U.S. cents, and holders of riyals sold them for bullion. Attempts to stop the outflow of silver were unsuccessful, and the silver riyal was demonetized in 1959.

The responsible officials at SAMA had long recognized that the Kingdom's system of coinage had to be improved to meet the needs of the growing economy. Unfortunately, the agency's charter prevented it from issuing paper currency. A solution to the growing shortage of cash had to be found despite the law's injunction against paper money. The problem was solved by the issue of "pilgrim receipts."

To meet the seasonal demand for cash associated with the annual influx of pilgrims, SAMA proposed the circulation of a pseudocurrency to be issued to the pilgrims in exchange for their currency. The notes were to be backed 100 percent by silver riyals. The government approved the scheme in 1953, and SAMA immediately issued a small amount of the notes in ten-riyal denomination. The following year more pilgrim receipts were issued in ten- and five-riyal denominations. The notes found immediate acceptance throughout the country because they were more convenient in larger transactions than the bulky, heavy silver riyal. Thus, the issue of pilgrim receipts increased the efficiency of the nation's monetary system.

In June 1961, following the successful conclusion of the reform program discussed earlier, SAMA issued an official paper currency with denominations of one, five, ten, 50, and 100 riyals. At the same time the number of quirsh in a riyal was reduced from 22 to 20. For accounting purposes the quirsh was divided into five halalah. Cupronickel coins of one-, two-, and four-quirsh value were also issued. On December 20, 1972, SAMA began issuing new coins of five-, ten-, 25-, and 50-halalah denominations. The new coins will replace the older one-, two-, and four-quirsh coins currently in circulation. Withdrawal of the older coins will be slow to avoid inconveniencing the public. Until completion of the withdrawal both types of coins will circulate side by side.

THE MONETARY BASE

Table 11.1 gives the sources and uses of the Kingdom's monetary base as reflected in SAMA's balance sheet as of the end of the Hijra years 1380, 1388, and 1393 (May 1961, February 1969, and December 1973). The sources of the monetary base are foreign exchange, gold, foreign bonds, and coins held by SAMA. In 1961, 77 percent of the monetary base was held in foreign exchange, 22 percent in foreign bonds, and 0.9 percent in coin. By 1969 the distribution of these funds had changed to 70, 14, 16, and 0.1 percent for gold foreign exchange, foreign bonds, and coin, respectively. The relative decline of foreign-exchange holdings and gold in favor of foreign-bond holdings reflects SAMA's attempt to maximize the return on the country's assets. By 1974 the distribution had changed back again in favor of foreign-exchange holdings, which accounted for 82 percent of the sources of the monetary base, followed by foreign bond holdings (14.4

TABLE 11.1

Sources and Uses of the Monetary Base, 1961, 1969, 1974, at End of Hijra Year (S.R. million)

	1961	1969	1974
Sources			
Foreign exchange	818	2,915	13,108
Gold	237	574	546
Foreign bonds	—	687	2,292
Coins	10	5	2
Subtotal	1,065	4,181	15,948
Government deposits	293	1,512	9,776
Reserve funds	14	20	21
Other (net)	18	880	1,907
Subtotal	325	2,412	11,704
Total sources	740	1,769	4,244
Uses			
Commercial bank deposits with SAMA	89	200	1,092
Notes held by commercial banks	70	111	208
Currency held by public	581	1,458	2,944
Total uses	740	1,769	4,244

Sources: 1961, 1969: Ahmed A. Malik, The Money Supply Process in Saudi Arabia (Ann Arbor: University Microfilms, 1974), p. 179; 1974: SAMA, Annual Report, 1392/93 A.H. (Jedda, 1973), pp. 78-79.

percent) and gold (3.4 percent). The recent increases in oil prices led to an increase of 140 percent in the monetary base. In addition to the effect on the monetary base, SAMA's balance sheet gives some insight into the way the large surpluses result from the recent increases in oil revenues. On January 23, 1974, SAMA held S.R. 15.4 billion in highly liquid international assets ($4.2 billion at the parity rate of S.R. 3.7 to the U.S. dollar).

Uses of the monetary base are distributed among three items: commercial bank deposits with SAMA, notes held by commercial banks, and currency held by the public.* By far the largest proportion of uses was currency held by the public, which accounted for 78.5, 82.4, and 69.4 percent in 1961, 1969, and 1974, respectively. During the same years, commercial bank deposits with SAMA accounted for 12, 11.3, and 25.7 percent, respectively, with the remainder in notes held by commercial banks. The large proportion of currency held by the public indicates that the use of demand deposits is still low and shows the continued preference for cash transactions by the general public. The decline in currency held by the public, from 82.4 percent in 1969 to 69.4 percent in 1974, does not invalidate that conclusion. The reason for the decline in relative standing rests in the more than fivefold increase in commercial-bank deposits with SAMA, reflecting the huge expenditures on development projects that increased the bank's needs for deposits with SAMA to facilitate business transactions and the need for greater amounts of reserve deposits, both of which are contained in the heading commercial bank deposits with SAMA. (Demand deposits rose 126.7 percent, from S.R. 977.8 million on February 15, 1972, to S.R. 2,217 million on January 23, 1974.) What it may indicate is the fact that the general public has not yet received the full benefit of the country's increasing wealth.

THE GROWTH OF THE MONEY SUPPLY

Table 11.2 shows the growth of the money supply as measured by changes in currency in circulation and demand deposits at the end of the Hijra calendar year and the corresponding Gregorian dates. The total money supply grew at an annual rate of 13.4 percent, from S.R. 892.3 million in June 1960 to S.R. 5,160.4 million in January 1974, an increase of 480 percent. During the same time, currency in circulation rose from S.R. 517.5 million to S.R. 2,943.4 million, an increase of 460 percent, at an annual rate of 13.2 percent, while demand deposits grew nearly fivefold at an annual rate of 13.5 percent.

---

*Currency is placed into circulation in three ways: First, the Ministry of Finance and National Economy makes currency available to the various government departments for payment of various obligations—e.g., wages for government workers, payments to businesses for services rendered, et., second, SAMA changes foreign exchange into riyals; third, there are transfers of cash from SAMA's banking department to commercial banks.

TABLE 11.2

Currency in Circulation and Demand Deposits, 1960-74
(S.R. million)

Hijra	Gregorian	Currency in Circulation	Demand Deposits	Total	Percent Change in Total Money Supply
12/30/79	6/23/60	517.5	374.8	892.3	—
12/29/80	6/13/61	584.0	353.9	937.8	5.1
12/29/81	6/2/62	659.1	405.4	1,064.5	13.5
12/30/82	5/23/63	787.4	394.6	1,182.0	11.0
12/29/83	5/11/64	915.1	469.7	1,384.8	17.2
12/29/84	4/30/65	963.8	510.3	1,474.1	6.4
12/29/85	4/20/66	1,061.7	555.5	1,617.2	9.7
12/30/86	4/10/67	1,219.5	650.9	1,870.4	15.7
12/30/87	3/29/68	1,370.2	738.7	2,108.9	12.8
12/29/88	3/18/69	1,466.1	778.1	2,244.2	6.4
12/29/89	3/7/70	1,566.9	816.6	2,383.5	6.2
12/29/90	2/25/71	1,655.8	834.1	2,489.9	4.5
12/30/91	2/15/72	1,788.2	977.8	2,766.0	11.1
12/30/92	2/3/73	2,296.3	1,418.0	3,714.3	34.3
12/30/93	1/23/74	2,943.4	2,217.0	5,160.4	38.9

Source: SAMA, Annual Report, various issues.

The year-to-year change in the money supply has been rather erratic. From June 1960 to June 1961 it rose by 5.1 percent. During the following three periods, from June 1961 to May 1964, the money supply rose 13.5, 11, and 17.2 percent, respectively, followed by increases of 6.4 and 9.7 percent, respectively, during the next two periods. The next two periods experienced increases of 15.7 and 12.8 percent, respectively. From March 1968 to February 1971 the money supply registered increases of 6.4, 6.2, and 4.2 percent, respectively, followed by changes of 11.1, 34.8, and 38.9 percent, respectively. Table 11.3 gives the year-to-year percent changes in the monetary base and the money supply, beginning in 1962. After an inspection of these data, a reason is not suggested for the variability of the money supply in terms of changes in the money base. The only pattern that suggests itself is that, with the exception of the changes from 1967 and 1968 to 1969, there is a one-year lagged relationship

TABLE 11.3

Percent Change in the Monetary Base and Money Supply, 1961/62 to 1973/74

	Monetary Base	Money Supply
1961-62	4.7	13.5
1962-63	20.1	11.0
1963-64	15.3	17.0
1964-65	27.0	6.4
1965-66	45.6	9.7
1966-67	- 5.4	15.7
1967-68	17.3	12.8
1968-69	37.3	6.4
1969-70	-11.7	6.2
1970-71	9.9	4.5
1971-72	16.3	11.1
1972-73	22.8	34.3
1973-74	35.5	38.9

Source: SAMA, Annual Report, various issues.

in the direction of change between the money base and the money supply. For example, the money base increased by 20.1 percent from 1962 to 1963, and the money supply rose 17 percent between 1963 and 1964, as opposed to an 11 percent change in the money supply from 1962 to 1963. From 1969 to 1970 the monetary base declined by 11.7 percent, and the money supply rose only 4.5 percent from 1970 to 1971. Although there was an increase in the money supply from 1970 to 1971, it was the smallest increase of any year, held down to that level by the large decline of the money base in the previous year. Additional investigations into the component parts of the monetary base yielded no further insights into the relationship between money base and money supply.

The division of the money supply into currency and demand deposits (see Table 11.2) shows that the population has been rather slow in accepting demand deposits as a form of holding and using money. Since June 1960 the proportion of currency in circulation has been around 57 percent, and that of demand deposits about 43 percent of the money supply. The reluctance to use demand deposits is still deeply embedded. Around four or five years ago the government considered the possibility of paying its employees by check to accelerate

TABLE 11.4

Growth of GDP and Money Supply, 1962/63 to 1972/73
(S.R. million)

	GDP	Percent Change		Money Supply	Percent Change
1962/63	8,603.7	—	5/23/1963	1,182.0	—
1963/64	9,205.2	7.0	5/11/1964	1,384.8	17.4
1964/65	10,257.5	11.4	4/30/1965	1,474.1	6.4
1965/66	11,775.6	14.8	4/20/1966	1,617.2	9.7
1966/67*	13,078.6*	11.1	4/10/1967	1,870.4	15.7
1966/67*	13,142.5*	0.5*	3/29/1968	—	12.8
1967/68	14,656.6	11.5	3/18/1969	2,108.9	—
1968/69	15,975.3	9.0	3/7/1970	2,244.2	6.4
1969/70	17,398.6	8.9	2/25/1971	2,383.5	6.2
1970/71	22,921.2	31.7	2/15/1972	2,489.9	4.5
1971/72	28,257.3	23.3	2/3/1973	2,766.0	11.1
1972/73	39,987.5	41.5	1/23/1974	3,714.3	34.8

*Overlap with old Series.

Sources: GDP: Table 4.1; money supply: Table 11.2.

the use of banks and demand deposits among the population. The scheme was never implemented because of considerable resistance by the employees. Even paper currency is still viewed with suspicion. Nearly all employees are paid weekly with paper riyals that many of the recipients change almost immediately into gold or silver coin. On payday the money changers in the suqs do a land-office business. The distrust of all non-full-bodied currency is underscored by the fact that once the paper currency has been exchanged for silver, the purchaser will take each coin and test its soundness by throwing it on a piece of steel (supplied by the money changer) and listening to each coin's ring. Only if this test is satisfactory will the holder pocket his wages.

GDP AND THE MONEY SUPPLY

From 1962/63 to 1972/73 the GDP rose 16.6 percent per annum, and the money supply increased at an annual rate of 12.1 percent (see

Table 11.4). During the same 11-year period the year-to-year change of GDP fluctuated between 7 and 41.5 percent, while increases in the money supply moved between 4.5 and 34.8 percent. (The 0.5 percent change in GDP is ignored because it resulted from the change between the old and new GDP series.) The pattern of change in the two series is entirely unrelated. GDP rose 7 percent from 1962/63 to 1963/64, and the money supply rose 17.2 percent. During the next two periods (1963/64 to 1964/65 and 1964/65 to 1965/66) GDP rose 11.4 and 14.8 percent, respectively, and the money supply rose 6.4 and 9.7 percent, respectively. The next four changes, between 1965/66 and 1966/67 and 1968/69 and 1969/70, display a closer relationship in the movement of GDP and money supply. The changes from 1969/70 to 1970/71 and from 1970/71 to 1971/72 are again rather unrelated, while the final change from 1971/72 to 1972/73 displays a closer relationship.

The failure to find a reasonable relationship between the monetary base, the money supply, and GDP forces the conclusion that the monetary authorities have not carried out a monetary policy to affect those variables. Thus, it seems that they have simply acted as paymaster to the government without any considerations of the effect of the money variables on the rest of the economy.

RESERVES AGAINST CURRENCY

The Saudi riyal is one of the world's strongest currencies. Royal Decree Number 6, dated December 29, 1959, required that currency in circulation must be backed 100 percent by gold and foreign exchange convertible into gold. The agency has been in compliance with this provision. Between June 1963 and February 1971 the ratio of gold to notes outstanding fluctuated between 44.7 percent in May 1962 and 15.5 percent in January 1974 (see Table 11.5). On the average the gold cover amounted to slightly over 31 percent of currency outstanding.

COMMERCIAL BANKS

The growth of the commercial banking system has proceeded along with the development of the economy. From one bank in 1948, the number of commercial banks operating in the nation has grown to 12, operating 72 permanent offices and branches and 13 seasonal offices by the end of 1974. (SAMA has issued licenses for the establishment of 12 additional branches that will be opened in the near future.) With the exception of the United Bank, Ltd., the head offices are lo-

TABLE 11.5

Notes Issued and Reserves Held by SAMA, 1961-74
(S.R. million and percent)

	Amount of Notes Issued	Gold Holdings	Foreign Exchange Convertible into Gold	Ratio of Gold to Notes Outstanding	Ratio of Foreign Exchange Convertible to Gold to Notes Outstanding
6/13/61	727.3	237.6	489.6	32.7	67.3
5/5/62	784.3	350.2	434.1	44.7	55.3
5/23/63	921.6	349.7	571.8	38.0	62.0
5/11/64	1,070.8	349.7	721.1	32.7	67.3
4/30/65	1,122.2	349.7	772.5	31.2	68.8
4/20/66	1,271.3	348.8[a]	922.5	27.4	72.6
4/10/67	1,428.8	348.8[a]	1,080.0	24.4	75.6
3/29/68	1,608.8	348.8[a]	1,260.0	21.7	78.3
3/18/69	1,812.7	574.2[a]	1,238.5	31.7	68.3
3/8/70	1,880.2	574.2[a]	1,306.0	30.5	69.5
2/25/71	2,083.0	574.2[a]	1,508.9	27.6	72.4
2/17/72	2,201.0	574.2	1,626.8	26.1	73.9
2/3/73	2,755.3	574.2[b]	2,195.8	20.1	79.7
1/23/74	3,536.5	546.4[b]	3,006.9	15.5	85.0

[a]Includes S.R. 39.4 million subscription to IMF.

[b]Includes S.R. 88.9 million subscription to IMF on February 3, 1973, and S.R. 84.6 million on January 23, 1974.

Source: SAMA, Annual Report, various issues, Table III.

cated in Jedda with branches spread over the Kingdom in every major city. Two banks, the National Commercial Bank and the Riyadh Bank, are Saudi owned; another three banks, the Arab Bank Limited, Banque du Liban et d'Outre-Mer, and Banque du Caire, are Arab owned; the remaining seven are non-Arab owned. Although there are no recent statistics available on the relative size of Saudi and non-Saudi banks, it is safe to assume that Saudi-owned banks account for more than 55 percent of the total banking business in the Kingdom.

SAMA has been encouraging the spread of banking facilities throughout the Kingdom. Branches of banks have been opened in almost all towns with a population of more than 10,000 and in some of the towns with populations between 5,000 and 10,000. To accelerate this progress SAMA has subsidized the establishment of private branches. If the operation of a branch in a given town is unprofitable, SAMA absorbs these losses to encourage the opening of banking facilities in marginal areas. In mid-1973, 24.3 percent of the banking facilities were located in the central region, 34.3 percent in the eastern region, and 41.4 percent in the western region. That pattern accurately reflects the distribution of nonoil economic activity in the Kingdom.

SAMA's current objective is to gain Saudi control over the commercial banks. The first step in the plan was taken in 1968 when the Jedda branch of the National Bank of Pakistan was converted into a Saudi joint-stock company with 60 percent Saudi participation.

The Legal Framework

On June 11, 1966, Royal Decree Number M/5 was issued defining the legal framework of the commercial banking sector: National banks must be licensed by the minister of Finance and National Economy; the establishment of foreign banks is subject to conditions laid down by the Council of Ministers as proposed by the minister of Finance and National Economy, and its deposit liabilities may not exceed 15 times its reserves and invested capital.*

National banks must be Saudi joint stock companies, must have a minimum paid-up capital of not less than S.R. 2.5 million, and subscriptions to the share capital are payable in cash. Banks estab-

*A national bank is defined as "a bank the head office and branches of which are situated in the Kingdom"; a foreign bank, as "a bank with branches in the Kingdom and its head office outside it"; invested capital, as "the capital assigned by a foreign bank for the use of its branches in the Kingdom."

lished prior to the issuance of the law are exempted from the provisions. However, the agency may require compliance with Article 3 within a certain time period to be fixed by it.

The deposit liabilities of any bank may not exceed 15 times its reserves and paid-up or invested capital. If this limit is exceeded, the bank must within one month "either increase its capital and reserves to the prescribed limit or deposit 50 percent of the excess with the Agency." Banks must maintain reserve deposits with SAMA of not less than 15 percent. In addition to the reserve deposits held by SAMA, banks must "maintain a liquid reserve of not less than 15 percent of its deposit liabilities. Such reserve shall be in cash, gold or assets which can be converted into cash within a period not exceeding 30 days." SAMA has the power to raise this percentage to 20 percent.

Banks may not make a loan or any other form of credit "to any natural or juristic person for amounts aggregating more than 25 percent of the bank's reserves and paid-up or invested capital." The agency may raise that ratio to 50 percent.

Banks may not engage in the following activities:

1. Engage in the wholesale or retail trade.

2. "Have any direct interest neither as stockholder, partner, owner or otherwise, in any commercial, industrial, agricultural or other undertaking exceeding ten percent of the paid-up capital of such company." If a bank acquires an interest in due course as settlement of a debt due to the bank, it must divert itself of such interest within two years.

3. Acquire stocks and shares of any bank conducting business in the Kingdom.

4. Acquire or lease real estate. If the bank acquires real estate as settlement of a debt it must divest itself of this property within three years.

Before distribution of any profit a bank must "transfer a sum equal to not less than 25 percent of its net profits to the statutory reserve, until the amount of that reserve equals as a minimum the paid-up capital." Furthermore, the amendment of March 3, 1971, states that a bank may not "pay any dividend, or remit any part of its profits abroad, until its aggregate capitalized exepnditures, including preliminary expenses and amounts of losses incurred, have been completely written off."

The Banking Control Law of 1966 is a solid base for the development of the commercial banking system. It guarantees that the banking sector will be a productive, stable, and safe factor in the growth of the economy. One point must be emphasized: The law does not prohibit commercial banks from charging or paying interest. That is a significant compromise between the needs of a modern economy and the conservative force of traditional religion. A modern financial system cannot operate without the interest mechanism. The omission of a legal injunction against the giving and taking of interest in commercial banking activities is a guarantee that the banking system will function efficiently.

The Growth of Commercial Banking

The commercial banking system grew not only in terms of facilities but also in the magnitude of its services (see Table 11.6). The bank's cash holdings rose fivefold at an annual rate of 16.3 percent, from S.R. 120 million in December 1960 to S.R. 735 million in August 1972. In the following 12-month period, August 1972 to July 1973, cash holdings rose more than 200 percent, to S.R. 2,416 million, reflecting the acceleration of business activity associated with the recent oil-price increases. Net foreign assets rose from S.R. -121 million in December 1960 to S.R. +1,483 in January 1974, with the largest single-period increase from August 1972 to January 1974.

The Kingdom's commercial banks have been active agents in its continued economic growth. Loans and advances to the private sector rose from S.R. 519 million in December 1960 to S.R. 1,706 million in July 1973, an increase of 228.7 percent at an annual rate of change of 8.4 percent. That rate compares with the 12.9 percent average annual growth rate of GDP from 1966/67 to 1972/73.

Total deposits held by commercial banks (excluding interbank deposits) rose from S.R. 423 million in December 1960 to S.R. 3,756 million in July 1973. The growth of deposits must be divided into two time periods: from 1960 to 1971 and from 1971 to mid-1973. Overall deposits grew 344.7 percent during the first period and doubled again in the second period. The accelerated rise in deposits has led to an increase in the system's liquidity ratio (total liquid assets over total liquid liabilities), which rose from 36.1 percent in August 1971 to 63.5 percent in July 1973. The rather sharp increase in deposits led to a relatively slow increase in loans and advances to the private sector. Loans and advances rose 3.8 percent from September 1970 to August 1972, and only 5 percent from that date to July 1973. It should also be noted that there was a slight decline in loans and advances during the 12-month period between August 1971 and August 1972. SAMA suggests that this relatively slow growth of loans and advances resulted from increased use of internal funds of enterprises for investment purposes.

TABLE 11.6

Commercial-Bank Assets and Liabilities, 1960-73
(S.R. million)

Year	Cash in Hand and with SAMA	Net Foreign Assets (+) or Liabilities (-)	Loans and Advances to the Private Sector	Total Deposits (excluding interbank deposits)
December 1960	120	- 121	519	423
December 1961	125	- 34	565	528
November 1962	146	- 45	642	596
November 1963	182	+ 68	625	685
November 1964	164	+ 93	737	784
October 1965	214	+ 26	915	895
October 1966	221	+ 2	1,091	1,045
October 1967	266	+ 27	1,260	1,236
September 1968	325	+ 113	1,373	1,361
September 1969	250	+ 171	1,329	1,475
September 1970	252	+ 323	1,565	1,616
August 1971	348	+ 471	1,634	1,881
August 1972	735	+ 817	1,624	2,540
July 1973	2,416	+ 321	1,706	3,756

Note: Gregorian calendar months are given, corresponding to mid-Hijri Year.

Source: SAMA, *Annual Report*, various issues.

The banks have also contributed to the regional redistribution of the available credit. In September 1970, 27.8 percent of total bank deposits originated in the central region, and 30.7 percent of the outstanding credit was provided to the same area. The eastern region accounted for 22.1 percent of the deposits but for only 13.5 percent of the credit extended. The western region was the beneficiary of this interregional flow of funds: It provided 50.1 percent of the deposits and received 55.8 percent of the credit extended.

The growth of clearing-house activity shows the banks' increasing participation in the growth of the economy. The first clearing house was opened on October 4, 1967. On August 10, 1968, the Riyadh Clearing House was opened, followed by the Dammam Clearing House on March 24, 1969. The number of checks cleared in all three clearing houses rose from 244,637 in 1969/70 to 413,522 in 1972/73, or 69 percent. During the same period, the value of cleared checks rose almost 123.5 percent, from S.R. 3.4 billion to S.R. 7.6 billion.

OTHER BANKS

Besides SAMA and the commercial banks a number of special banks already operate or will soon operate in the Kingdom. The Agricultural Bank is the oldest of these facilities. Its role in the economy is discussed with the agricultural sector.

Royal Decree Number M/44 established the Saudi Credit Assistance Bank on November 9, 1971. Its function is to "grant interest-free loans to people of limited means who are unable to borrow through normal banking channels." The bank has an authorized capital of S.R. 5 million, half of which will be supplied by SAMA and the other half by the government. Additional finance will be provided through government deposit of S.R. 10 million and other funds provided by the government, interest-free loans granted by SAMA, and noninterest bearing deposits of the public insured by the government. The establishment of this bank is an attempt to reconcile the dictates of Islam and the realities of a modern economy. The Koran prohibits the taking of interest. Yet a smoothly functioning interest rate is required to achieve an efficient distribution of scarce resources. The establishment of the Bank for People of Small Means deals with the problem by differentiating between two basic types of loan: the type that is made by the businessman with the intent of gaining profits from the use of the loan, and the nonbusiness loan, which is designed to help the less fortunate of society. The former transaction may involve the granting and taking of interest; the latter should not, because it implies that the lender makes a profit from dealings with people in distress. Furthermore, the possibility of keeping deposits at a bank without interest receipts, makes it possible to use needed banking services while at the same time complying with the Koran's injunction against the taking of interest.

On March 20, 1974, the establishment of an Industrial Development Fund was approved by Royal Decree. Capitalized initially at S.R. 500 million, it will grant interest-free medium- and long-term loans for the development of the private sector. The loans will be extended up to a certain percentage of the capital requirements for a given private venture. To complement the government bank the establishment of an investment bank is under consideration. The investment bank will "extend loans for the promotion and development of industries, real estate, mining, transportation, and in certain circumstances even agriculture, including fisheries and poultry farming."[7]

THE BANKING TRAINING CENTER

The Banking Training Center was established to alleviate a serious shortage of qualified bank personnel. Since its establishment in July 1965 more than 200 people have successfully completed the program. In addition to the teaching of clerical skills, such as typing in Arabic and English, and instruction in English, the center has set up a program for the training for assistant-cashier and other management positions. The expansion of the center's activities is expected to continue.

NOTES

1. SAMA, Annual Report, 1380 A.H. (Jedda, n.d.), p. 3.
2. Ibid., p. 31.
3. Ibid., p. 5.
4. Ibid.
5. The following discussion of the development of a system of coinage and currency is based on Thomas W. Shea, "The Riyal: A Miracle in Money," Aramco World Magazine 20, no. 1 (January-February, 1969): 26-33.
6. Ibid., p. 28.
7. SAMA, Annual Report, 1392/93 A.H. (Jedda, 1974), p. 36.

CHAPTER

12

THE REVENUE SYSTEM

In addition to oil revenues, the government collects revenues from a number of sources. Estimates of all revenues are published annually in the budget documents, divided into major accounts and subaccounts. In this chapter we will present a discussion of the Kingdom's total revenue system. Although oil revenues have already been discussed in Chapters 7 and 8, the most important aspects of oil revenues will be repeated here to present a complete picture of the revenue structure.

REVENUES BY BUDGET CODE CLASSIFICATION

The revenue side of the budget is divided into 12 major accounts, some of it are divided into subaccounts (see Table 12.1). The major classifications are oil royalties (account number 8,000), income tax (8,100), Tapline transit fees (8,200), oil products tax (8,300), customs duties (8,400), transport tax (8,500), services (8,600), papers of value (8,700), government sales (8,800), rents and installments (8,900), miscellaneous revenues (9,000), and Zakat (10,000). A thirteenth tax, the Jihad tax, was added for the budget year 1970/71 but was repealed the following year, owing to rising oil revenues.

Oil Royalties (8,000)

Aramco (8,001)

Aramco royalty payments are based on Article 14 of the Original Concession Agreement of May 29, 1933, which states:

TABLE 12.1

Revenue Classifications, by Control and Subaccounts

Control Account Number	Subaccount Number	Classification
8,000		Oil Production
	8,001	Aramco
	8,002	Getty Oil
	8,003	AOC
8,100		Income Taxes
	8,101	Aramco
	8,102	Getty Oil
	8,103	AOC
	8,104	Other companies
	8,105	Individuals
8,200		Tapline Fees
8,300		Petroleum Product Tax
8,400		Customs Tariffs
	8,401	On value
	8,402	Specified
8,500		Transportation Tax
	8,501	Railroad and Dammam port
	8,502	Vehicles licenses
	8,503	Roads tax
8,600		Services
	8,601	General service fee
	8,602	Municipalities
	8,603	Ports fees
	8,604	Airports fees
	8,605	Landing fees
	8,606	Post
	8,607	Telegram
	8,608	Telegraph
8,700		Papers of Value
	8,701	Publications
	8,702	Stamps
	8,703	Drivers licenses, work permits
	8,704	Residency and passports
8,800		Government Sales
8,900		Rents and Installments
	8,901	Public property rents
	8,902	Employees housing installments
9,000		Miscellaneous
	9,001	Profits
	9,002	Fines and penalties
	9,003	Other revenues
10,000		Zakat
10,100		Jihad Tax

> The Company shall pay the Government a royalty on all net crude oil produced and saved and run from field storage, after first deducting:
> (1) water and foreign substances; and
> (2) oil required for the customary operations of the Company's installations within Saudi Arabia; and
> (3) the oil required for manufacturing the amounts of gasoline and kerosene to be provided free each year to the Government in accordance with Article 19 hereof.
>
> The rate of royalty per ton of such net crude oil shall be either:
> (a) four shillings, gold, or its equivalent; or
> (b) (in United States currency subject to certain conditions to take account of exchange rate fluctuations).

On October 10, 1948, an agreement between the government and Aramco provided "the royalty payable for oil produced from the offshore of Saudi Arabia . . . shall be the royalty as provided in Article 14 of the Saudi Arab Concession signed in Jedda on 29 May 1933 . . . plus five cents, United States of America currency (U.S. $.05) per barrel." Royalties are paid on or about the fifteenth day of the Gregorian month following the month in which the crude oil was run from field storage. In January 1965 the company agreed to expense a portion of the royalty paid equal to 12.5 percent of the Ras Tanura posted price of each grade of crude and crude equivalent of refined products sold for export.

The Getty Oil Company (8,002)

Formerly the Pacific Western Oil Corporation, Getty Oil also pays royalties to the government. Getty's royalty payments consist of two parts: "a royalty of fifty-five ($.55) cents in currency of the United States of America for each United States barrel of crude oil which it obtains from [the] Neutral Zone"; "a royalty of twelve and one-half (12.5%) percent of the gross proceeds received by the Company for its own account from the sales of any natural gas or natural gas products and by-products produced, manufactured and sold from said Neutral Zone" less cost of handling and transportation to the point of consumption (Article 5).

AOC (8,003)

The company's royalty payments are based on Article 14 of the Agreement of December 10, 1957, which provides that the company pay for each calendar year:

> (a) A royalty equal to 20 percent (20%) of the crude oil produced from the Government's undivided one-half interest as gauged in the producing field. . . .
> (b) A royalty of twenty percent (20%) on the natural asphalt extracted from the Government's undivided one-half interest each year measured in the producing field.
> (c) A royalty of twenty percent (20%) on the value of the natural gas alienated or used as fuel each year from the Government's undivided one-half interest.

The royalties referred to under (a) and (b) are payable in cash or in kind depending on the government's decision. Conversion to cash payments is made by multiplying the 20 percent of production by the posted price for each grade of crude produced. If the royalties under (a), (b), and (c) amount to less than $2.5 million, the company must make an additional payment to bring total payments to that amount.

Income Taxes (8,100)

The Saudi government collects three types of income tax: income tax due from non-Saudi individuals and firms; additional tax levied on oil companies; Zakat, the sharia tax on capital and income payable by all Moslems, from which non-Moslems are exempt.

The Oil Companies

Aramco (8,101). Until 1965 Aramco income tax payments were based on Royal Decrees Number 12/2/28/3321 and Number 17/2/28/7634. Article 1 of the latter imposes on "every company . . . engaged in the production of petroleum or other hydrocarbons in the Kingdom of Saudi Arabia . . . an income tax of fifty percent (50%) of the net operating income." Article 3 provided for the subtraction of "all taxes (except the income tax imposed by this decree), royalties, rentals, duties, and all other sums paid or payable to the Saudi Arab Government," from the income tax payable to the government.

The provisions were included in the Agreement of December 30, 1950 between the government and Aramco, Article 1 of which states:

> Anything in Article 21 in Aramco's Concession Agreement not withstanding, Aramco submits to the income taxes provided in Royal Decrees No. 17/2/28/3321 and No. 17/2/2817634, . . . it being understood
>
> (a) that in no case shall the total of such taxes, royalties and exactions of the Government exceed fifty percent (50%) of the gross income of Aramco, after such gross income has been reduced by Aramco's cost of operation, including losses and depreciation.

This agreement governed Aramco's basic income-tax liability until 1965; on January 25, 1965, the "expensing" of royalties was introduced into the calculation of the company's income-tax liability. Prior to that date royalties were subtracted from the income tax liability, while in the new agreement royalties were treated as an expense deductible from gross income in computing the tax liability. The tax rate was raised to 55 percent on February 14, 1971.

In addition to the income tax on Aramco sales, the 8,101 classification contains the transit fee payments due from Tapline for delivering oil to Sidon. The fees are computed on a miles-per-barrel basis.

The Getty Oil Company (8,102). Article 49 of the agreement between the government and the Getty Oil Company provides that "neither the Company nor any property imported into, used or held for use in said Neutral Zone or in Saudi Arabia . . . shall be subject to any taxes or charges whatever by or on behalf of the Government." This provision was introduced into the agreement to protect the company from double taxation in the United States and in Saudi Arabia. This "tax-free" status was modified in the same article to the extent "that a tax or taxes may be levied by the Government against the company, . . . if and only to the extent that a credit of the full amount of such tax is allowed against the amount of any tax otherwise payable by the company to any other government." In actual practice this means if the company can negotiate a tax credit on its Neutral Zone operating profits with the U.S. government, the amount of tax not paid in the United States is payable to the Saudi Arabian government.

The 8,102 classification includes an additional payment by the Getty Oil Company that should not be recorded as an income tax, because conceptually it is a nontax receipt. Article 7 of the agreement provides:

> Within 90 days after each anniversary of the date of the signing hereof, the Company will pay to the Government:
>
> (a) An amount in currency of the United States of America equivalent to twenty-five (25%) percent of the net profits realized by the Company . . . from the sale of products and by-products, including gas and gas products and by-products, obtained . . . by the company and not refined by the Company at any refinery built . . . in said Neutral Zone; and
>
> (b) An amount in currency of the United States of America equivalent to twenty (20%) percent of the net profits obtained by the Company during such year from the operation of any refinery or refineries built . . . in said Neutral Zone.

AOC (8,103). Income taxes are based on the provisions as specified in Royal Decrees Number 17/2/28/3321 and Number/7/2/28/574. Article 14(d) of the agreement between the government and the company states that the income tax is: "imposed . . . on all the operations of the Company inside and outside Saudi Arabia, including sale of crude oil, refinery, transportation and marketing." The same article further provides:

> (c) If after the royalties mentioned in (a), (b) and (c) [see p. 261] and the taxes mentioned in (d) have been received by the Government, the Government's share does not amount to fifty-six (56%) percent of the Company's net income from all the phases of operations. . . , the Company shall pay . . . an additional tax which shall make the Government's share fifty-six percent (56%) of the Company's net income during the taxable year.

In a letter of agreement dated September 12, 1963, the government's share was raised to 57 percent, and the expensing of royalties for income tax liabilities was introduced.

The tax liability is calculated as follows: All operating costs are deducted from gross receipts to determine net taxable income. Royalties paid are deducted from net income and the residual is subject to income taxes according to the tax brackets established for the taxation of non-Saudi firms. After income taxes and royalties have been calculated the amount owing at 57 percent of net income is determined. Income taxes and royalties actually payable are subtracted from that amount, and any additional taxes are calculated so that the sum of royalties, income taxes, and additional tax equal 57 percent of the company's net taxable income.

Nonoil Companies and Individuals*

Saudi law differentiates between three types of income: personal income (such as wages); individual income, earned from capital, from work and capital, or derived from professional work (for example, in the case of a lawyer, physician, plumber, and so on); income earned from financial firms (joint stock companies, joint ventures). Until the budget year 1970/71 (beginning September 1, 1970) Saudi firms and Saudi individuals were exempted from income taxation; however, foreign-owned companies and foreigners working in the Kingdom have always been liable to taxation. Owing to budget problems associated with the Arab-Israeli conflict, changes in the tax rates and brackets payable by foreigners were made, and temporary income taxes were levied on Saudi citizens. The income tax on Saudi citizens was repealed the following budget year.

Foreigners earning a wage or salary are subject to personal income taxation if their earnings (or income on capital invested) exceed S.R. 6,000 per annum. The exemption of the first S.R. 6,000 may only be claimed if the recipient resides in the Kingdom for one full year, or if he is considered a one-year resident. For residence of less than one year the exemption is prorated for the length of the stay. The following tax rates (and net brackets) apply for earnings of individuals of more than S.R. 6,000 since September 1, 1970:

S.R. 6,000 to S.R. 15,999	5 percent
S.R. 16,000 to S.R. 35,999	10 percent
S.R. 36,000 and over	20 percent

Foreign companies are subject to income taxes on their total net profits. (Loss carryover is prohibited; that is, if the taxpayer suffers

*For a more detailed discussion of Saudi income taxes, see Nizar Rafai, "Income Tax in Saudi Arabia," Bulletin for International Fiscal Documentation 23, no. 10 (1969): 482-87.

a loss, he is not allowed to carry it into the next year. Losses are considered a liability in the year during which they were incurred.) The following rates apply:

Less than S.R. 100,000	25 percent
S.R. 100,000 to S.R. 499,999	35 percent
S.R. 500,000 to S.R. 999,999	40 percent
S.R. 1 million and over	45 percent

Tapline Fees (8,200)

Payments by Tapline Company have three aspects: (1) "make-up" payments, if the government's revenue from company operations falls below a certain minimum per barrel transported, (2) the Badanah Agreement payment for the maintenance of the amirates along the Tapline, and (3) some service fees paid to the government.

The make-up payments are based on the Supplemental Agreement of March 24, 1963, which specifies that Tapline will pay the government

> the amount if any, per barrel of crude oil transported . . . by which
> (a) $0.097 per barrel . . . exceeds
> (b) Fifty percent of the amount by which the Sidon published price exceeds the sum of the Ras Tanura published [posted] price applicable to such barrel and Tapline charges.

This provision means that whenever the return to the Saudi government on crude oil sold at Sidon falls below 9.6 cents per barrel the company is liable to a make-up payment that is recorded under budget classification 8,200. The make-up payment rests on the idea that the government should be guaranteed one-half of the difference in the return on deliveries between Ras Tanura and Sidon, owing to the higher posted prices at Sidon, or at least 9.7 cents per barrel.

The make-up payments arise because of changes in the costs incurred by the Tapline Company. For example, in 1969 Tapline incurred a liability of about S.R. 16 million in the payments, which were calculated as shown in the following pro forma example:

Posted price at Sidon (34°API crude	$2.17
Less Posted Price at Ras Tanura	$1.80
Differential Sidon over Ras Tanura	$0.37

Less estimated costs (including payments to other governments)	\$0.233
Net taxable income per barrel	\$0.137
Tax rate: 50 percent	
Transit fee per barrel due	\$0.685
Contractual minimum fee	\$0.09619
Make-up payment due per barrel	\$0.0276

If total costs per barrel had been, say, \$0.15, no make-up payment would have been due:

Differential in posted prices, Sidon over Ras Tanura	\$0.37
Less all costs (assumed for example)	\$0.15
Net taxable income per barrel	\$0.22
Tax rate: 50 percent	
Transit fee per barrel due	\$0.11
Contractual minimum fee	\$0.97
Make-up payment due per barrel	None

Petroleum Products Tax (8,300)

This is an excise tax paid by all buyers of petroleum products on seven major types of petroleum. The tax is collected on the wholesale level but is shifted to the consumer. Until the end of budget year 1967/68 two-thirds of the tax on gasoline was recorded in the national budget and one-third in the municipalities budget. Since that time all receipts have been recorded under 8,300. To meet the rising demands for funds the gasoline tax was raised from 8 halalas to 14 halalas per liter for the budget year 1970/71. At the same time a tax of 2.5 halalas per liter was levied on diesel fuel. Both these changes were eliminated the following years. Petroleum products other than gasoline—products that used to be imported but are now produced locally—are still subject to "customs duties." Ninety percent of the receipts are recorded under the Customs on Value (8,401) classification, and the remainder is distributed among Municipalities Fees (8,602), Quay Fee (8,605), and School Subsidies (9,003).

Customs Duties (8,400)

Two types of customs duties are collected: customs on value (8,401) and specified customs (8,402). The schedule of duties has undergone two changes in recent years: On June 7, 1968, a new, lower schedule of duties went into effect; to meet the pressure on the budget associated with the deficit of 1970/71 selected increases in customs duties were decreed, starting in September 1970. The increases were abolished, effective January 3, 1972.

Transportation Tax (8,500)

This classification contains three items: revenues from railroad and Dammam port (8,501)p vehicle licenses (8,502); roads tax (8,503).

Railroad and Dammam Port (8,501)

Since the budget year 1966/67 revenues derived from these two organizations have not been recorded in the general budget because they have been combined into an independent government corporation with its own budget.

Vehicle Licenses (8,502)

Subgroup 8,502 consists of (1) revenues collected by customs when a car is imported (the fees are levied at the following rates: S.R. 400 on cars weighing one ton or less; S.R. 500 on each car weighing between one and two tons, plus S.R. 200 for any additional ton or fraction of a ton above two tons); (2) temporary licenses issued for an automobile or truck registered in a foreign country but driven in the Kingdom (in the case of trucks making regular runs into the Kingdom a flat fee is charged twice yearly); (3) registration fees of S.R. 5 collected by the traffic departments annually; and (4) S.R. 15 for license plates.

Roads Tax (8,503)

This subgroup contains at least two items. By far the largest portion of the revenue is derived from a 2-percent payroll tax (roads tax), levied on all persons earning S.R. 400 or more. The amounts shown in the budget are cash receipts only. Payments by government employees, which are deducted from the payroll, are not recorded. A small amount is realized from fees charged pilgrims for transportation during the Hadj.

Service Fees (8,600)

This classification contains eight unrelated revenue items.

General Service Fees (8,601)

These fees are collected from seven different revenue sources:

1. The S.R. 63 general service fee. Formerly levied on all foreigners entering the Kingdom, on January 17, 1970, the fee was abolished for all "foreigners entering the Kingdom for the purpose of work, business or visit." It has been retained for the Hudjaj.
2. Investing company services. The revenues derived from this fee are paid by the oil companies for services rendered to them by the government. The Aramco payments are based on Article 7 of the Agreement of December 30, 1950. They are fixed at $700,000, payable in four equal installments. Payments are also made by the Getty Oil Company, AOC, and Tapline.
3. The Badanah Agreement payment. This is a payment of S.R. 2.9 million made annually by the Tapline Company in support of the Amirates along the Tapline.
4. Ministry of Agriculture Services. These fees are charged for services, such as plowing, rental of agricultural machinery, and water supply.
5. In addition to the above fees, the yield from a number of minor revenue sources is recorded in this classification. They are trade registration fees, quarantine fees, export certificate fees, and fees charged for the publication of notes in Um-Al Qura.

Municipalities Fees (8,602)

These revenues are derived from a 6-percent surcharge on the amount of customs duties. They are paid by the importer and earmarked as municipal revenues. For example, if the customs duties on a given import are calculated at S.R. 100, a surcharge of S.R. 6 is made for the municipalities and is transmitted to them via SAMA. In this class 6 percent of the "customs duties" collected on locally produced petroleum products other than gasoline are also recorded.

Ports Fees (8,603)

This item contains a group of fees, license fees, and taxes levied in connection with port and other maritime activities. The largest portion of the revenues recorded under this classification comes from charges against cargo collected in (all) ports, except for

Dammam. They are service fees, based on Royal Decree Number 425 for transferring goods from the ship to customs and from customs to merchants. Under modern port administration practices payments for these services rendered are usually included in the wharfage charge. For the Dammam port these charges are part of the Saudi government railroad tariff schedule.

In November 1970 the government announced the imposition of port dues on tankers calling at Saudi ports. Retroactive to August 1, 1971, tankers calling at Saudi ports will pay a fee of S.R. 0.57 per gross register ton of capacity.

In addition, at least the following fees collected by the Coast Guard Department are recorded under this classification: shamandarah, koshan, marsa (anchoring, tending boats, dubah, and launch and sailing boats), manifest tax (arrival and departure), boat owner's (license), fishing licenses, hori boat fee, fishing ticket, muzawariah fee, and lighterage fee for any boat. Marsa and shamandara are service fees. They are related to the dockage fee charged in modern port-administration practices. Both are charges for using (tying up to) pier space. Koshan and manifest tax do not appear to be service fees: they are attempts to raise revenue by taxing various maritime activities. The remaining items are probably license fees.

Airport Fees (8,604)

These fees, based on Royal Decree Number 12, are (1) aircraft fees (landing fee, lighting fee for landing and takeoff during the night, sheltering fee for use of hangar space); (2) observation fee; (3) departure fee (S.R. 6 due from every passenger going abroad); (4) aircraft service equipment fee; (5) aircraft towage; (6) land equipment fee; (7) clearance fee (for entry of aircraft into airport area); (8) aircraft requisition certificate; and (9) pilots and engineers license fee.

Quay (Maintenance) Fees (8,605)

Quay fees are a customs surcharge of 3 percent on the duties due on all dutiable goods discharged in the Kingdom (see 8,602). In addition, it includes 3 percent of the "customs duties" levied on all locally produced petroleum products other than gasoline.

Postal (8,606), Telegram (8,607), and Telephone (8,608)

These fees are the gross receipts of the government paid by the users of these services.

Papers of Value (8,700)

All documents or contracts, permits, licenses, and government publications are called "papers of value." Revenues derived from the sale or taxation of papers of value are recorded under four headings: sale of government publications (8,701), financial fee stamps (8,702), drivers licenses and working permits (8,703), and residency and passports (8,704).

Government Publications (8,701)

Most of the Royal Decrees and other important publications are printed by the government press and sold by the Ministry of Finance and National Economy. The price varies with the size of the publication, and the receipts from these sales are recorded under subaccount number 8,701.

Financial Fee Stamps (8,702)

Financial fees are levied against most activities requiring some form of contract or other documentation. In theory, financial fees of varying amounts are levied on at least eight different types of document, ranging from "permits to establish factories," "documents of lease and loan," manifests submitted for customs clearance of exports and imports, to "receipts given by offices [for] whatever [purpose]." Financial fees can be divided into 11 classes: (1) permits (ten items); (2) documents (33 items); (3) contracts and agreements (eight items); (4) manifests (five items); (5) warrants (three items); (6) certificates (five items); (7) petitions and requests (three items); (8) documents and papers (12 items); (9) wills and notifications (ten items); (10) receipts (two items); and (11) fines.

There appears to be no general organizing principle underlying the concept of financial fees, either as to the amounts charged or the choice of items taxed. As far as the amounts charged are concerned, they appear to have been based on the "ability-to-pay" idea. With few exceptions, the amounts charged are small. They range from 500 qirsh for "internal regulations for limited companies registered by the government" to several one-qirsh charges, such as "insurance cash-bills for the amount of 100 P.S. and less."

The revenue generated from these fees is collected by means of financial stamps. For example, a lease for a house renting for 5,000 P.S. calls for the payment of a financial fee of two qirsh. The fee is paid by pasting on the document a two-qirsh stamp purchased from the government.

Drivers Licenses and Working Permits (8,703) and Residency and Passports (8,704)

These are mostly permits and licenses. Revenues arising out of these two sources are collected through the sale of financial and/or special stamps or by payment for the document. For example, residence permits are used as a source of revenue. When the permit is issued for the first time, a charge of S.R. 40 is levied and collected by payment for the residence passbook itself. Thereafter, a fee of S.R. 40 is levied for every extension of the residency permit. The renewal fee is collected through the sale of residency renewal stamps.

Papers of value can be divided into nine groups, the majority of which are recorded under subclasses 8,703 and 8,704: (1) passports (14 items); (2) residence (eight items); (3) traffic (nine items); (4) health (one item); (5) Coast Guard (14 items); (6) labor (five items); (7) public security (two items); (8) commerce (one item) and (9) miscellaneous (eight items). Most of the revenues collected under the papers-of-value classification by the Coast Guard are probably recorded as ports fees (8,503) and miscellaneous revenues (9,003).

Government Sales (8,800)

These are the receipts from the sale of surplus government property and forced sales by customs authorities of confiscated goods. As of April 22, 1963, the classification also includes the cash payments made by Aramco under Article 6 of the December 30, 1950, Agreement, made in lieu of deliveries in kind of free kerosene and gasoline.

Rents and Installments (8,900)

Only public property rents (8,901) should be recorded as a revenue receipt. Housing installments (8,902) are transfer payments from government employees to the government for a mortgage loan made to the employee in previous years.

Public Property Rents (8,901)

In addition to rental receipts from leases of public property, this subaccount records two other items: (1) a portion of the Tapline Company's Badanah payments and (2) payments of exploration fees by Auxirap, Agip, and Sinclair-Natomas-Pakistan. Until 1968 it also contained an annual payment of $165,000 by Aramco as a rental of exploration rights for the southern half of the Neutral Zone between the Kingdom and Iraq.

Miscellaneous Revenues (9,000)

Government Profits (9,001)

This class includes two sources of revenues: (1) profits on investments by SAMA, dividends on the shares of AOC held by the government, and returns on stocks of Saudi Arabian electric companies and local banks held by the government (9,001A), and (2) Petromin profits (9,001B).

Fines and Penalties (9,002)

This item is self-explanatory.

Other Revenues (9,003)

These are various items not listed elsewhere. Among them are the cash payments made by Aramco for salaries of teachers employed in schools, schools built by the company in the Eastern Province, the tonnage fee, revenues from government-owned hospitals and electric companies, quarantine fees, landing fees (collected by customs), and a few other items.

Zakat (10,000)

This tax is an obligation placed on all Moslems by the Prophet Mohammed. It is divided into two parts: Zakat of Al-Fitr and Zakat of Wealth. According to Moslem Law, non-Moslems are excluded from payment of Zakat. The government has attempted to collect Zakat in various ways in the past. Currently (April 1973) the Department of Income Tax and Zakat is responsible for the collection of one-half of Zakat on articles of trade. The payment of the remainder is left to the individual as a moral obligation at the time of Eid-el-Fitr.

Payments in Kind

The following payments are received in kind and are not recorded in the budget: (1) road maintenance by Aramco and the Tapline Company; (2) deliveries of petroleum products by Aramco under

Article 6 of the Agreement of December 30, 1950; (3) school buildings erected by Aramco in the Eastern Province.

Nontax, Nonrevenue Receipts

In addition to housing installments (8,902), several other nonrevenue items are included. It is difficult to determine where they are listed. However, one of the largest items, included in the miscellaneous revenue (9,003) classification, consists of overpayments on invoices submitted by government employees for expenses incurred during the execution of their duties. Another item, also listed under 9,003, is the return of unused advances at the end of the fiscal year. The amounts recorded probably do not exceed S.R. 1,000 in any one year and can be safely ignored.

In view of the huge amounts of oil revenue received by the government collection of these taxes appears to be at first glance unnecessary. Many of these items are a holdover from the days when the government was so strapped for funds that occasionally it could not pay the civil servants. There is, however, one reason why the government will continue to collect those minor revenues: The Kingdom has been a united country for only about 40 years, and despite the harmony currently prevailing among the regions, there still exists considerable loyalty to the tribe and the region; in many places the government is a remote presence that does not impinge on the population's everyday activities. Under those conditions it becomes important to the government to make its presence and power known throughout the Kingdom. There is no better way to remind the population of the national government's existence than the payment of taxes to the government. Thus, it seems likely that most of the small revenue items will be kept on the books.

CHAPTER

13

THE BUDGET: REVENUES

This chapter presents a discussion of the government's current revenues. The first section deals with the classification of revenues. Following a brief mention of the classification of revenues as published by the government's Department of Statistics, an alternative classification scheme is presented to facilitate understanding of revenue receipts. The second section is a discussion of budget receipts from 1948 to 1972/73.

Information on the budget is published in the Statistical Yearbook, issued annually by the Central Department of Statistics. Unfortunately, the statistics, particularly revenue statistics, are presented in an obscure and often even misleading manner. The revenue statistics used in the budget, as well as those published in the Statistical Yearbook, are not based on generally accepted criteria, and reliance on the classification scheme may well lead to incorrect conclusions about the Kingdom's current revenue. For example, the item called "roads tax" (number 9 in Table 13.1, listed under the heading of "transport tax") is not an excise tax on transportation; instead, it is a form of income taxation, as shown in Chapter 12. Furthermore, as published, the revenue statistics do not lend themselves to international comparisons.

THE CLASSIFICATION OF REVENUES

The revenue statistics published in the Statistical Yearbooks must be divided into two periods: from 1948 to 1957/58 and from

---

Portions of this chapter have been previously published in Public Finance 28, no. 3-4 (1973): 435-53.

1961/62 to the present. The data given for the earlier period are not organized in accordance with any unifying principle; rather, they are a compilation of various taxes and accounts collected throughout the Kingdom. Beginning in 1961/62, the revenue statistics are published on the basis of the classifications discussed in Chapter 12. Although the classification system is a distinct advance when compared to the earlier years, it is still unsatisfactory.

Given that the currently published revenue data are difficult to use for meaningful analysis, this section presents an alternative classification scheme based on various commonly accepted definitions of public revenues, outlined as follows:*

I. Current general revenues
    A. Oil-sector revenues
        1. Royalties
        2. Income tax
        3. Tapline
    B. Tax revenue
        1. Direct taxes
        2. Indirect taxes
        3. Fees and licenses
    C. Nontax revenue (charges and miscellaneous)
    D. Other revenue (n.l.c.)
    E. Total current general revenues
II. Special-fund receipts
    A. Additional receipts
        1. Housing installments
        2. Railway and Dammam port
        3. Saudi Airlines
III. Total current receipts: general and special funds
IV. Estimation of error
V. Nonrevenue receipts
    A. Other sources of budget finance
        1. Drawn from development fund
        2. Drawn from reserve
VI. Total sources of finance

Oil-Sector Revenues

Methodologically, the oil-sector revenues listed under this heading should be divided between tax revenues and nontax revenues.

*This classification scheme has benefited from comments by Phillip E. Taylor.

Income taxes should be classified under direct-tax revenues, and royalties and Tapline payments under nontax revenues. However, because oil revenues account for such a disproportionate part of the Kingdom's total revenues, it is best to treat them as a special item.

Tax Revenues

The division of tax revenues into direct and indirect taxes has been a subject of debate. Nevertheless, the concept of direct and indirect taxes is a useful analytical tool and has been retained. The classification rests not on incidence, however, but on the rule that "taxes which are based on the receipt of income are . . . direct [taxes], whereas those levied on expenditure are . . . indirect [taxes]."[1] Based on that rule, income taxes on individuals and nonoil companies and the roads tax are considered direct taxes. The rule has been expanded to allow the classification of the Zakat (the Koranic tax on wealth), because that source of revenue cannot be readily classified as a tax on income or expenditure. Customs duties and some customs-associated revenues have been classified as indirect taxes. The category "fees and licenses" has been added to take account of those revenues that arise neither out of levies on income nor out of expenditure for goods and services offered in the marketplace.

Nontax Revenues

Nontax revenues are the income from services rendered by the government for which a payment is charged that may or may not cover the cost of providing the service. In one or two cases inclusion in this category may be questioned. For example, the public service fee (item number 10 in Table 13.1) contains several items that are closely related to licenses and should be included under tax revenues. Because it is impossible to differentiate between the various parts recorded under this heading, and because it is known that more than half the yield was generated by the S.R.-63 general service fee and certain oil-company nontax payments, it has been included in the nontax classification.

Other Revenues, Not Elsewhere Classified

Other Revenues, not elsewhere classified, include fines and penalties and a group of miscellaneous fees. Among the latter are such items as al-Fallah School fees and overtime charges made by customs for loading and unloading ships outside normal working hours. If the Kingdom's revenue-recording system were improved, most of these items would be recorded until Sections I.B and I.C.

Exclusions

An important drawback of the published revenue data is that no distinction is made among current revenues, nonrevenue receipts, and other sources of budget finance. The total is considerably less than that given by the Central Department of Statistics, because a number of items have been excluded. Railroad and Dammam port (item 7) and Saudi Airlines (item 25) have been excluded, because those agencies have been turned into independent government corporations with their own budgets. Exclusion of those items makes the time series of current revenues more consistent over time. Installments (item 20) are repayments of housing loans to government employees and should be considered transfer payments, which by definition are not revenues. Those items are included under number II.A, additional receipts. Finally, the entries, drawn from the development fund (item 22) and drawn from the reserve (item 23) are excluded because they are not current revenues.

Other Sources of Budget Finance

The government received a number of one-time special payments in settlement of claims associated with changes in the Aramco Concession Agreement in 1963, 1965, and 1966. Those funds were not recorded as revenues at the time of receipt. Instead they were set aside in an economic development fund and used to finance special development projects.[2] Since its inception this fund has been slowly drawn down, and it was exhausted by March 1969.[3] An argument can be made for the inclusion of funds drawn from the development fund in the way in which they were allocated for expenditure. So long as they were not recorded at the time of receipt, there is no double counting, and thus the amount of revenues received over time is not distorted.

There is no reason, however, to label funds drawn from the reserve as <u>current</u> revenues. These reserves were accumulated partly from surplus cash payments by the oil companies (March 1963) and "shortfalls in overall Government spending."[4] That is, funds that had been allocated for major development projects but not paid out as scheduled during a given budget year because of delays in meeting target dates, were transferred to reserves to be used as the

TABLE 13.1

Estimated Budget Receipts of the Kingdom of Saudi Arabia, 1967/68
(S.R. million)

As Published			As Reorganized			
Item Number	Description	Amount	Class	Description	Published Item Number	Amount
1	Royalties from oil	1,126.6	I	Current general revenues		
				A. Oil-sector revenues		3,515.4
	Income tax			1. Royalties	1	1,126.6
2	Oil companies	2,388.8		2. Income tax	2	2,388.8
3	Other companies and individuals			3. Tapline	4	—
		44.0		B. Tax revenue		327.4
	Total	2,432.9		1. Direct taxes		78.0
				a. Income tax	3	44.0
4	Tapline fees	—		b. Roads tax	9	29.0
5	Tax on oil products	21.0		c. Zakat	24	5.0
6	Customs duties	192.0		2. Indirect taxes		232.5
	Total	213.0		a. Customs duties	6, 11, 14, 21	211.5
	Transport tax			b. Petroleum products tax	5	21.0
7	Railway and Dammam port	—		3. Fees and licenses		16.9
8	Plates of cars	10.0		a. Drivers licenses and work permits	18	0.7
9	Roads tax	31.0		b. Residency, passports	18	2.8
	Total	41.0		c. Vehicle licenses	9	10.0
				d. Revenue stamps	18	3.4

	Services			C. Nontax revenue		211.0
10	Public service fee	27.0		1. Post	15	6.0
11	Municipalities fee	12.0		2. Telegram	16	14.0
12	Ports fees	14.0		3. Telephone	17	7.0
13	Airport fees	3.0		4. General service fee	10	27.0
14	Quay fees	5.0		5. Ports fee	12	14.0
15	Post	6.0		6. Airports fees	13	3.0
16	Telegraph	14.0		7. Sales of government property	19	4.0
17	Telephone	7.0		8. Government profit	21	124.6
	Total	88.0		9. Government press	18	1.3
				10. Rents	20	2.5
	Others			11. Nontax revenue, n.e.c.	21	7.6
18	Papers of value	8.3		D. Other revenue, n.e.c.		10.9
19	Government sales (properties)	4.0		E. Total current general revenues		4,064.7
20	Rents and installments	4.0	II.	Special-fund receipts		
21	Miscellaneous income	141.7		A. Additional receipts		1.5
22	Drawn from the development			1. Housing installments	20	1.5
	fund	—		2. Railway and Dammam port	7	—
23	Drawn from the reserve	871.6		3. Saudi Airlines	25	—
24	Zakat	6.0	III.	Total current receipts		4,066.2
25	Saudi Airlines	—	IV.	Estimation errors (+ or -)		- 0.8
	Total	1,035.6	V.	Nonrevenue receipts		
				A. Other sources of budget finance		871.6
				1. Drawn from development fund	22	—
	Grand total	4,937.0		2. Drawn from reserve	24	871.6
			VI.	Total sources of finance		4,934.0

Source: CDS, Statistical Yearbook, 1388 A.H., vol. 4 (Riyadh, 1968), Table II-2, p. 374.

projects are completed in subsequent budget years. Thus, the revenue is counted twice: once, when it is recorded in the budget year in which it was received, and again, when it is "transferred from the reserve" to pay for development projects.

Table 13.1 presents the Kingdom's estimated budget receipts as published in the Statistical Yearbook and as reorganized according to the classification suggested in this section for the budget year 1967/68. The estimation error results from double counting of some small items listed under miscellaneous income (item 22) that cannot be identified.

REVENUE RECEIPTS, 1948 to 1973/74

Estimated Budget Receipts, 1948 to 1957/58

Table 13.2 presents estimate revenue receipts for the years 1948, 1951/52, 1954/55, and 1957/58. A number of comments are in order regarding the quality of these statistics. First, all figures given are based on estimated receipts. Second, despite the reorganization of the statistics of this period according to the method discussed in the previous section, the figures for 1948 to 1957/58 are considerably less reliable than those given for the period beginning in 1961/62. Third, the various allocations of certain catchall revenue items shown in the right-hand section of Table 13.1 are based on unpublished material developed by the author. It is possible to allocate the components of item 18, papers of value, among four categories in the latter period by calculating the percentage distribution of the components of the papers-of-value classification and fit them into the new scheme. Here, the estimation error arises because it is not always possible to assign an item to its proper class. It is impossible to treat the figures for 1948 to 1957/58 in the same manner. The whole published category had to be allocated to one or the other class in the new classification scheme, thus avoiding estimation errors. At any rate, the estimation error is small enough in any given year to be of no great concern.

In the decade 1948 to 1957/58 oil revenues rose 758 percent, from S.R. 144.6 million to S.R. 1,241 million. Of the S.R. 214.6 million in current revenues collected in 1948, 67.4 percent were produced by the oil sector, and the remaining 32.6 percent came from the other revenues collected. Although oil revenues outranked nonoil revenues, the Kingdom's income still hinged in part on the collection of traditional taxes. By 1957/58 the distribution of current revenues showed that 86.8 percent of total revenues originated in the oil

TABLE 13.2

Estimated Budget Receipts by Major Categories, 1948 to 1957/58
(S.R. thousand)

Type of Revenue	1948	1951/52	1954/55	1957/58
I. Current general revenues				
A. Oil-sector revenues	144,600[a]	340,005[a]	966,625	1,241,000
1. Royalties	140,000	180,000	274,375	375,000
2. Income tax	—	160,005[b]	692,250	866,000
3. Tapline	—	—	—	—
B. Tax revenues	29,254	70,965	92,586	143,216
1. Direct taxes	3,362	8,500	5,450	6,600
2. Indirect taxes	25,000	60,000	80,000	126,000
3. Fees and licenses	892	2,465	7,136	10,616
C. Nontax revenue (charges and miscellaneous)	37,937	39,765	26,100	25,606
D. Other revenues, n.e.c.	2,796	2,705	5,100	20,378
E. Total current general revenues	214,587	453,400	1,090,411	1,430,200
II. Special-fund receipts				
A. Additional receipts	—	7,560	52,600	68,000
III. Total current receipts: general and special funds	214,587	461,000	1,143,011	1,498,200
IV. Estimation error	—	+ 3,900	—	—
V. Other sources of budget finance	—	25,000	211,990	—
VI. Total sources of finance	214,587	489,900	1,355,001	1,498,200

[a]Includes value of deliveries in kind.

[b]Includes an unknown amount of income tax paid by nonoil firms and individuals.

Sources: 1948 and 1951/52: CDS, Statistical Yearbook, 1385 A.H., vol. 1 (Riyadh, 1965), pp. 250-51; 1954/55 and 1957/58: Ibid., p. 256.

TABLE 13.3

Estimated Total Sources of Finance by Major Categories, 1961/62 to 1973/74
(S.R. million)

Type of Revenue	1961/62	1962/63	1963/64	1964/65
I. Current general revenues				
A. Oil-sector revenues	1,648.8	1,917.8	2,267.9	2,571.8
1. Royalties	564.3	674.5	721.4	813.4
2. Income tax	1,084.5	1,243.3	1,528.0	1,756.6
3. Tapline	—	—	18.5	1.8
B. Tax revenues	229.6	214.8	219.3	234.7
1. Direct taxes	66.8	65.5	58.0	59.5
2. Indirect taxes	153.5	140.2	152.2	163.0
3. Fees and licenses	9.3	9.1	9.1	12.2
C. Nontax revenue (charges and miscellaneous)	61.0	77.8	121.5	140.1
D. Other revenues, n.e.c.	—	—	—	—
E. Total current general revenues	1,939.4	2,210.4	2,608.7	2,946.6
II. Special-fund receipts				
A. Additional receipts	67.3	55.6	17.3	15.5
1. Housing installments	1.1	1.2	1.3	1.5
2. Railway and Dammam port	36.2	24.4	16.0	14.0
3. Saudi Airlines	30.0	30.0	—	—
III. Total current receipts: general and special funds	2,006.7	2,266.0	2,626.0	2,962.1
IV. Estimation error	+ 0.3	—	—	- 0.1
V. Nonrevenue receipts				
A. Other sources of budget finance	159.0	186.2	60.0	150.0
1. Drawn from development fund	—	—	—	50.0
2. Drawn from reserve	159.0	186.2	60.0	100.0
VI. Total sources of finance	2,165.7	2,452.2	2,686.0	3,112.0

1965/66	1966/67	1967/68	1968/69	1969/70	1970/71	1971/72	1972/73
3,144.2	3,944.1	3,515.4	4,198.3	5,197.8	5,440.0	9,859.4	12,106.0
954.4	1,160.7	1,126.6	1,177.0	1,738.5	1,573.0	2,226.7	2,528.9
2,186.5	2,783.4	2,388.8	3,018.8	3,459.3	3,863.5	7,628.2	9,568.8
3.3	—	—	2.5	—	3.5	4.5	8.3
272.9	308.5	331.2	392.7	441.3	654.0	583.2	595.5
62.0	76.7	81.0	88.1	110.4	202.5*	150.0	157.5
198.5	215.0	233.3	286.0	303.7	421.7	403.1	408.6
12.6	16.8	16.9	18.6	27.2	29.8	30.1	29.4
176.0	188.3	211.0	299.1	316.2	275.9	327.6	482.7
4.9	7.4	6.4	8.5	8.0	6.2	8.0	11.8
3,598.0	4,448.3	4,064.0	4,898.6	5,963.3	6,376.1	10,778.2	13,196.0
15.7	1.6	1.5	1.5	3.0	3.4	3.4	5.2
1.7	1.6	1.5	1.5	3.0	3.4	3.4	5.2
14.0	—	—	—	—	—	—	—
—	—	—	—	—	—	—	—
3,613.7	4,449.9	4,065.5	4,900.1	5,966.3	6,379.5	10,781.6	13,201.2
- 0.1	+ 0.1	0.1	- 0.1	- 0.3	+ 0.5	+ 0.4	- 1.2
347.4	575.0	871.6	635.5	—	—	—	—
100.4	10.4	—	200.0	—	—	—	—
247.0	564.6	871.6	435.5	—	—	—	—
3,961.0	5,025.0	4,937.1	5,535.5	5,966.3	6,379.5	10,781.6	13,201.2

*Including S.R. 55.0 million in interim Jihad tax.

Sources: 1961/62 to 1962/63: CDS, Statistical Yearbook, 1388 A.H., vol. 4 (Riyadh, 1968), p. 374; 1963/64 to 1969/70: Ibid., 1390 A.H., vol. 6 (Riyadh, 1970), p. 380; 1970/71 to 1972/73: Ibid., 1393 A.H., vol. 9 (Riyadh, 1973), p. 362.

sector, and 13.2 percent in the nonoil sector. The effect of the imposition of an income tax on the oil producers is reflected in the rapid rise of that tax as compared to royalties. In 1948 royalties accounted for almost all of the oil revenues recorded. Royalties rose about 168 percent during the period under discussion. Income taxes on the other hand accounted for less than 50 percent of oil revenues in 1951/52. By 1957/58 income tax payments from oil producers had risen more than eightfold and accounted for 69.8 percent of total oil revenue.

Tax revenues rose almost 390 percent, from S.R. 29.3 million in 1948 to S.R. 143.2 million in 1957/58. Of this total the largest increase, 404 percent, was recorded by indirect taxes, and because customs revenues comprise the largest portion of these taxes, this rise reflects the growing prosperity of the population. During the same time, nontax revenues declined and other revenues, n.e.c., rose from S.R. 2.8 million to S.R. 20.4 million.

Estimated Budget Receipts, 1961/62 to 1972/73

Table 13.3 gives estimated budget receipts for the years 1961/62 to 1972/73. Although we lack actual receipts, these figures can be used with confidence. By far the largest item is oil-sector revenues, and in the past these estimates have been remarkably close to the actual payments made. The remaining classifications are less accurate; unfortunately, the two major statistical series of oil revenues give these data in different form. The series offered in Table 13.3 is based on the figures published in the Statistical Yearbook, which gives a breakdown between royalty and income tax payment but does not enable us to differentiate by company. The statistics published by SAMA offer a breakdown by company and not by type of revenue. Therefore, our discussion will be based on both sets of oil revenue data. For the purpose of overall analysis of total budget revenue receipts the data in Table 13.3 will be used, while the more detailed analysis of oil revenues alone will be based on the data provided by Zuhayr Mikdashi[5] and SAMA and reproduced in Table 13.5.

From 1961/62 to 1972/73 oil revenues rose 634 percent, from S.R. 1,648.8 million to S.R. 12,106 million. As a percentage of total current revenue oil-sector revenues rose from 85.1 percent in 1961/62 to 19.7 percent in 1972/73 (see Table 13.4). The share of royalties with respect to total current revenues declined steadily during this period, falling from 34.2 percent to 20.9 percent. At the same time the share of income tax from oil rose correspondingly.

TABLE 13.4

Percent Distribution of Estimated Current Budget Receipts, by Major Category and Within Major Categories, 1961/62 to 1972/73
(percent)

Type of Revenue	1961/62	1963/64	1965/66	1967/68	1968/69	1969/70	1970/71	1971/72	1972/73
Oil-sector revenue	85.1	86.9	87.4	86.5	85.7	87.2	85.3	91.5	91.7
Royalties	34.2	31.8	30.4	32.0	28.0	33.4	28.9	22.6	20.9
Income tax	65.8	67.4	69.5	68.0	71.9	66.6	71.0	77.4	79.0
Tapline	—	0.8	0.1	—	0.1	—	0.1	0.0	0.1
Tax revenue	11.8	8.4	7.6	8.1	8.0	7.4	10.3	5.4	4.5
Direct taxes	29.1	26.4	22.7	24.5	22.4	25.0	31.0	25.7	26.4
Indirect taxes	66.8	69.5	72.7	70.4	72.9	68.8	64.4	69.1	68.7
Fees and licenses	4.1	4.1	4.6	5.1	4.7	6.2	4.6	5.2	4.9
Nontax revenue (charges and miscellaneous)	3.1	4.7	4.9	5.2	6.1	5.3	4.3	3.0	3.7
Other revenue, n.e.c.	—	—	0.1	0.2	0.2	0.1	0.1	0.1	0.1
Total current general revenues	100.0	100.0	100.0	100.0	100.0	100.0	100.0	100.0	100.0

Source: Table 13.3.

REVENUE RECEIPTS BY CLASSIFICATION

Oil Revenues

Total oil revenues received are determined by five factors: total output of crude and refined products, the output "mix" of various types of crude and refined products, costs of production, posted prices, and contractual factors. Table 13.5 presents current oil revenues from 1938 to 1972 by producing company. To bring the series as close as possible to estimated current revenue special one-time payments by Aramco resulting from retroactive application of contract changes have been excluded from this series. They.were, therefore, earned in the years preceding the actual payments. To be consistent these payments should be prorated and included in the year for which they were made. Unfortunately, it is impossible to tell how much of a given special payment was incurred in any given year. Therefore, they have been recorded as special payments in the year in which they were received.

Aramco

Aramco's payments can be divided into five time periods. From 1938 to 1944 revenues rose from less than $200,000 to $2.5 million; the disruptions associated with World War II explain the relative constancy of revenues. The second period extends from 1945 to 1950; payments rose more than tenfold, from $5 million to $56.7 million. Worldwide recovery from the war led to an increase in oil demand. The 224 percent increase, from $17.5 million in 1947 to $56.7 million in 1950, resulted primarily from European economic recovery under the Marshall Plan. The third period began in 1951 and ended in 1963; revenues received from Aramco nearly doubled from 1950 to 1951 owing to the imposition of the income tax and from increased demand associated with the Korean conflict. The 93-percent increase from 1951 to 1952 resulted from the elimination of the offset provision for taxes paid by Aramco in the United States. The decline of revenues from 1955 to 1959 was caused by an oversupply of crude oil on the world markets. During this period, posted prices were lowered several times, causing a decline of revenues of 14.5 percent from the high of 1955, remaining about constant at $286 million from 1956 to 1958. By 1959 a slight increase in revenues was registered. It was the decline in revenues caused by the lower posted prices that led to the unification of the oil-producing nations and the establishment of OPEC. The decline was also the cause of the political crisis that ended in the replacement of ibn Saud by the Crown Prince, Faisal Ibn

TABLE 13.5

Oil Revenues, by Company, 1938-73
(U.S. $ million)

Year	Aramco	Getty Oil	AOC	Other	Total	Special Receipts
1938	0.2	—	—	—	0.5	—
1939	2.0[a]	—	—	—	2.0	1.16
1940	2.5	—	—	—	2.5	—
1941	2.0	—	—	—	2.0	—
1942	2.0	—	—	—	2.0	—
1943	2.0	—	—	—	2.0	—
1944	2.5	—	—	—	2.5	—
1945	5.0	—	—	—	5.0	—
1946	12.5	—	—	—	12.5	—
1947	17.5	—	—	—	17.5	—
1948	31.5[b]	—	—	—	31.5[b]	19.32
1949	39.0	—	—	—	39.0	—
1950	56.7	—	—	—	56.7	—
1951	110.0	—	—	—	110.0	—
1952	212.2	—	—	—	212.2	—
1953	169.8	—	—	—	169.8	—
1954	234.8	1.5	—	—	236.3	—
1955	338.2	2.6	—	—	340.8	—
1956	286.8	3.4	—	—	290.2	—
1957	286.5	9.8	—	—	296.3	—
1958	287.4	10.2	—	—	297.6	—
1959	295.3	15.3	2.5	—	313.1	—
1960	312.8	18.4	2.5	—	333.7	—
1961	352.2	22.9	2.5	—	377.6	—
1962	381.7	25.0	3.0	—	409.7	—
1963	418.6[c]	23.0	13.6	—	455.2[c]	152.5
1964	482.1	23.7	17.4	—	523.2	—
1965	572.4[d]	23.8	20.4	—	586.2[d]	46.0
1966	716.1[e]	20.6	22.3	1.3	760.3[e]	29.4
1967	830.1[f]	17.8	31.8	0.1	879.8[f]	29.3
1968	872.0	13.6	34.3	6.9	926.8	—
1969	895.2	15.2	37.1	1.5	949.0	—
1970	1,088.4	17.2	40.3	3.8	1,149.7	—
1971	1,866.4	20.6	44.2	13.7	1,944.9	—
1972	2,677.9[g]	28.0	68.7	4.7	2,779.3[g]	—
1973	4,209.7	22.0	91.4	7.8	4,330.9	—

[a]Excludes $1.16 million due under 1939 supplementary agreement.
[b]Excludes $19.32 million settlement of gold-pound controversy.
[c]Excludes $152.5 million due under March 24, 1963, agreement.
[d]Excludes $46 million due under January 1965 agreement.
[e]Excludes $29.4 million due under September 30, 1966, agreement.
[f]Excludes $29.3 million due under September 30, 1966, agreement.
[g]Includes $45.2 million value of royalty crude delivered to Petromin.

Sources: 1938-49: Zuhayr Mikdashi, A Financial Analysis of Middle Eastern Oil Concessions: 1901-1965 (New York: Praeger, 1966), p. 122; 1950-54: SAMA Reports, 1384/85 A.H. (Jedda, 1966), p. 48; 1955-63: Ibid., 1390/91 A.H. (Jedda, 1972), p. 8; 1964-72: SAMA, Statistical Summary, Shawwal 1393 (December 1972), p. 55; 1973: SAMA, Annual Report, 1392/93 A.H. (Jedda, 1973), p. 93.

Ibn Abdul Aziz Al Saud. The fourth period starts with the Sidon Settlement and ends in 1970, and the fifth period began with the Teheran Settlement.

Aramco's total payments to the government are the sum of two separately calculated types of revenue: royalties and income taxes. The amounts of royalties and income taxes paid are affected differently by the five factors mentioned above. Royalty payments are determined by total production because their calculation is still based on the four gold shillings per ton agreed upon in 1933, except for offshore oil, for which an additional five cents per barrel is paid. The current practice that royalties are equal to 12.5 percent of posted price has had some effect on royalty payments, but the basic determinant of the amount paid is still the flat rate agreed upon in 1933. Posted prices, costs of production, contractual factors, and OPEC discounts and allowances determine the tax base and thus the government's average receipt per barrel. Past changes in any of these factors have shifted the tax base in favor of the government.

Posted Prices

Saudi Arabia's crude exports falls into three gravity ranges, and the posted price of a given grade of crude depends on its API gravity; the higher the gravity, the greater the posted price. Thus, given the range of grades of crude and their posted prices, it is clear that, ceteris paribus, oil revenues will be higher, the greater the proportion of high-gravity oil lifted.

During the 22 years from 1948 to 1970 posted prices remained relatively stable (see Table 9.9, p. 209). Arabian Light crude posted prices fluctuated between $2.12 and $1.75 per barrel for that period. For the decade of 1960-70 all posted prices stayed the same, reflecting the absolute control that the international oil companies had over the price of oil. While tax-reference prices remained constant, world prices for manufactured goods and general services rose dramatically. Thus, it is not surprising that the OPEC nations demanded a new deal from the oil companies. The result was the Teheran Agreement, which raised tax-reference prices for Arabian Medium and Arabian Heavy crude and provided for additional increases until 1975. Owing to the increasing rate of inflation in the industrialized countries, and for political reasons, Saudi Arabia rejected the schedule of posted prices agreed upon in Teheran and negotiated new and higher tax-reference prices. Table 9.9 gives the posted prices for crude oil since August 31, 1970. From August 1970 to January 1974 posted prices rose 547, 588, and 633 percent for Arabian Light, Arabian Medium, and Arabian Heavy, respectively.

Contractual Factors

The various changes in the agreement between the exploiting companies and the government have been thoroughly discussed in Chapters 7 and 8, so we will concentrate our attention on a series of pro forma examples, showing the effect on the tax base resulting from the Sidon Agreement and the royalty-expensing agreement of 1965.

The "Sidon Price Settlement" of March 24, 1963, called for an increase of the posted price of Arabian Light crude delivered at Sidon from $1.80, the Ras Tanura posting, to $2.17, retroactive to October 6, 1953. The agreement raised the tax base by 14 percent, from $1.361 to $1.555, and increased the government's take by 14 percent, from $0.681 to $0.778 per barrel (see Table 13.6).

The agreement change of January 25, 1965, called for the expensing of royalties. This means that royalties became deductible from gross income rather than from income tax liability. The overall effect of this agreement was a reduction of the tax base but it resulted in an increase in actual income tax receipts for all grades of crude oil produced (see Table 13.7). The changes in per-barrel tax receipts from the two contractual changes are summarized in Table 13.8.

Costs of Production

Very little is known about the actual costs of lifting crude oil, and the more we retreat into the past, the less available accurate information becomes. It has been established, however, that up to a certain point, increases in output will lower production costs per barrel. Based on partial information and informed opinion, it is our estimate that the cost of crude f.o.b. Ras Tanura fell about 37 percent for Arabian Heavy and 27 percent for Medium crude, and the cost of Arabian Light ex-Ras Tanura declined about 50 percent and ex-Sidon about 25 percent during the 1960s.

Output mix, OPEC discounts, and Tapline "make-up" payments have been discussed above. They are, therefore, not included in the general discussion of factors affecting government oil revenue receipts.

The Getty Oil Company

Getty began production in 1954. From that year to 1965 oil revenues received by the government rose by an average of 14.9 percent per annum. The decline of payments from 1966 to 1968 resulted from a shift in demand to the lighter crudes, lowering demand for

TABLE 13.6

Tax Liability Calculation on Sidon Sales
(pro forma example)

Before January 1, 1963

Posted price per barrel of Arabian Light at Sidon		$1.800
Less marketing allowance	$0.005	
Less OPEC allowance	0.100	
	$0.105	
Net selling price		$1.695
Plus Tapline cost	$0.176	
Adjusted posted price		$1.871
Less cost to Quisumah (estimated)	$0.109	
Less royalty	0.225	
Less Tapline cost (estimated)	0.176	
	$0.510	
Tax base		$1.361
Tax rate = 50 percent		
Income tax payable		$0.681

After January 1, 1963

Posted price per barrel of Arabian Light at Sidon		$2.170
Less marketing allowance	$0.005	
Less OPEC allowance	0.100	
	$0.105	
Net selling price		$2.065
Adjusted posted price		$2.065
Less cost to Qaisumah (estimated)	$0.109	
Less royalty	0.225	
Less Tapline cost (estimated)	0.176	
	$0.510	
Tax base		$1.555
Tax rate = 50 percent		
Income tax payable per barrel		$0.778

TABLE 13.7

Tax Liability Calculation on Ras Tanura Sales
(pro forma example)

Before January 1, 1965

Posted price per barrel of Arabian Light at Ras Tanura		$1.800
Less marketing allowance	$0.005	
Adjusted posted price		$1.795
Less total production costs to shipping point (estimated)	$0.150	
Tax base		$1.645
Tax rate = 50 percent		
Total income-tax liability		$0.8225
Less royalties paid	$0.2250	
Total income tax payable		$0.5975

After January 1, 1965

Posted price per barrel of Arabian Light at Ras Tanura		$1.800
Less OPEC allowance (8.5 percent)	$0.153	
Less marketing allowance	0.005	
Less gravity allowance (0.13235 x 7)	0.009	
	$0.167	
Adjusted posted price		$1.633
Less royalties expense ($1.80 x 0.125)	$0.225	
Less production costs to shipping point (estimated)	$0.150	
	$0.375	
Tax base		$1.258
Tax rate = 50 percent		
Income tax payable		$0.6290

TABLE 13.8

Government Take per Barrel Before and After Sidon-Agreement and Royalty-Expensing-Agreement Changes
(in U.S. dollars)

Type of Payment	Before	After
Sidon Agreement (January 1, 1963)		
Royalty	0.2250	0.2250
Income tax	0.6810	0.7780
Total receipts	0.9060	1.0030
Royalty-Expensing Agreement (January 1, 1965)		
Royalty	0.2250	0.2250
Income tax	0.5975	0.6290
Total receipts	0.8225	0.8525

Source: Tables 13.6 and 13.7.

Getty's heavier-crude output. The contractual factors that applied to Aramco did not affect Getty's payments to the government until 1970. However, the Teheran Agreement forced a considerable increase in Getty payments to the government, owing to higher posted prices.

AOC

AOC began payments in 1959. For the first three years the company paid the minimum required by agreement. Oil in commercial quantities was discovered in 1962, and thereafter payments to the government rose from $3 million in that year to $68.7 million in 1972. Again, the large increase in payments from 1971 to 1972 resulted from the higher posted prices set by the Geneva Agreement.

The Other Companies

At this writing (February 1974) the other companies have not yet found oil in commercially exploitable quantities, and the payments received from this source since 1966 have been in the nature of rental payments.

TABLE 13.9

Average Revenue Receipts per Barrel, 1948-73
(dollars)

Year	Amount	Year	Amount
1948	0.220	1961	0.743
1949	0.224	1962	0.738
1950	0.284	1963	0.766
1951	0.396	1964	0.833
1952	0.703	1965	0.793
1953	0.551	1966	0.871
1954	0.679	1967	0.926
1955	0.968	1968	0.895
1956	0.804	1969	0.869
1957	0.818	1970	0.888
1958	0.803	1971	1.185
1959	0.784	1972	1.262
1960	0.731	1973	1.562

Sources: Tables 9.2 and 13.5.

Government Take

Table 13.9 presents average revenue receipts per barrel from 1948 to 1973 (the data are presented graphically in the accompanying chart). The figures best reflect the five factors affecting the government's oil-revenue receipts. Per barrel receipts rose about 600 percent, from $0.22 in 1948 to $1,562 in 1973. The major contractual changes are clearly reflected in the statistics. From 1951 to 1952 average revenues per barrel rose 77.5 percent, reflecting the imposition of the income tax. The decline in per barrel revenues from 1956 to 1960 resulted from the fall in posted prices during that period. Finally, the Sidon Agreement, the Expensing-of-Royalties Agreement, and the Teheran Agreement are clearly associated with increases in per barrel revenue receipts.

Tax Revenues

The Kingdom's nonoil tax revenues have been divided into three groups: direct taxes, indirect taxes, and fees and licenses. Direct

FIGURE 1

Average Revenue Receipts per Barrel, 1948-73

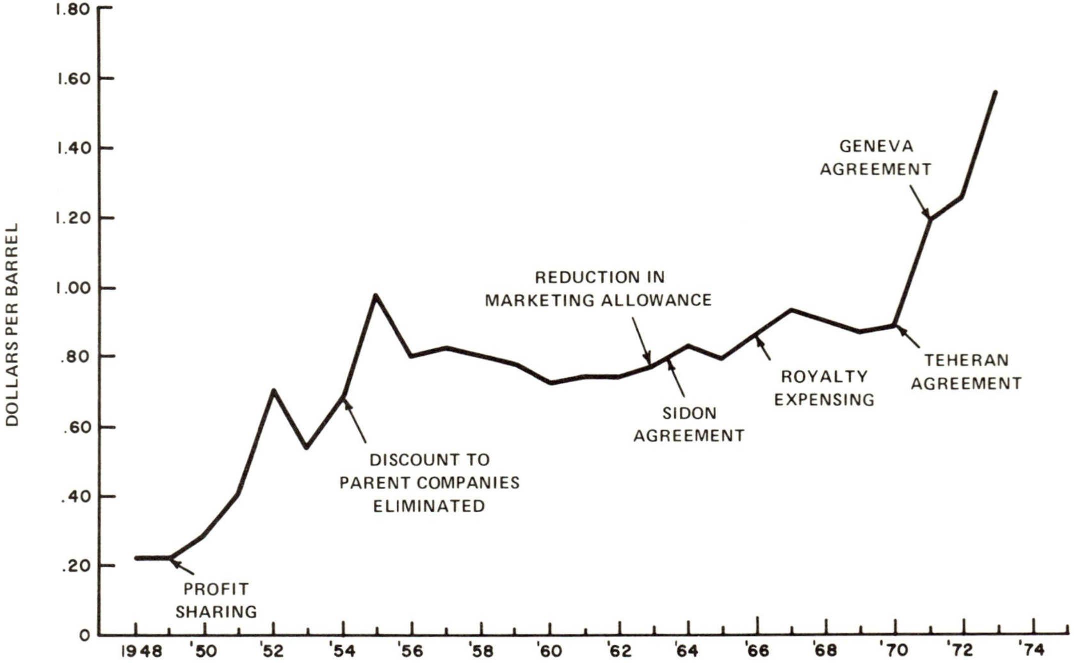

Source: Table 13.9.

TABLE 13.10

Estimated Direct-Tax Revenues, by Source, 1961/62 to 1972/73
(S.R. million)

	Nonoil Income Tax	Roads Tax	Zakat	Total
1961/62	33.0	30.0	3.5	66.8
1962/63	33.0	30.0	2.5	65.5
1963/64	35.0	23.0	[a]	58.0
1964/65	36.5	23.0	[a]	59.5
1965/66	38.0	24.0	[a]	62.0
1966/67	42.7	29.0	5.0	76.7
1967/68	44.0	31.0	6.0	81.0
1968/69	46.7	35.4	6.0	88.1
1969/70	62.6	41.3	6.5	110.4
1970/71	99.5	41.5	6.5	147.5[b]
1971/72	100.5	41.5	8.0	150.0
1972/73	105.0	41.5	11.0	157.5

[a]Not collected in this year.
[b]Plus S.R. 55 million of Jihad tax in 1970/71.

Sources: 1961/62 to 1970/71: Ramon Knauerhase, "A Survey or the Revenue Structure of the Kingdom of Saudi Arabia, 1961/62 to 1971/72," Public Finance 23, no. 3-4 (1973): 443; 1971/72 to 1972/73: CDS, Statistical Yearbook, 1393 A.H., vol. 9 (Riyadh, 1973), p. 362.

taxes are levied on the taxpayer's income; indirect taxes are those that are levied against expenditures; fees and licenses are those levies that do not fall directly on income or expenditures for goods and services in the marketplace. Owing to the unreliability of the data on all nonoil revenues before 1960, the following discussion will concentrate primarily on the period after that date.

Direct-Tax Revenues

Total direct-tax revenues rose 135.8 percent at an annual rate of 8.1 percent, from S.R. 66.8 million in 1961/62 to S.R. 157.5 million in 1972/73, with the sharpest increase from 1968/69 to 1970/71 (see Table 13.10). This increase of S.R. 59.4 million reflects the attempt to close a threatened budget deficit in 1970/71 by manipulation of the rates assessed.*

Within this class income taxes on non-Saudi individuals and business enterprises accounted for almost 50 percent in 1961/62 and for two-thirds in 1972/73. The roads tax has been a more variable source of tax revenue: It fell from S.R. 30 million in 1961/62 to S.R. 23 million in 1963/64, rose slowly back to its original level in 1966/67, and continued its rise to S.R. 41.5 million in 1972/73. The cause of the decline from 1962/63 to 1963/64 is unknown. The increase since that year has been the result of the larger number of foreigners working in the country as well as of the rising income of those guest workers.

Collections from the Zakat have risen slowly. The government has experimented with various ways of collecting the tax without much success. More than any other tax on Saudi citizens, the Zakat depends on voluntary reporting of income on assets by the populace. It is known that the payments made are considerably lower than required.

By far the most important single item in the direct-tax category was the Jihad tax (Holy War Tax). Levied for the budget year 1970/71, it was repealed in the following year, owing to rising oil revenues.

Indirect Revenues

Indirect taxes originate from two major sources: customs duties and the petroleum products tax (see Table 13.11). As in the case of direct taxes, the analysis of this component is complicated by the lack of precise information.

Customs duties are collected under two headings: customs on value and specific customs. Of these two classes the former contributed by far the largest portion. Customs duties rose from S.R. 155.7 million in 1961/62 to S.R. 320 million in 1972/73, about 105 percent. On June 7, 1968, a new, lower schedule of tariffs went into effect. That schedule was amended in September 1970, increasing the duties on luxury imports as part of the previously mentioned attempt to cover a deficit in the 1970/71 budget.

The decline in customs revenues in 1962/63 and 1963/64 resulted from certain tariff adjustments made with Lebanon. Actual receipts in 1967/68 were probably less than the estimates shown, because the Kingdom's trade was interrupted by the Arab-Israeli War of June 1967. The 24 percent increase in collections from 1967/68

---

*The increase is actually S.R. 114.4 million when the S.R. 55 million yield of the Jihad Tax is included. See Chapter 14 also.

TABLE 13.11

Estimated Indirect Revenues, by Source, 1961/62 to 1972/73
(S.R. million)

Year	Customs Duties	Petroleum Products Tax	Total Indirect Revenues
1961/62	155.7	n.a.	155.7
1962/63	142.2	n.a.	142.2
1963/64	142.2	12.0	154.2
1964/65	150.0	15.0	165.0
1965/66	182.5	16.0	198.5
1966/67	194.5	20.0	214.5
1967/68	211.5	21.0	232.5
1968/69	262.0	23.5	285.5
1969/70	275.4	27.0	302.4
1970/71	333.5	89.0	422.5
1971/72	351.0	49.0	400.0
1972/73	320.0	52.0	320.0

Sources: 1961/62 to 1970/71: Ramon Knauerhase, "A Survey of the Revenue Structure of the Kingdom of Saudi Arabia, 1961/60 to 1971/72," Public Finance 23, no. 3-4 (1973): 446; 1971/72 to 1972/73: CDS, Statistical Yearbook, 1393 A.H., vol. 9 (Riyadh, 1973), p. 362.

to 1968/69 resulted from the lower schedule introduced on June 7, 1968, as well as from the population's rising prosperity. Finally, the increase in the 1970/71 budget year can be traced to an increase in duties on luxury imports.

The petroleum products tax is imposed on eight major petroleum products ranging from kerosene to aviation gasoline. Until the budget year 1970/71 more than 90 percent of this tax was derived from gasoline sales. To help finance the deficit of the budget year 1970/71 the tax on gasoline was raised from S.R. 0.014 to S.R. 0.024 per liter. At the same time a S.R. 0.025 tax on diesel fuel was imposed.

Also included under indirect taxes should be three items, two of which are recorded in the Statistical Yearbooks as "service fees" and the other is included in the "miscellaneous income" category.

Municipalities fees, quay fees, and Al Fallah school fees are surcharges on customs duties earmarked for special purposes. Those three customs-associated levies should amount to 10 percent of all duties collected. In practice the amounts collected are slightly higher, because they are due on all dutiable goods. That is, even if a given shipment of goods is exempted from duties, the 10-percent surcharge for the three items must be paid.

Fees and Licenses

The following items fall into this category: drivers' licenses and work permits, residency permits and passports, automobile registration, and revenue stamps. Because of poor collection and enforcement methods the yield has been low and nowhere near its potential.

Nontax Revenues

These revenues range from postal-service income to a small amount collected from the rental of certain government-owned properties. Most of the items contained in this class yield very little revenue, therefore we will discuss only government profit.

TABLE 13.12

Estimated Government Profits, 1961/62 to 1970/71
(S.R. million)

Year	Amount
1961/62	—
1962/63	0.7
1963/64	60.3
1964/65	66.3
1965/66	90.7
1966/67	103.2
1967/68	124.6
1968/69	200.0
1969/70	214.9
1970/71	145.6

Source: Ramon Knauerhase, "A Survey of the Revenue Structure of the Kingdom of Saudi Arabia," Public Finance 23, no. 3-4 (1973): 447.

Table 13.12 gives estimated government profits for the period from 1961/62 to 1970/71. It is the largest single item received in the nontax category. It represents the profit earned on various government funds invested outside the Kingdom. In addition, a small amount of Petromin profits is also included. Most of the funds invested abroad originated from special payments made by Aramco during the 1960s in settlement of claims associated with contract changes in March 1964, January 1965, and September 1966. As has been pointed out, those funds were not recorded as revenues at the time they were received. Instead, they were set aside in the Economic Development Fund and used to finance special development projects.

NOTES

1. A. R. Prest, Public Finance (London: Weidenfels and Nicholson, 1960), p. 24.
2. SAMA, Annual Report, 1382/83 A.H. (Jedda, 1964), p. 5; Ibid., 1384/85 A.H. (Jedda, 1966), p. 4; Ibid., 1385/86 A.H. (Jedda, 1967), pp. 20-21.
3. SAMA, Statistical Summary, Shawwal 1390 A.H. (December 1970), Table III, pp. 28-29.
4. SAMA, Annual Report, 1382/83 A.H., p. 5.
5. Zuhayr Mikdashi, A Financial Analysis of Middle Eastern Oil Concessions, 1901-1965 (New York: Praeger, 1966), p. 122.

CHAPTER

14

THE BUDGET: EXPENDITURES

This chapter deals with the expenditure side of the national budget. It begins with a brief discussion of some of the difficulties inherent in the available data. Next, government expenditures are presented by budget chapters to throw some light on the overall expenditure patterns. This discussion is followed by a reclassification of the published data into three major functional groups: administration and defense, social and economic, and other expenditures. An analysis of these data shows that the relative share of outlays for defense and support of the royal family has declined since 1959, and has been offset by an increase in allocations to the Interior Ministry. Expenditures by the ministry are dedicated to law enforcement (police, prisons, frontier police and so on) and maintenance of the amirates (provincial administration). Among the appropriations for social purposes, education ranked highest, followed by public health. The first section ends with an examination of the projects budget.

The rest of the chapter deals with the relationship between revenues and expenditures. It shows that the drain of the Khartoum payments in support of Egypt and Jordan depleted the nation's financial reserves and led to a cash deficit in fiscal year 1969/70. Faced with the possible reduction of the development effort and the Arab subsidies, the government began its effort to increase oil revenues by assuming complete control over oil pricing. The process began with the Teheran conference and will end in 1975 with the complete takeover of Aramco.

The budget is divided into four basic chapters.[1] Chapter 1 contains salaries and allowances, including civil and military employees, fixed salaries, day laborers' wages, and indemnity payments (overtime-injury compensation), subsidies for pilgrimage, radio and television broadcasting, visiting academicians, agricultural organizations, imams, muezzins' allowances, and more. Chapter 2 deals with general expenses, including travel and transportation expenses, stationery and printing supplies, maintenance of airports, roads and government installations, furniture, and so on, permanent contracts with nongovernment organizations for roads and airports maintenance, utilities expenses, and miscellaneous items. Chapter 3 covers special appropriations: expenses of the privy purse, government contributions to the civil-service retirement fund, national defense, and subsidies of imported necessities. Chapter 4 is the projects budget; it contains social-overhead capital formation, directly productive projects, and defense projects.

A detailed record of actual expenditures is not available. The only source of expenditures is a short statement of cash expenditures published by SAMA. The detailed data available are budget appropriations issued at the beginning of each fiscal year. In addition to the budget document, which is restricted in circulation, there are two sources of appropriations data: CDS's Statistical Yearbook, and the Annual Report of SAMA. In 1966 CDS published a time series of appropriations by chapter, from 1959 to 1965/66, based on revised classifications; the data have been updated annually since then. In the following presentation we will use the data published in the Statistical Yearbook for the chapter-by-chapter analysis and those published by SAMA for the analysis of the main government-spending agencies. That discussion will be followed by an examination of the cash-expenditure data published by SAMA.

The budget year covers one Hijra year from the first day of Rajab (the seventh Hijra month) to the last day of Jumada II (the sixth Hijra month). The Ministry of Finance and National Economy is in complete control of the budget-preparations process. Formulation of the budget begins when the Ministry of Finance and National Economy issues a call to all ministries and agencies to submit their estimated needs for the coming fiscal year. The information originates at the lowest level, where estimates are made of anticipated needs based on past experience, current and projected needs, and actual, current expenditures. Once the budget has been formulated at the department or section level within each ministry, it is forwarded to the budget department of the individual ministries or agency where it is examined within the context of the ministry's overall objectives. Following that review, the ministry budget is forwarded to the budget department of the Ministry of Finance and National Economy, which has the power to add or eliminate items. Following the integration of the various ministry budgets into a budget for the whole nation, the document is forwarded to the King and the Council of Ministers for final approval. As the budget progresses through the hierarchy it is subject to review and revision. Responsibility for control of expenditures also rests with the Ministry of Finance and National Economy.

Until the budget year 1970/71 there was little, if any, input from CPO. With the completion of the first development plan guidelines have been developed, focusing the budget-making process on the long run, thereby providing a means to integrate overall expenditures to achieve national development goals.

EXPENDITURES

Appropriations by Chapter

Table 14.1 gives an overall look at expenditure appropriations, by budget chapters. Total appropriations rose from S.R. 1,410 million in 1959 to S.R. 22,810 million in 1973/74, an increase of about 1,500 percent. During the same period, salaries and allowances rose 823 percent, and general expenses, 860.9 percent.

Because there are no detailed data available for 1959 for Chapters 3 and 4, comparison for those two items is based on the budget year 1959/60. In that budget year special appropriations amounted to S.R. 205.8 million; they rose to 3,224.4 million by 1973/74. Chapter 4, the projects budget, registered the most dramatic change during the period under discussion. It rose nearly 23-fold, from S.R. 592.2 in 1959/60 to S.R. 14,263 million in 1973/74. The slight decline of S.R. 86 million from 1969/70 to 1970/71 resulted from the depletion of the development fund, the interruption of the Tapline in Syrian territory, and a decline of reserves. The dramatic increase of projects appropriations the following year was made possible by the increased revenue receipts following the Teheran and Geneva agreements.

In 1959/60, salaries and allowances accounted for 29.2 percent of appropriations, while Chapters 2, 3, and 4 accounted for 14, 14.6, and 42.1 percent, respectively. By 1973/74 the percentage share of the chapters had changed radically. The share of the first three chapters had declined to 15.7, 7.6, and 14.1 percent, respectively, while the projects budget's share had risen to 62.5 percent.

Appropriations by Main Government Sectors

The budget is the expression of the government's fiscal policy and thus allows us to observe the course and direction of the development planned for the Kingdom. To facilitate the analysis appropriations have been broken down into the following functional categories:

TABLE 14.1

Expenditure Appropriations, by Budget Chapter, January 1959 to August 1973
(S.R. million)

Year	Chapter 1	Chapter 2	Chapter 3		Chapter 4	Total
1959	388.2	181.0		840.8		1,410.0
1959/60	410.0	196.1	205.8		592.2	1,405.0
1960/61	482.5	237.0		1,066.5		1,786.0
1961/62	577.5	299.3		1,289.2		2,166.0
1962/63	650.3	423.3		1,378.6		2,452.2
1963/64	1,016.8	556.8		1,112.4		2,686.0
1964/65	1,111.5	632.8	605.7		762.0	3,112.0
1965/66	1,254.7	621.4	682.4		1,402.4	3,961.0
1966/67	1,368.9	691.4	1,247.2		1,717.4	5,025.0
1967/68	1,432.9	624.6	732.7		2,146.8	4,937.0
1968/69	1,600.5	806.7	908.3		2,222.0	5,535.5
1969/70	1,688.0	711.5	884.5		2,682.0	5,966.0
1970/71	1,791.0	746.3	1,408.7		2,596.0	6,380.0
1971/72	2,537.1	1,015.8	2,193.4		5,035.7	10,782.0
1972/73	3,122.8	1,365.1	2,462.3		6,717.6	13,200.0
1973/74	3,583.4	1,739.2	3,224.4		14,263.0	22,810.0

Sources: 1959 to 1960/61: CDS, Statistical Yearbook, 1386 A.H., vol. 2 (Riyadh, 1966), p. 289; 1961/62 to 1970/71: Ibid., 1391 A.H., vol. 7 (Riyadh, 1971), p. 339; 1971/72 to 1973/74: Ibid., 1393 A.H., vol. 9 (Riyadh, 1973), p. 361.

I. Administration and defense
   A. Administration (private treasury, Royal cabinet, Council of Ministers, ministries of Foreign Affairs, Interior, Finance and National Economy, and Justice)
   B. Defense (defense and civil defense)
II. Social and economic
   A. Social (health, information, education, labor, and social affairs, subsidies for basic commodities, ministry of the Hadj, and religious organizations)
   B. Economic (ministries of Agriculture, Communications, Petroleum and Minerals, Commerce and Industry, and Projects)
III. All other (emergency expenses, other expenditures, and general budgetary reserve)

Administration and defense expenditures are a form of social overhead outlay that benefits the body politic as a whole rather than the individual. The maintenance of law and order through the judiciary and the administration of monetary policies are examples of the collective nature of the usefulness generated by these expenditures.

Defense expenditures are somewhat further removed. They generate a service called national security, benefiting the population as a whole. In a sense, however, expenditures on missiles are sterile. That is, once they are installed, they do not directly facilitate and encourage the productive process. In developing countries the one exception to the rule is in the education of the soldiers: To the extent that schooling in the army raises the general educational level, the productive process is furthered. Unfortunately, there is no way to isolate the educational portion of the military budget. Finally, it must be mentioned that whenever the army gives civil-disaster relief it contributes in a positive way to the productive effort.

Expenditures on social services affect the members of society directly and contribute to the overall well-being of the society. Appropriations for health and education benefit the recipients directly by raising their general health through expenditures on public-health programs, as well as on direct medical care in case of individual illness. By raising the level of health, productivity of labor is increased, leading to higher levels of output. A similar argument can be made for public education, social affairs, and subsidies of basic commodities.

Table 14.2 presents budget appropriations, by functional categories, from 1959 to 1973/74. By far the majority of the ministries and agencies listed received approximately the same share of the budget throughout the period. Under the heading "administration and defense" two trends are registered. Allocations for the private treasury (the King's purse) declined from S.R. 236 million in 1959 to S.R. 173 million in 1964/65 and has remained constant at this level, resulting in a fall of its share in the budget, from 21.2 percent in 1959 to 0.7 percent in 1973/74. Total defense outlays rose absolutely, from S.R. 262 million in 1959 to S.R. 1,711 in 1973/74, while its share of the allocations fell from 23.6 percent to 7.5 percent in the same years. The decline reflects the change of priorities introduced by King Faisal following his assumption of the administration, first as Prime Minister and later as King, as well as the large total increase in budgeted outlays. The decline of the share of allocations to the private treasury and defense was offset by a rise in allocations to the Interior Ministry. The more than 13-fold increase of expenditures of the Ministry of Interior's budget between 1959 and 1973/74 and the fall in the ministry's share of the total budget, from 8.1 percent to 5.5 percent, are probably somewhat overstated with respect to allocations for administration by the inclusion of civil defense and other nonadministrative items. The reduced emphasis on military expenditures may not be as large as the measured decline in defense expenditure's share of the budget suggests. The budget classification "other expenditures" is rather high, and it is not unreasonable to assume that this class hides a portion of defense expenditures.

Education was by far the largest item of the appropriations for social purposes. It rose from S.R. 118 million in 1959 to S.R. 1,677 million in 1973/74. Education's share of the total budget fluctuated between 10.1 percent in 1963/64 and 7.4 percent in 1973/74. Given the need for an increase in the level of education, the average share of 8.8 percent of the budget appears to be rather small. Increasing the level of education is a social as well as an economic problem. If the government commands the needed resources, it should find it relatively easy to build the physical plant required. The social problem, however, is more difficult. It appears that the need for education has met with some indifference on the part of a considerable portion of the population. Despite the ease with which anyone can acquire at least a basic primary education, many people refuse to take advantage of the opportunity, because it has not been a tradition in the society to give children a secular education; the Koran and the sunna are still the only source of learning for the conservative Saudi. Only in recent years has there been a lessening of this resistance. Thus, the total outlay is limited by a social constraint, and it would be redundant to raise expenditures in this area as long as this constraint exists.

The second-largest recipient of funds under the social classification is the Ministry of Health. Appropriations declined from 5.4 percent of the total budget in 1959 to 2.2 percent in 1973/74. That does not indicate a decline in the level of medical care available to

TABLE 14.2

Budget Appropriations, by Functional Categories, 1959 to 1972/73
(S.R. million)

	1959	1959/60	1960/61	1961/62	1962/63	1963/64
Administration						
Private treasury	236.0	248.0	248.0	248.0	199.0	183.0
Royal cabinet	0.5	5.0	7.0	10.0	10.0	10.0
Council of Ministers	7.0	9.0	8.0	9.0	11.0	11.0
Foreign affairs	19.0	28.0	34.0	43.0	50.0	39.0
Interior	90.0	103.0	104.0	129.0	162.0	228.0
Finance and National Economy	39.0	53.0	43.0	41.0	46.0	61.0
Justice	18.0	18.0	20.0	21.0	21.0	24.0
Total	409.5	464.0	464.0	501.0	499.0	556.0
Defense						
Defense	262.0	266.0	259.0	340.0	392.0	502.0
Civil defense	—	—	—	—	40.0	28.0
Total	262.0	266.0	259.0	340.0	432.0	530.0
Social						
Labor and social affairs	—	—	—	47.0	77.0	55.0
Education	118.0	130.0	149.0	171.0	223.0	271.0
Health	60.0	55.0	58.0	69.0	87.0	103.0
Information	—	—	—	—	31.0	32.0
Religious affairs	23.0	23.0	25.0	29.0	61.0	66.0
Subsidies	—	78.0	35.0	25.0	30.0	30.0
Total	201.0	286.0	267.0	341.0	509.0	557.0
Economic						
Agriculture	20.0	23.0	21.0	34.0	43.0	58.0
Communications	24.0	8.0	9.0	18.0	21.0	79.0
Petroleum and minerals	—	—	11.0	11.0	11.0	11.0
Commerce and industry	3.0	4.0	4.0	5.0	6.0	10.0
Projects	55.0	110.0	291.0	400.0	550.0	550.0
Total	102.0	145.0	336.0	468.0	631.0	708.0
All other						
Emergency expenses	—	—	—	—	60.0	60.0
Other expenditures	138.0	112.0	105.0	115.0	174.0	251.0
Budgetary reserve	—	—	—	—	—	—
Total	138.0	112.0	105.0	115.0	234.0	311.0
Grand total	1,112.0	1,273.0	1,431.0	1,765.0	2,279.0	2,686.0

1964/65	1965/66	1966/67	1967/68	1968/69	1969/70	1970/71	1971/72	1972/73	1973/74
173.0	173.0	173.0	173.0	173.0	173.0	173.0	173.0	173.0	173.0
6.0	8.0	8.0	15.0	13.0	14.0	15.0	17.0	18.0	20.0
14.0	19.0	19.0	17.0	19.0	18.0	19.0	25.0	29.0	33.0
49.0	51.0	56.0	52.0	65.0	56.0	57.0	70.0	80.0	94.0
276.0	345.0	370.0	406.0	528.0	546.0	589.0	850.0	1,071.0	1,267.0
63.0	57.0	62.0	58.0	71.0	68.0	69.0	105.0	104.0	120.0
25.0	31.0	33.0	32.0	36.0	36.0	37.0	51.0	53.0	57.0
606.0	684.0	721.0	753.0	905.0	911.0	959.0	1,291.0	1,528.0	1,764.0
548.0	572.0	1,163.0	723.0	841.0	831.0	925.0	1,138.0	1,427.0	1,711.0
39.0	31.0	31.0	20.0	30.0	20.0	20.0	—	—	—
587.0	603.0	1,194.0	743.0	871.0	851.0	945.0	1,138.0	1,427.0	1,711.0
62.0	78.0	87.0	84.0	92.0	92.0	98.0	125.0	144.0	198.0
305.0	360.0	399.0	383.0	483.0	558.0	646.0	1,031.0	1,300.0	1,677.0
117.0	128.0	154.0	122.0	156.0	155.0	166.0	250.0	375.0	499.0
34.0	39.0	42.0	43.0	44.0	43.0	44.0	60.0	74.0	92.0
73.0	81.0	90.0	91.0	68.0	67.0	69.0	92.0	109.0	123.0
30.0	20.0	20.0	20.0	20.0	15.0	—	—	—	—
621.0	706.0	792.0	743.0	863.0	930.0	1,023.0	1,558.0	2,002.0	2,589.0
67.0	84.0	88.0	80.0	89.0	82.0	82.0	113.0	136.0	177.0
87.0	103.0	119.0	98.0	111.0	106.0	109.0	149.0	189.0	231.0
12.0	14.0	17.0	16.0	19.0	19.0	19.0	26.0	31.0	39.0
11.0	12.0	15.0	13.0	16.0	14.0	15.0	21.0	40.0	45.0
762.0	1,402.0	1,717.0	2,146.0	2,570.0	2,682.0	2,596.0	5,036.0	6,718.0	14,263.0
969.0	1,615.0	1,956.0	2,353.0	2,805.0	2,903.0	2,821.0	5,345.0	7,114.0	14,755.0
60.0	44.0	46.0	31.0	40.0	41.0	41.0	60.0	61.0	201.0
311.0	313.0	339.0	322.0	396.0	328.0	749.0	1,131.0	1,227.0	1,338.0
—	—	—	—	—	—	—	250.0	300.0	452.0
371.0	357.0	385.0	353.0	436.0	369.0	790.0	1,216.0	1,318.0	1,991.0
3,112.0	3,961.0	5,025.0	4,037.0	5,885.0	5,966.0	6,542.0	10,782.0	13,668.0	22,810.0

Source: Appendix Table C.7.

the population. As is the case in education, it is a sign that much of the basic structure of infirmaries and hospitals has been built. Providing the qualified personnel to supply the required services is a slower process than erecting buildings and stocking them with medications and equipment. There is an acute shortage of nurses and physicians. The shortage of nurses is particularly serious, because women are not allowed to enter the labor force.

In recent years the lion's share of the economic classification has been assigned to the projects budget. Its share has shown the most dramatic leap: allocations rose from 4.9 percent in 1959 to more than 60 percent of the budget appropriations in 1973/74. The relatively small increase from 1968/69 to 1969/70 resulted from the loss of oil revenues caused by an extended interruption of deliveries through the Tapline. The rather sharp decline in the share of projects, from 45 percent of the total budget in 1969/70 to 39.7 percent in 1970/71, was associated with the fiscal difficulties of that period.

A line-by-line examination of the projects budget is constrained by the large portion of the expenditures classified under "other projects" (see Table 14.3). As has been suggested before, that classification probably includes expenditures on military projects. As for the remainder of the items shown in Table 14.3, three trends are apparent. First, the share of education and health in the projects budget declined between 1959 and 1973/74. Education accounted for 5.2 percent of the projects budget in 1959 and for 4 percent in 1973/74. Over the same time period projects for health and Red Crescent fell from 3.8 percent to 0.6 percent. Second, agriculture's share of projects rose from 2.9 percent of the projects budget in 1959 to 6 percent in 1973/74, with a high of 15.4 percent in 1968/69. Third, the second- and third-largest shares of the projects budgets in 1973/74 were communications and municipalities, with 14.4 percent and 11 percent, respectively. Communication's share of the projects budget reached a high of 36.8 percent in 1964/65; municipalities reached its high in 1966/67. Both these classes reflect the government's aim to improve the social overhead-capital structure. Included in the communications classification are roads and ports construction, post, telephone and telegraph, the railroad, and airlines. Municipal projects concentrated on the paving of streets and the building of water and sewage facilities. The remaining categories listed retained about the same share of the projects budget in 1973/74 as they did at the beginning of the period.

REVENUES AND EXPENDITURES

According to law the Kingdom's budget cannot be submitted to the King and the Council of Ministers if it is in deficit. If expected revenues do not cover anticipated expenditures, the latter must be reduced to bring revenues and expenditures into line. Examination of the officially published revenue and expenditures data indicate that the obligation has been met, but that conclusion is incorrect: Between 1966/67 and 1968/69 the Kingdom's budget was in deficit (the deficit was covered by transfers from previously accumulated surpluses), and in 1969/70 the budget generated a cash deficit.

One of the reasons for the change in the presentation of the revenue figures in Chapter 13 was the fact that the statistics as published failed to distinguish between current revenues and total spendable funds available. Since 1963 the Kingdom's available funds have come from two sources: current oil and other revenues and transfers from the economic development fund, which contained the various one-time retroactive payments made by Aramco in response to agreement changes. Thus, it was possible to estimate anticipated expenditures and match them with anticipated revenues by covering any shortfall in revenues by transfers from reserves and from the economic development fund.

Table 14.4, presenting revenues and appropriations for the period 1965/66 to 1970/71, clearly shows that for the five-year period beginning in 1966/67 the Kingdom's budget, as reorganized for our purposes, was in deficit. In the budget year 1965/66 estimated current revenues amounted to S.R. 3,598 million, and appropriations amounted to S.R. 3,961; the difference of S.R. 360.7 million was made up with transfers from the development fund and general reserves.* In 1966/67 total current revenues and total budget appropriations were balanced again with additions to current revenues from reserves and the development fund. There was, however, a serious omission on the expenditure side of the budget: The appropriations did not include Arab subsidies. The inclusion of this expenditure item in the budget shows clearly that the Kingdom had incurred a deficit in its budget.

The government's cash flows clearly show how the subsidy payments depleted the Kingdom's reserves. When the decision was taken to subsidize Egypt and Jordan to offset the losses those countries had sustained owing to Israeli occupation of the West Bank of Jordan and the closing of the Suez Canal, it was decided to finance the expenditures "through domestic borrowing to be repaid out of budgetary surpluses within a period of three years. This procedure was adopted to provide for extraordinary payments while maintaining a reasonable level of expenditures on which the economy is largely dependent."[2]

---

*The internal difference in the data results from our manipulation of the revenue time series. See Table 13.4.

TABLE 14.3

Percent Distribution of Major Classes of the Projects Budget, 1960/61 to 1972/73

	1960/61	1961/62	1962/63	1963/64	1964/65	1965/66	1966/67
Education	5.2	3.1	6.4	8.7	6.1	8.7	6.5
Health and Red Crescent	3.8	3.2	2.1	2.3	1.9	2.2	1.6
Labor and social affairs	—	0.9	2.3	0.9	1.2	1.3	0.8
Municipalities	—	—	14.3	15.7	13.8	16.2	16.3
Hadj and Awqaf[a]	1.5	1.9	1.6	1.7	1.3	1.4	1.2
Communications	27.4	33.6	32.0	27.6	36.8	26.7	30.9
Agriculture and water	2.9	6.3	6.2	12.3	12.4	11.2	12.6
Finance	21.5	10.1	10.1	9.1	5.5	7.4	6.5
Commerce and industry	b	b	0.3	1.3	0.7	0.8	0.9
Petroleum and minerals	1.4	1.5	1.4	3.3	7.8	2.7	2.6
Information	3.4	0.9	1.1	3.2	3.1	2.8	4.9
Foreign affairs	b	—	—	—	0.5	0.3	0.5
Interior (except for municipalities)	1.4	12.5	0.7	2.8	2.6	2.5	1.7
Other projects	31.2	26.2	21.5	11.1	6.3	15.7	13.1

	1967/68	1968/69	1969/70	1970/71	1971/72	1972/73	1973/74[c]
Education	3.4	2.3	1.6	2.7	2.9	4.4	4.0
Health and Red Crescent	1.0	0.5	0.5	0.4	0.6	0.7	0.6
Labor and social affairs	0.5	0.3	0.3	0.3	0.5	0.4	0.3
Municipalities	10.9	11.6	9.3	7.2	8.7	9.4	11.0
Hadj and Awqaf[a]	0.7	0.7	0.4	0.4	0.6	0.7	0.4
Communications	23.3	30.7	26.0	23.3	28.9	21.8	14.4
Agriculture and water	13.9	15.4	11.1	8.7	9.0	8.4	6.0
Finance	4.6	6.4	5.3	5.1	7.8	9.4	n.a.
Commerce and industry	0.3	0.6	0.3	0.3	0.6	0.4	0.3
Petroleum and minerals	1.8	2.2	2.1	1.5	1.6	1.3	1.0
Information	3.2	2.0	2.0	1.1	1.0	1.2	1.1
Foreign affairs	0.1	0.1	0.1	0.1	0.2	0.4	n.a.
Interior (except for municipalities)	1.0	0.6	1.6	1.8	1.8	2.3	n.a.
Other projects	35.3	26.4	39.2	47.1	36.0	39.3	57.7

[a]A special trust set up by an individual for the benefit of the religious establishment.
[b]Less than one-half of 1 percent.
[c]Add 3.3 percent for civil aviation.
Source: Appendix Table C.8.

TABLE 14.4

Estimated Revenues and Expenditures, 1965/66 to 1970/71
(S.R. million)

	1965/66	1966/67	1967/68	1968/69	1969/70	1970/71[a]
Current revenues						
Oil	3,144.2	3,944.1	3,515.4	4,198.3	5,197.8	5,440.0
Other	453.8	504.2	548.6	700.3	765.5	936.1[a]
Total	3,598.0	4,448.3	4,064.0	4,898.6	5,963.3	6,376.9
Additional receipts						
Transfers from development fund	100.4	10.4	—	200.0	—	—
Transfers from general reserves	247.0	564.6	871.6	435.5	—	—
Other, n.e.c.	15.7	1.6	1.5	1.5	3.0	3.4
Total additional receipts	363.1	576.6	873.1	637.0	3.0	3.4
Total funds available[b]	3,961.0	5,024.9	4,937.0	5,535.6	5,966.3	6,380.3
Total budget appropriations	3,961.0	5,025.0	4,937.0	5,535.6	5,966.0	6,380.0
Arab subsidies[c]	—	150.0	630.0	630.0	630.0	662.0
Total expenditures	3,961.0	5,175.0	5,567.0	6,165.0	6,596.0	6,542.4
Surplus (+) or deficit (-)	—	-148.0	-630.0	-629.4	-629.7	-142.1

[a]Includes S.R. 55 million from interim Jihad tax.
[b]Total does not agree with the sum of the items in this table because of the estimation error. See Table 13.3.
[c]SAMA, Annual Report, 1386/87 A.H. (Jedda, 1968), p. 8.

Sources: Table 13.3 and Appendix Table C.7.

TABLE 14.5

Government Cash Flows, 1969/70 to 1971/72
(S.R. million)

		Expenditures			
	Revenues	General, from Budget	Other	Arab Subsidies	Total
1969/70	6,009[a]	5,417	—	662	6,079
1970/71	7,940	5,756[b]	—	662	6,418
1971/72	11,120	7,291	350[c]	662	8,303

[a]Includes transfer of S.R. 341 million from reserves.
[b]Excludes S.R. 70 million paid to local bank.
[c]Transferred to the general investment fund at the end of 1971/72.

Source: SAMA, Annual Report, 1392/93 A.H. (Jedda, 1974), p. 22.

To separate the payments, they were not recorded in the general budget on the expenditure side.

Table 14.5 gives the government cash flows for the period 1969/70 to 1972/73. In 1969/70 revenues amounted to S.R. 6,009 million, including S.R. 341 million transferred from the reserves. On the other hand, total cash expenditures amounted to S.R. 6,079 million, resulting in a cash deficit of S.R. 70 million. Additional evidence of the deteriorating financial position can be found in a footnote to the official oil revenues for the budget year 1969/70. Oil revenues were recorded at S.R. 5,198 million, which included "additional oil revenues of Rls. 5,198 million *expected to be realized during the fiscal year*"[3] (italics added). This unusual assumption was necessary to meet the anticipated deficit for fiscal year 1969/70 in the budget estimates. Finally, the use of accumulated reserves to meet the extraordinary subsidy expenditures is further substantiated by SAMA in the Annual Report for 1389/90: "The reserves accumulated in the past rendered extremely useful service in sustaining economic growth by enabling government expenditures to be maintained at a sufficient level in the wake of the Middle East War [of 1967] when the growth in oil revenues was relatively negligible."[4]

Following the Arab-Israeli War of 1967, the Arab leaders met in Khartoum to lay plans for the future. Among other agreements

King Faisal pledged a subsidy totaling S.R. 630 million to the United Arab Republic and to Jordan as compensation for losses incurred by those countries. It is unknown whether or not the Khartoum payments were viewed as a long-term commitment. The payment has, however, continued year after year since 1967. It is certain that the failure to anticipate the need for subsidies beyond 1967/68 was the cause of the fiscal difficulties of the budget years 1969/70 and 1970/71 and that these difficulties led the Saudi Arabian government to demand higher payments from the oil companies by seizing control over the tax-reference (posted) prices. Given the desire to avoid budget deficits and the ever-increasing demands for larger budgets to finance the economic development effort, the Khartoum payments constituted a considerable drain on the Kingdom's resources. The expected budget savings did not materialize, owing to the unexpectedly small increases (1.9 and 2.4 percent for the years 1966/67 to 1967/68 and 1967/68 to 1968/69, respectively). Instead the general reserve was reduced, and in February 1969, the economic development fund was depleted.[5]

The subsidy payments presented no problem in fiscal year 1966/67. Hostilities broke out in June 1967, and the budget year ended on October 4, 1967. The precise amount of payment for the remainder of that fiscal year is unknown, but it appears that the subsidy payments amounted to only S.R. 150 million. Similarly, the next two fiscal years, 1967/68 and 1968/69, passed without a deficit, but in fiscal 1969/70 all financial resources available to balance the budget had been exhausted.

In 1970/71 estimated total current revenues amounted to S.R. 6,376.9 million, and total budget appropriations to S.R. 6,542 million, including S.R. 400 million of the S.R. 662 earmarked for Arab Subsidies. A budget saving of S.R. 162 million lowered total appropriations to S.R. 6,380 million. Current revenues could not be augmented by transfers from reserves or the development fund. Balance was achieved by subtracting S.R. 162 million of "expected savings"—i.e., funds that had been appropriated but were not expected to be used. To raise the required revenues additional taxes were levied. That step was taken reluctantly, but it could not be avoided. A Jihad tax, an income tax on salaries of government employees and Saudi employees in the private sector and on profits of Saudi-owned firms, an increase in gasoline taxes, and a tax of 2.5 halala per liter of diesel fuel were imposed. In addition customs duties were raised on many items. The seriousness ascribed to the budget crisis was underscored by the levy of an income tax on Saudi citizens and the tax on diesel fuel. It had been a cornerstone of fiscal policy since 1950 that Saudi citizens should not be subject to income taxation because they paid the Zakat and that diesel fuel should not be taxed because that fuel is used primarily by farmers (it was felt that a tax on diesel fuel would reduce the already low income of farmers). Nevertheless, those taxes were imposed and the government decided to demand a larger share of oil profits; the second could only be achieved by eliminating the middleman and gaining control over the pricing of oil.

NOTES

1. For a more detailed content listing of the aviours budget chapters, see CDS, Statistical Yearbook, 1386 A.H., vol. 2 (Riyadh, 1966), pp. 282-85.
2. SAMA, Annual Report, 1386/87 A.H. (Jedda, 1967), p. 8.
3. Ibid., 1389/90 A.H. (Jedda, 1971), p. 10.
4. Ibid., p. 13.
5. SAMA, Statistical Summary, Rajab 1389 (September-October 1969), pp. 28-29.

CHAPTER

15

PLANNING ECONOMIC DEVELOPMENT

Economic-development planning has become an integral part in the government's effort to improve living standards and the preparation for the day when the oil resources have been depleted. The first step in the creation of a planning apparatus was taken in August 1958, when the late Anwar Ali, the head of the IMF mission that had prepared the plan for the restoration of fiscal soundness, suggested the establishment of an economic development committee.

Formal planning began in 1959, when the Prime Minister expanded the economic development committee and established it as the Committee for Economic Development. The committee was replaced in 1961 by the Supreme Planning Board, because its members had not functioned successfully. Charged with the design of an economic-development policy, the committee members had been involved in customs problems brought to them by the business community, rather than economic planning. The Supreme Planning Board was to design an economic-development policy in cooperation with various ministries and agencies and was to supervise the execution of development projects. The board was replaced in 1965 by the Central Planning Organization (CPO).

THE CENTRAL PLANNING ORGANIZATION

The CPO was established by Royal Decree 19, dated 17 Ramadan, 1384 A.H. (1965), and its functions were defined in Council of Ministers Resolution 430, dated 11/12 Ramadan, 1384 A.H.:

1. To write a periodic economic report;

2. To formulate economic development plans (the first plan was to be of five-year duration, and it was to be approved by the Council of Ministers before implementation);

3. To estimate the overall resources needed to implement the plan (these estimates are to be the basis for the preparation of the state budget and the budgets of public corporations);

4. To assist the various ministries and government agencies in their economic planning;

5. To assist in the establishment of planning units in each ministry and public agency; and

6. To supply the King with needed technical advice (furthermore, the president of the CPO reports directly to the King).

The organization consists of four departments: the Planning Department, the Research Department, the Follow-up Department, and the Administrative Department. The Planning Department prepares economic reports and formulates development plans. It is divided into six sections, each entrusted with a particular phase of planning. The Research Department is responsible for the coordination of research, and the Follow-up Department monitors and reports on program implementation. The General Administration Department handles the day-to-day control of the organization. A branch office has been opened to facilitate the CPO's operations in the western part of the nation.

The CPO's power is circumscribed by its reliance on the Ministry of Finance and Economy and SAMA. Ministerial Resolution 430(5.a) provides that "the Budget Department in the Ministryof Finance and National Economy is responsible for studying and preparing the budget for projects [,] . . . following in this concern the same procedures applied for the preparation of the other parts of the budget." Because the funding of projects is controlled by the minister of Finance, the plans prepared by the CPO in cooperation with the ministries and agencies are subject to a financial review based on available resources.

Close cooperation with SAMA is needed because the agency collects all information on banking and the balance-of-payments and issues statistics in those areas. Furthermore, it carries out both monetary and banking policy, which affect the development plan and which are in turn affected by the plan.

The role of the CPO in the economic-planning process is also complicated by its position vis-a-vis the ministries. Section 5(d) of Resolution 430 provides that "planning units are [to be] established in each ministry and independent agency." The CPO, in cooperation with each ministry and independent agency, sets up the organization of those units. The planning units become a liaison in the planning business between the CPO and the ministries.

Clearly, the CPO is an integral part of the government structure. It leads in the design of economic policy and coordinates the needs of various government agencies, and at the same time its actions are influenced by the realities of day-to-day operations of the ministries that uncover the actual needs of the country in various economic sectors. In addition, its plans are constrained by the Ministry of Finance and SAMA. Inputs by those two agencies ensure that the plan does not exceed the available resources and that monetary and banking policy is carried out in a manner that will accelerate development without endangering the fiscal and monetary stability of the country. Finally, access to the King guarantees that the CPO is aware of the thinking of the highest level of policy makers and offers a means to the resolution of disputes involving the partners in the planning process.

To carry out its assignment the CPO has developed a set of four planning procedures. First, the CPO analyzes the state of the economy and publishes the findings in a report. Second, on the basis of the economic report and in cooperation with the ministries the organization makes up broad outlines "for resolving current economic and social problems, for attaining a high and sustained rate of economic growth, and for achieving steady improvement in the welfare of the people." The strategy is submitted to the Council of Ministers for final sanction. Third, upon approval of the general strategy the CPO assists and coordinates the transformation of that strategy into action by the various ministries and agencies. Following the development of targets, projects, and actions to be carried out in the implementation of the overall strategy, the CPO combines the various elements into a single plan to be submitted to the King for approval. Finally, acting in concert with the Ministry of Finance, the CPO assists the Ministry in reviewing past events, the current situation, and the possible course of future events as outlined in the planned projects and policies.

THE COURSE OF PLANNING

From 1960 to 1968 the planning effort was characterized by a number of half-hearted starts. In November 1960 a team from IBRD submitted a report entitled "Approach to the Economic Development of Saudi Arabia," in which an interim program of two years, covering 1961 and 1962, was recommended. The program outlined and proposed the following actions:

1. The creation and staffing of a central planning body in the office of the Prime Minister, responsible for the planning, coordina-

tion, execution, and operation of economic development activities;

2. The establishment of a separate ministry to prepare and carry out a program for the development and conservation of the Kingdom's water resources;

3. A reorganization of the Ministry of Agriculture to improve its efficiency in carrying out a more comprehensive program for the improvement of the rural welfare and eventually to make the Kingdom largely self-sufficient in food and fiber;

4. The accelerated completion of a number of infrastructure projects in progress;

5. The undertaking of preinvestment surveys for certain water, agricultural, communications, and mining projects and the beginning of various projects already in the planning stages;

6. The expansion of education programs, with special emphasis on teacher training, technical training, and vocational agriculture; and

7. The stimulation of private enterprise in power and industrial ventures, and giving monopolistic franchises in order to ensure adequate services at reasonable rates.

The cost estimates for these projects were set at S.R. 400 million, with one-half of the total to be spent in each budget year.

In March 1961 a UN industrial economist submitted a report suggesting various industrial projects to be developed immediately. Among the suggested projects was a soap factory in Jedda, a slaughterhouse industry, and, associated with it, tanning and leather works.

The first comprehensive document developed for use by the CPO was circulated under the title "Planning for Growth." It was a joint effort between the CPO and a number of advisers working under the auspices of the Public Administration Project of the Ford Foundation. The report was "an attempt to provide broad guidelines for the economic development of Saudi Arabia, general programs for each sector and some specific suggestions to be incorporated into the programs of ministries over the next five or more years." It is known that some of the proposals made in this plan were adopted in budget year 1966/67.

Unfortunately, none of the above reports was used in the budget-making process. There are four reasons for this failure. First, the plans were not detailed enough and failed to provide for precise guidelines for implementation. Second, with very few exceptions neither the CPO nor the ministries and agencies had enough trained personnel to take the advice offered and translate it into action. Third, there was little support for the CPO's mission among the top policy makers and executives. Finally, the CPO lacked strong leadership that could sell its goals to the government officials.

By 1968 it had become apparent that the existing planning structure was inadequate to do its job. However, instead of changing the bureaucracy and creating another useless government planning agency, the King appointed Hisham Nazer, a young, intelligent, able upper-level official in the Ministry of Petroleum and Minerals as President of the CPO. Nazer put together a staff of Saudi economists assisted by a team of advisers from the Stanford Research Institute, and under his leadership the CPO became an active, aggressive planning body. The CPO set out to formulate a new development plan, and this time it was destined for success.

Although the early attempts to plan economic development met with failure, the task of creating a more efficient bureaucracy on all levels of government and the rationalization of the government's administrative structure progressed rapidly. A Central Department of Organization and Management was established in the Ministry of Finance and National Economy. At the same time organization and management units were also established in all public corporations and all ministries. With the assistance of advisers from the Ford Foundation's Public Administration Program, the ministerial O and M department (coordinated by the Central O and M Department) studied the details of the ministries' and agencies' administrative structure and provided rational alternatives to improve the overall administrative efficiency.

To further raise the efficiency of the government's administrative functions an Institute of Public Administration (IPA) was established in 1962 to improve the quality of civil service employees. The IPA's task is threefold: to train government employees, to encourage administrative improvements, and to conduct research in administrative affairs. The institute is probably the best-run government office in the Kingdom, and it has been highly effective in the training of civil servants. By the use of the most modern teaching devices the IPA trains typists, teaches English, and runs numerous classes on administrative reform. Its effort is not concentrated on lower-echelon employees only. Special seminars and special courses for middle- and upper-government officials keep those men informed of the latest developments in their area of expertise and also help them to refresh their skills.

The relative success of the Administrative Reform Program stems from the fact that the effort was supported and nurtured by the highest-level policy makers. To ensure that all the necessary steps to facilitate the reforms are taken the High Committee for Administrative Reform was established in 1963. Currently, the committee consists of the King, the Minister of Defense, the Presidents of the CPO and the General Personnel Bureau, and the Ministers of Agriculture, Communications, Information, and Petroleum. The high committee has the same authority and powers as the Council of Ministers in the areas of government organization and administration. The high committee has in recent years been developing a general reorganization plan of the government's administrative structure as well as specific plans for changes in the Ministries of Health, Finance, Education, and others.

THE ECONOMIC DEVELOPMENT PLAN FOR 1970/71 TO 1974/75

On August 16, 1970, the CPO submitted to the King its development plan for the five-year period 1970/71 to 1974/75. It contained a plan for systematic action in all fields of the economy, including the policies, programs, and projects necessary to achieve the desired results. Its overall objectives were to be reached by increasing the rate of growth of GDP, developing human resources so that the several elements of society will be able to contribute more effectively to production and participate fully in the process of development, and diversifying sources of national income and reducing dependence on oil through increasing the share of other productive sectors in GDP.[1]

Planned Growth Rates

Table 15.1 gives the average growth rates from 1965/66 to 1968/69 and those projected for the plan period. The actual growth rate for the four-year preplan period of GDP was 7.9 percent per annum, and the projected rate for the plan period is 9.8 percent. Clearly, it is expected that the plan will have a significant effect on the nation's economic growth. Except for those of the petroleum-refining and public administration and defense sectors, the growth rates of all sectors are expected to be accelerated by the plan effort. By far the largest increases in the growth rate are planned for mining and quarrying (from 6.4 percent in the preplan period to 23.3 percent during the plan period) and education (from 7.2 percent to 19 percent). It is assumed by the planners that by 1973/74 one of the many potential mineral finds will become commercially feasible and that thereafter that sector will grow substantially. (Because this sector is the smallest in GDP the high anticipated growth rate is probably a function of the small base rather than any actual increases in activity in this sector.)

The high anticipated growth rate of education reflects the fact that the Kingdom has a rather small base of skilled workers in all fields. The magnitude of the problem is placed into perspective by

TABLE 15.1

Average Annual Growth Rates of Value Added by Sector and GDP for 1965/66 to 1968/69 and the Plan Period, 1970/71 to 1974/75, in Constant Prices
(percent)

Sector	1965/66 to 1968/69	Plan Period
Agriculture	1.7	4.6
Crude oil and natural gas	8.2	9.1
Mining and quarrying	6.4	23.3
Petroleum refining	11.7	9.1
Manufacturing	12.1	14.0
Construction	4.2	10.4
Electricity, gas, water, and sanitation	12.1	13.2
Transportation, communications, and storage	11.1	12.9
Wholesale and retail trade	10.3	12.8
Banking, insurance, and real estate	10.7	11.0
Ownership of dwellings	7.0	8.6
Public administration and defense	5.4	5.0
Education	7.2	19.0
Health	2.4	9.5
Other services	8.1	10.0
GDP	7.9	9.8

Source: CPO, Development Plan, 1390 A.H. (Riyadh, n.d.), p. 38.

the large number of non-Saudi workers in nearly all skilled positions and by the fact that toward the end of the 1960s more than 80 percent of all workers hired by private businesses were non-Saudi. To overcome the problem the plan's overall objective is the "continued expansion of opportunities for education at all levels to provide the capability at each level of accepting all qualified graduates from subordinate levels who seek employment."[2]

Included in the education plan is the acceleration of vocational education. The planned expansion goes against the experience of the International Labour Office, which found that vocational education does not necessarily lead to accelerated economic development, because the forecasting techniques used in manpower-needs projections are not reliable enough to yield accurate estimates of the number of skilled persons needed in the various trades and professions.[3] However, that fact presents no problem in the Kingdom, where the manpower shortage is so great that any trained person can find a job in his field. The problem may arise as time passes and the vocational-training program creates an adequate pool of skilled labor to cover the nation's basic needs.

The remaining planned sector-growth rates are much more in line with their preplan growth rates. That is, except for the petroleum-refining and public administration and defense sectors, whose growth rates were reduced slightly for the duration of the plan, the sectors' planned growth rates are only slightly higher for the plan period than that before, which suggests that the overall strategy guiding the planners was relatively balanced growth. That strategy makes sense, because the leading sector—oil—generates all the necessary capital for the expansion of the rest of the economy.

Financing the Plan

The distribution of the financial allocations for the plan suggest a modification of the conclusion stated in the previous section (see Table 15.2). In terms of the projected expenditures defense stood in first place with 23.1 percent of total allocations, followed by administration (18.6 percent), transport and communications (18.1 percent), and public utilities and urban development (11.1 percent). The remaining four sectors together accounted for the rest of the allocations (11.4 percent). Thus, it appears that next to defense and administration the plan concentrated on the continued development of social and physical infrastructure (excluding health and social affairs). The reason for this priority structure is not hard to find. About the time the plan was in its formative phase the Kingdom felt its security threatened on four sides, by Yemen, Syria, Iraq, and Iran. The plan was completed several years before the settlement of the disputes between Iran and Saudi Arabia in the Arabian Gulf Area, and before the Arab Summit Meeting of late 1974. The position of administration in second place follows from the fact that for some time to come the real force in advancing the development of the nation will have to come from the government. The private sector is still far too small to contribute significantly to economic development. Thus, increases in the efficiency of the administration promise gains in the economic development.

TABLE 15.2

Distribution of Financial Allocations for the Plan
(S.R. million)

Sector	Recurrent[a]	Project[b]	Total	
			Amount	Percent
Administration	6,794.6	922.8	7,717.4	18.6
Defense	3,980.0	5,575.0	9,555.0	23.1
Education, vocational training, and cultural affairs	6,150.2	1,227.5	7,377.7	17.8
Health and social affairs	1,612.9	308.2	1,921.1	4.7
Public utilities and urban development	1,246.9	3,325.4	4,572.3	11.1
Transport and communications	1,767.3	5,709.2	7,476.5	18.1
Industry	321.8	776.7	1,098.5	2.7
Agriculture	973.8	493.9	1,467.7	3.6
Trade and services	83.5	43.8	127.3	0.3
Total	22,931.0	18,387.5	41,313.5	100.0

[a]Expenditures covered in Chapter 1 (salaries), Chapter 2 (all other current expenses), and Chapter 3 (miscellaneous special expenses) of the state budget.

[b]Covered in Chapter 4 of the state budget.

Source: CPO, Development Plan, 1390 A.H. (Riyadh, n.d.), p. 43.

The emphasis on the physical and social infrastructure (excluding health and social affairs) is related to the nature of planning itself and to the needs of the nation. The creation of an adequate physical infrastructure, by avoiding bottlenecks, guarantees the success of development planning. Furthermore, it is somewhat easier to plan in the area of infrastructure because of the large base of development projects in place already upon which further advances can be based. The high position of education is explained by the extreme shortage of skilled manpower, which has been a severe constraint on the Kingdom's advancement.

An examination of the changes in the percentage shares of the financial allocations by sectors further strengthens the conclusion of the tripartite structure of the plan and at the same time deemphasizes somewhat the importance of the defense sector (see Table 15.3).

TABLE 15.3

Changes of the Percentage Shares of Financial Allocations, by Sector, 1969/70 and 1974/75

Sector	1969/70	Last Plan Year
Administration	22.3	18.3
Defense	30.7	21.3
Education, vocational training, and cultural affairs	12.0	21.7
Health and social affairs	4.4	5.0
Public utilities and urban development	9.7	10.9
Transport and communications	15.7	16.0
Industry	1.4	2.7
Agriculture	3.6	3.8
Trade and services	0.2	0.3
Total	100.0	100.0

Source: CPO, Development Plan, 1390 A.H. (Riyadh, n.d.), p. 44.

Again, there is a distinct pattern in the distribution of financial allocations. The education, vocational training, and cultural affairs sector is expected to rise to first place (21.7 percent of allocations), with defense in close proximity in second place, followed by transport and communications (16 percent), and public utilities and urban development in third with 10.9 percent of allocations. The pattern is clear: A relatively large initial effort in the early part of the plan to gain greater military security is reduced in subsequent years; a somewhat lower initial effort in the early years of the plan with education and vocational training rises as the plan progresses. Administration is expected to stay about the same in terms of share of allocations; next is physical infrastructure, followed by the remaining sectors.

Evaluation of Plan Effectiveness

One aspect of the planning process remains to be discussed: How successful was the plan? Did it achieve its projected goals? Unfortunately, there is no direct answer to the question. The available statistics are not sufficient to evaluate the plan. The change from the old to the new classification of GNP, the lack of detailed data for the diverse sectors of the economy, and the lag in statistical reporting—all prevent an analysis of the possible success or failure of the plan. To attempt such an analysis despite the small data base would simply be an exercise in futility.

NOTES

1. CPO, Development Plan, 1390 A.H. (Riyadh, n.d.), p. 23.
2. Ibid., p. 95.
3. Mark Blaug, Education and the Employment Problem in Developing Countries (Geneva: ILO, 1973), pp. 21-23.

APPENDIXES

APPENDIX A

THE ISLAMIC AND GREGORIAN CALENDARS

Saudi Arabia uses the Islamic calendar, which is based on the lunar year. A lunar month is the time between two new moons. Thus, the Islamic year has 12 months of about 29.5 days, giving the lunar year 354 days—11 days fewer than the solar year. The Islamic calendar compensates for the slight overlap of time that occurs in the distribution of 354 days over the 12 months by adding one day 11 times during a 30-year cycle, making 11 leap years of 355 days and 19 normal years per cycle.

An additional discrepancy with the Gregorian year results from the different starting dates for the calendars. The Islamic Year One, the year of the Prophet's flight (Hijra) from Mecca to Medina, corresponds to the Gregorian year 622 A.D.

To find the corresponding Gregorian year for the Hijra year 1390 the following calculation must be made. Multiply the Hijra year by .03, subtract the result from the Hijra year, and add 622:

1390	1390
x .03	- 41
41.7	1349
	+ 622
	1971

The Hijra year has no fixed relation with the seasons. The month makes a complete circuit of the seasons once every 33 years approximately. For example, the first day of Muharram (the first month of the Hijra year) fell on July 18, 1958, for the year 1378 A.H. Fifteen years later the first day of the Hijra year fell on February 4, 1973. The names of the 12 months of the Hijra calendar are Moharram, Safar, Rabi al-Awwal (Rabi I), Rabi ath-Thani (Rabi II), Jumada al-Ula (Jumadi I), Jumada ath-Thani (Jumadi II), Rajab, Shaban, Ramadan, Shawwal, Dhu al-Quadah, and Dhu al-Hijjah.

The existence of two calendars creates some difficulty in the time reference of the data. The data available are collected and expressed in three time references: the Hijra year (Moharram through Dhu al-Hijja), the Hijra fiscal year (Rajab through Jumada II), and the Gregorian calendar year. No attempt was made to convert the data into Gregorian dates with the method given above. Rather, dates given in Hijra fiscal years were translated into the corresponding overlapping year. Thus, Hijra fiscal year 1385/86 becomes 1965/66 without determination of the precise day-and-month time horizon in the Gregorian calendar. For Hijra years the same general approach was adopted unless the corresponding combination of Gregorian years contained fewer than three months of one of the two Gregorian years. For example, since the Hijra year 1380 covers the Gregorian calendar period June 25, 1960, to June 13, 1961, it is given as 1960/61. On the other hand, Hijra year 1390 covers the period from March 8, 1970, to February 24, 1971; because the portion of 1971 overlapped by 1390 contains only two months, the year 1390 is given as 1970.

It is possible to convert the Hijra year into the Hijra fiscal year by the use of a two-period moving average. The Hijra fiscal year includes the second one-half of the preceding and the first one-half of the following Hijra year of two successive Hijra years. Thus, the value for a Hijra fiscal year can be found by taking one-half of the value of a series in the earlier year and adding one-half of the value of a series in the subsequent year.

To convert a Gregorian year into a Hijra fiscal year the following crude procedure can be used. Step 1: Split each successive pair of values expressed in Gregorian terms by taking one-fourth of the earlier year and three-fourths of the following year of any pair of Gregorian years and recombine them into the corresponding Hijra fiscal year. Step 2: Because the Hijra year is about 3 percent shorter, reduce the result of step one by that amount. A word of caution is necessary. This method is crude at best, and because of the moving nature of the month within the Hijra year the method will be reasonably accurate only for the period from about 1960 to 1973.

To facilitate the reader's attempt to translate Hijra dates into a Gregorian time horizon Appendix Tables A.1 and A.2 give the starting and ending Gregorian dates for the regular Hijra year and for the Hijra fiscal year (accurate to within a day or two).

APPENDIX TABLE A.1

Gregorian Dates of Regular Hijra Years

Hijra Year	Gregorian Calendar	
	Starts	Ends
1380	June 25, 1960	June 13, 1961
1381	June 14, 1961	June 2, 1962
1382	June 3, 1962	May 23, 1963
1383	May 24, 1963	May 12, 1964
1384	May 13. 1964	April 30, 1965
1385	May 11, 1965	April 19, 1966
1386	April 20, 1966	April 9, 1967
1387	April 10, 1967	March 30, 1968
1388	March 31, 1968	March 18, 1969
1389	March 19, 1969	March 7, 1970
1390	March 8, 1970	February 24, 1971
1391	February 25, 1971	February 13, 1972
1392	February 12, 1972	January 31, 1973
1393	February 1, 1973	January 21, 1974
1394	January 22, 1974	January 10, 1975
1395	January 11, 1975	December 29, 1976

APPENDIX TABLE A.2

Gregorian Dates of Hijra Fiscal Years

	Gregorian Calendar	
	Starts	Ends
1380/81	December 19, 1960	December 8, 1961
1381/82	December 9, 1961	November 27, 1962
1382/83	November 28, 1962	November 16, 1963
1383/84	November 17, 1963	November 4, 1964
1384/85	November 5, 1964	October 25, 1965
1385/86	October 26, 1965	October 14, 1966
1386/87	October 15, 1966	October 3, 1967
1387/88	October 4, 1967	September 22, 1968
1388/89	September 23, 1968	September 11, 1969
1389/90	September 12, 1969	September 1, 1970
1390/91	September 1, 1970	August 20, 1971
1391/92	August 21, 1971	August 9, 1972
1392/93	August 10, 1972	July 29, 1973
1393/94	July 30, 1973	July 20, 1974
1394/95	July 19, 1974	July 9, 1975

APPENDIX B

THE GENEVA DEVALUATION AGREEMENT

The most important reason for the Geneva Agreement was the need to defend the purchasing power of the oil-revenue receipts. Worldwide inflation and the dollar devaluation had led to a decline of more than 8 percent in the purchasing power of oil revenues. To prevent further purchasing-power erosion a formula was developed that allowed for quarterly adjustments of posted prices. Below, we attach the formula as it was used beginning June 1, 1973, as published in OPEC, Selected Documents of the International Petroleum Industry (Vienna: OPEC, 1972), pp. 133-35.

Annex 2

1. As of the Effective Date the present posted price for each crude oil exported from the Gulf States will be increased by 8.49%. With regard to posted prices for Eastern Mediterranean Exports, the increase will be applied separately to the posted prices (excluding Suez Canal Allowance and Temporary Freight Premium) and to whatever Suez Canal Allowance and Temporary Freight Premium is applicable from time to time.
2. Thereafter posted prices will be further adjusted as follows:
   (a) The arithmetic average of the Exchange Rate changes of the nine other Group of Ten currencies is 11.02% against the U.S. dollar (in terms of central rates against 30th April, 1971 IMF parities) as shown in attachment "A," and such arithmetic average is hereinafter referred to as the "Starting Average."
   (b) On the 1st of March, 1st of June, 1st of September, and 1st of December in each year the arithmetic average of the Exchange Rate change of the said nine currencies against the U.S. dollar against the April 30, 1971 IMF parities shall be recalculated. If such recalculation shows a variation of two whole points or more up or down from the Starting Average (or the latest Effective Average, as the case may be) the new average resulting from such recalculation shall become the Effective Average commencing on the first day of the following calendar quarter. "Exchange Rate" as used herein means

the rate of exchange existing between any one of the nine currencies by virtue of that currency's rate and the rate for the U.S. dollar, notified to the IMF resulting from the realignment of exchange rates agreed by the Group of Ten countries or any successors to such rates. If any of the nine currencies concerned is hereafter permitted to float in relation to the Dollar (that is to say it is no longer being maintained by the Central Bank of the country concerned within the margins of general application to members of the IMF) the Exchange Rate for that currency to be used in the aforesaid calculation shall be the arithmetic average as certified by the National Westminster Bank Limited in London of the mean of the buying and selling rates in respect of telegraphic transfers for the currency concerned into U.S. dollars quoted by the Bank at 10:30 a.m. G.M.T. for those days in the calendar month preceding the month of calculation on which the London Foreign Exchange Market is open.

(c) Effective with establishment of a new Effective Average the posted price for each crude oil shall be adjusted in the manner indicated below:

(i) With respect to posted prices of crude oils exported from the Gulf: Posted price (including the effect of all periodic increases which have become applicable as provided for in the appropriate Related Agreement)

$$\frac{+ .0849\ (T \times B - A)}{11.02} = \text{adjusted posted price}$$

that would have applied on first day of the quarter absent this latest adjustment.

(ii) With respect to posted prices for Eastern Mediterranean exports, the formula set forth in (i) above shall be performed separately for the posted prices (excluding any Suez Canal and Temporary Freight Allowances but including the effect of all periodic increases which have become applicable as provided for in the appropriate Related Agreement). The sum of such allowances, whenever applicable, shall be multiplied by the following formula and the result added to the separate posted price calculation performed under the first sentence of the sub-paragraph (c)(ii):

$$\text{Adjusted Suez Canal Allowance plus Temporary Freight Premium} = \text{Suez Canal Allowance and Temporary Freight} \times 1 + \left(\frac{B \times .0849}{11.02}\right)$$

Premium as determined under appropriate Related Agreement, excluding the effect of any adjustments under this Agreement.

Where T = Posted price as of day before the Effective Date as provided under the appropriate Related Agreement.

A = The most recent prior Effective Average preceding the currency change (or the Starting Average if no prior Effective Average had superceded it), and

B = The new Effective Average.

(d) Notwithstanding sub-paragraph (c) above, no posted price in respect of any period shall be below the level which would have prevailed in respect of that period under the appropriate Related Agreement excluding the effect of any adjustment under this Agreement. If the calculation in sub-paragraph (c) produces an adjusted posted price below such level the calculation will continue to be made from time to time as if the posted price had been reduced to this adjusted posted price and the posted price will be adjusted whenever the calculation again produces an adjusted posted price exceeding such level.

Attachment "A" to Annex 2

Exchange Rate Changes Against U.S. Dollar: Central Rates as of Effective Date Against April 30, 1971 IMF Rates

Belgium	11.57%
France	8.57%
Germany	13.58%
Italy	7.48%
Japan	16.88%
Netherlands	11.57%
Sweden	7.49%
United Kingdom	8.57%
Switzerland	13.50%
	99.21

$$\text{Arithmetic average} = \frac{99.21}{9} = 11.02\%$$

APPENDIX C

APPENDIX TABLE C.1

Percent Relatives and Annual Average Growth Rates of Real GDP, by Industry Group, 1962/63 to 1971/72
(percent relatives, 1962/63 = 100)

Industry Group	1962/63	1963/64	1964/65	1965/66	1966/67	1967/68	1968/69	P 1969/70	P 1970/71	Annual Average Growth Rates 1962/63-1970/71 (percent)
Agriculture, forestry, fishing	100.0	101.8	100.9	99.8	98.1	102.1	105.1	108.4	112.2	1.5
Mining, quarrying										
Crude oil, natural gas	100.0	107.1	121.7	143.2	157.5	171.0	181.4	207.2	253.6	13.0
Other	100.0	114.9	152.0	186.3	202.3	220.6	224.6	220.0	226.3	10.7
Manufacturing										
Petroleum refining	100.0	107.4	119.8	124.7	133.1	157.7	173.8	212.5	224.5	10.5
Other	100.0	110.1	121.8	135.3	151.0	169.2	190.4	211.5	236.8	11.4
Construction	100.0	112.7	145.9	175.1	185.8	198.8	198.1	189.8	191.2	3.5
Electricity, gas, water, sanitary services	100.0	116.2	137.7	169.9	191.6	214.9	239.2	265.2	290.6	14.3
Transport, storage, communications	100.0	118.2	137.6	159.2	181.7	197.3	218.1	243.3	266.8	13.0
Wholesale and retail trade	100.0	114.2	137.1	153.6	156.8	176.6	206.0	210.7	216.8	10.2
Banking, insurance, real estate	100.0	109.9	133.4	149.3	173.2	190.1	202.3	207.8	214.2	10.0
Ownership of dwellings	100.0	104.0	108.2	114.0	119.5	129.2	139.8	149.5	159.5	6.0
Public administration, defense	100.0	112.3	119.1	120.5	138.6	135.1	141.1	141.3	142.8	4.6
Services										
Education	100.0	122.6	133.1	149.0	178.1	185.8	183.7	187.5	202.0	13.8
Medical and health	100.0	114.4	122.2	130.8	148.0	141.3	140.4	139.8	140.6	4.3
Other services	100.0	100.4	110.3	127.2	134.5	152.3	160.6	157.2	167.1	6.6
GDP at factor cost	100.0	108.8	122.0	137.2	149.5	161.5	172.4	189.1	214.5	10.0
Less net factor payments abroad	100.0	93.5	106.2	134.3	137.4	145.4	154.6	175.1	218.8	10.0
GNP	100.0	113.8	127.1	138.1	153.4	166.8	178.2	193.7	213.1	10.0

P = preliminary.

Sources: 1962/63 to 1968/69: CDS, Gross Domestic Product of Saudi Arabia, 1382/83 Through 1388/89 A.H. (Riyadh, September 1970), p. 41; 1969/70 to 1970/71: SAMA, Annual Report, 1391/92 A.H. (Jedda, 1973), p. 106.

APPENDIX TABLE C.2

Real GDP, by Industrial Origin, 1966/67 to 1972/73
(1969/70 S.R. million)

Industry Group	1966/67	1967/68	1968/69	1969/70	1970/71	1970/72	1973/73*
Industries and Producers, Except for Producers of Government Services							
Agriculture, forestry, fishing	884.6	924.8	956.5	984.1	1.017.8	1,050.1	1,088.7
Mining, quarrying							
Crude oil, natural gas	6,177.0	6,695.8	7,084.9	8,106.3	9,922.1	12,427.0	16,707.1
Other	39.7	46.1	50.4	46.7	48.8	55.3	61.4
Manufacturing							
Petroleum refining	780.4	920.4	1,015.5	1,240.9	1,355.3	1,304.4	1,389.0
Other	308.9	344.1	385.3	431.2	483.6	543.0	610.3
Electricity, gas, water	198.0	219.2	247.0	273.1	297.9	328.6	381.0
Construction	846.8	961.4	1,027.8	933.9	957.2	1,052.7	1,185.2
Wholesale and retail trade, restaurants, hotels	755.0	840.9	960.7	1,007.5	1,051.3	1,145.9	1,264.6
Transport, storage, communications	918.9	1,012.7	1,139.5	1,242.5	1,467.7	1,544.4	1,631.6
Finance, insurance, real estate, business services							
Ownership of dwellings	520.5	564.8	602.2	661.0	693.0	731.9	773.6
Other	289.1	330.0	341.5	354.7	360.3	377.6	396.5
Community, social, personal services	180.2	198.3	215.1	238.3	253.0	271.8	291.9
Less imputed bank service charge	-38.5	-42.3	-44.9	-46.0	-47.7	-46.0	-45.0
Subtotal	11,860.6	13,019.3	13,981.5	15,474.2	17,860.3	20,776.1	25,735.8
All producers of government services	1,475.3	1,515.6	1,646.5	1,678.4	1,722.0	1,834.4	1,980.4
Total public and private output	13,335.9	14,534.9	15,628.0	17,152.6	19,582.3	22,621.1	27,716.3
Import duties	228.3	237.9	276.3	246.0	324.5	342.2	240.8
GDP	13,564.2	14,772.8	15,904.3	17,398.6	19,906.8	22,963.3	27,957.1

*Preliminary.

Source: SAMA, Annual Report, 1392/93 A.H. (Jedda, June 22, 1974), pp. 114-15.

APPENDIX TABLES C.3 AND C.4

Methodology for Capital Formation Estimates and Total Capital Formation in Current Riyals

The estimate of capital formation is based on three assumptions. First, it is assumed that the construction component of GDP (old series) accurately reflects additions to capital by the building industry. Second, the values given for capital goods other than building are probably understated because of the omission of in-country costs, such as transportation, installation costs, and so on. To adjust for this omission it is assumed that these costs amount to 30 percent of the value of capital goods imported. Third, nearly all machinery and other capital goods are imported from abroad.

To determine an index of total values of investment goods imported, the index of unit values of imports (1383 = 100) was multiplied by the index of the quantum of imports (1383 = 100) and the result was converted to the base (1384 = 100). To calculate a riyal value for the total value of imports the index was multiplied by S.R. 375.2 million, the estimated value of capital imports in 1384 A.H. The resulting riyal values must be used with some care, because the whole series is based on only one year for which the money value of capital imports is known. To account for in-country costs that were not included in the index of imports, the total value of capital goods imported was raised by 30 percent, the estimated value of in-country costs. Finally, the adjusted value of capital goods was converted into Hijra budget years by the moving-average method.

Appendix Table C.4 gives total capital formation in current prices, as calculated in Appendix Table C.3, and construction, as presented in the old GDP figures.

The capital-goods series was changed to the 1386/87 base by use of the index of unit values. The constant 1386/87 construction figures were taken from the old GDP series (CDS, The Gross Domestic Product of Saudi Arabia, 1382/83 to 1388/89 A.H. [Riyadh, n.d.], p. 39; SAMA, Annual Report, 1390/91 A.H. [Jedda], p. 107). Finally, the projection of the real-capital-goods-imported series for the years 1389/90 and 1390/91 was based on an annual average growth rate of 19.5 percent, for the period 1383/84 to 1388/89.

APPENDIX TABLE C.3

Methodology for Capital Formation Estimates

Year	Index of Unit Values of Imports[a] (1)	Index of Quantum of Imports[a] (2)	Index of Total Values of Imports[a] (3)	Index of Total Value of Imports[b] (4)	Value of Capital Goods Imported[c] (5)	Adjusted Value of Capital Goods Imported[c] (6)	Capital Goods Imported in Budget Years[c] (7)
1383	100.00	100.00	100.0	78.6	294.9	383.4	435.6
1384	110.12	115.50	127.2	100.0	375.2	487.8	601.2
1385	113.31	164.40	186.3	146.5	549.7	714.6	735.8
1386	119.35	165.40	197.4	155.2	582.3	757.0	778.3
1387	124.03	168.10	208.5	163.9	615.0	799.0	1,017.8
1388	142.90	225.60	322.4	253.5	951.1	1,236.0	1,490.8
1389	152.60	298.30	455.2	357.9	1,342.8	1,745.6	—

[a]1383 = 100.

[b]1384 = 100.

[c]S.R. million.

Note on Method: Col. 3 = Col. 1 x Col. 2; Col. 4 = Col. 3 ÷ 127.2; Col. 5 = Col. 4 x S.R. 375.2 million; Col. 6 = Col. 5 x 1.3; Col. 7 = two-year moving average of Col. 6.

Sources, Cols. 1 and 2: 1383-87: CDS, Statistical Yearbook, 1390 A.H. (Riyadh, 1970), p. 312; 1388-89, SAMA, Annual Report, 1390/91 A.H. (Jedda, 1972), p. 99.

APPENDIX TABLE C.4

Total Capital Formation in Current Riyals
(S.R. million)

	1383/84	1384/85	1385/86	1386/87	1387/88	1388/89	1389/90	1390/91
Construction	368.3	501.7	633.4	707.1	796.1	837.8	841.4	890.0
Imported capital goods	435.6	601.2	735.8	778.3	1,017.8	1,490.8	n.a.	n.a.
Total	803.9	1,102.9	1,369.2	1,485.4	1,813.9	2,328.6	—	—

Sources, Construction: 1383/84: CDS, Gross Domestic Product of Saudi Arabia, 1382/83 Through 1388/89 A.H. (Riyadh, September 1970), p. 2; 1384/85 to 1390/91: SAMA, Annual Report, 1391/92 A.H. (Jedda, June 1973), p. 106. Imported Capital Goods: Appendix Table C.3.

APPENDIX TABLE C.5

Budget Appropriations for Transport and Communications, 1960/61 to 1972/73
(S.R. million)

	Ministry of Communi-cations	Post, Telephone, and Telegraph	Railways	Roads, Bridges, and Ports	Civil Aviation, Saudi Airlines, and Meteorologi-cal Department	Total
1960/61	12.3	42.6	33.7	66.2	55.1	209.9
1961/62	3.3	46.5	44.3	106.8	157.9	358.8
1962/63	3.3	55.0	37.4	152.3	131.0	379.0
1963/64	4.2	78.4	36.4	149.0	146.7	414.7
1964/65	5.1	122.5	38.0	370.4	178.4	714.4
1965/66	2.3	79.0	31.8	359.1	193.7	665.9
1966/67	2.2	78.6	49.1	474.1	302.0	906.0
1967/68	1.9	74.9	35.3	473.9	318.6	904.6
1968/69	2.0	145.7	38.7	647.2	365.9	1,199.5
1969/70	2.0	160.5	40.8	539.0	369.5	1,111.8
1970/71	1.9	141.7	40.8	489.0	361.6	1,035.0
1971/72	2.3	380.6	41.1	1,099.7	470.4	1,994.1
1972/73	2.9	329.2	55.1	1,072.1	653.7	2,113.0
Percent change 1960/61 to 1972/73	-76.4	672.8	63.5	1,519.5	1,086.6	966.7
Average annual growth rate	—	18.6	4.2	26.1	22.9	21.2

Sources: 1960/61 to 1963/64: CDS, Statistical Yearbook, 1387 A.H., vol. 3 (Riyadh, 1967), p. 181; 1964/65 to 1972/73: Ibid., 1393 A.H., vol. 9 (Riyadh, 1973), p. 265.

APPENDIX TABLE C.6

Development of the Road System, December 1964 to August 1972
(kilometers)

Month and Year	Total Length of Roads, Asphalted and Open to Traffic	Total Completed (provisional handover)	Total Construction Started	Total Submitted for Tender	Total of Design Completed	Length of Roads to Be Constructed
December 1964	n.a.	n.a.	810	810	1,540	4,842
October 1965	n.a.	n.a.	1,646	2,590	2,779	5,435
November 1966	485	n.a.	2,525	3,167	3,958	6,306
October 1967	1,265	621	3,084	3,095	4,608	6,337
November 1968	2,309	1,583	4,206	4,481	5,557	7,670
December 1969	3,142	2,311	4,102	4,753	7,414	9,014
December 1970	3,569	3,199	4,446	4,770	7,881	9,031
August 1971	4,096	3,321	4,453	5,569	9,089	9,089
August 1972	5,356	3,828	5,433	5,766	9,302	10,707

Source: CDS, Statistical Yearbook, 1393 A.H., vol. 9 (Riyadh, 1973), p. 270.

APPENDIX TABLE C.7

Annual Budget Appropriations, 1959 to 1973/74

The table gives annual budget appropriations for the period 1959 to 1973/74, by major category. During this period a number of changes have occurred, affecting the consistency of the data. Most important of these changes was the creation of a number of government agencies with independent budgets. To make the appropriations time series consistent the following adjustments have been made:

1. From 1959 to 1963/64 Ministry of Defense and Royal Body Guard have been combined into a single item. The Royal Body Guard entry does not appear after 1963/64, and it is assumed that it was added thereafter into the Ministry of Defense category.
2. For the years 1959 to 1962/63 the regular budget contains two entries, "Emirates of Provinces" and "Saudi Airways, Railways and Post, Telegraph, and Telephone," that are omitted after the latter budget year. The first item was included under Ministry of Labor and Social Affairs for 1960/61 and 1962/63; it was omitted for the years 1959 to 1960/61. The second was omitted from 1959 to 1962/63, because Saudi Airlines became an independent government corporation with its own budget. Because railways and PTT cannot be separated from the category, they were dropped, too. Beginning in 1966/67, the railroad became an agency with an independent budget. PTT appears to have been included under the Ministry of Communications category.

Two entries, "Expected Savings" and "Repayment of Government Debt," need additional explanation. The first is meant to bring appropriations and estimated revenues into line. Appropriations in 1968/69, 1970/71, and 1972/73 exceeded projected revenues. To balance the budget it was assumed that appropriations exceeded actual requirements because delays in completion or changes in policies would lead to a shortfall in spending below the planned levels. These unspent funds are saved, and thus appropriations can be reduced by this amount.

APPENDIX TABLE C.7

Annual Budget Appropriations, 1959 to 1973/74
(S.R. million)

	1959	1959/60	1960/61	1961/62	1962/63	1963/64
Private Treasury	2.0	248.0	248.0	248.0	199.0	183.0
Royal Cabinet	0.5	5.0	7.0	10.0	10.0	10.0
Council of Ministers	7.0	9.0	8.0	9.0	11.0	11.0
Ministry of Defense	262.0	266.0	259.0	340.0	392.0	502.0
Ministry of Foreign Affairs	19.0	28.0	34.0	43.0	50.0	39.0
Ministry of Labor and Social Affairs	—	—	—	47.0	77.0	55.0
Ministry of Interior	90.0	103.0	104.0	129.0	162.0	228.0
Ministry of Education	118.0	130.0	149.0	171.0	223.0	271.0
Ministry of Communications	24.0	8.0	9.0	18.0	21.0	79.0
Ministry of Agriculture	20.0	23.0	21.0	34.0	43.0	58.0
Ministry of Finance and National Economy	39.0	53.0	43.0	41.0	46.0	61.0
Ministry of Petroleum and Minerals	—	—	11.0	11.0	11.0	11.0
Ministry of Health	60.0	55.0	58.0	69.0	87.0	103.0
Ministry of Commerce	3.0	4.0	4.0	5.0	6.0	10.0
Ministry of Hadj and Awqaf	—	—	—	—	31.0	32.0
Ministry of Justice (judiciaries)	18.0	18.0	20.0	21.0	21.0	24.0
Ministry of Information	—	—	—	—	5.0	17.0
Religious organizations, muezzins, and so on	23.0	23.0	25.0	29.0	30.0	34.0
Civil defense	—	—	—	—	40.0	28.0
Emergency expenses	—	—	—	—	60.0	60.0
Projects	55.0	110.0	291.0	400.0	550.0	550.0
Other expenditures	138.0	112.0	105.0	115.0	174.0	251.0
General budgetary reserve	—	—	—	—	—	—
Cost increase and subsidies due to riyal devaluation	—	78.0	35.0	25.0	30.0	30.0
Total	1,112.5	1,273.0	1,431.0	1,765.0	2,279.0	2,686.0
Less expected saving	—	—	—	—	—	—
Repayment of government debt	160.0	235.0	225.0	225.0	15.0	—
Grand total	1,272.5	1,508.0	1,656.0	1,990.0	2,294.0	2,686.0

Sources: 1959 to 1960/61: SAMA, Annual Report, 1382/83 A.H. (Riyadh, 1964), pp. 42-43; 1960/61: Ibid., 1383/84 A.H. (Riyadh, 1965), pp. 38-39; 1962/63: Ibid., 1384/85 A.H. (Riyadh, 1966), pp. 44-45; 1963/64: Ibid., 1385/86 A.H. (Riyadh, 1967), pp. 44-45; 1964/65: Ibid.,

1964/65	1965/66	1966/67	1967/68	1968/69	1969/70	1970/71	1971/72	1972/73	1973/74
173.0	173.0	173.0	173.0	173.0	173.0	173.0	173.0	173.0	173.0
6.0	8.0	8.0	15.0	13.0	14.0	15.0	17.0	18.0	20.0
14.0	19.0	19.0	17.0	19.0	18.0	19.0	25.0	29.0	33.0
548.0	572.0	1,163.0	723.0	841.0	831.0	925.0	1,138.0	1,427.0	1,711.0
49.0	51.0	56.0	52.0	65.0	56.0	57.0	70.0	80.0	94.0
62.0	78.0	87.0	84.0	92.0	92.0	98.0	125.0	144.0	198.0
276.0	345.0	370.0	406.0	528.0	546.0	589.0	850.0	1,071.0	1,267.0
305.0	360.0	399.0	383.0	483.0	558.0	646.0	1,031.0	1,300.0	1,677.0
87.0	103.0	119.0	98.0	111.0	106.0	109.0	149.0	189.0	231.0
67.0	84.0	88.0	80.0	89.0	82.0	82.0	113.0	136.0	177.0
63.0	57.0	62.0	58.0	71.0	68.0	69.0	105.0	104.0	120.0
12.0	14.0	17.0	16.0	19.0	19.0	19.0	26.0	31.0	39.0
117.0	128.0	154.0	122.0	155.0	155.0	166.0	250.0	375.0	499.0
11.0	12.0	15.0	13.0	16.0	14.0	15.0	21.0	40.0	45.0
34.0	39.0	42.0	43.0	44.0	43.0	44.0	60.0	74.0	85.0
25.0	31.0	33.0	32.0	36.0	36.0	37.0	51.0	53.0	57.0
23.0	35.0	39.0	35.0	49.0	45.0	48.0	69.0	83.0	92.0
39.0	42.0	48.0	48.0	24.0	24.0	25.0	32.0	35.0	38.0
39.0	31.0	31.0	20.0	30.0	20.0	20.0	—	—	—
60.0	44.0	46.0	31.0	40.0	41.0	41.0	60.0	61.0	201.0
762.0	1,402.0	1,717.0	2,146.0	2,570.0	2,682.0	2,596.0	5,036.0	6,718.0	14,263.0
311.0	313.0	339.0	322.0	396.0	328.0	749.0	1,131.0	1,227.0	1,338.0
—	—	—	—	—	—	—	250.0	300.0	452.0
30.0	20.0	20.0	20.0	20.0	15.0	—	—	—	—
3,112.0	3,961.0	5,025.0	4,937.0	5,885.0	5,966.0	6,542.0	10,782.0	13,668.0	22,810.0
—	—	—	—	350.0	—	162.0	—	468.0	—
—	—	—	—	—	—	—	—	—	—
3,112.0	3,961.0	5,025.0	4,937.0	5,535.0	5,966.0	6,380.0	10,782.0	13,200.0	22,810.0

1386/87 A.H. (Riyadh, 1968), pp. 56-57; 1965/66: Ibid., 1387/88 A.H. (Riyadh, 1969), pp. 72-73; 1966/67: Ibid., 1388/89 A.H. (Riyadh, 1970), pp. 78-79; 1967/68: Ibid., 1389/90 A.H. (Riyadh, 1971), pp. 84-85; 1968/69: Ibid., 1390/91 A.H. (Riyadh, 1972), pp. 84-85; 1969/70: Ibid., 1391/92 A.H. (Riyadh, 1973), pp. 82-83; 1970/71: Ibid., 1392/93 A.H. (Riyadh, 1974), pp. 88-89.

APPENDIX TABLE C.8

Projects Budget, 1960/61 to 1973/74
(S.R. million)

	1960/61	1961/62	1962/63	1963/64	1964/65	1965/66	1966/67
Education	15.2	12.3	35.4	60.8	74.0	124.4	113.4
Health and Red Crescent	11.0	12.6	11.6	16.0	23.5	31.2	28.3
Labor and social affairs	—	3.7	12.4	6.2	14.3	19.0	13.8
Municipalities	—	—	78.7	110.4	166.0	231.7	284.0
Hadj and Awqaf	4.5	7.5	8.7	12.2	15.6	19.4	21.7
Communications	79.8	134.5	175.9	193.9	443.4	382.0	538.8
Agriculture and water	8.4	25.0	34.3	86.6	149.0	160.4	220.0
Finance	62.5	40.3	55.5	63.9	65.9	105.6[a]	112.8
Commerce and industry	0.2	0.1	1.8	8.9	7.9	11.1	15.8
Petroleum and minerals	4.2	5.9	7.5	23.3	94.6	38.2	45.7
Information	10.0	3.4	6.3	22.4	37.1	40.4	85.0
Foreign affairs	0.2	—	—	—	6.2	4.6	7.9
Interior (except municipalities)	4.2	50.0	3.8	19.6	31.3	36.1	30.1
Other projects	90.0	104.8	118.2	77.6	76.3	224.7	228.7
All projects	291.1	400.0	550.0	701.7	1,205.3[b]	1,428.6[c]	1,746.1[d]

	1967/68	1968/69	1969/70	1970/71	1971/72	1972/73	1973/74
Education	76.6	60.1	42.2	72.9	144.7	298.4	565.5
Health and Red Crescent	21.8	14.1	13.9	10.9	30.1	47.0	84.2
Labor and social affairs	11.1	8.0	8.8	8.2	24.1	26.4	36.4

Municipalities	247.0	301.0	252.3	190.1	438.8	640.5	1,575.3
Hadj and Awqaf	16.4	19.0	10.7	9.4	28.2	45.7	57.5
Communications	527.0	794.4	705.6	620.4	1,463.6	1,481.8	2,051.7
Agriculture and water	314.2	398.9	300.0	230.1	456.0	572.5	855.0
Finance	105.3	164.8	143.0	136.4	396.1	640.6	n.a.
Commerce and industry	7.5	14.4	8.7	9.2	28.9	29.9	46.0
Petroleum and minerals	41.7	56.2	57.7	39.6	82.3	86.7	136.3
Information	72.4	50.9	53.5	28.2	48.8	82.2	158.8
Foreign affairs	3.0	3.0	3.6	2.5	8.9	27.5	n.a.
Interior (except municipalities)	21.9	16.3	43.2	48.8	91.0	155.8	n.a.
Other projects	800.2	682.9	1,057.3	1,251.8	1,823.1	2,672.6	8,229.8
All projects	2,266.2[e]	2,583.9[f]	2,700.4[g]	2,658.6[h]	5,064.7[i]	6,807.5[j]	14,263.0[k]

[a]Includes through 1964/65 appropriations for extension of Holy Harams.

[b]Total includes S.R. 122 million added by Royal Decree. Also includes S.R. 321 million drawn from the development fund.

[c]Total includes S.R. 26.2 million owing to the inclusion of the projects of the autonomous department.

[d]Total includes S.R. 28.7 million of autonomous departments' projects.

[e]Total includes S.R. 100 million expected saving and projects of independent departments aounting to S.R. 19.4 million.

[f]Total includes S.R. 13.9 million of projects resulting from the inclusion of projects of autonomous corporations with those of the various ministries.

[g]Total includes S.R. 18.4 million for the same reason given in note e.

[h]Total includes S.R. 62.6 million for independent department projects.

[i] S.R. 28.9 million for same reason as given in note h.

[j] Total includes S.R. 90 million for projects of permanent establishments since included in ministry projects.

[k] Total includes S.R. 466.8 for civil aviation.

Sources: 1960/61 to 1965/66: CDS, Statistical Yearbook, 1386 A.H. (Riyadh, 1966), pp. 300–301; 1966/67 to 1969/70: Ibid., 1390 A.H. (Riyadh, 1970), pp. 391-92; 1970/71 to 1972/73: Ibid., 1393 A.H. (Riyadh, 1973), pp. 374–75; 1973/74: SAMA, Annual Report, 1393 A.H. (Jedda, 1974), p. 90.

BIBLIOGRAPHY

SAUDI ARABIAN GOVERNMENT SOURCES

The two major statistical publications are CDS, Statistical Yearbook, and SAMA, Annual Report. Of the two sources the Annual Report is the more informative for the general reader. It is divided into two parts. Part 1 deals with the whole economy by major sectors; it gives a detailed review of the events of the past year and often suggests possible explanations for given events. Part 2 consists of a series of statistical tables of which the most important are the monetary and the foreign trade statistics. The Annual Report complements the Statistical Yearbook, which contains a wealth of statistical data on the Saudi economy. The third important source of statistical information is the Petroleum Statistical Bulletin. The three sources are published in English and contain the most important data. In addition, there are reports and bulletins; they are harder to obtain, because the issuing authorities are not set up to disseminate the data widely. The best approach is simply to write to the government agency directly, requesting all public information, and hope that the request will be answered.

Embassy of Saudi Arabia. Statement of Industrial Policy of Saudi Arabia. Washington, D.C., n.d.

Kingdom of Saudi Arabia, Central Planning Organization. Development Plan, 1390 A.H. Riyadh, n.d.

______. Foreign Capital Investment Code. Washington, D.C., n.d.

Kingdom of Saudi Arabia. Agreements Between the Saudi Arab Government and the Arabian American Oil Company. Mecca: Government Press, 1964.

Ministry of Finance and National Economy, Central Department of Statistics. Gross National Product.

______. Statistical Yearbook, 1385/93 A.H., vols. 1-9. Riyadh, various dates.

______. Gross Domestic Product of Saudi Arabia, 1382/83 Through 1388/89, A.H. Riyadh, September, 1970. This is in reference to the old GDP series. As of December 1974 the only citation of the revised GDP series can be found in SAMA, Annual Report, 1392/93.

Ministry of Information. Saudi Arabia, Land of Achievement. n.d.

Ministry of Petroleum and Mineral Resources, Economic Department. Petroleum Statistical Bulletin, 1970-74, vols. 1-5. Dammam: Al Mutawa Press, various dates.

Saudi Arabian Monetary Agency, Central Bank. Annual Report 1390/91, A.H. Jedda, 1972.

Saudi Arabian Monetary Agency. Annual Report, 1380 to 1392/93. Jedda, various dates. This is the only source of monetary statistics as well as of the continuation of the GDP series beginning in 1389/90.

______. Statistical Summary. Jedda, various dates. This source is published several times annually. It is a means to update some of the information presented in SAMA's Annual Report.

OIL COMPANY SOURCES

Published information on the oil companies is very sparse. The most readily available sources of basic information are the Annual Reports and the Aramco Handbook. They are listed below.

Arabian American Oil Company. Aramco 1962 to 1973. These are the company's annual reports; they contain interesting information on the company's economic and social impact in its area of operation. Furthermore, they give the most important production statistics.

______. The Saudi Arab Government and the Arabian American Oil Company Basic Agreements and Selected Documents Pertaining Thereto. No place or date of publication.

______. Folio of Background Petroleum Data. January 1969.

______. "A Dam in Saudi Arabia." Aramco World Magazine 25, no. 2 (March-April 1974): 4-9.

______. Summary of Middle East Oil Developments, 2d ed. (1948).

______. Annual Review of Operations, 1949. No date or place of publication.

Lebkicher, Roy, et al. Aramco Handbook. Arabian American Oil Company, 1960.

Petromin. Progress Report. These reports have been issued at irregular intervals; they summarize the company's achievements. A complete report on Petromin's activities is to be issued in the summer of 1975.

JOURNALS

All the major journals serving the oil industry give some information on the Saudi Arabian oil industry. The best source of current information is the Middle East Economic Survey. Published in Beirut, the MEES gives weekly accounts of all development and, in addition, publishes numerous supplements that are highly accurate and very informative.

GENERAL SOURCES

A selection of sources follows, listing those that the author cited or consulted in the course of the preparation of this work. A number of well-written, general sources on Islam and the Middle East have been included.

Adelman, Morris A. The World Petroleum Market. Washington, D.C.: Resources for the Future, 1973.

Asfour, Edmond Y. Saudi Arabia: Long Term Projections of Supply of and Demand for Agricultural Products. Beirut: American University of Beirut, 1965.

Assah, Ahmed. Miracle of the Desert Kingdom. London: Johnson, 1969.

Blaug, Mark. Education and the Employment Problem in Developing Countries. Geneva: International Labor Office, 1973.

Bradley, Paul G. The Economics of Crude Petroleum Production. Amsterdam: North-Holland, 1967.

DeGaury, Gerald. Faisal, King of Saudi Arabia. London: Barker, 1966.

Doughty, Charles M. Travels in Arabia Deserta, vols. 1 and 2. London: Cape, 1964.

Frank, Helmut J. Crude Oil Prices in the Middle East. New York: Praeger, 1966.

Gibb, H.A. R. Modern Trends in Islam. Chicago: University of Chicago Press, 1947.

______. Mohammedanism, 2d ed. New York: Oxford University Press, 1962.

Guilliaume, Alfred. Islam. Baltimore: Penguin Books, 1956.

______. The Traditions of Islam, Khayats Oriental Reprint no. 13. Beirut: Khayats, 1966.

Hamilton, Charles W. Americans and Oil in the Middle East. Houston: Gulf, 1962.

Hartshorn, J. E. Politics and World Oil Economics, rev. ed. New York: Praeger, 1967.

Hitti, Said H., and George T. Abeel. "The Economy and Finances of Saudi Arabia." International Monetary Fund Staff Papers 21, no. 2 (July 1974): 247-306.

Hodkin, E. C. The Arabs. London: Oxford University Press, 1966.

Hopwood, Derek, ed. The Arabian Peninsula. Totowa, N.J.: Rowman and Littlefield, 1972.

Howarth, David. The Desert King. London: Collins, 1964.

Issawi, Charles. Oil, the Middle East and the World. New York: Library Press, 1972.

______, and Mohammed Yeganeh. The Economics of Middle Eastern Oil. New York: Praeger, 1962.

Kelley, J. B. Eastern Arabian Frontiers. New York: Praeger, 1964.

Klebanoff, Shoshona. Middle East Oil and U.S. Foreign Policy. New York: Praeger, 1974.

Leeman, Wayne A. The Price of Middle East Oil. Ithaca, N.Y.: Cornell University Press, 1962.

Lipsky, George A., et al. Saudi Arabia. New Haven, Conn.: HRAF Press, 1959.

Longrigg, Stephen H. Oil in the Middle East, 3d ed. London: Oxford University Press, 1968.

Lubell, Harold. Middle East Oil Crisis and Western Europe's Energy Policy. Baltimore: The Johns Hopkins Press, 1963.

Malik, Ahmed Abdullah. The Money Supply Process in Saudi Arabia. Ann Arbor, Mich.: University Microfilms, 1970.

Mikdashi, Zuhayr. The Community of Oil Exporting Countries. Ithaca, N.Y.: Cornell University Press, 1972.

______. A Financial Analysis of Middle Eastern Oil Companies: 1901-1965. New York: Praeger, 1966.

______, Sherrill Clelland, and Ian Seymour. Continuity and Change in the World Oil Industry. Beirut: The Middle East Research and Publishing Center, 1970.

Organization of Petroleum Exporting Countries. Selected Documents of the International Petroleum Industry, 1967. Vienna: OPEC, 1968.

______. Selected Documents of the International Petroleum Industry, 1972. Vienna: OPEC, 1973.

Penrose, Edith. The Growth of Firms, Middle East Oil and Other Essays. London: Cass, 1971.

Philby, H. S. St.-J. B. Arabian Days. London: Hale, 1948.

______. The Land of Midian. London: Benn, 1957.

Rahman, A. "Outlines of an Islamic Bank." The Journal of the Moslem World League 1, no. 9 (1974): 43-48.

Rahman, Fazlur. Islam. New York: Holt, Rinehart and Winston, 1966.

Rauf, M. A. A Brief History of Islam. Kuala Lumpur: Oxford University Press, 1964.

Rifai, Taki. The Pricing of Crude Oil. New York: Praeger, 1974.

Rouhani, Fuad. A History of OPEC. New York: Praeger, 1971.

Rugh, William. "Emergence of a New Middle Class in Saudi Arabia." Middle East Journal 27, no. 1 (1973): 7-20.

Sayegh, Kamal S. Oil and Arab Regional Development. New York: Praeger, 1968.

Schurr, Sam H., Paul T. Homan, et al. Middle Eastern Oil and the Western World. New York: American Elsevier, 1971.

Schwadran, Benjamin. The Middle East, Oil and the Great Powers. New York: Praeger, 1955.

Secretariate of the Asian-African Legal Consultation Committee. Constitutions of Asian Countries. Bombay: N. H. Tripathi Private, 1968.

Shea, Thomas W. "Measuring the Changing Family Consumption Patterns of Aramco's Saudi Arab Employees, 1962 and 1968." in The Arabian Peninsula, Derek Hopwood, ed. Totowa, N.J.: Rowman and Littlefield, 1972.

Smith, Wilfred C. Islam in Modern History. Princeton, N.J.: Princeton University Press, 1957.

Sparrow, Judge Gerald. Modern Saudi Arabia. London: Vernon, 1970.

Stocking, George W. Middle East Oil. Nashville, Tenn.: Vanderbilt University Press, 1970.

Taher, Abdulhady H. Income Determination in the International Petroleum Industry. Oxford: Pergamon Press, 1966.

Tanzer, Michael. The Political Economy of International Oil and the Underdeveloped Countries. Boston: Beacon Press, 1969.

Thomas, Alfred. Saudi Arabia, A Study of the Educational System of the Kingdom of Saudi Arabia. American Association of Collegiate Registrars and Admissions Officers, International Activities Group, 1967.

Tugendhart, Christopher. Oil, the Biggest Business. New York: Putnam's, 1968.

Twitchel, K. S. Saudi Arabia, 3d ed. Princeton, N.J.: Princeton University Press, 1958.

Van der Menlen, D. The Wells of Ibn Saud. New York: Praeger, 1957.

Vicker, Ray. The Kingdom of Oil. New York: Scribner's, 1974.

Walpole, Norman C., et al. Area Handbook for Saudi Arabia. Washington, D.C.: Government Printing Office, 1971. This volume contains an excellent bibliography.

Winder, Bayly. Saudi Arabia in the Nineteenth Century. New York: St. Martin's Press, 1965.

Yamani, Ahmed Zaki. Islamic Law and Contemporary Issues. Jedda: Saudi Publishing House, 1968.

Xydix, Dorothy Peaslee. Constitutions of Nations, rev. 3d ed., vol. 2. The Hague: Nihoff, 1965.

INDEX

ABOUT THE AUTHOR

RAMON KNAUERHASE is an Associate Professor of Economics at the University of Connecticut. From August 1968 to August 1970 he served as a Project Specialist with the Ford Foundation Public Administration Project in Riyadh, Saudi Arabia.

Dr. Knauerhase has published in the areas of comparative economic systems, economic development, and European economic history. He has published An Introduction to National Socialism, 1920-1939, and his articles have appeared in The Journal of Economic History and the International Review of the History of Banking.

Dr. Knauerhase holds a B. A. from Temple University and an M.A. and Ph.D. from the University of Pennsylvania.

RELATED TITLES
Published by
Praeger Special Studies

ECONOMIC GROWTH AND EMPLOYMENT PROBLEMS IN VENE-ZUELA: An Analysis of an Oil Based Economy
Mostafa F. Hassan

ECONOMIC GROWTH IN DEVELOPING COUNTRIES--MATERIAL AND HUMAN RESOURCES: Proceedings of the Seventh Rehovot Con-ference
edited by Yohanan Ramati

MIDDLE EAST OIL AND U.S. FOREIGN POLICY: With Special Ref-erence to the U.S. Energy Crisis
Shoshana Klebanoff

THE ENERGY CRISIS AND U.S. FOREIGN POLICY
edited by Joseph S. Szyliowicz
and Bard O'Neill

THE ECONOMIC DEVELOPMENT OF IRAN: A Recent Survey with Projections to 1981
Robert E. Looney